NGOS

AND POLITICAL CHANGE

A HISTORY OF THE AUSTRALIAN COUNCIL
FOR INTERNATIONAL DEVELOPMENT

NGOS

AND POLITICAL CHANGE

A HISTORY OF THE AUSTRALIAN COUNCIL
FOR INTERNATIONAL DEVELOPMENT

PATRICK KILBY

Australian
National
University

PRESS

ANU PRESS

Published by ANU Press
The Australian National University
Acton ACT 2601, Australia
Email: anupress@anu.edu.au
This title is also available online at http://press.anu.edu.au

---

National Library of Australia Cataloguing-in-Publication entry

Creator:	Kilby, Patrick, author.
Title:	NGOs and political change : a history of the Australian Council for International Development / Patrick Kilby.
ISBN:	9781925022469 (paperback) 9781925022476 (ebook)
Subjects:	Australian Council for International Development--History. Non-governmental organizations--Australia--History. Non-governmental organizations--Australia--Political aspects.
Dewey Number:	361.76

Cover design and layout by ANU Press

Contents

List of Figures

'… what's past is prologue, what to come. In yours and my discharge.'
(William Shakespeare, *The Tempest*, act 2, scene 1, line 244)

Preface

Writing a book about the 50 years of the Australian Council for International Development (ACFID) is not without its challenges. The main one is what to include and what to leave out; what themes to emphasise and what to downplay or even ignore. The readers of this book who know ACFID will no doubt suggest I overplayed or overdramatised some things at the expense of talking about some of the other good work ACFID has done. Sometimes people are too close to the action, and sometimes memory is all too faulty. In the end, this book is ACFID's story as I have experienced it, as an insider through the 1980s, 1990s and 2010s on many of its committees. ACFID's story is also told through the memories of the people involved, to whom I am very grateful, and ACFID's records of the time, now held in the National Library of Australia.

The caveat, of course, is that the inclusions and exclusions are mine alone. The 10 chapters of this book pick up what I regard as the key themes that built ACFID but also challenged it: its relationship with government, global education, its work with emergencies, human rights, the Code of Ethics/Code of Conduct, and gender and development. Some of these themes were a product of their time, such as global education, and were successful for a period; some ACFID probably should not have undertaken, such as disaster work, and others, like gender and development, ACFID has struggled with throughout its life.

Acknowledgements

Writing this book has been on my mind for a long time. The idea of a 50th anniversary book probably first occurred to me in 1990 at the time of the 25th anniversary council, but it was not until around 2005 that I undertook the first set of interviews and put some thoughts down. After 2010, as the 50th anniversary loomed, the intensity picked up. I remember at a conference putting some chapter headings down on a piece of paper and passing it to Marc Purcell and Susan Harris-Rimmer, who commented, changed the order, added one or two and nodded encouragingly, and so began the race to finish it in time.

I would like to thank those who gave me the necessary nudges over the past few years to make this publication possible; in particular, Marc Purcell, the executive director of ACFID, and his staff who gave me their full support without any editorial 'guidance' as to what should or should not be included. This presented its own set of challenges as then it was up to me to make those decisions. The staff at the Special Collections Reading Room at the National Library of Australia were always helpful in retrieving boxes from 'off site'. The NLA's archiving staff (together with ACFID staff) did a fantastic job of cataloguing 40 years of archives, from enigmatic handwritten notes to ground-breaking reports. It is these manuscripts of the official record that are the primary sources for the book and against which interviews were checked when there was an occasional difference in accounts. Special thanks go to Jim Richards who provided some valuable research assistance for Chapter 6 on human rights.

The interviewees were chosen on the basis of their leadership role in ACFID or their insights into particular issues they were involved with during their time with the organisation. I spoke to all former executive directors, who generously gave their time: Mick Sullivan, Bob Whan, Russell Rollason, Janet Hunt, Graham Tupper and Paul O'Callaghan. In particular, I would like to thank Russell Rollason and Janet Hunt, who provided valuable comments on earlier drafts and kept me anchored to the reality of the times. I would also like to thank former presidents and chairmen: the late Major General Paul Cullen, Richard Alston, Bill Armstrong and Gaye Hart; former executive committee members: Wendy Rose, Elizabeth Reid, Wendy Poussard, Ruth Pfanner,

Andrew Hewitt, Jeremy Hobbs, and Jack de Groot; Chris Franks from the Code of Conduct Committee; and James Ensor from the Advocacy Committee. In addition, thanks are also due to former foreign ministers Andrew Peacock and Gareth Evans, and former staff of ACFID Brendan O'Dwyer, Kate Moore, Christine Vincent, Cath Blunt, Pat Walsh and Susan Harris-Rimmer. The late Jim Webb and Nancy Anderson, who I had the opportunity to speak to, deserve a special mention as they were present at the meetings and workshops that led to the establishment of ACFID.

The three anonymous reviewers and the Social Sciences Editorial Board led by Emeritus Professor Marian Sawer provided constructive feedback and kept me focused. Special thanks go to Helen Topor for copyediting the manuscript and to the ANU Press for publishing the book. Last, but by no means least, I am grateful to my wife Joyce Wu whose constant support made this task possible. She provided much-needed proofreading and made valuable editorial comments.

Naming conventions

In a history such as this, the names of agencies invariably change. ACFID began as the Australian Council for Overseas Aid (ACFOA), the name it had until 2004. The convention I have adopted is to use the current name or terminology (for example, ACFID and global education rather than ACFOA and development education) except where material is cited and in direct quotes. For the Australian government aid agency I use the name AusAID, as it had that name for over 20 years until the agency was absorbed into the Department of Foreign Affairs in 2014. References to ADAA, ADAB and AIDAB refer to the former names of the Australian aid agency. In the case of the East Pakistan crisis of 1971, I have used the name Bangladesh (which came into existence in early 1972) for consistency. Further explanation is made in the text. The term NGO will be used throughout this book to refer to international development NGOs rather than the less-often-used term INGO. The term 'local NGOs' will be used for developing country NGOs and 'domestic NGOs' for those NGOs which operate solely within Australia. I have used the generic name the Red Cross rather than Australian Red Cross or ARC, as it is more familiar to the reader. Other Red Cross societies or agencies will be referred to by their full names.

Glossary

ACC	Australian Council of Churches
ACFID	Australian Council for International Development
ACFOA	Australian Council for Overseas Aid
ACR	Australian Catholic Relief
ADAA	Australian Development Assistance Agency
ADAB	Australian Development Assistance Bureau
AFFHC	Australian Freedom from Hunger Campaign
AIDAB	Australian International Development Assistance Bureau
ANCP	Australian NGO Cooperation Program
ANTaR	Australians for Native Title and Reconciliation
APCMCOE	Asia Pacific Civil-Military Centre of Excellence
ASEAN	Association of Southeast Asian Nations
AusAID	Australian Agency for International Development
AWD	Action for World Development
BiNGO	Bilateral NGO Scheme
BOAG	British Overseas Aid Group
BRICS	Brazil, Russia, India, China, South Africa – a loose political grouping of emerging economies involved in global development issues
CAA	Community Aid Abroad
CCIC	Canadian Council for International Cooperation
CDC	Committee for Development Cooperation
CEDAW	Convention on the Elimination of all Forms of Discrimination against Women.
CERD	Convention on the Elimination of all Forms of Racial Discrimination
CID	Council for International Development
CIDA	Canadian International Development Agency

COPAC	Code of Practice Advisory Committee
CSW	(UN) Commission on the Status of Women
DAC	Development Assistance Committee (of the OECD)
DAWN	Development Alternatives with Women for a New Era
DEC	Disasters Emergency Committee
DEDAW	Declaration on the Elimination of Discrimination against Women.
DFAT	Department of Foreign Affairs and Trade
DND	*Development News Digest*
ECA	(UN) Economic Commission for Africa
ECOSOC	UN Economic and Social Council
EPLF	Eritrean People's Liberation Front
ESCAP	(UN) Economic and Social Commission for Asia and the Pacific
FAO	(UN) Food and Agriculture Organization
FFHC	Freedom from Hunger Campaign
GDP	Gross Domestic Product
ICCC	Interim Code of Conduct Committee
ICCPR	International Covenant on Civil and Political Rights
ICESCR	International Covenant on Economic, Social and Cultural Rights
ICRC	International Committee of the Red Cross
ICVA	International Council of Voluntary Agencies
IDEC	International Disasters Emergency Committee
ILO	International Labour Organization
INSTRAW	(UN) International Research and Training Institute for the Advancement of Women
IPA	Institute of Public Affairs
IWDA	International Women's Development Agency
JANIC	Japan Centre for International Cooperation
JCFADT	Joint Parliamentary Committee on Foreign Affairs, Defence and Trade
MDGs	Millennium Development Goals
MSF	Médecins Sans Frontières
NGDO	Non-Governmental Development Organisation
NIEO	New International Economic Order
NWAC	National Women's Advisory Council

NZADDS	New Zealand Aid and Development Dialogues
ODA	Overseas Development Assistance
ODI	Overseas Development Institute
OECD	Organisation for Economic Cooperation and Development
OSB	Overseas Service Bureau
PVO	Private Voluntary Organisation
RPF	Rwandan Patriotic Front
RSL	Returned and Services League
UNDG	United Nations Development Group
UNESCO	United Nations Educational, Scientific and Cultural Organization
UNGA	United Nations General Assembly
UNHCR	United Nations High Commissioner for Refugees
UNIFEM	United Nations Development Fund for Women
USAID	United States Agency for International Development
VCOAD	Voluntary Committee on Overseas Aid and Development
WADNA	Women and Development Network of Australia
WCC	World Council of Churches
YCW	Young Catholic Worker

01 | A Greek Chorus

All but the most hard-core cynics will admit that there is such a thing as altruism which inspires people to invest time and money in helping others without any hope of tangible returns ... But altruistic intentions must be translated into concrete actions. In a world of conflicting interests, that means making choices which are political, accepting compromises which are debatable, and influencing public opinion in one direction or another.

— Lissner 1977, Preface

This book looks at NGO development through the lens of the first 50 years of the Australian Council for International Development (ACFID), from its very humble beginnings in 1965 to the respected peak body it has become in 2015. This period coincided with the optimism of the first Development Decade of the 1960s through to the emergence of developing countries as rising political powers in the 2010s, many with their own aid programs, and with quite different views from the West on what development means for them and what role NGOs might play.

While the story of ACFID is common to most national NGO groups and peak bodies in Europe and North America since the 1960s, it is also a story of nuanced responses to the issues of the time. For example, as much as there have been increases in government funding of NGOs, such as in the 1980s, there have also been real cuts in government funding to NGOs at other times, such as in the early 2000s in Australia and the early 2010s in Europe. In the 1980s, NGOs were seen as a solution to the need for service provision in 'weak' developing countries, while in the 2000s there has been much more pressure from the politically strong developing countries to limit the NGO 'voice' (Howell and Lind 2009a; Smillie 2012; van der Borgh and Terwindt 2012).

This book engages with the complex histories that shaped NGOs. It tries to avoid sweeping generalisations and catchy slogans such as NGOs are 'too close [to government funding] for comfort' (Edwards and Hulme 1996), or that there is an inexorable growth in numbers, scale and importance of NGOs (McGann and Johnstone 2004; Reimann 2006; Elkington and Beloe 2010). While these generalisations may be true for certain periods, they tend to suggest that there is an inevitable path-dependent process of 'NGO-ization' of civil society involved in development (Lang 2012). I will argue that this process is not the case, rather NGOs and their peak bodies such as ACFID respond to the changing contexts their members face, while still hanging on to their founding vision and values.

This book discusses how NGOs responded to the social and political mood of the times, the changing ideologies of the governments of the day with their differing priorities for aid, in general, and for dealing with NGOs, in particular, as part of the broader political cycle. Each chapter examines key themes that shaped ACFID. Chapter 1 provides an overview of ACFID and how it has developed. Chapter 2 outlines the origins of ACFID and traces its formative processes and the work of Sir John Crawford. Chapter 3 looks at the central role global education and later campaigning has had in ACFID's work. Chapter 4 questions the progress that ACFID and its members have made in realising gender justice in their programs. Chapter 5 examines how NGOs shaped and are shaped by humanitarian interventions, and the work that ACFID undertook through its International Disasters Emergency Committee (IDEC) and later the Emergencies Forum. Chapter 6 analyses the leadership ACFID took on human rights, particularly on East Timor but also more generally. Chapters 7 and 8 examine ACFID's relations with government and how these are affected by not only the political cycle but also other events outside ACFID's control. The penultimate chapter deals with the role ACFID has had globally in developing NGO self-regulation and the use of robust codes of conduct to argue for NGO legitimacy. This book concludes with a look into the future and what a changing global and local context may mean for ACFID.

What is ACFID?

ACFID is the peak organisation representing Australia's aid and development NGOs. It is 'a single, united Australian voice for global fairness' (ACFID 2013a). ACFID's 140 members are involved in providing development assistance (or aid) mainly to local NGOs and civil society organisations such as religious groups, trade unions and activist groups in developing countries. The purpose of this aid is mainly for community level work that ranges from livelihood programs, such as microcredit or training programs, to the provision of health or education services, or to address human rights and social justice issues. ACFID members are also involved in public awareness and advocacy campaigns on social justice and poverty issues in developing countries and in Australia. ACFID members range from small NGOs run entirely by volunteers to the large household names such as World Vision, CARE or Oxfam, who are part of global coalitions of NGOs. ACFID provides a forum for its members to discuss issues affecting NGOs. It also runs campaigns on their behalf and, most importantly, offers a single, united voice to government and to the Australian public on major aid, development and social justice issues.

ACFID was founded in 1965 with a handful of members. It now has members operating in 100 countries and spends over $1 billion per annum on overseas aid, most of which comes from donations from the Australian public and the rest from government grants and subsidies. As a proportion of GDP, ACFID's aid programs funded by public donations have been remarkably stable over the past 50 years, with NGO aid expenditure of 0.035 per cent of GDP in 1970, 0.02 per cent in 1988, and 0.03 per cent in 2000. A big jump in the 2000s was due to Indian Ocean tsunami expenditure. Unlike the early 1970s, when there was no government support for NGO work, by the late 1980s NGOs were able to lever significant government funding. While government grants to Australian NGOs represents around 20 per cent of their total aid expenditure, the government, as both a regulator and funder, has a large influence on NGO work and the approach ACFID takes in its relations with government (ACFID 2013b) – a theme that recurs throughout this book.

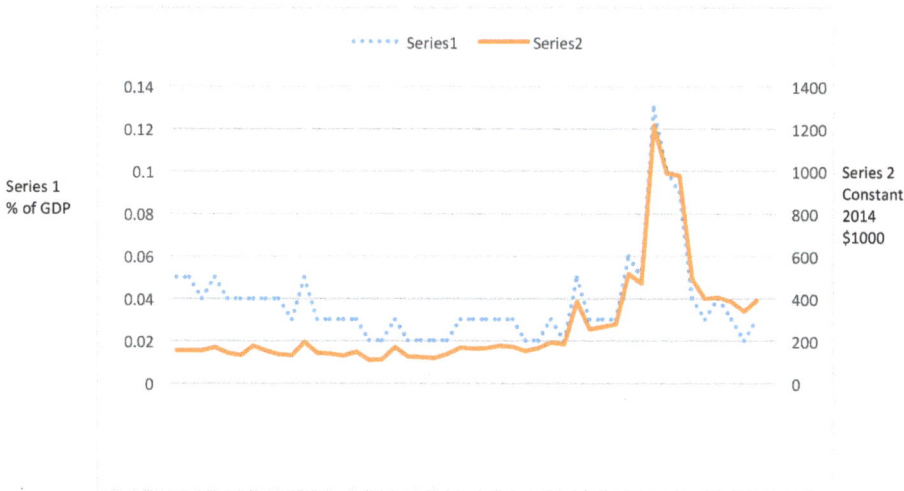

Figure 1 Australian NGO aid levels and as a percentage of GDP 1968–2014.

Source: Author's composition.[1]

---

[1]   This expenditure was calculated from ACFID Annual Reports, and Lissner (1977) for the 1970s figures. The jump in the 2000s was also due, in part, to the Indian Ocean tsunami of 2004, which lifted both the profile and income of NGOs for the next eight years after which expenditure returned to the long-term trends.

ACFID has a secretariat in a part of Canberra often referred to as 'lobby valley', where a large number of industry peak bodies have been corralled by the town planners. A staff of around 20 people look after a broad set of issues, including advocacy, members, policy, and the Code of Conduct. At the time of writing, ACFID was working on three major themes: human rights, gender, and civil society. On top of this there are about another dozen specific issues looked after by member working groups which network and share information.

ACFID has counterparts in most donor countries, the main ones being Bond in the UK, InterAction in the US, the Canadian Council for International Cooperation (CCIC), the Council for International Development (CID) in New Zealand, and the Japan NGO Center for International Cooperation (JANIC). ACFID is one of the strongest of these peak bodies in that it represents the largest proportion of national member NGOs working in international development, and it derives a high proportion of its income from member fees – both good indicators of the strength of member support.[2]

The challenge for peak bodies such as ACFID is how to represent the diversity of membership, which invariably includes global NGO networks, such as Oxfam, CARE and World Vision, and small locally based NGOs that might be involved in a small program in one part of a country, or be involved in controversial advocacy work which other NGOs or their international affiliates might disagree with. In the UK, New Zealand and Canada, divisions occurred in the peak bodies so that they became vulnerable to either internal or external pressures. In the UK it was over the direction of global education in the 1970s which forced the Voluntary Committee on Overseas Aid and Development (VCOAD) to close (Burnell 1991). In the case of Canada and New Zealand, both CCIC and CID were significantly reduced in size due to sharp cuts in government funding in 2010, compounded by a perceived loss of support of the larger agencies (Smillie 2012; McGregor et al. 2013).

The historical context

The history of NGO aid since World War II can be divided into four periods. The first, until the 1960s, was mainly about sending volunteers, and in some ways was a colonial relic in that it followed the former colonial practice of sending young administrators to the colonies (Webb 1971). The second period was from the mid-1960s until the 1980s, when NGOs were recognised as development actors, and they were part of the movement for development alternatives. This followed the launch of the first Development Decade in 1960, the global Freedom from Hunger Campaign in 1962, and the 1963 United Nations

---

2   Based on the 2012 annual reports for each.

General Assembly (UNGA) call for more recognition of the role NGOs play in development (UNGA 1963a). The third period, from the early 1980s until the mid-1990s, saw more formalised government relationships with NGOs and a rapid expansion of official funding of NGO work. Finally, the fourth period, from the mid-1990s until into the 2010s, has been characterised by:

> a persistent and public set of concerns about practice, direction, and focus of NGOs. It is a period in which NGOs have had to come to terms with their entry, at scale, into the reform agenda, as well as increasing diversification within the NGO sector (Mitlin, Hickey et al. 2007, p. 1709).

While voluntarism and development work have been a part of the historical evolution of many societies, in the West this can be traced back to the seventeenth century (Lissner 1977). A notable example of early NGO work is the advent of service delivery, such as health and education by missionaries. Another is public advocacy, such as the anti-slavery movement in the early nineteenth century. Development as we currently understand it, however, is essentially a post-World War II phenomenon where 'individuals and groups within the field of development derived … their motivation from an ideological and spiritual commitment to social reform and change' (Tandon 2000, p. 319). In the 1950s and early 1960s the major development paradigm was state building, with a focus on infrastructure and industrial development. This approach to development typically ignored the more local community contexts, with NGOs being at the margins involved mainly with missionary-based welfare work, sending volunteers, or involvement in disasters and emergencies work (OECD 1988; Webb 1971; Smillie 1995). It was also a period of what was seen as Western neocolonial domination:

> In the 1960s and 1970s, the problems of war and famine in the non-Western world were predominantly seen in the context of Western domination and Cold War clientelism. The existence of broad social and political movements based on Third World solidarity or critiques of Western market domination meant that the problems were seen in a broader international context (Chandler 2001, p. 681).

NGOs were part of the response to this paradigm through their aid programs and advocacy so that by the late 1960s and into the 1970s NGOs were demanding alternatives focused on local level development. This demand was driven in part by Schumacher's *Small is Beautiful* (1973) and Paulo Freire's *Pedagogy of the Oppressed* (1970), and was enthusiastically picked up by NGOs through small-scale, integrated community development activities, and promoted through public awareness programs (Tandon 2000; Chandler 2001; Mitlin, Hickey et al. 2007). Underlying this approach was the strong belief that people can and should develop themselves, and that 'their own involvement, engagement, and contribution are an essential foundation for sustainable development' (Tandon 2000, p. 320). Non-formal education, community organising, and local leadership building were the types of interventions being promoted, and it was out of this experience that emerged the 'rights-based approach' to development (see Chapter 6).

By the 1980s the idea of state building was cast aside and a new development paradigm emerged. The basis of this paradigm was to pare down the size and role of the state under what was called a New Policy Agenda, picking up the central tenets of neoliberalism: deregulation, privatisation, and liberalisation (Newman et al. 2002; Stokke 2013). In this framework of a smaller state, NGOs were being asked and supported to perform many local and state functions. This was the period of the NGO 'boom', characterised by broader relationships among state, market and civil society, and the promotion of practices such as strengthening 'civil society' and 'people's participation', which were a central part of NGO arguments around aid quality. NGOs at the time were also highly critical of structural adjustment policies of aid donors, particularly the World Bank, but at the same time there were high expectations of NGOs to provide a better alternative. These criticisms were perhaps unfair and certainly unrealistic, given the relatively small scale of most NGO work.

> While there was some discourse space and there were financial resources for collaborative projects, there was little to no space to pursue large-scale, or system-questioning, or alternative projects (Mitlin, Hickey et al. 2007, p. 1706).

The final phase of NGO engagement can be tracked from the mid to late 1990s until the 2010s. This phase is characterised by a persistent and public set of concerns about the practice, direction and focus of NGOs. This was related to the failure of much of the neoliberal agenda in the mid-1990s, exemplified by the Asian economic crisis, to be replaced in the 2000s with an increased security agenda and the rise of a nationalistic, more centralised, development state (Hallsworth and Lee 2011; Bloodgood and Tremblay-Boire 2011). With this came more cautious, uncertain and risk-averse donor governments, and the re-emergence of both donor and recipient national interest in a more complex donor world.

It is in this historical context that ACFID has grown and developed, and to which it has responded. There has been a shift from the activism for alternatives in the 1970s and 1980s to the adoption of a more circumscribed role in an uncertain NGO world of the 2010s where government and, to some extent, the public have become more sceptical.

An overview of the Australian Council for International Development

This book tracks the history of how ACFID got to where it is today, and be as strong in the 2010s as it has ever been, but with a different voice to reflect the times. This chapter looks at how ACFID has developed since 1965 and its work as a commentator and a voice for NGOs in Australia – a bit like a Greek chorus or conscience. The idea of ACFID as a Greek chorus arose from a conversation with Jack de Groot, a long-standing AFCID executive member, about what ACFID was.[3] In Greek tragedy the role of the chorus was to express the fears, hopes, questions, judgements and feelings of the spectators who made up the civic community (Vernant and Vidal-Naquet 1990). The challenge for the Greek chorus was to comment on the dramatic action in a collective way with a balanced sound of all the voices – to curb individual choristers from drowning out the whole (Black 1988, p. 282). Over its 50 years of existence, ACFID has been at times a sharp and loud commentator on the events around aid and development in ways that both reflected and led public opinion. There have also been times when some of the choristers have tried to sing from different song sheets. At these times, ACFID has had to manage the disharmony among the 'choristers' with some deep soul-searching, most notably in the 1970s around the issue of global education (see Chapter 3).

At ACFID's 25th anniversary conference in 1990, Doug Porter used the metaphor of a Jazz Band: 'one of the more enigmatic of musical forms that never respects any of the perceived truths about itself, and is neither composed nor purely extemporised music' (Porter 1990). He also noted that the tradition of NGOs parallels the tradition of jazz, with the strong role of the Christian church in both, and certainly religious NGOs (mainly Jewish and Christian) have played a central role in ACFID's development, particularly in the early years, when they provided much of ACFID's leadership. The metaphor was also used as a critique of ACFID, with Porter (1990) suggesting that ACFID had become set in its ways by playing traditional jazz and 'what the punter wants to hear … with a tempo that is too fast and a volume too low', suggesting that ACFID had strayed from its 'radical' roots.

Doug Porter seemed to have been pining for the activist era of ACFID in the mid-1970s when it seemed to take on a more radical hue, or as Rolf Gerritson noted, ACFID 'was a home for left over student radicals' (quoted by Rollason 2013). Of course this begs the question of whether or not ACFID's roots were indeed radical, which is dealt with in detail in the following chapter on ACFID's

---

3   Marc Purcell, an ACFID executive director, took the metaphor a step further and suggested that at times the organisation had all of the elements of a full-blown Greek tragedy.

origins. While the roots of ACFID may have been set down in the radical times of the late 1960s, few of the founding members would have called themselves radical, and certainly not Sir John Crawford, ACFID's founder, academic and public service icon. What may have been in people's minds was that the ACFID executive committee may at times have been 'courageous' in employing the passionate and outspoken staff that it did.

ACFID has to juggle a number of competing interests: it has to not only represent the broad set of views of its constituency – its member NGOs in Australia – but it also has to inform and challenge both the membership and the government of the day. In doing so, ACFID must strive not to alienate either. In the 1970s there was a strong perception that it alienated many of its members (ACFOA 1979c), and in the late 1990s and early 2000s it at times alienated elements of the government (see Chapter 8). The problem seemed to be that the messages did not resonate with the audiences in those times. In either case, the audience – be it the ACFID membership or government – could not simply switch off, as they were in part paying for the messages being delivered, either through member fees or AusAID grants. The paradox, as Lang argues, is that the 'stabilisation of an organisation ... to confer predictability ... tends to turn down the volume of public advocacy' (2012, p. 205). Forty years earlier, Lissner argued in the same vein that the 'opportunity cost of income maximization poses a greater threat to the credibility [of NGOs] than does doctrinaire idealism' (1977, p. 227). Perhaps 'turning down the volume' is not bad thing, if being too strident leads to people either not listening or to merely preaching to the converted.

This book is heavily influenced by Jorgen Lissner's *The Politics of Altruism* and Sabine Lang's *NGOs, Civil Society and the Public Sphere*. Their two works serve to bookend this history. Lissner's (1977) work looks at the issues facing NGOs in the 1970s while Lang's (2012) looks at the state of NGOs in the 2000s. While Lang focuses on relations between NGOs and government as regulator and funder, and what she refers to as the 'tacit co-dependency among unequals' (p. ix), Lissner focuses less on government and more on the tension between fundraising and advocacy, or 'voice'. What the two books share is a critique of social movements which become institutionalised – Lang calls this the 'NGO-ization' of social justice movements. While ACFID did not directly emerge from the social justice movements of the 1960s and before, many of its members did, such as Oxfam, Caritas, OSB, Act for Peace, Overseas Service Bureau (OSB), which all have had a strong influence on ACFID and its work.

Lissner (1977, p. 74) and Lang (2012, p. 4) both argue that an integral part of being an NGO is that it is a public benefit organisation driven by a world view or Weltanschauung (such as humanism or religious beliefs), from which it draws legitimacy by communicating messages to the public about this world view. While NGOs can and do communicate individually on social justice issues, there is also a big advantage in communicating with a common voice, such as that provided by ACFID. This also enables individual NGOs to be a bit 'hands off' in their advocacy work and avoid the tension Lissner mentioned that comes with NGO funding, whether from the public or government. This still leaves the question as to whose voice ACFID should represent − is it just about 'normative claims about the common good … [and being] a public expert in variously scaled civic spaces'? (Lang, p. 13).

The issue of moral hazard is one consequence of 'whose voice?', as ACFID and its members may be articulating their own values as being the values of those they purport to represent (Kilby 2011). This is the major criticism of NGOs: that the universal public good and set of values they claim to represent may be more contested (Staples 2008). Is a peak body like ACFID able to enter these spaces and argue that the social justice agenda is not about the self-interest of a few NGOs but represents a broad public view and gives voice to the voiceless? This is a theme to be explored throughout this book. This question goes to the effectiveness of ACFID in the role of a commentator with a strong values base, or what Landolt (2004) and O'Neill (2000) refer to as a 'constructivist' analysis of the world, which sees change as adopting norms around social justice and equity.

Maintaining harmony

From the outset ACFID has had the challenge of maintaining the harmony of a good chorus. The international NGO sector has never been homogenous but rather it represents a diverse set of values, beliefs and world views. A conservative religious NGO may have quite a different world view from a secular activist NGO and, while they can agree on broad principles around social justice, the devil lies in the detail of what each might say on these issues. A simple characterising of NGOs into left and right, or conservative and progressive on a political spectrum, is neither sufficient nor helpful. Similarly, the views of the broader society that ACFID's members represent are also in a state of flux, and their sympathy or hostility to the social issues of the day shifts over time. The challenge that ACFID has had over its 50 years has been that of providing leadership in the international development NGO sector. It has had to provide ideas and resources, as well as a forum, without being captured by the particular interests of its members, or fall into the trap of irrelevance by meekly following the membership.

Chapter 2 discusses how ACFID members in 1965 had to be dragged into a council by the indefatigable Sir John Crawford, and how they struggled for the next few years to find a purpose until the opportunity of being involved in global education emerged in the 1970s. This opportunity, however, was also to set the scene for division in the mid-1970s, which Chapter 3 looks at. Divisions emerged again in the mid-1990s when the government was questioning ACFID and NGO legitimacy more broadly, prompting the suggestion that the larger NGOs form their own council or network, much like what happened in the UK following the break-up of the VCOAD in the 1970s (Miles 1978). Certainly government would prefer dealing with the larger agencies only, and AusAID has often encouraged regular discussions among the bigger agencies. In the end, however, the divisions of the 1970s and 1990s were never deep enough to split ACFID, and in the 2010s it remains probably more united and with more members than ever. The divisions that occurred were probably inevitable in a diverse council, and keeping everybody 'in the tent' has been a major challenge over the 50 years of ACFIDs' life.

Mick Sullivan, executive director in the mid-1970s, noted at the time of a major review of the Australian Council for Overseas Aid (ACFOA), the precursor to ACFID:

> ACFOA is not a healthy organisation because it was never planned that way; [and] the consensus on what it is, is inadequate. [It] has been necessary for ACFOA's continued existence that it be ambiguous, and be many things to many people (ACFOA 1977a, p. 1).

The idea of ACFID being 'many things to many people' is an inevitable issue for any peak body that provides a range of services. Some members are there to be part of the lobbying, others for the legitimacy that membership brings, while for others again it is access to the resources that ACFID provides. Furthermore, many see the networking as essential for them to be effective in their work. The review that Sullivan refers to followed deep divisions in part around what was seen as 'a rapid growth in increasingly dissident views of aid and development problems' while at the time not being responsive to member needs (Tiffen et al. 1979, p. 29). The key finding from the review was simply that 'ACFOA had survived', but the review also noted the successful relations ACFID had built with government, its being a forum for members and the positive role the work on global education work had achieved. For some members at the time, ACFID was not sufficiently useful or of interest to them to command a greater commitment. It was seen as sending them an overload of written communication but not providing enough personal links, very necessary if complex and controversial ideas were to be 'sold' to the members.

Figure 2 Mick Sullivan meets Pope Paul VI who blesses ACFOA (Mnsgr Coveney translates).

Source: Felici (Rome).

The outcome of the 1979 review was to temper the voice of the chorus, and it led to some steps by ACFID to ensure the members were more or less singing from the same song sheet. The review, however, meant much more than survival; it also put ACFID in good stead for the following 20 years when a new set of tensions arose. These, however, were less internal and more about changes in the external environment, and how AusAID and the government saw NGOs in general and ACFID in particular. The outcome of the 1979 review led to the 'good' years of ACFID through the 1980s, when the enduring legacies of ACFID emerge: the code of ethics/conduct, and the discourse on good development practice for NGOs. In both of these areas ACFID was a world leader, discussing these issues many years before its European and North American counterparts.

In the 1980s ACFID was able to be a commentator and challenger of both government and NGOs. It was prolific, putting out roughly one press release a week, usually critical of government policy on a whole range of matters to do with international issues, often human rights or conflict related, but also on Aboriginal and Torres Strait Islander issues in Australia. The commentary went beyond aid and development issues, with ACFID arguing that human rights abuses, international conflict and domestic indigenous issues were all related to broader questions of development and social justice. By the 1990s, however, government felt this was going beyond commentating on aid, was outside the mandate of ACFID and, more importantly, was outside the scope of the funding provided by government. By the mid-1990s AusAID was starting to define very sharply what it was paying for in the ACFID secretariat funding agreements, and advocacy and global education were no longer to be part of it. By the 2000s, government was largely hostile to such adverse commentary from ACFID and believed it was inimical to their role of service providers and based on a view that 'only elected representatives are accountable through the electoral process' (Staples 2007, p. 6). This view of the role of NGOs presented a challenge for ACFID and its members as it ignored the argument that the very purpose of NGOs is to give voice to the marginalised, that an advocacy role is central if NGOs are to be true to their values and mandate – that is, to take a social justice rather than a welfare focus (Lissner 1977; O'Neill 2000; Korf 2007).

'Biting the hand that feeds.' This was the phrase used by Andrew Thompson, the Parliamentary Secretary for Foreign Affairs and Trade, responsible for aid and development when ACFID briefed him on its advocacy work: 'ACFOA was on AusAID's payroll and so [by doing advocacy] they were biting the hand that feeds' (ACFOA 1996a). This has been an ongoing problem for ACFID as it receives a substantial part of its income from government. This pressure was to continue to varying degrees up to and through the 2010s.

The idea of a publicly funded critic of government was seen as important in promoting public debate on key development issues through the 1970s and 1980s (Melville 1999; Sawer 2002; Maddison, Hamilton et al. 2004; Staples 2007). The rationale was 'to strengthen weak voices, the sections of the community that would otherwise be unheard in public debate and policy development' (Sawer 2002, p. 39). While industry bodies had the resources to put their case and provide policy advice to government, the more marginalised groups in society did not. While government funding of ACFID dated back to the late 1960s (see Chapter 2), by the mid-1970s this had risen sharply when the Whitlam Labor government provided support for a large range of domestic welfare and other peak bodies, including ACFID.

Although this philosophy of government providing support to NGO peak bodies was reiterated in 1991 at a parliamentary inquiry which noted that government support for peak bodies 'reinforces the democratic nature of Australian society' (Parliament of the Commonwealth of Australia 1991, p. 4), by the 1990s and 2000s this view began to change. The more managerial Labor government in the early 1990s saw a cooling of relations with welfare peak bodies, including ACFID, as results-based management clauses were applied to their contracts

(Maddison et al. 2004; Martinez and Cooper 2013). This went a step further in the late 1990 under a conservative Coalition government when NGO critics and right-wing think tanks asserted a conservative agenda more forcefully, part of which was attacking NGO legitimacy. Using public choice theory to bolster their case, these critics argued that ACFID's 'biting the hand that feeds' was merely ACFID and the NGO sector acting out of self-interest (Johns 2000; Staples 2007, 2008). The self-interest argument was hard to maintain given the ongoing support by the public for NGO work that was clearly driven by values based on social justice and human rights. The public could also see the rising level of inequality in the world at the time, in part driven by the neoliberal policies of the late 1980s and 1990s. NGOs and ACFID argued that 'an ethical theory of global responsibility needs to take account of structural relations in our global world' (Korf 2007, p. 373). The implication was that it commits NGOs, as O'Neill (2000) argues, 'to seeing those on the far sides of existing boundaries, distant strangers though they be, as having moral standing for us' (p. 202), which was to conservative critics, a 'dangerous form of idealism' (p. 201).

This ideologically based criticism of NGO advocacy work brought a different set of pressures into play which ACFID hitherto had not had to deal with. The role of ACFID as a result of its government funding became an issue not only for government but also within ACFID (Rollason 1994; ACFOA 1994b). On the one hand, government questioned what it saw as the high levels of funding it provided to ACFID vis-a-vis member contributions (Terrell 1994) while, on the other, larger NGOs felt that some of their interests were being overlooked in favour of smaller agency interests. The bigger agencies saw any threat to ACFID as also being a threat to them, and they were thinking about ways of reducing that threat. While there were some meetings in the mid-1990s of larger agencies to discuss alternative structures, in the end these talks came to nothing and ACFID remained (Smillie 1999a; Hobbs 2013; Hunt 2011). ACFID, however, continued to be a vocal critic of the government's record on aid delivery until the early 2000s, when perhaps the last straw was the 'bawling out' of the ACFID executive director by the foreign minister Alexander Downer in front of the Indonesian Ambassador over its criticism of Indonesia's human rights record in West Papua (Harris-Rimmer 2013). As a result of these pressures from AusAID, and government more broadly, ACFID became more muted, and, for a time in the mid-2000s, it took more of a lobbying role rather than public advocacy sharply critical of government (O'Callaghan 2013).

ACFID was not alone in having at times a tense relationship with government. Canada followed a similar trajectory through the 1990s and into the 2000s, with attacks from government at the highest levels on both domestic and international NGOs and their legitimacy to be advocates (Sawer and Laycock 2009; Smillie 2012). CCIC, the sister organisation of ACFID in Canada, had similar experiences to ACFID a few years earlier. In the early 1990s,

> CIDA did not like being hectored about their political stances on Southern Africa much less on the volume and quality of their aid program. Measured criticism was acceptable but only up to a point. Nor did they [CIDA] like being asked in Parliament why the government was supporting voices that came across as shrill, radical and sometimes abusive (Smillie 2012, p. 279).

This came to a head in 1991 when the head of CCIC was given a dressing-down by the head of CIDA for a 'report card' they had produced critical of CIDA's performance. The head of ACFID was to receive a similar dressing-down a decade later over a report they did, which was similarly critical of a DAC[4] peer review (see Chapter 8).

ACFID has always struggled with funding, and finding the 'right' balance between what members paid and any government subsidy they received. One executive director has suggested a whole chapter of this book could be spent on budgeting alone. In its early days, ACFID's members felt that as the government seemed to have a big hand in ACFID's establishment (see Chapter 2) then government should pay for its running costs. It was through some skilful negotiation that Sir John Crawford, ACFID's founder, managed to get some money earmarked for coordinating aid to South Vietnam (a project which was both unwanted and unworkable) to be used to cover the running costs of ACFID (ACFOA 1967a; Webb 1971). Ever since then ACFID has been funded to varying degrees: by a government grant, by members' fees, by special projects (usually funded by government), and from time to time from its own income generation through the sale of services and resources to its members and others. This is a balancing act that other international NGO peak bodies have to manage, with ACFID having much of its advocacy work, for the first 25 years at least, covered by government funding. However, changes in governments, with a shift in philosophy against funding NGO advocacy on behalf of the marginalised, saw much of that funding curtailed in the 2000s (Staples 2007).

From the mid-1990s the constant threat to funding and AusAID's approach of putting limits around its support to ACFID's budget, saw ACFID over time take a reduced government grant for its core operations from 60 per cent of the budget in the early 1990s to 40 per cent in the 2000s (Hewett 2013). AusAID had funded ACFID 'projects' since its inception. Funding aid coordination in South Vietnam was the first of many ACFID 'projects' up until the early 2010s, when

---

4   Development Assistance Committee of the OECD (DAC).

it provided ACFID with support for NGO research and Code of Conduct-related work as a special project. At the time of writing, the ACFID secretariat was staffed in such a way that while project-related staff might lose their jobs when projects were completed, a cut in government funding would not stop the core operations continuing. In other parts of the world, precipitate funding cuts by government to peak bodies created serious problems. In 2010 neither CCIC in Canada nor CID in New Zealand were really prepared for the sudden loss of their government grants, which reduced CID to a single staff person and CCIC having to mortgage its office space to cover the redundancies of two thirds of its staff (CCIC 2010a; Ed Challies, McGregor et al. 2011; Smillie 2012).

The work of ACFID

Histories such as this one can get caught up in the struggles that organisations go through and the politics surrounding them and forget the day-to-day work. For ACFID this is about networking among members and keeping the ear of government. While the other chapters of the book look at the work of ACFID, it is by necessity selective in picking up only some of the key themes and issues which shaped it. The rest of this chapter attempts to look at some of the everyday work of ACFID, as well as introduce the bigger issues touched on in subsequent chapters.

Advocacy

Whether it was under the guise of global education and the *Development News Digest* (the ACFID magazine through the 1970s) or through more direct advocacy targeting government, ACFID was a regular commentator and advocate for change in government development policy. It has continually pushed a poverty and human rights focus on bilateral aid, as well as government support for NGO approaches to aid. While ACFID has shifted from being a strong critic of government in its advocacy work in the 1970s and 1980s to having an uneasy alliance with government on advocacy in the 2000s with Make Poverty History, ACFID has remained an influential voice.

At the everyday level there are regular meetings between ACFID staff and government policymakers, whether in the Department of Foreign Affairs and Trade (DFAT) or other government departments such as Defence and Treasury. ACFID meets regularly with ministers and politicians to talk about aid policy issues. The first major advocacy campaign in 1972 was for the McMahon Coalition government to increase its aid effort to the Bangladesh refugee crisis in 1971 (see Chapter 3). With the election of the Labor government in 1972 both aid policy and the level of aid became an important issue for government, to the extent that Gough Whitlam mentioned aid in his election campaign launch (Rollason 2013).[5] Some 40 years later, in 2013, the incoming conservative Coalition government did not release its policy to cut the aid program until two days before the election, to avoid any public debate.

From the mid-1970s there were, and still are, regular meetings with government about the level and direction of aid, and ACFID, being an *ex officio* member of Aid Advisory Councils, has a seat at the 'table' set up from time to time to advise ministers on aid issues.[6] Advocacy work, however, depends on having someone to listen and the interest of the minister in the issues, and even being aware of their moods. Russell Rollason tells the story of Bill Hayden (Labor foreign minister 1983–88) not talking to him for a year over some real or imagined slight, then calling from Finland (while Rollason was visiting AusAID) seeking his urgent views on a fairly non-controversial issue. Gareth Evans for his part largely delegated aid issues to his junior minister, arguing that NGO aid issues 'were below his pay grade' (Evans 2013). Likewise Andrew Peacock, as foreign minister in the 1970s, blamed Mick Sullivan for a leak to the opposition (Sullivan 2013), and Alexander Downer, when foreign minister in the late 1990s and early 2000s, had a prickly relationship with ACFID. Mick Sullivan makes the point, however, that keeping the channels of communication open at all times to both political parties was most important, as was avoiding being tarred by some ideological brush (Sullivan 2013) – sage advice which ACFID has generally followed.

ACFID has had some important 'wins' with government: the work on Africa, particularly South Africa; East Timor; and Cambodia probably being the main ones. ACFID was one of a small number of voices who fought against the political injustices of South Africa's apartheid regime; the invasion and occupation of East Timor through the 1970s, 1980s and into the 1990s; the isolation of Cambodia by the West in the 1980s; and the treatment of Aboriginal and Torres Strait Islanders in Australia and their land rights since the 1970s. ACFID often provided both a venue and a way of opening doors to many of the spokespeople for these movements. For a time in the 1980s, José Ramos-Horta, who was to become East Timor's president and Nobel Laureate, had some space in an office

---

5   This was to be the first and last time an Australian prime ministerial candidate put overseas aid into a campaign speech.
6   The first of these aid advisory councils was chaired by Sir John Crawford, who resigned as ACFID President to take up the role of chair of the first of these councils which had a number of iterations over time. Public servants tended to think these councils were interfering in their work and a waste of time, while ministers had mixed views of their usefulness (Viviani and Wilenski 1978; Tupper 2012). In 2015 an Innovations Hub was set up with a high level Reference Group to advise government on innovative aid approaches with ACFID being represented on it.

in the ACFID building, as did Fessahaie Abraham, the representative of the Eritrean Relief Association. Eddie Funde, the African National Congress official representative in Australia, was also a welcome visitor when he was in Canberra.

ACFID's work on Cambodia, which had been isolated following the defeat of the Khmer Rouge in 1979, was important to the Australian government at a time when the only Australian and other donor country presence was through their NGOs (Utting 1994). As Bill Hayden (1990) put it somewhat delicately at the ACFID 25th anniversary conference: '[S]ome of the organisations were able to monitor Australian interests, much as an unofficial consulate might do.' It was probably a little more than this as Lyndall McLean, head of the Joint Australian NGO Office in Pnom Penh for three years from 1989 and a former (and subsequent) diplomat, played no small role in opening communications for the Australian foreign minister Gareth Evans and others to negotiate the comprehensive 1991 peace settlement in Cambodia (Evans 2011). Having a friendly Australian presence in Cambodia was very important at the time, and ACFID member agencies performed that role. At the same time, ACFID lobbied at home and was relentless in its push for a comprehensive settlement and a normalisation of relations between Australia and Cambodia and Vietnam – the hostility with Vietnam and Cambodia being more of a US-defined Cold War relic rather than a result of substantial security or other issues in either country (Utting 1994; Brown and Zasloff 1998; Rollason 2013).

The quality of aid

The linked issues of aid quality and aid effectiveness became very important in the 2000s as increasing aid budgets were demanding some justification (Knack et al. 2011; Birdsall and Kharas 2012; Ndikumana 2012). The key guiding process has been the Paris Principles on Aid Effectiveness, which emphasises transparency, local participation, and alignment of aid programs with recipient government priorities and recipient government ownership (Booth 2012). After 10 years the results of the Paris Principles are mixed, due mainly to donor countries being reluctant to give up power and control over their foreign aid (Eyben 2010; Booth 2012; Brown et al. 2012; Hughes and Hutchison 2012).

None of this is new, and in Australia the debates around aid effectiveness started in 1982 as a global education issue when a Quality of Aid seminar that year criticised AusAID's development programs. In particular, it focused on the use of food aid as a support to Australian producers, and two controversial bilateral projects in the Philippines: the Zamboanga Del Sur and North Samar projects, which were seen to have a more strategic security focus that a development one (ACFOA 1982a). It followed the old and ongoing argument that:

the neo-colonial business of aid silences the autonomy and agency of local communities and citizens by the power of its representation and maintains the status quo of under-development (Gulrajani 2011, p. 202).

The clear implication was that NGO aid was somehow different. This ongoing critique of official government aid programs by NGOs raised the obvious question as to whether NGO aid was any more effective or appropriate. This led to some work by ACFID with regard to the quality of projects in the Australian NGO Cooperation Program (ANCP) subsidy scheme and another Quality of Aid seminar in 1983 focusing on NGO aid (Birch 1983; ACFOA 1983b). One outcome of this seminar was a 'quality bonus' of 20 per cent within the ANCP to those agencies that could demonstrate they could meet quality criteria, including directly targeting poor women. The aim of the subsidy was to shift NGOs away from the very common, but usually poorly thought out and unsustainable village craft projects (ACFOA 1983b; Rollason 2013). The Quality of Aid seminar was the first in a series of debates on NGO effectiveness, which still engages ACFID some 30 years later. To some extent these debates are difficult to resolve as the starting points are so different. NGOs can never be mainstream players in national level aid delivery, but rather can be important marginal players with targeted small-scale interventions (Ndikumana 2012).

In 1984 the ACFID secretariat was asked by its members to help 'verify NGO claims of effectiveness' (ACFOA 1984d). In 1985 the booklet *Questioning Practice: NGOs Project Evaluation* (Porter et al. 1985) prompted further debate and led to the establishment of a Development Project Appraisal and Evaluation Unit (ACFOA 1985a; 1985b; 1985g), with a quality of aid committee of ACFID members set up to support the unit. The first adviser, who was employed in 1987, prepared a set of manuals to assist NGOs with developing viable development projects (Zivetz 1988). The unit, however, was aimed at not only improving quality but also establishing ACFID and NGO legitimacy in commenting on the quality of government aid programs (ACFOA 1986a). By the early 1990s the unit was renamed the Development Advice and Training Unit with a mandate to be more active with NGOs in building their program management capacity (Ross 1992).

This work did not stem the criticism from AusAID and others completely; the NGO effectiveness review of 1995 found, somewhat paradoxically, that while the ANCP was very effective, NGOs were, nevertheless, too 'dependent' on AusAID and so no additional funding should be provided to the ANCP (AusAID 1995a). By 2000 the AusAID 'mood' had changed and the quality of NGOs' work had 'improved'. Another AusAID review found that NGO work was appropriate to development context, focused on marginalised people and effective partnerships, and addressed long-term development needs of beneficiaries, with no mention of NGO dependency. Similar to the 1995 report, gender issues were identified as a weakness, with the impact of projects on gender relations in general, and women in particular, neither understood or known, and monitoring remained weak (AusAID 2002). The development effectiveness debate continues into the 2010s with the new mantras being 'value for money' and 'benchmarking' effectiveness (AusAID 2012). As Lewis notes, the general view on NGO effectiveness at a global level was that:

> many NGOs were only weakly accountable to communities and governments, that their 'impact' on poverty reduction, where the attempt had been made to assess it, was lower than expected and that NGO efforts to scale up their work beyond piecemeal efforts or islands of success were largely unsuccessful (Lewis 2010b, p. 337).

While Riddell (2007) argues that NGOs are effective, the problem remains of the high expectations of NGOs, which is driven in part by the view that large-scale efforts are what is required and these are beyond the capability of most NGOs. Also NGOs themselves not only do not like admitting failure but they also do not like even admitting partial success (Kraeger 2011; Lang 2012). For many NGOs it is about an all-or-nothing approach, and being effective is an article of faith fundamental to establishing their legitimacy (Smillie 1996; Lecy ct al. 2012). Of course this does little to assuage the scepticism of governments.

Professionalism

Part of the quality debate was also linked to the perceived need by NGOs to 'professionalise', which is essentially to meet the needs of the state and, to a lesser extent, the private sector (Lang 2012), but at a cost.

> Professionalization of the aid sector into a sizable industrial complex has privileged managerial values of efficiency and impartiality at the expense of civic orientations and moral purposes. This turn of events is not unique to foreign aid; increasingly modern public administration is sacrificing the social meaning of the ends for the technical efficiency of the means (Gulrajani 2011, p. 212).

Implicit in the argument that NGOs need to professionalise is a view that has always been around: that NGOs and their work were somehow intrinsically not professional, and that being 'professional' was seen as a path to legitimacy (ACFOA 1994c). Professionalism also seems to suggest that 'the language of development has become depoliticised; power analysis and conflict are removed, contradictory ideas, concepts and approaches are robbed of their differences' (Wallace et al. 1997, p. 16). Almost at any stage through ACFID's 50 years there are statements to the effect that ACFID members were now professional, implying that before they were not. In 1997, a decade after the Code of Ethics was developed and was being replaced by a Code of Conduct, Rudy von Bernuth from the International Council of Voluntary Agencies (ICVA) noted that the Code was not only about professional standards but also about increased efforts by governments North and South to regulate NGOs (ACFOA 1997b). A decade earlier, Neville Ross, who was ACFID chair at the time, put it succinctly when he said:

> NGOs have been sucked in by the new emphasis on professionalism to believing that professionalism means doing things the way professionals do. Professionalism does not mean accepting AIDAB claptrap automatically (Ross 1988).

This continuing discussion about professionalism is also about NGO identity, and what they are really about (Lissner 1977). They are caught in the middle of being part of a social movement and being part of an aid 'industry' with its own language, rituals and behaviours. Over the years, ACFID has had links with social movements such as the anti-apartheid movement and various national liberation movements. While these links might be accepted to varying degrees by much of the supporter public, they are, however, looked at askance by government. NGOs are in a bind as they do need the support of government not only for formal approval via regulation, but also for 'some' funding. Some years back Michael Edwards (1999) pointed out:

> At a deeper level, most NGOs are still confused about their identity ... [and they] tend to import the philosophy of the market uncritically, treating development as a commodity, measuring market share as success, and equating being professional in their work with being businesslike ... [but NGO] legitimacy is derived from the NGO's social roots (its domestic constituency) and from demonstrable adherence to the values that hold the movement together (p. 28).

Lang (2012) more recently goes on to argue that a lot of the discussion around professionalisation leads to a corporate view of NGOs as a 'firm' with a product to sell. NGOs themselves can fall into the trap of inadvertently supporting the public choice theories touched on above rather than Lissner's (1977) notion of a public benefit based on values. 'The sector's function as an assembly for organised citizen engagements ... have little place in the firm logic of instrumental accountabilities' (p. 115). The evidence from Australia is probably not as clear-cut as Lang (2012) and Edwards (1999) argue; while the language of professionalism is still in vogue there may be enough checks and balances in place to ensure there remains a strong values base behind the work of most NGOs.

The reason for this continuing strong values base may be the relatively low levels of government funding for most NGOs vis-a-vis their domestic and many of their international counterparts. In addition, some of the regulatory processes in place, such as accreditation, have an emphasis on values and the nature of NGOs' partnerships with their counterparts in developing countries. Since the late 1980s, however, a set of controls and procedures have been put in place by AusAID through funding contracts which have limited the more innovative aspects of social change work, what Martinez and Cooper (2013) refer to as 'management and accounting control' (p. 1).

The Australian Council for International Development committees

Most of ACFID's most effective work is the activities and the networking that occurs through its committees. A measure of success is that the demand for committees has always outstripped the supply of ACFID staff to service them. Quite early on, in 1969, ACFID set up a committee structure to replace the unworkable commissions that were part of its founding structure. In retrospect, it was hard to have a secretariat plus two semi-autonomous commissions working, which is what the founding fathers of ACFID created in 1965 (see Chapter 2). The ACFID committee structure went through a number of iterations. At the time of writing there were four main committees dealing with development practice, advocacy, humanitarian response, and the University Network. There are also a number of ad hoc working groups dealing with the important issues of the day, which are largely run by members with ACFID staff having a communications role.

In the early days, however, there seemed to be committees for everything. Mick Sullivan said that at one point in the mid-1970s ACFID had 16 subcommittees, and he was secretary to them all (Sullivan 2013). By 1985 they had been rationalised a little, but there were still committees dealing with the Pacific, Africa, Education, Indochina, North–South issues, East Timor, human rights, and women and development (ACFOA 1985f). Later, environment and HIV/AIDS were added to the list. The problem was that the number of committees grew like Topsy, and ACFID staff had to service them despite regular attempts to cut them back, such as Janet Hunt's (1998) attempt to have just two committees: Development Practice and Advocacy, the rest being self-managed working groups.

There was always a tendency to add a new committee to look at the latest urgent issue without getting rid of those committees that may have run their course. For example, Janet Hunt (1998) noticed that there were few major agencies on the environment committee, and gender had been flagged as an issue after the Beijing World Conference on Women in 1995. While most people who have been associated with ACFID probably have their favourite committees, I would argue that apart from the ones which have dedicated chapters in this book (gender, human rights, code of conduct, and humanitarian response), probably the most effective over the longer term were the Africa Committee for keeping Africa on the AusAID agenda for so long, the Mekong Committee on its work with Cambodia through the 1980s, and the North–South Committee for keeping global justice issues alive, particularly in the neoliberal period of structural adjustment in the 1980s. The work of the Environment Committee and the HIV and AIDS Development Network of Australia (HIDNA) played a key role in bringing these issues to the fore in the 1990s to the point that environment and HIV/AIDS were mainstream issues in most NGO work in the 2000s.

The choir masters

Of course any Greek chorus requires a choir master. In the case of ACFID, while the executive director is in charge of the choir, the ACFID executive committee calls the tune. In a governance sense this causes difficulty as the ACFID executive committee has a more hands-on role than a regular NGO board, and from time to time this has led to tensions as the executive directors have always been a little constrained in what they could do. The other issue is that with advocacy, and for some type of programming, such as advice and training, there was always the possibility of a conflict of interest where ACFID was competing for the same resources as its members, and so the executive committee tried to make sure that the ACFID secretariat did not become 'operational'.

There were a couple of times when ACFID did become operational: one was with IDEC (see Chapter 5), which functioned reasonably well on and off for over 20 years; the other was global education, which also ran for 20 years and morphed into campaigns for a further 10 years or so. In other cases, where ACFID attempted to recoup some staff costs through consultancies, the executive committee was more nervous (Rollason 2013).[7] The issue of ACFID's role and the extent to which it can become 'operational' is an ongoing issue. At the end of the day, ACFID has to be able to maintain its identity with the public, and more importantly connect with its ACFID values in a meaningful way and avoid the danger Lang (2012) cautions against of being turned into primarily a lobbying business. Other aid NGO peak bodies, such as InterAction in the US, derive a much larger proportion of their income from services 'sold' to members.

---

7   For example, in 1994 the HIDNA staff person's role was able to be extended by a year through the consultancy work of the development advice and training team, but this income was capped at 60 days per year (ACFOA 1994e), and then faded all together.

The public face of ACFID is its executive director, who has to lead and represent members' interests to government, build the membership and ease tensions among members. Of the 10 executive directors ACFID has had over its 50 years, only one has been a woman. Three came out of church member agencies, two from secular member agencies, one was an ex-politician, one had military connections, one was a lobbyist, one an ex-government official, and one was an internal promotion from staff. Of the first five executive directors, two were sacked, two left through ill health, and one died in office. While not all of these 'casualties' were directly related to the pressures of the job, most were – giving some indication of the fluid nature of the organisation at the time and the growing pains ACFID was having. From the early 1980s ACFID was more stable, and the executive directors have all left of their own volition and timing. It is worth noting that despite it being a peak body, unlike its US counterpart InterAction, the executive director does not come from the ranks of the executive directors of the large member agencies, but rather from their staff. Whether this is constraint or not is hard to say (Harris-Rimmer 2013).

The chorus

Throughout its history ACFID has been a broad representative body, with most NGOs as members, so as to have as many voices as possible in the chorus. However, there have been NGOs who have been either indifferent or opposed to being members of ACFID. In the early years, World Vision Australia was reluctant to join, not seeing the benefit and feeling that too many of the existing members were opposed to its way of working. At various times the Australian Red Cross has been a member, an associate member, or not a member at all. The Red Cross, as part of an international organisation, has restrictions on membership of peak bodies, particularly if they are involved in advocacy work. It formally withdrew from ACFID in 1975 over what it saw as ACFID's partisan stance on the Indonesian invasion of East Timor, but rejoined in 2013. In the early 1990s CARE Australia was not a member and did not see any advantages, but joined when the Code of Ethics became a Code of Conduct, and code compliance was mandatory for accreditation to receive government funds. In the 2010s neither Compassion nor Médecins Sans Frontières (MSF), the third and fourth largest NGOs in Australia in terms of funding from the public (Wulfsohn and Howes 2014), were members of ACFID or code signatories, as they did not receive government funding and felt the Code of Conduct would restrict the way they worked.

Conclusion

This chapter has attempted to give a flavour of ACFID's history and a taste of what is to come in this book. The key role of ACFID as commentator, advocate, lobbyist, and networker has stood the test of time. The key question this book will look at is how adaptable ACFID has been to an ever-changing environment, and how it can keep up with the changes. A former staff member questions whether ACFID deserves the name of being the peak of the NGO 'sector', as the sectoral voice is not coherent enough, and criticises it for not taking the debate forward and setting the agenda as much as it might have in the past. In the 2010s ACFID may be more of a collective bound by a Code of Conduct rather than a sectoral leader. In the 1970s and 1980s the general community knew a little bit about ACFID through its public advocacy and global education programs, but now in the 2010s there is much lower public recognition (Harris-Rimmer 2013; Hewett 2013).

This is a harsh criticism, maybe a little unfair, and probably something that staff have said of ACFID throughout its history, but it does raise the question of how the 'chorus' can keep up with changing times and changing tunes, and when to be loud and when to be quiet. The stakes are much higher than they were in the early years when NGOs were barely noticed by government, let alone regulated or funded. In the 2010s the level of funding is much the same as what it was (in real terms) in the 1990s, but the conditions attached to the funding are seeking answers to much harder questions about effectiveness and value for money, and the NGO mantra of 'doing good' and 'it is all about the values' does not wash as much as in earlier times. Also, while NGO funding has grown the ACFID secretariat has not grown in the same way so it is being asked to do more with the same staff as 20 years ago. The chorus song sheet and requests may have grown, but the choir remains the same.

02

The Origins and Establishment of the Australian Council for International Development

In Canberra, where the Australian Council for International Development is located, whole suburbs are devoted to industry associations and peak bodies there to capture the ear of government. It is often assumed that these industry peak bodies' own members drove the process of coming together to advocate for their cause. The case of ACFID is quite different: it was a determined individual, Sir John 'Jack' Crawford, a former public servant with no NGO connections, who brought a disparate group of Australian development NGOs together into a single council in the mid-1960s. Without him there may not have been a single peak body for NGOs with the near universal representation of Australian development NGOs it has today; or at the very least it may have formed much later. In 1965 there was scepticism among NGOs about the need for a peak body, and it was not until the early 1970s that ACFID was able to establish a clear identity and become a very active council. This chapter describes how ACFID came about.

Part of the rationale for establishing ACFID lies in the post-war aid scene in which newly independent countries and their international supporters, including NGOs, were struggling to meet the post-war and postcolonial challenges. While there were aid programs before World War II, and some of the common NGOs today such as the Red Cross, Save the Children, and others have their origins in the nineteenth or early twentieth centuries, these were largely concerned with disaster relief, health, education, and welfare. Lissner (1977) dates the first international NGO to 1653, when a missionary society from Quebec started work in Latin America, followed by other missionary and educational institutions that worked in all European colonies over the next 300 years. Since those early missionary NGOs, the growth in NGO numbers has been slow, with their focus remaining narrow and welfare based. Notions of development did not get much currency until US President Roosevelt's 1941 call for 'four freedoms' – of speech and worship, and from want and fear; the creation of the United Nations in 1945; and US President Truman's Point Four Program[1] for development in 1949 (Chant and McIlwaine 2009; James 1993). The post-war reconstruction efforts in war-ravaged Europe and Japan through the 1950s spilt over to meeting the needs of the newly independent developing countries and sought to transplant rapid industrial development models from the West (Gubser 2012; Thorbecke and Tarp 2000; Tarp 2010; Dwivedi and Nef 1982). The 1950s also saw NGOs responding to the needs of local populations in the emerging developing countries and starting their own programs there, most often with volunteers. This nascent development work by Australia started in Asia in the 1950s and in Africa in the 1960s (Australian Aid Abroad 1967).

In the 1950s developing countries were either fighting for independence or developing the political formations and administrative machinery necessary for government, and so it was not until the 1960s that economic development and aid programs began to expand and assume much greater importance (Abdel-Rahman 1970; Pearson 1969; Fukuda-Parr 2004; Kanbur 2006). A notable exception was the 1950s' Colombo Plan,[2] which was very much part of a Cold War strategy to keep the emerging Asian nations in the Western sphere of influence, and to help them fight communism at home with economic development (Hasluck 1966; Taylor 1965; Tarp 2010; Oakman 2001; Howell 2014).

The first Development Decade

The first Development Decade (1961–70) was an attempt to have a more focused and directed approach to development (Thorbecke and Tarp 2000). The key elements were an agreement that developed countries would provide 1 per cent of their GDP as aid and foreign direct investment, and developing countries would achieve a 5 per cent real rate of growth (Quataert 2013; Hulme 2013). The decade was launched by the UN General Assembly in 1961 and was characterised by a shift in focus to include agricultural development and the Green Revolution, as well as the large-scale industrial development so favoured in the 1950s. This was a response to the problem that economic growth in general, and agricultural output in particular, were not able to keep up with rapid population growth. It would simply take too long for industrial development to produce enough jobs in the context of a looming food crisis. The problem with these approaches,

---

1   It was called the Point Four Program because it was the fourth objective (point) of Truman's foreign policy.
2   Its full title at the time was the Colombo Plan for Cooperative Economic Development in South and Southeast Asia.

which still persists, is that they depend on imported technocratic solutions rather than adapting local approaches and addressing global structural issues of inequality and access to resources (Meier 1971; Quataert 2013; Gubser 2012).

US President John F. Kennedy was a champion of the Development Decade and picked up the Truman idea of the Point Four Program. He sought to expand it with what he referred to as a Marshall Plan for development.

> To those people in the huts and villages of half the globe struggling to break the bonds of mass misery, we pledge our best efforts to help them help themselves, for whatever period is required – not because the communists may be doing it, not because we seek their votes, but because it is right. If a free society cannot help the many who are poor, it cannot save the few who are rich (from John F. Kennedy's Inauguration speech quoted in Birdsall and Sowa, 2013, p. 3).

Kennedy enacted the US Act for International Development in 1961, from which the Peace Corps, the Alliance for Progress, and Food for Peace emerged as the US response to the first Development Decade (Black 1992; OECD 1988; Council of Europe 1963; Labouisse 1961). Under the leadership of the prime minister of India, Jawaharlal Nehru, 1965 was declared the Year of International Cooperation (Kowalski 2011; Cumming 2013). Most importantly for ACFID's story, 1963 saw NGOs first recognised by the UN as being important players in developing a constituency of support for aid programs in Western donor countries (UNGA 1963a).

Despite the optimism of the first half of the Development Decade, development practice did not measure up to the rhetoric, and the decade ended in failure. As Lester Pearson (1969), the former prime minister of Canada who reviewed the first Development Decade, noted: 'the climate surrounding foreign aid programs is [now] heavy with disillusion and distrust' (p. vii). Neither the targeted aid and investment flows nor the growth targets were reached, and developing countries felt they had been short-changed (Odén 2010; Gubser 2012). The decade also marked the start of some fundamental questioning of the nature of development, with writers such as André Gunner Frank and the radical social movements of the time having a strong influence on development discourse (Legum 1970; Schmidt and Pharo 2003; Frank 1969). This all set the scene for a greater focus on direct poverty alleviation programs by addressing basic human needs, and a role for NGOs emerged as a way to ensure a greater and improved focus on development (Ziai 2011; Gubser 2012; Harries Committee 1979).

Australia's aid program

While Australia's overseas aid program began in earnest in 1950, it did not develop a strong and coherent development focus until the 1970s. In 1950 the Australian foreign minister Percy Spender, who was concerned at Australia's lack of engagement with Asia, put the idea to a Commonwealth Conference in Colombo of a plan of development for the three newly independent countries of South Asia: India, Pakistan, and Sri Lanka (Sullivan 1976; Taylor 1965; Oakman 2010).[3] This program was established partially to counter the communist inclinations of many of the newly independent countries of the time through the use of soft power, as part of a broader Cold War strategy (Waters 1999; Taylor 1965; Jones and Benvenuti 2012) to project an 'image of Australia as a purposeful and strong Pacific power which, assuming appropriate and resolute action, could assert a stabilising presence in Asia' (Oakman 2010, p. 44).

The other important aspect of the Colombo Plan was to strengthen the cultural ties between Australia and Asia, which would build the enduring bilateral relationships that exist today (Lowe 2013). An important aspect of building these cultural ties was the sending of volunteers to provide technical assistance to Colombo Plan projects, which led to the burgeoning NGO volunteer programs of the 1960s (Oakman 2010). The placement of these enthusiastic young volunteers in the 1950s was fairly ad hoc, an example of which was a volunteer program to Indonesia proposed by Herb Feith and Jim Webb to be run by the Australian Committee of the World University Service in 1953 (Webb 1971). This was probably the first instance of an Australian government funding an NGO: 'the Australian Government provided the airfare, £50 and a bicycle' (Smillie 1995, p. 41). The ad hoc volunteer programs of the 1950s were part of a trend that led to the American Peace Corps, British VSO, and Australian Volunteers Abroad, which were all set up in the early 1960s and largely funded by their respective governments. They were seen as a way to foster cultural exchanges and build a positive image of the West at the height of the Cold War (Webb 1971; Georgeou and Engel 2011).

The 1950s was also a period when Australia, the UK and the US were involved in a number of postcolonial and Cold War conflicts. The main ones were the Korean War, 1950–52; the Malayan Emergency, 1955–60; the Indonesian Confrontation (*Confrontasi*) with Malaysia over Borneo, mid-1960s; and the war in Vietnam, 1962–75. Development aid was often linked to these conflicts as part of 'winning hearts and minds' or, as Oakman (2001) described it, 'fighting the Cold War in Asia through propaganda and development projects' (p. 260). In the United

---

3   The idea may have had its origins in an idea of the Indian Ambassador to China, Kavalam Madhava Panikkar, who in 1949 proposed to the Australian and the UK ambassadors a multilateral fund largely funded by the US (Fisher 1971).

States, NGOs were often part of the Cold War mix, with the Asia Foundation for example being set up in 1954 by the US government and funded by the CIA for this purpose (Department of State 1966; Wu 2012; Kilcullen 2005; Keck 2011; Oakman 2001). For Australia, its development programs went to the Southeast Asia Treaty Organisation countries to complement military aid – mainly to Malaysia but later to Vietnam as well (Wolf 1957; Hasluck 1964; Oakman 2001; Howell 2014).

Aid programs to Southeast Asia at the time were not without their problems, with emerging countries suffering the twin problems of too little investment and too much tied aid (Government of Malaysia 1969). Overall, the growth in aid in the 1960s was found to be ill-directed, not sufficient to kick-start the emerging economies of the region, and tied more to the donor's strategic self-interest rather than the development needs of recipients (Pearson 1969; Easterly and Williamson 2011).

NGO aid

Before World War II there were 655 international NGOs around the world, which quickly doubled in the postwar years to over 1,300 when ACFID had its first meetings in 1965 (Lissner 1977). This rapid growth in NGOs had its origins in community responses to war and the voluntary rebuilding efforts that follow conflict (TR Davies 2012; Kane 2013). As Fowler (2000) put it,

> in this early stage, the inspiration and moral grounding for civic action arose principally from religiously informed and culturally conditioned values of compassion and from conventions of mutual obligation within groups both at home and abroad (p. 639).

The Catholic Relief Services and CARE,[4] originally a US 23-agency network, had their origins in rebuilding Europe after World War II. Oxfam was originally founded in Oxford by a group of Quakers, social activists and Oxford academics in response to the famine created by the British blockade of Greece in 1942. Save the Children Fund had its origins in the 1919 blockade of Germany following World War I; World Vision had its origins in the Korean War in 1950; and, of course, the Red Cross with the Battle of Solferino in 1859 nearly a century before. With the exception of World Vision, which came later, these NGOs were very involved in the huge refugee flows from 1947–50, and the relief efforts in the mainly European war-ravaged countries (OECD 1988; Hilton 2012).

---

4   CARE was initially the Cooperative for American Remittances to Europe. Later it became the Cooperative for American Relief Everywhere and, as it globalised, the Cooperative for Assistance and Relief Everywhere.

NGO aid did not have a development focus until the 1950s, when the refugee and rehabilitation work of the postwar period was completed. At the same time there was limited government support for NGO work, with only Sweden providing public funds for NGOs in 1952 and the US government supporting some NGO work from 1954, mainly through food aid (Lindin 1976; Sommer 1977; Cullather 2010; OECD 1988). While the strong growth in support and interest in NGOs after the war was in the areas of post-conflict reconstruction, they soon became involved in responding to the devastating famines in India in the early 1950s, and in China later that decade. This work, while growing rapidly, was still ad hoc and privately funded, involving what Wright (2012) refers to as 'importing Northern ways to the South' (p. 124), much in the same way that bilateral programs were run at the time.

The 1960s saw NGOs shift more clearly to development aid, spurred on in part by the UN and the first Development Decade with its call for stronger public involvement in aid programs globally, and fostering a public voice for aid and development (Lockwood 1963; Hilton 2012). One example of this was the World Council of Churches (WCC) advocacy work from 1958, which adopted the position that Western donors provide 1 per cent of their GDP for both aid and foreign direct investment. This position was adopted by the UN in 1961. In 1972 this was revised to a 0.7 per cent target for official aid only (Clemens and Moss 2007; Tomasevski 1993). This nascent advocacy work took on an official guise with the formation of the Freedom from Hunger Campaign (FFHC), which started in 1961 as a five-year global campaign movement sponsored by the UN's Food and Agriculture Organization (FAO) to raise funds and awareness of the issues of global injustice among mainly the general public of Western donor countries (Lissner 1977; FAO 1961; Jachertz 2012).

The aim was to build a political constituency for development to enable the very large amounts of aid required. This and other calls for voluntary action came from a perceived moral obligation at the time to act on the very large levels of poverty, hunger and injustice around the world not being addressed in the postcolonial context (Opeskin 1996; Lockwood 1963; Tarp 2010; Huntington 1970). The aim was to not only go beyond governments in the FFHC but also to ask governments to be part of the campaign together with the community.

> FFHC became, therefore, about people rather than politics. While British campaign patrons talked up national characteristics, FAO publicity material promoted Freedom from Hunger as a global campaign, encouraging its participants to identify as international actors (Bocking-Welch 2012, p. 890).

In the UK, Oxfam was a major player in the FFHC and had set up 1,000 FFHC committees, so that by 1965 they had raised £7 million while at the same time driving a new way of thinking about development. For example, Oxfam/FFHC produced their first teachers' guide on development in 1962 (Bocking-Welch 2012; Black 1992).

The impetus provided by FFHC resulted in 1963 being a pivotal year in NGO coordination globally. The FFHC had a global week of action against hunger in March (FFH Editorial 1962; Sen 1962); and in July of that year the Council of Europe held a seminar in Strasbourg which sought increased cooperation among NGOs, given the fast-growing public interest in aid (Council of Europe 1963). In December 1963 there was a conference in Berlin to bring together agencies across the world to report on how they were working together (Kidd 1963). To cap it off a UN General Assembly resolution, also in December, called on:

> all non-governmental organisations to put their increased enthusiasm, energy and other resources into a world campaign in the basis fields of food, health and education to start in 1965 and continue for the remainder of the development decade (UNGA 1963a, p. 32).

In the UK, Volunteer Services Overseas (VSO) started in 1962. At the same time a coordination process, the Lockwood Committee, was put in place to coordinate the various UK volunteer-sending agencies. Following its establishment, the UK Ministry for Overseas Development had discussions with the eight major agencies on the need for more cooperation and coordination of their activities, and for improving the climate for aid. This led to the establishment of VCOAD in 1965, which brought together the development and volunteer-sending agencies, with the ministry covering half the cost of the secretariat and having observer status (Ministry of Overseas Development 1965; Anderson 1964a). There were similar committees in New Zealand and the US dating back to the 1940s (Anderson 1964b).

The churches also played a role. For example, there were three Papal Encyclicals in the 1960s which moved the Catholic Church to a much stronger social justice stance,[5] and which had a profound impact on Catholic development agencies. They rapidly expanded their reach and the type of work they became involved in, moving from welfare to social justice and development, and to undertaking social justice advocacy in their home countries (Clark 2012; Donaldson and Belanger 2012; see Chapter 3). For its part, the WCC adopted a policy in 1968 that 2 per cent of churches' income would go towards overseas aid (OECD 1988; Clemens and Moss 2007). It was these events of the 1960s that set the scene for

---

5   *Mater et Magistra*, (on Christianity and social progress) 1961; *Pacem in Terris* (Peace on Earth) 1963; and *Populorum progressio* (Progress of Peoples) 1967.

the rapid growth of NGO work through the 1960s and 1970s; their increasing involvement in government aid programs; and their advocacy work for social justice. With the increase in both the number and activities of NGOs, there was a need for NGO peak bodies to present a strong united voice.

The origins of ACFID

In Australia, international NGOs had seen a rapid expansion from the early 1950s. Initially there was a strong volunteer component with a focus on building cultural connections to challenge the xenophobia of the time (Webb 1971). Jim Webb was a passionate advocate of Australian community involvement in aid programs through the 1950s; he was involved with the UN, and from the early 1950s with the Volunteer Graduate Association for Indonesia, which expanded its focus in 1962 to become what is now Australian Volunteers International (Arndt 1970; Manning and Maxwell 2011). Funding for NGO work from the public also climbed quickly in the 1950s so that by 1963, for example, the National Missionary Council received $2,114,000; Australian Catholic Relief $1,120,000; and the Australian Council of Churches (ACC) $600,000 (Anderson 1964a; Black 1992).[6]

The Freedom from Hunger Campaign provided an important impetus to Australian NGOs. The Australian government supported the campaign by providing seed funding, arranging a committee to manage it and, importantly, agreeing to provide tax relief for those who donated to the campaign for its first five years. The campaign was an outstanding success and in 1963, its first year of fundraising, it raised over $2 million – around $100 million in 2010 figures,[7] and boosted NGO income by 50 per cent. The campaign became the major fundraising arm for development NGOs, with the funds raised being distributed through them to their partners in developing countries (Anderson 1964a; AFFHC 1963; Kilby 2014). This funding provided a major shot in the arm to the NGOs so that by the mid-1960s these NGOs were well-established development agencies.[8]

---

6   Converted from British pounds at the prevailing rate of 2:1; a multiplier of 12 would convert it to 2010 Australian dollars based on CPI changes.

7   This estimate takes into account not only the value of the dollar in constant price terms, but also the relative size of the economy at the time.

8   The main NGOs at the time were World Christian Action, World University Service, Community Aid Abroad, Austcare, Australian Catholic Relief and Freedom from Hunger (Sullivan 1976).

The growth of NGO support was such that there was even a perceived proliferation of Australian NGOs involved in aid, for example, in a letter from Lord Casey, former foreign minister, to John Crawford, complaining: 'I would expect it would be almost beyond the wit of man to get them to come together into an organisation of size and consequence that would ring a bell with a wide range of people' (Casey 1965, p. 1). This assertion of a proliferation of NGOs persists to this day. Even though their numbers were small by today's standards (around 30), and some were quite new on the scene, the larger Australian NGOs were beginning to engage with government on matters of aid policy, including increasing aid and foreign direct investment to 1 per cent of GDP in line with UN resolutions (Clunies-Ross 1963). This increased visibility of NGOs, especially the increased public support for NGOs, would not have gone unnoticed by the Australian government with its increasing aid program. In addition, there was not only the UNGA call for a greater role for the NGOs in 'alleviating hunger disease and ignorance', but also that member governments report to the UN Economic and Social Council (ECOSOC) on progress in 'stimulating a campaign by NGOs ... on food, health, and education' (UNGA 1963a, p. 32).

It was the coming together of this unique set of global and local changes for NGOs in the early 1960s that set the scene for the establishment of a coordinating body for NGOs in Australia. However, despite these international factors, the push for coordination did not come from the Australian NGOs, but rather from the persistent drive of a former leading public servant with strong links to government.

Enter Sir John Crawford

Sir John Crawford, who had been involved in some of the global issues around development in the 1950s and 1960s, picked up on the UN call in the early 1960s for a greater commitment to development and aid, both public and private, and for closer cooperation among NGOs. Crawford was an eminent scholar and leading public servant. He was responsible for many of the enduring public institutions in Australia of the postwar era: he was the founding Director of the Bureau of Agricultural Economics in 1945 (now ABARE); Secretary of the Department of Commerce and Agriculture in 1950; and then Secretary of the new Department of Trade. He was responsible for the Australia–Japan Agreement on Commerce of 1957, for which there was strong opposition with the war then being a recent memory, but his pioneering work broke Australia's isolation of Japan, thus setting up an enduring trade relationship (Miller 2009; Ingram 2010).

In 1960 Crawford left the government service to become director of the
Research School of Pacific Studies, now the College of Asia and the Pacific
at The Australian National University. He stipulated that he must be free to
undertake government inquiries and international commitments. The most
important of these was the World Bank's economic mission to India in 1964–65;
from there he played an important role in the implementation of its strategy for
Indian agricultural development and the Green Revolution.[9]

Crawford's concern about development (and in particular agricultural
development) was undoubtedly an important driver in his interest in NGOs,
and why it was important for them to have a consultative mechanism with
government as well as achieving greater synergies among themselves.
The process of bringing the Australian NGOs together started in 1963 at the
height of the growing global interest in NGOs (Perkins 1965). The first step
was a lunch with Jim Webb from the Overseas Service Bureau in late 1963 in
Canberra, hosted by Crawford. Included were David Scott from Community Aid
Abroad, who was leading the 1 per cent campaign in Australia at the time,
and Alan Manning, a journalist and friend of Crawford (Webb 2006; Blackburn
1993; Crawford 1964c).[10] Jim Webb later recalled he had the feeling that Garfield
Barwick, the then External Affairs Minister, was probably behind the move,
and certainly others at the time felt the strong hand of government (Webb 2006;
Sullivan 1976).

There was a belief some years later that the Department of External Territories'
motive was to engage Australian NGOs in aid to South Vietnam as part of the
war effort (Cullen 1986; O'Dwyer 2011). This Crawford initiative, however,
predated Australia's major involvement in the war in Vietnam by a couple of
years, and its major ally, the United States, did not seek to actively engage
with NGOs in Vietnam until 1965 (Flipse 2002; Howell 2014). While there was
a substantial Colombo Plan program to South Vietnam in the early 1960s, the
Australian government had little, if any, understanding of NGO work, and there
was very little NGO aid to South Vietnam at the time. So the idea of using
NGOs to provide aid to South Vietnam was an unlikely motive for bringing the
NGOs together (Oakman 2001). While the Department of External Territories
did provide support in the ACFID planning processes, particularly for the
second planning conference in July 1964, the evidence points to Crawford
being the major driver, given his very active and continuing interest in ACFID,
where he was to remain president until 1974. The government, however, did
have an interest by virtue of the increased profile of NGOs with the public face

9   It was this initiative he was most proud of, contributing as it did to the making of a world where people
would have enough to eat, and setting the stage for India's subsequent success (Miller 2009).
10   According to Sue Blackburn (1993), Harvey Perkins from ACC was at the lunch, but Jim Webb is adamant
it was Manning not Perkins.

of the Freedom from Hunger Campaign, and the UN's call for governments to 'stimulate' the role of NGOs (UNGA 1963a). It is easy to speculate that having a council of NGOs would be one way the government could meet its obligations under this UN resolution.

The interest from the NGOs in having a coordinating body at the time was lukewarm at best. They had just had their fingers burnt with the perceived duplicity by government on the issue of tax deductibility for the FFHC, which had been prematurely withdrawn just as these negotiations about forming a peak body were beginning. This was a sore point, as the NGOs felt the government had reneged on its five-year commitment to provide tax relief to the FFHC, and in the end only provided it for two years (Hobbin 1964; Webb 1964a).[11]

What emerged from the lunch in 1963 was a two-day workshop funded by the Myer Foundation and convened by Crawford at ANU's University House in April 1964. Sixteen agencies attended and reported on their activities.[12] This was where, as Jim Webb (2006) put it, Crawford 'charmed them into cooperation', or from Nancy Anderson (2011), '[Crawford] would not stand for any nonsense'. Jim Ingram (2010) also noted Crawford's consummate skill in getting people to agree to things they may not have thought possible. However, the NGO aid activities over the previous 10–15 years, and in particular the growth in support NGOs had received since 1960, while being substantial and rapid, did not provide a strong argument for many NGOs for coming together. The arguments in favour of forming a peak body were to overcome public apathy; foster greater understanding of the issues of development; stir government to greater efforts; and, most interestingly, be able to present a more disinterested image of Australia in the minds of the recipient country. The effectiveness of small- and large-scale aid, tax deductibility and government funding were also touched on (Anderson 1964b; Webb 1964b).

In the end there was some general agreement for a Standing Conference of Private Organisations Engaged in Voluntary Overseas Aid which, among other things, would have led to a very clumsy acronym. It was shortened to ACFOA in later meetings, and the basic governance structure moved to it being a council rather than a conference. The key purposes agreed to were cooperation and consultation; exchange of ideas among members; suggesting projects for joint

---

11   The decision to withdraw the tax concession was based on the rather spurious argument that the five-year timeline was from the international agreement to set up the campaign made in 1959. The more likely explanation might be that the success of the campaign resulted in a significant amount of tax revenue foregone.

12   These were the Apex Club; the Australian–Asian Association of Victoria; the Australian Council of Churches; the Australian Red Cross; the Catholic Bishops Coordinating Committee; Community Aid Abroad; the Freedom from Hunger Campaign; the Friends of Vellore; the Junior Chamber of Commerce; Lions International the National Missionary Council; the National Union of Students; the Overseas Service Bureau; Save the Children Fund; the Volunteer Graduate Program in Indonesia; and the World University Service.

funding being an organisation for channelling government funds; advising on training; acting cooperatively on publicity; and providing hospitality to visitors. Given the breadth of the wish list of functions, it was agreed that a permanent staff and secretariat would seem necessary, and that the council of member agencies would meet twice a year, with an executive committee to coordinate the work of the council (Anderson 1964b).

The meeting agreed that Jim Webb and OSB would convene a further meeting two months later and the minister would be invited. While the records at the time do not indicate what was expected from the minister, the issues of funding and tax deductibility were probably at the front of people's minds. It was after the first meeting that FFHC had its tax deductibility removed (Hobbin 1964) and, as Webb (1964a) pointed out in correspondence, this had the effect of 'muddying the waters' and leading to some resistance to the very idea of coming together for a second meeting. Another suggestion at the time was that just the larger agencies (FFHC, ACC, and Australian Catholic Relief (ACR)) come together on an ad hoc basis only, rather than have a council open to all agencies (Webb 1964a, 1964b). This idea was to emerge again 30 years later in the mid-1990s (Hobbs 2013; Smillie 1995).

Clearly Crawford prevailed upon these large agencies, and the second meeting was held on 27 July 1964 with 15 agencies attending. Paul Hasluck, the new minister for External Affairs, was also supportive and attended the meeting briefly, and there were observers from the department. Jim Webb opened the meeting, pointing out the very favourable climate for aid at the time and, while Crawford acknowledged the tensions within the group, he urged that the awareness-raising work that ACFID could do still had to go on (Anderson 1964c). The feedback from agencies to this second meeting was also cautious. The Lions Club was nervous at the thought of a coordinating body, but felt that regular meetings were desirable; the Missionary Council felt the idea was premature and that more work was required on the issues, and broader policies, of foreign aid before a council could be set up; Apex was cautiously supportive of a coordinated group, but noted that it was important that agencies not lose their identity; and the Australian Asian Association, who supported it, suggested that the Department of External Affairs might have a liaison officer as part of the organisation.

It was here, however, with the urging of Crawford that the larger key agencies began to come on board. Crennin (Catholic Overseas Relief) was supportive provided there was no fundraising role; he also suggested the membership could extend to trade unions and industrialists and be on a semi-government basis. Jim Webb (OSB) indicated the need for such a body, but he was not sure of the form it should take, arguing that the Australian community was not yet mobilised behind the government aid program, and more awareness work was still needed. David Scott (Community Aid Abroad (CAA)) noted that the UN resolution of December 1963 asked governments to support NGOs, and that the Australian government, at the very least, should have a funding role in the proposed organisation. Noreen Minogue from the Red Cross liked the idea of a coordinating body, but was not sure the Red Cross could be a member, given their constitution prevented them from being members of other organisations. Minogue preferred an Overseas Development Institute (UK)-type structure, which was less a membership organisation and more a think tank. An interesting suggestion, possibly reflecting a generation gap, was that it should have a youth focus to get the 18–35 age group 'off the sand'. But a subsequent youth focus in the 1970s with their 'radical' ideas proved a step too far for some (see Chapter 3). The minister, Paul Hasluck, spoke off the record: 'There is a strong streak of idealism in the Australian character, and it behoves us to see that it can find an outlet in the best possible way' (Anderson 1964c).

Crawford noted, somewhat delicately, that the government 'would not look askance' at the idea of a council of some sort, and it was on that basis he put forward a motion for further consideration of the idea. He picked up on David Scott's suggestion that a committee be set up to look in more detail into establishing a body. Crawford agreed to have three papers prepared: one on what happens in other countries, in particular the United Kingdom and Canada; a second on possible aims and structure; and, finally, a paper on implications for members. The plan was that these papers would be prepared by Crawford in consultation with DFAT, so it did not seem to be a 'government thing' (Webb 1964a p. 1), but in the end DFAT did much of the drafting work for him. Crawford also wrote directly to Australian embassies and high commissions in the major donor countries seeking information on NGO coordinating bodies in those countries.

Initially the thought was to link ACFID with the Australian Freedom from Hunger Campaign (AFFHC) (which only became an organisation in its own right in 1964), which would do the fundraising for the other NGOs, while ACFID focused on advocacy through two semi-autonomous commissions: relief and development, and refugees and migration. The idea was that ACFID would do research, consultation, education and government relations through each of these commissions (Webb 1964c).

Crawford suggested a two-stage process for the formation of ACFID. The first was the establishment of a six-person group to discuss the proposal, and the three discussion papers, with other agencies.[13] The second step was a full meeting of proposed founding members in 1965 to take a formal decision. This agreement was seen to be quite a breakthrough and a press release went out at the time saying:

> there was a strong feeling evident amongst those attending the meeting that much more must be done by Australians to help underdeveloped countries, and the general task of creating public interest in the support for foreign voluntary aid activities might well be one of the tasks of any co-operating organisation (Crawford 1964a).

The discussion papers were circulated in November 1964, with meetings convened by the planning group held in Sydney and Melbourne at the end of 1964 and early 1965 to finalise the draft constitution and structure (Webb 1964b, 1965; Crawford 1964b). The key sticking point was whether to include refugees and migration in the mandate as a separate commission or not. In the end it was included but the structure of having commissions was in any case to be relatively short lived.

The formation of ACFID

ACFID held it first official meetings on 5 and 6 April 1965, and had its first executive meeting a few days later on 12 April (ACFOA 1965a, 1965d). Twenty NGO representatives met at University House at ANU in Canberra. Crawford, in opening the meeting, referred to a letter from Lord Casey expressing concern on the lack of cohesion among aid organisations. Crawford went on to urge that as aid had to be as concrete as possible there was a role in having rational aid policies and ACFID could support that (ACFOA 1965a, Casey 1965). After some discussion at the planning group meetings it was agreed to establish ACFOA with a 'formula ... of collaboration not integration' and a structure not be too elaborate (ACFOA 1965d). ACFID stated:

> The common objective of all members is to work for social and economic justice, to respond to human needs and to help produce conditions through which people can realise their full potential as human beings (ACFOA 1965e).

---

13   The six-person group included Crennan (ACR), Hobbin (FFHC), Scott (CAA), Tuckey (Apex), Perkins (ACC), Herbert (SCF), and Webb (OSB). This grouping represented the major agencies as well as a smaller service agency in the form of Apex. The group became seven with Bill Hobbin included later as he was absent from the July meeting.

The seven founding agencies were Australian Council of Aid to Refugees; Australian Council of Churches; Catholic Overseas Relief; Community Aid Abroad; Federation of Australian Jewish Welfare Societies; Overseas Service Bureau; and World University Service (Perkins 1965). A further 14 NGOs were to be admitted by the first council in August 1965. They included the major agencies with the exception of the Red Cross and Save the Children Fund, which could not join due to constitutional constraints preventing them from joining other organisations.

The key areas for ACFID's early work were identified as aid effectiveness, the relationship with government, and education of the public. It is worth noting that these three priorities have not substantially changed 50 years on. At the outset, ACFID was seen as a mechanism for collaboration among agencies rather than integration of the agencies (ACFOA 1965a). The role of government in this whole process was seen as important, and one of the first acts of the ACFID executive was to seek a grant of £1,750, or 50 per cent of ACFID's running costs, from the Department of External Affairs (ACFOA 1965d). While this request was not immediately agreed to, the department did cover the cost of the first council meeting in August 1965 and has continued to cover, with some variation depending on government priorities, around half of ACFID's running costs since 1967.

At the first council meeting in August 1965 the ACFID executive committee was formally confirmed, with Sir John Crawford as foundation president and Syd Einfeld as chairman. Syd Einfeld was a good choice as chairman as Crawford's other commitments would keep him away from the day-to-day running of the council. Einfeld was not only a tireless advocate for refugee rights but also the Deputy Leader of the Australian Labor Party in the New South Wales Parliament, which gave him the stature and authority to provide ACFID leadership through those difficult early years. For the first council meeting there were 14 members, with invitations sent out to another 11 agencies. Initial membership fees were set at £1,750 (ACFOA 1965c).

Figure 3 The founding office bearers of ACFID.

Clockwise from top left: Sir John Crawford, Syd Einfeld, Monsignor George Crennin and David Scott.

Source: Australian News and Information Bureau. National Archives of Australia A1200 L68147; A1200 L54364; A1200 L54365; A1200 L54366.

While there was an organisation there was not an effective structure to make ACFID work. Agencies had agreed to be on the executive and the two main commissions, but the resources for the work were limited, with no staff or premises. The first year was spent not only on developing an identity and clear policies, but also on holding a flagship event. A conference by the Relief and Development Commission on the respective roles of government, the UN and NGOs was held in November of that year as a first step in building an identity (ACFOA 1965b). In 1966 further policy was agreed, the first being a Standing Policy on Development that recognised:

> That the huge and widening gap between the poorer and wealthier nations of the world and between rich and poor people within nations which result in deprivation of basic human rights for more than half the world's population constitutes a denial of natural justice and is a continuing threat to world peace (ACFOA 1966c, p. 1).

The policy statement on NGO relations with government was a carefully crafted document to ensure that it did not adversely affect ACFID, given the financial support that was being hoped for in those early years. The policy stated that relations with government were to 'represent the interests of members, and to enter into formal arrangements with Government to further the interest and activities of the Council'. The government, however, saw ACFID's role as being a 'filter, or a point of reference for consultation' (ACFOA 1966b, p. 1).

Building a secretariat

Once the structure was in place ACFID had to find a way to fund a secretariat when members were reluctant to pay the higher fees necessary to provide the services being asked for. They probably took the view that given the hand of government in this venture then government should pay for it. The government was ready to exploit this conundrum facing ACFID, and in the latter half of 1966 made ACFID an offer that it would fund a position and a secretariat if ACFID would take on the role of coordinating aid to what was then South Vietnam. This followed the lead of the US government the previous year, which had supported a NGO fact-finding mission so they could undertake work in South Vietnam (Flipse 2002; Howell 2014). There were informal meetings among agencies in September 1966 followed by a special meeting of the council, which agreed to accept the offer, and so ACFID was able to appoint an executive director and establish an office. Interestingly, ACFID was to consult with DFAT on 'matters relating to the appointment', and the minister of External Affairs would make an announcement, giving an indication of the hand government had those days in these early organisational processes (ACFOA 1966d). The relationship with government thus became closer, and in some ways fraught as early as 1966 as there was increasing concern about Australia's growing involvement in the Vietnam conflict. In 1967 students were starting to organise aid to the South Vietnamese communist National Liberation Front through North Vietnam, which some of the church agencies would later follow, with warnings from government that this might amount to treason (Saunders 1982). This was an era when social justice issues were reaching the mainstream, folk protest songs were on the popular music play lists, and the war in Vietnam was becoming a focus of protests everywhere.

In September 1966, John Crawford, David Scott and Syd Einfeld met with the Department of External Affairs about the Vietnam project, with a follow-up meeting in Melbourne. It was agreed that key criteria for the project were that there were to be no links with military and that ACFID would only appeal for members to be involved. They also noted the inherent difficulties of operating in South Vietnam (ACFOA 1966e; 1966f). The first step was a high-level ACFID executive visit by Einfeld, Scott and Harvey Perkins to South Vietnam in late 1966 to look at the scale of NGO aid to Vietnam (*Canberra Times* 1966). Their report was noncommittal on how ACFID would proceed, and they recommended that no further work be done until after the secretariat was established. There had been experiences elsewhere where NGOs had been engaged in partisan activities around the war in Vietnam. For example, Catholic Relief Services of the US was providing 80 per cent of the USAID food aid it sent to the families of the armed forces of South Vietnam (Casey 1973; Lissner 1977; Flipse 2002). There was a real risk that there could be similar 'mission creep' in the ACFID program; it could also be seen to be partisan and part of a 'hearts and minds' war strategy.

In early 1967, ACFID appointed Brian Hayes as the first executive director, with a salary of $6,000. He had been with the World Youth Assembly in Brussels and returned to Australia in 1965 without a job. His background was as a moulder from Brisbane who had got involved in trade union work and from there the Young Catholic Worker (YCW) movement, of which he was elected its first full-time president in 1959 (Hinton 1971; Armstrong 2011). YCW at the time was a large Catholic youth organisation based on a philosophy of experiential learning, which was to be the source of global education in later years, and would play an important part in ACFID's life in the 1970s. Hayes was elected Secretary of the World Council of Youth in 1963 and went to Brussels as a full-time officer. When he came back to Australia without a job he was an obvious candidate and was appointed to ACFID in early 1967.

Brian Hayes' first task was to set up an office in Melbourne and then finalise the Vietnam project. He visited a heavily militarised South Vietnam in July 1967 and quickly found that NGOs could not operate safely there, so he suggested to the department, as an alternative, that ACFID could produce a bulletin on members' work in Vietnam (Hayes 1967a, 1967b). Further meetings were held with the department in which Crawford played a key role, emphasising the nervousness about the Vietnam project among members, particularly in maintaining independence from government and its involvement in the war (Hinton 1968).

The government agreed that the secretariat's work on Vietnam be reduced to a quarter of its time (ACFOA 1967a); in return ACFID held a Vietnam Appeal in early 1968, which raised a relatively modest $70,000 that was distributed to the larger agencies' programs in Vietnam and effectively ended the Vietnam project for ACFID (*The Age* 1968; Hayes 1968; ACFOA 1968a; 1968b; 1968c).

ACFID in the late 1960s

While the Vietnam project took up a lot of ACFID's time in the early years, given that its resourcing was tied to it, ACFID was also struggling with the issue of coordination among members and seeking out a clearer role for itself as a nascent organisation. This was a period in which Brian Hayes was thinking about the internationalisation of NGOs and development issues, and the direction ACFID should go (Develtere and De Bruyn 2009; Lindenberg 1999). The idea of a development education focus came out of this thinking, as Hayes tried to bring the agencies into a more cooperative framework.

Membership

The day-to-day work was spent on building a constituency and ensuring a growing and broad membership. While the Red Cross did not join immediately, in 1967 they saw their way clear to join the Relief and Development Commission, and World Vision was approached to join after it noticed it was not included in the ACFID report on aid to Vietnam (Irvine 1969). Hayes was trying to get as broad a membership as possible, representing a diverse set of views across the political spectrum to build ACFID's legitimacy. A broad membership, however, did pose a risk in the day-to-day operations of ACFID if a consensus on particular issues was unable to be reached. Tensions were inevitable between older, more established conservative organisations and the younger, more radical NGOs riding the wave of liberation theology and the social activism of the time. In a letter to Vaughan Hinton, Crawford (1969b) refers to conflict among the diverse set of NGOs and was pleased that a couple of agency representatives 'for whom particular difficulties have been evident, are now members of the Executive'. Crawford took a close interest in ACFID when he was vice-chancellor of ANU (1968–73). Throughout this period he kept a guiding eye on its work, with his door always open to the ACFID staff and executive committee, playing an important role in diffusing issues as they arose (O'Dwyer 2011).

Issues of the time

One of the early challenges for ACFID was how to coordinate activities among agencies, and in particular fundraising. ACFOA (1967a) reported that 'a state of bewilderment exists due to the fragmentation of effort by organisations, particularly in the field of fundraising'. This was to be an ongoing issue with the resolution being an agreement among some of the larger agencies to talk among themselves about the issue. A starting point was the publication of a member directory, *Not by Government Alone*, funded by the Myer Foundation. It not only listed the agencies but also outlined what they did, and so introduced the reader to ACFID and its members (ACFOA 1967d). The other main ACFID activity at the time was holding regular seminars and conferences by each of the commissions. The purpose of the conferences at the time was to build the credibility of ACFID and the NGO sector more broadly by facilitating public debate. From 1968 there was a conference as part of the council, and this set a trend for subsequent councils, enabling ACFID members to engage in the debates of the time as a group.[14]

Constitutional change

By 1969 problems with the original structure of ACFID began to emerge as the idea of having an executive plus two commissions was found to be unworkable. The Relief and Development Commission tended to have the same membership as the executive and so had trouble finding a role separate to that of the executive, and 'lapsed as an effective entity' (Scott 1968). The Refugee and Migration Commission, on the other hand, undertook important work but generally outside of ACFID's membership, tending to operate independently (Hinton 1969). It went its own way, becoming a forerunner of the Refugee Council of Australia. David Scott suggested the idea of subcommittees of the executive committee rather than commissions with their own funding base as a better way forward. In 1969 the structure of commissions was abolished and replaced with committees that could look at a broader range of activities (ACFOA 1969b; Hayes 1969a). The first new committee to be established was on education and publicity; other committees to be considered by the executive were on trade and tariffs; the second Development Decade, which the government was keen on (ACFOA 1970b); and Australian official aid.

---

14 The conference themes included a Refugee and Migrant Service conference in February 1966; the Respective Roles of Government, UN and NGOs at the end of 1965; Aid and Development in 1965 and 1967 (ACFOA 1965b, 1967c); the Human Factor in Development (ACFOA 1968a); and in 1969 Australia's Role in Joint Ventures and Investment in Developing Countries of Asia and the Pacific (Hinton 1971; ACFOA 1969a).

By the late 1960s concerns were also emerging about membership. As originally envisaged, there was to be one category of membership but with different fees based on size. There was, however, a strong desire to expand membership to those agencies that while having an interest in aid and development may not have it as their primary interest. The category of Associate Member was created, which was to remain until the 2010s when ACFID reverted back to a single category of membership for NGOs, with a new affiliate membership being restricted to universities. The other major issue at the council in 1969 was the future role of the secretariat. Hayes (1969b) had put to the council that the secretariat had to expand from being a one-person operation, with the addition of a research and information officer, that there was a need for a comprehensive information centre and last, but not least, to move to Canberra in order to engage with government more closely.

In 1970 these changes were implemented but not without some controversy. There was some debate on the role of the education committee, whether it should be linked with fundraising and whether it should go beyond aid in its mandate to a more social justice focus, a topic that was to come back in the mid-1970s as a continuing source of division. The council agreed that the office transfer to Canberra would occur by January 1971 (Hayes 1970a). As an interim measure they approached Crawford in his role as vice-chancellor at ANU and asked if there was temporary space available. They were offered accommodation in an old army hut where other NGOs were located at ANU for ACFID's first six months in Canberra in late 1971, while it found alternate accommodation (Hayes 1970b).

The end of an era

On 16 March 1971 Brian Hayes died suddenly, and his loss was felt deeply among the NGO community. As Vaughan Hinton (1971) reported to the 1971 ACFID Council in 1967, the council was struggling to establish its identity and purpose, but:

> [Brian's] determination to break down parochialism and build a true internationalism of outlook and action … [and the] cooperation and sharing that exists among us as organisations and as individuals results also from the strong personal friendships so many of us shared with Brian.

Operating from a one-person office in Melbourne, Hayes built ACFID to become what Crawford (1972b) called 'an authoritative body for making statements about aid policy generally … ACFOA does have a public standing and a public audience'. Brian Hayes set up the changes that were to endure: a structure that remains largely unchanged to this day; an education program that was to identify ACFID through the 1970s; and the move to Canberra, the seat of government, which represented a subtle shift from building a network of NGOs to being an advocate for their cause.

The loss of Hayes at this time of rapid expansion and moving proved to be a challenge. Interim measures were put in place to make the move before employing a new executive director. Brendan O'Dwyer, who was on the executive committee at the time representing the World University Service, was asked to act as an executive officer. The office moved to a room in an ACC house in the inner suburb of Glebe, Sydney, pending the move to Canberra in September 1971 and its permanent base (ACFOA 1971b; O'Dwyer 2011).

Conclusion

The achievements of ACFID in the first five years were considerable given the level of suspicion about the venture and what its functions would be. It drew on the ground-breaking work of Australian NGOs in the 1950s and the global movement for social justice. It was a voice for NGOs in the big development debates of the 1960s, and benefitted greatly from the vision of Sir John Crawford. While it was finding its feet, ACFID managed to stimulate the development and migration debate in Australia with regular programs of conferences through the early years. NGOs started working together, sharing information and undertaking joint programs. The leadership of Crawford, who saw himself as a 'sleeping partner' (1972b), was evident throughout. He was available for key meetings with politicians, was aware of the internal tensions, and his door was open to the executive director and executive committee at all times.

The relationship with government was tenuous through this early period with the arguments for tax deductibility falling on deaf ears. Government funding was, for a period, tied to coordinating aid to Vietnam, which was not seen by members as a task for ACFID. Hayes and Crawford navigated ACFID through this in a way that both preserved their funding and their independence – no small feat. It was Crawford's leadership as the 'founder' and first president, his links with government and NGOs and the substantial authority he exerted on them that made ACFID happen. Later, when tensions were high between ACFID and government, he was instrumental in easing them. It would seem that the government, rather than leading the process, was led within the process by an extraordinary individual (Webb 2006; Anderson 2011).

03 From Global Education to Campaigning

An informed public in Australia is a prime asset in the struggle for justice and social equity in world development.

— John Crawford, Vice-Chancellor ANU and President ACFOA, 1972

In the twenty-first century, global education is seen as a way of promoting aid programs and to some extent as a propaganda arm for official aid agencies. This current perception, however, is a relatively recent phenomenon. From the late 1960s until the late 1990s the main thrust of global education was quite different from that of the official aid programs, and very much focused on promoting a social justice agenda. Official aid agencies such as AusAID, which once funded this broader development agenda, now use school and adult education curricula to push the benefits of their national overseas aid programs and limit discussion of social justice issues within the global system (AusAID 2013; Weber 2013; Selby and Kagawa 2011; Biccum 2011). This chapter will look at the growth and development of global education since the 1960s, and how it has evolved into campaigns such as Make Poverty History and the global education programs of the 2000s.

The first Development Decade (1961–1970) offered much hope but in the end failed, leaving both developing countries and many international and local NGOs disillusioned (Pearson 1969; Legum 1970; Gubser 2012). The upshot was a reinforced need for greater awareness of the public in developed countries to pressure their governments to use aid to create a more just world. In Australia it was the drive from Brian Hayes, ACFID's first executive director, with European experience of working on awareness raising (see Chapter 2). Hayes' drive led to ACFID's establishment of the development education (Dev Ed) program. The 1970 ACFID Council agreed to set up an education committee to develop a program to commence in 1972 (ACFOA 1970b). This was to become the main focus of ACFID's work for the following 20 years, and the most controversial. The main activities of the nascent program were to be a resource centre; produce a bi-monthly newsletter; and organise a series of conferences to drive Australian state and federal government policy to ensure development issues were taught in schools.

This program continued in one form or another until the early 1990s, after which it was replaced by more focused, issues-based campaigning, such as Make Poverty History, and a much smaller aid and development-focused global education program. This chapter will largely focus on the first five years to 1975, as they set the scene for ACFID's relations with its members and government in later years and led to ACFID having a credible voice in development policy, and then conclude with the shift to campaigning in the 1980s onwards.

Global education: Some background

The idea for global education had its origins in the 1930s and the nascent idea of community education, a response to community demands for greater relevance of education to their needs (Bennett 1969). The basis of community education was helping people resolve problems by understanding them, rather than being told the answer. Organisations such as the Council for Education on World Citizenship founded in 1939 (Rendall 1976; Heater 1984) had a focus on 'education for international understanding' (Hicks 2003, p. 266). Christian social justice teaching of the 1960s had its 'origins in a desire to educate the public into effective concern for the Third World [with] the inherent logic that … development begins at home' (Rendall 1976, p. 2). Biccum also traces this desire to educate the public back to nineteenth-century humanism and what she calls its 'civilising mission' (2011, p. 1344). While the notion of a 'civilising mission' is probably only partly true, it did underpin some of the tensions that arose in the 1970s between those who were driven by a social justice concerns, and those whose altruism was based on notions of welfare and charity. It was the coming together of these various strands of thinking that led to the sharp focus on global education in the 1960s and 1970s, and was also the source of the division that accompanied it.

Following the failure of the first Development Decade, building support for increases in development aid and fair and equitable development policies was seen as the way forward for the second Development Decade from 1971 (Meier 1971; Gubser 2012; Trebilcock et al. 2012; Weber 2013). By the mid-1960s economic growth was slower than population growth for many developing countries, who were struggling to feed their growing populations. The spectre of a chronic food crisis was very real, with famines having occurred in India and China in the 1950s and 1960s (Gráda 2011; Cheek 2012), and industrial output was low. Some of the blame was levelled at the protectionist trade policies of the West and, as an alternative, the idea of a New International Economic Order (NIEO) to 'overcome developmental hurdles rooted in historically constructed patterns of dependence and inequality' (Golub 2013, p. 1003) was gaining traction. It was no surprise then that the political focus in developing countries was on central planning and a healthy scepticism of Western driven market processes (Meier 1971; Hilton 2012; Golub 2013).

As a result of these fundamental structural development issues many activists, and not a few policymakers in the West such as John Crawford in Australia, felt the solution was in garnering public support for a fairer world through public education on social justice and development issues. This public support would then drive the political processes for donor and developed country policy change. In the UK, after the first flourish of the very successful Freedom from Hunger fundraising campaign, the 'zeitgeist of the 1960s which was marked by a widespread political awakening' was picked up (Saunders 2009, p. 43). The major British agencies had agreed in 1966 to work together on global education, noting (rather idealistically) that they should not subordinate the 'educational responsibility to any money making campaigning considerations' (VCOAD 1966, p. 1). In both the UK and Australia in the 1960s there was a noticeable change in broader social norms, which included not only changes in social mores but also a greater public awareness of social justice issues (Chalmers 2012; Shragge 2013).

The 1960s also saw the Christian churches (both Protestant and Catholic) providing important leadership in global education, which arose from a concern at the injustices they saw emerging from decolonisation and the Cold War in the 1950s and 1960s. Liberation theology emerged in the Catholic Church in Latin America, with its radical Christian agenda (Brouwer 2010; Mackin 2012). At the same time, the WCC argued that they should be active in promoting worldwide opposition to new forms of colonialism and oppression that the West, with its capitalist political and economic system, was imposing on developing countries (Abrecht 1968; Kim 2011; Petrou 2012). The groundbreaking papal encyclical Populorum Progressio (on the development of peoples), enunciated a set of rights including wages, conditions and access to resources for all peoples (AWD 1970; Donaldson and Belanger 2012).

This move to a stronger social justice philosophy by the two leading Christian churches led to the development of a joint approach to achieve it: the program of Action for World Development (AWD 1970; Fernandes 1970). The AWD program started in the UK in 1969 as the World Development Movement (De Waal 1997; Saunders 2009), which was very influential in changing public opinion at the time (McDonald 1972). It coincided with an international youth assembly at the General Assembly of the United Nations (Hill 1970). By 1970 the role of global education was well established internationally, with both the WCC and the FAO Second World Food Congress emphasising the need for community education on issues such as self-determination, social justice, as well as trade, employment, and investment (Lissner 1977; Lemaresquier 1987).

It was only a matter of time before the Australian churches took up the call for action. In April 1969 the ACC and the Australian Catholic Bishops Conference agreed to set up a planning committee for AWD (Fernandes 1970; ACC 1972; Herbert 1973). After a year's planning, a joint conference between the ACC and the Catholic Church was held in February 1970 with the exhortation that 'it is necessary to instil social and economic processes with a new dynamism of human solidarity and justice' (AWD 1970, p. 49). The conference had a strong focus on aid, and resolved that *inter alia* 'aid and trade must be grounded in justice, and used to eliminate root causes of the disparity in wealth, which threatens the peace of the world' (p. 18). The meeting also resolved to campaign to eliminate poverty and racial injustice, not only overseas but also in Australia.

The national campaign was started with coordinated study group meetings in homes across the country over a week in July 1971 to study an education kit prepared by the program (O'Dwyer 1972a). The campaign even gained tacit support from the federal government, reporting favourably that AWD had 20,000 groups with 200,000 supporters (AIS 1972). The AWD program provided a strong synergy and impetus for the ACFID global education program, which had started earlier that year.

Establishment of the Development Education Unit

John Crawford, the founder of ACFID (see Chapter 2), continued his influence and support for the global education program at the ACFID Annual Council in 1971, where he made the point that education of the public is key, especially for the needs of the second Development Decade. He also said that:

> Australian Governments seem too prone to attach conditions to their acceptance of international obligations. Education of the people and the application by them of pressure on our Government to give more aid and more generously and promptly, is absolutely vital if Australia is to mount an aid effort commensurate with her increasing affluence, and worthy of her international image (Crawford 1971, p. 1).

The Dev Ed Unit was very timely as the Bangladesh civil war became the major development event through 1971 and into 1972. This war created the largest global refugee crisis since the breakup of India in 1948. The massacre of hundreds of thousands of people, and nearly 10 million people fleeing to India led to global outrage, triggering the first global fundraising event for a development crisis – The Concert for Bangladesh (Cullen 1971; O'Dwyer 1971a; Bose 2005; West 2007; Salehyan 2008; Mookherjee 2011; Wolf 2013). Australia's poor official response to the crisis added to the storm of protest, and the Australian government 'received a lashing from public opinion' (O'Dwyer 1971a). There were large demonstrations across the country, including a hunger strike by Paul Poernomo and a large rally of 5,000 in the rain outside Parliament House, at a time when Canberra was much smaller than it is in the 2010s (Canberra Times 1971; O'Dwyer 1971a). There had already been a groundswell among the Australian public about poverty and ethnic problems in Australia through 1971, and the Bangladesh crisis provided a strong catalyst for ACFID's Dev Ed Unit (ACFOA 1972b).

Figure 4 Paul Poernomo is helped into Parliament House by other fasters.

Source: Fairfax Media.

After a year of planning and some funding hiccoughs, the Dev Ed Unit was launched in February 1972 with John Crawford taking a particular interest in its planning (ACFOA 1971). The focus was still Brian Hayes' idea of a resource centre, a newsletter, and a series of regular conferences. ACFID's role in global education from the government's viewpoint was to be 'encouraging an informed questioning of public opinion on the issues of world development, particularly as they effect Australian policies in trade and aid' (News and Information Bureau 1972, p. 2).

Despite the international events and Crawford's support, there was still reluctance among member agencies to increase fees to cover the Dev Ed Unit's costs. Some ACFID members felt that education was not ACFID's role and were reluctant to continue their membership if their fees were used to support it. While ACFID had received a $12,000 grant from the government in 1971 for the promotion of the second Development Decade (O'Dwyer 1971b), any government support was to be for specific activities rather than as a grant for the Dev Ed Unit. In late 1971, four agencies agreed to fund a shortfall so there was a budget to cover one staff person and associated program costs (Solomon 1971, 1972a). It was also agreed that global education be managed out of a separate unit within ACFID, with the result that the Dev Ed Unit saw itself as being semi-autonomous from the rest of the secretariat. This was not helped by it being also physically separate in another part of the building a couple of years later.

The *Development News Digest*

The bi-monthly *Development News Digest* (DND) was the flagship of the unit with a print run of 5,000 copies going into selected bookshops and Melbourne newsagents, as well as to NGOs and other subscribers (O'Dwyer 1972d). The first issue in 1972 opened with the provocative headline 'Aid as a Political Issue', which was to set the tone for DND and the Dev Ed Unit through its early years (O'Dwyer 1972a). The front page went on to report the events in Bangladesh and its neglect by the Australian government, the major political issue of the time. The tone was deliberately provocative and challenged existing shibboleths. It also challenged a lot of established NGO aid practice, and from the very beginning this took a toll on its support from some ACFID members (O'Dwyer 1972b). ACFID had already sought legal advice on how to avoid litigation arising from DND articles (Solomon 1972b), and even at that time considered having the Dev Ed Unit made a separate legal entity from ACFID.

John Crawford (1972), who was no doubt aware of the tensions caused by the Dev Ed Unit, made a point of congratulating DND in his keynote address at the 1972 Annual Council in which he referred to himself as a 'sleeping partner', noting how ACFID members:

[in the] face of Government's non-support, have rallied round to support the beginning of an education program ... and ACFOA had become an authoritative body for making statements about aid policy generally ... [with] a public standing and a public audience.

DND in subsequent issues went on to deal with the issues of the time, such as the war in Vietnam and apartheid in South Africa, and had its stories regularly picked up by the mainstream media (ACFOA 1973b). The second issue of DND, with the provocative headline 'Racism in Australian Schools', was particularly important as it dealt with how development issues and the Third World were presented in education curricula (O'Dwyer 1972b). This prompted interest from the ABC and other media, but most importantly it led to discussion with state education departments on curriculum development (O'Dwyer 1972f). This was the start of a long-standing global education activity of ACFID and its member agencies working on how development issues were presented in schools. This work has continued into the 2000s, but it is less about social justice and more about supporting government aid policy, and with much less direct funding from NGOs (Bracken 2011; Kagawa 2011; Bryan 2011; Biccum 2011).

Global education conferences

The second main activity of the Dev Ed Unit was organising global education conferences to raise public awareness, particularly within the educator community. This followed the lead of the World Studies project in the UK, which from 1973 ran a series of innovative conferences attended mainly by secondary teachers and NGO educators to look at the global issues of the time (Hicks 2003). There were also similar events held by FAO and UNESCO in Sweden and VCOAD in London and Washington in 1971 (O'Dwyer 1972e). ACFID organised two such conferences in Australia: one in Canberra in 1973 and one in Hobart in 1978. The 1973 conference was funded by DFAT and held over a week from 19–24 January. The conference looked at the basic question of what is development and, emerging from discussion, how education methods and developing country studies could be included in the various curricula to the get message of social justice more clearly into the formal education sector (O'Dwyer 1972c).

The conference was not only a success but it also inflamed passions. Some speakers called for aid to be ended as it was neocolonial, while others challenged the conference participants' role in what was seen as an exploitative system, and the complacent racism of Australian society. Sekai Holland, the Zimbabwean activist, put out the challenge:

One day the feelings your society has meted to you will be restored to you when you wake up to what you are collectively involved in doing in Vietnam and Southern Africa, but particularly to the Aboriginal and Islander peoples, then perhaps we can meet as equals. At the moment it is not yet time (ACFOA 1973d).

This challenge was followed up with a resolution that Australians were guilty of oppression by association with the government's trade policies. This was heady stuff and 'many aid people started to radically rethink their concept of development' (Moore and Tuckwell 1975, p. 11). There were important recommendations for the formal school education system which were taken up over time, including having Aboriginal studies, the treatment of other cultures, and other social justice issues in school curricula and, finally, that the Federal government should fund the recommendations (ACFOA 1973b; O'Dwyer 1973).

The second conference was to be ACFID's biggest undertaking: the Tasmanian Summer School in February 1978. Held over a week in Hobart, it was more than double the size of the Canberra event, with 500 delegates from around the country and 75 leading speakers. The key development issues it covered were trade and employment, human rights, lifestyles, the international economic order, militarism, and education; and how these issues could be better incorporated into global education (Curtis 1977; Sullivan 1978; ACFOA 1978c). This conference, while a great success, lacked the fire and passion of the 1973 event. It was to be the last nationwide global education conference, with questions being asked of the usefulness of such large and expensive events. Following the Tasmanian Summer School, the focus moved to more local and agency-based initiatives, which were the hallmark of global education in the 1980s.

Growing tensions about the Development Education Unit

In 1973 there was a rapid growth in global education among member agencies with AFFHC and CAA both having full-time education officers, as well as a growth in specialist global education agencies.[1] The unit's funding was by then integrated into the ACFID budget, rather than as a separate part of it, with member agencies accepting global education as a legitimate core activity of ACFID (ACFOA 1973a). In 1974 it had a more assured budget, with a very substantial $50,000 government grant from the Labor government, and so was able to increase staff numbers and broaden its role to undertake advocacy (Webb

---

1   For example, Action for World Development (AWD), International Development Association (IDA), World University Service (WUS) and Australian Student Christian Movement (ASCM).

1974; ACFOA 1974b).[2] The year 1974 was to prove to be the halcyon year for global education: it was well resourced, both internally and from the federal Labor government, and there was an increased demand for new ideas and information on development issues from the public, some of which sowed the seeds for the unit's crisis a year later.

While funding for the Dev Ed Unit was assured, the ongoing tensions within ACFID about its work began to grow, reflecting international trends on development issues (Sullivan 1974a; Smillie 2012; Weber 2013; Lissner 1977). Even though tensions were very real there was no major split, and Mick Sullivan, the executive director at the time, believes one of the reasons ACFID did not fall apart like VCOAD in the UK was because of the leadership of the Development Education Committee by two church leaders (Catholic and Protestant). Sullivan recounts that on the Sunday immediately before the education committee agenda item came up at the Annual Council, the two leaders of the committee each held a religious service. Now Sullivan believes that this made it hard for the churchgoing agency representatives hostile to the Dev Ed Unit and its work to accuse the program of being 'communist', the usual cry of the influential Catholic lobby group – the National Civic Council (Sullivan 2013).

The attitudes on both sides of the debate, however, were becoming more entrenched with the Dev Ed Committee report to ACFID Council in 1974 noting the split in voluntary agencies around global education with a plea for some understanding. The report also noted a similar division emerging among agencies in Europe:

> one that could be roughly summed up as a gap between the basically fund raising agencies, and those concerned with global education and social change. I see a similar gap developing in Australia within the ACFOA member agencies ... [It is] unfortunate ... if the issue became one of radical versus conservative, as both need each other ... (O'Dwyer 1974).

Lissner (1977, p. 190) identified three sets of opinions within and among agencies: the fundraisers who maintained that 'the overriding purpose of a voluntary agency is to provide social services to the third world'; the educationalists who argued that 'voluntary agencies have a responsibility for promoting social change there [in the home country] too'; and the middle-of-the-roaders who agreed to a concerted educational effort 'as long as it did not jeopardise agency income'. So they shied away from direct criticism of people and policies of high-income countries. These issues came to a head in Europe

---

2   In parallel, Community Aid Abroad had set up the Light, Powder, and Construction Company, and AFFHC had established The Ideas Centre, both of which undertook global education not only among their supporters but with the broader public as well.

in 1972 and led to the Frascati Consultation, which aimed to bring about some kind of understanding among the various groups of NGOs (Lissner 1977). This did not succeed, in part, because the NGOs did not see global education as a core activity, but rather as a specialist activity, and so NGO leadership did not attend these meetings.

Government funding for global education in many countries, including Canada, Germany, Denmark and Sweden, as well as Australia was readily available, but there was no appreciable change in NGO supporter values. Lissner argued that this was due to the 'middle-of-the-road' agencies merely wanting more education, not different education to challenge basic causes of injustice (Lissner 1977, p. 195). A solution to the conundrum of agencies not wishing to have their education work affect their fundraising evolved into 'constituency education work by proxy', whereby education campaigns were jointly funded, without agencies actually lending their names to it (Lissner 1977, p. 197).[3]

> The agencies satisfy their left-of-centre supporters by backing such initiatives; at the same time the agencies are able to appease their conservative and moderate supporters by assurances that the actions and views of the proxies are not officially endorsed (p. 198).

The problem with this approach was that the global education activities of the proxy agencies were invariably underfunded; and they developed a separate identity, separate values and separate objectives. The result is that communication with the host NGOs was hampered to the point of breaking down, often resulting in alienation and animosity. The global education NGOs developed separate constituencies and fell into the trap of 'preaching to the converted', which defeated the purpose of the exercise, that is, raising the awareness of constituencies of the larger, more mainstream development NGOs.

These issues were at the forefront of ACFID debates at the time. On the one hand, ACFID did provide the role of a proxy for agencies, but the ACFID Dev Ed Unit itself was developing into a proxy within a proxy, creating divisions not only within the ACFID secretariat but also across the agency membership. Despite these tensions the Dev Ed Unit actually expanded through 1974: it set up the anti-apartheid campaign (including calling for boycotts of South African goods); ACFID women's committee prepared for International Women's Year (see Chapter 4); and it also managed a $10,000 community education grant to be made available for worthwhile global education projects in the community (ACFOA 1974c).

---

3   The main proxies in the UK at the time were VCOAD, the World Development Movement, and the *New Internationalist* magazine, which still continues.

It was secure government funding, similar to what was happening in Europe, which tipped the balance for ACFID to maintain its lead in global education, but without solving the inherent tensions that were coming to a head.

In late 1974 Brendan O'Dwyer, the ACFID education officer, went to North Vietnam representing church groups as part of a peace delegation which also had delegates from the ACTU and the Women's Union, both with left-leaning and communist affiliations. The visit also included travel to Viet Cong-controlled areas in South Vietnam. On his return, O'Dwyer gave a number of interviews to the press and on radio, in which he gave unqualified support for the Provisional Revolutionary Government (the Viet Cong) and called on the Australian government to recognise it as the legitimate authority in South Vietnam. Even though O'Dwyer was representing the churches, rather than ACFID, it still led to a storm of protest from ACFID members and the executive (Byrne 1974; Cullen 1974). This set in train a series of incidents the following year which brought matters regarding the Dev Ed Unit to a head.

In 1975 the ACFID report from the Dev Ed Unit, *Aid in a Changing Society: A Handbook of the Australian Aid Debate* (Moore and Tuckwell 1975), was highly critical of Australian NGOs, and when it was debated at ACFID Council in 1975 there were moves for it to be pulped.[4] The Dev Ed Unit was challenging NGOs and their approach to aid, suggesting a need for much stronger participatory approaches and clearer support for social movements (O'Dwyer 1975a; ACFOA 1975h; O'Dwyer 1975c). If this was not enough, there was also an ongoing argument with the Returned and Services League (RSL), also an ACFID member, about the Dev Ed Unit's South African Campaign (Keys 1975; Cullen 1975a; O'Dwyer 1975b).

These divisions, which were becoming more prominent within ACFID, sparked a sense of crisis leading to a series of emergency executive meetings on what do about the unit (ACFOA 1975a, 1975b, 1975c, 1975g, 1975h). Ardent supporters of the unit, including Vaughan Hinton and Sir John Crawford, had resigned their positions for personal (Hinton) and conflict of interest reasons (Crawford).[5] While General Cullen, the chair of ACFID, had been supportive of the unit, the trip to Vietnam, ongoing arguments with the RSL, plus perhaps a reading of a change in the political wind by the ACFID executive (the Whitlam Labor government was sacked in November 1975) led Cullen and the executive to support a restructure of the Dev Ed Unit.

---

4   It was the fact it was government funded from the Office of Women that saved it.
5   Crawford had been appointed chair of the Aid Advisory Council in 1974.

A discussion paper by two executive members suggested having the unit as a separate entity, as some of the larger agencies could not be party to the perceived political activities of the unit (Minogue and Burns 1975). The paper went on to question whether ACFID, as a representative body of all agencies, was best placed for global education at all, given the 'growing political activities of the Education Unit' (p. 1). The paper recommended that an institute of development studies could take over the role with departments on aid, research, and education. This paper only served to worry the ACFID executive more as it could have led to a split, with the larger agencies leaving. John Mavor from the Uniting Church responded to the discussion paper, arguing that to separate the unit from ACFID and constitute it as a Third World Centre would be counterproductive as ACFID needed the challenge and thrust of the Dev Ed Unit, uncomfortable though this was. He went on to rather drily note that the opinions of the unit were 'mild compared to the expressions given by Third World Delegates' at a Christian conference he had attended the previous year (Mavor 1975, p. 2). The executive agreed that the unit should remain within ACFID and be able to present recipient views on aid issues, noting that this may upset some members, but as for the future of global education a broader discussion was required among the membership.

> We cannot have aid without development, we cannot have development without development education, we cannot have development education without action and we cannot have action without being political – and ACFOA cannot avoid living with this tension (ACFOA 1975g, p. 1).

This, however, was not enough and some in the ACFID executive wanted a scalp – and it was to be O'Dwyer's (Nation Review 1975; *The National Times* Editorial 1975; Juddery 1975a). The executive felt that action against him was not only necessary to ease the ongoing tensions, but there was probably nervousness about the possibility of a change of government, and some in ACFID felt they needed more politically neutral credentials (Hill 1975a). O'Dwyer was sacked with no specific reasons provided (Roberston 1975; Hill 1975a; Cullen 1975b; ACFOA 1975c). The sacking was later put down to a personality clash between O'Dwyer and the executive director, and divisions on the role and future of global education within the executive (Sullivan 2013).

The dismissal created a furore particularly at ACFID Council, which was held only two weeks after the sacking, with resolutions supporting his dismissal only being 'noted' and an alternative resolution to have O'Dwyer reinstated being passed. He declined the offer (ACFOA 1975d). At the same a new executive was elected, which was less divided and more supportive of the Dev Ed Unit and its work (Juddery 1975b). This story, however, created considerable press interest (*The National Times* Editorial 1975; Juddery 1975a; Hill 1975a; Juddery 1975b), with questions in parliament as to the possible involvement of the shadow foreign minister Andrew Peacock in influencing the executive, particularly General Cullen who was chair and a prominent member of the opposition Liberal Party (Kerin 1975). While Peacock's meeting with the executive actually occurred after the sacking, it did not remove the suspicion in those politically volatile times that there may have been some behind-the-scenes 'influence' by opposition politicians.

While the dismissal was to some extent inevitable, it did highlight that for ACFID to have a wide membership it had to accommodate the views of a broad range of agencies, lest they leave. It was also clear that the development community itself was divided between the social activists, who saw themselves seeking a different and more just social order, and the traditional aid agencies in favour of preserving the existing social order, but ameliorating its excesses (ACFOA 1975f). While this divide narrowed in the 1980s and 1990s, it was very wide in the 1970s.

Helen Hill, in summarising the era, said that global education at the time was promoting a more just world by pushing for changes within education systems and campaigning on the social justice issues of the time, such as racism, colonialism and sexism, while at the same time agencies were appealing to the public for donations – which led to natural tensions (Hill 1980). Echoing Lissner, Hill argued that it was the lack of internalising the importance of global education within ACFID and its members, which made it always vulnerable:

> [D]oes the fact that they give generously mean that they will also respond to information and want to know more about why such aid is necessary … I would say that the opposite is true, that those who give the most are the least interested in finding out more about the situation and may in fact give to rid themselves of the bother of finding out. The aid agencies … have assumed the reverse to be true (1980, p. 14).

In 1978 a group of seven agencies led by Bill Armstrong, deputy chair, held a review and recommended the continuation of the Dev Ed Unit with some mechanism for more inclusion of agencies through a liaison officer, and an additional publication: *Inside ACFID* (ACFOA 1977a, 1978a). A broader review of ACFID a year later found the key criticisms of the Dev Ed Unit fell into four broad areas: political bias; being a separate entity within ACFID; poor response to member agency needs; and only concentrating on activities with a select few (Tiffen et al. 1979). It was inevitable that the Dev Ed Unit could not continue as such, and it would have to spend more of its resources in serving member agencies. ACFID's global education program continued to challenge the development issues of the day, such as East Timor and South Africa; however, DND, the unit's flagship became too expensive and was wound up with its last issue in November 1979.

Global education in the 1980s

In the late 1970s and early 1980s, global education was maintained at a relatively low profile. Despite some lobbying of the foreign minister (ACFOA 1981b), there was little support from the more conservative Coalition government for global education, and AusAID was reluctant to fund it outside of the ACFID grant or mention it at the annual consultation with ACFID (Ingram 1981). Despite the review of 1979 there were still further reviews (Hodges 1980), and questions kept being asked as to whether global education should have a separate budget or even the need for ACFID to run a separate public awareness program, and instead focus on supporting member agencies' own work (ACFOA 1981c, 1981d).

In 1983 a new executive director, Russell Rollason, reinvigorated the global education program and moved the approach to a more focused, campaign-based strategy (Armstrong 1981; Rollason 2013). The origins of ACFID's move to a more comprehensive campaigning strategy lie in some of the weaknesses of conventional global education, which was mainly about providing broad-based information on social justice issues: 'publishing stuff where it sat on shelves – doing kits and sending them to your mates would not get you anywhere' (Rollason 2013). His experience from a 1974 Right to Eat campaign, and a 1977 campaign on what was thought an obscure topic, the Common Fund, had worked well. As an approach he felt campaigning had better prospects than more general global education. While working with schools was a worthwhile long-term investment, change was also needed more immediately (Rollason 2013). While there was still a view that ACFID had 'done its job' – as global education had been mainstreamed into most agencies' work with ACFID members spending $2 million on global education in 1982 (ACFOA 1983b) – ACFID still argued for a leadership role, albeit in the form of specific campaigns on global education issues.

The advent of a Labor government in early 1983 provided new opportunities. There was a renewed push for global education funding from government with submissions to the Jackson Committee on Aid for more support for community education (ACFOA 1983a). This recommendation was largely supported, as the Jackson Committee saw global education as a complementary activity to aid; this was important to maintaining a constituency for official aid (Fujikane 2003; Hicks 2003; Jackson Committee 1984). In 1985 AusAID funded resource centres in each state capital city. They were a hub for getting information not only out to the public but also to schools (Moxon 1985). There were regular liaisons with agencies such as the global education officers' conference in 1985 (ACFOA 1985c), and ACFID also did some work on the formal curriculum in that year, giving ACFID an opportunity to work with teacher groups such as the Geography Teachers Association in much the same way the UK did in the late 1970s (Fujikane 2003; Hicks 2003). Work on curriculum grew through the

1980s and at the end of the decade culminated in a three-year project funded by AusAID to continue its support of global education in the school system (Hunt 2012).

The campaigns

In the UK, NGO-led campaigns started earlier than in Australia, with Christian Aid Week in 1959 and the '1 per cent' campaign in 1965[6] by British NGOs' War on Want and Christian Aid being some of the first (Hilton 2012; Saunders 2009). As noted above, ACFID's first campaigns were the anti-apartheid campaign following the 1971 Springbok tour (Ross 1990) and the Bangladesh famine campaign of 1971–72. Later the Campaign Against Racial Exploitation emerged from another ACFID anti-apartheid campaign in 1974 (Minogue 1974; Roberston 1975), which then picked up Aboriginal issues in Australia. In the late 1970s, however, apart from aid budget campaigns, there was no coherent campaigning strategy for ACFID. Rollason pushed for a more direct campaigning approach and he slowly won the global education advocates over (Armstrong 1981).

Figure 5 ACFID stalwarts Russell Rollason and John Mavor eat pet food as part of a Right to Eat campaign in 1974.

Source: Ted Golding; Fairfax Media.

---

6   This was a campaign for British ODA and Direct Foreign Investment in developing countries to be 1 per cent of GDP.

In 1982 a community awareness campaign One World or No World was proposed and advised by prominent advertising executive and ACFID supporter Philip Adams, who presented an advertising-type pitch to the Council based on pithy slogans. This was too much for the traditional educationists and the response was lukewarm, with AWD, for example, saying such an approach would put global education back 10 years (ACFOA 1982a). But the seeds of change were sown, and a few years later campaigning was to become entrenched in ACFID's work.

The aim was for ACFID to focus on public awareness through its campaigns. Campaigning was about both focus and the use of mass media, and it was the Live Aid phenomenon in the mid-1980s that changed the mindset.

> Many NGOs have often felt uncomfortable with events based primarily on mass communication techniques. Their criticism focuses on the over-simplistic presentation of issues, on the fact that most such presentations portray the Third World as helpless, and on the lack of a long-term perspective on issues. Live Aid succeeded in conveying simple messages to large numbers of people because it based its approach on the public's perceptions and needs, rather than the causes and issues; it showed that the public needed to feel that they were part of a larger movement (Lemaresquier 1987, p. 197).

By the 1990s campaigning came into its own, with the One World campaign and later the Make Poverty History campaign the two major ones. These were large campaigns and effectively were the global education strategy for ACFID to get the message of development and social justice issues out (ACFOA 1990d; Rollason 2013). The only reason Dev Ed stayed as a name for another few years was that it was in the ACFID constitution (ACFOA 1990b). In 1998, however, 'development education' was formally replaced by the term 'advocacy' (ACFOA 1998a).

While campaigns were more tightly focused, with more direct messages, they tended to direct what the answer to a problem should be rather than enable a more open conversation – the basis of global education (Ni Chasaide 2009). Campaigns also tended to take the priorities and agenda from Southern NGOs to be 'owned' by Northern NGOs. For example, the trade justice agenda was being driven by what groups and campaigners in the North perceived to be the problem rather than what those in the South wanted or needed (Lloyd 2005; Murphy 2012). Southern NGOs tend to push for structural change against what they see as neocolonial economic structures, while Northern NGO advocates prefer a 'tweaking' of the system.

the strong justice agenda that underpinned the campaign at the start became incrementally replaced by an 'empathy' agenda which tended to appeal to Western politicians with relatively little consideration of the causes or nature of poverty, let alone the ways in which the British public might relate to Africans or African societies (Harrison 2010, p. 392).

Campaigns often serve as a shell into which a wide range of information could be poured. Their focus and project nature made it easier for ACFID to budget and plan while providing a mechanism to ensure a necessary profile. As Rollason said to the Campaigns Committee in 1993: '[ACFID was] adopting a strategy to ensure that aid would be the second or third issue on the prime minister's agenda and acknowledge that change would need to come over a longer period was very important' (ACFOA 1993b, p. 1).

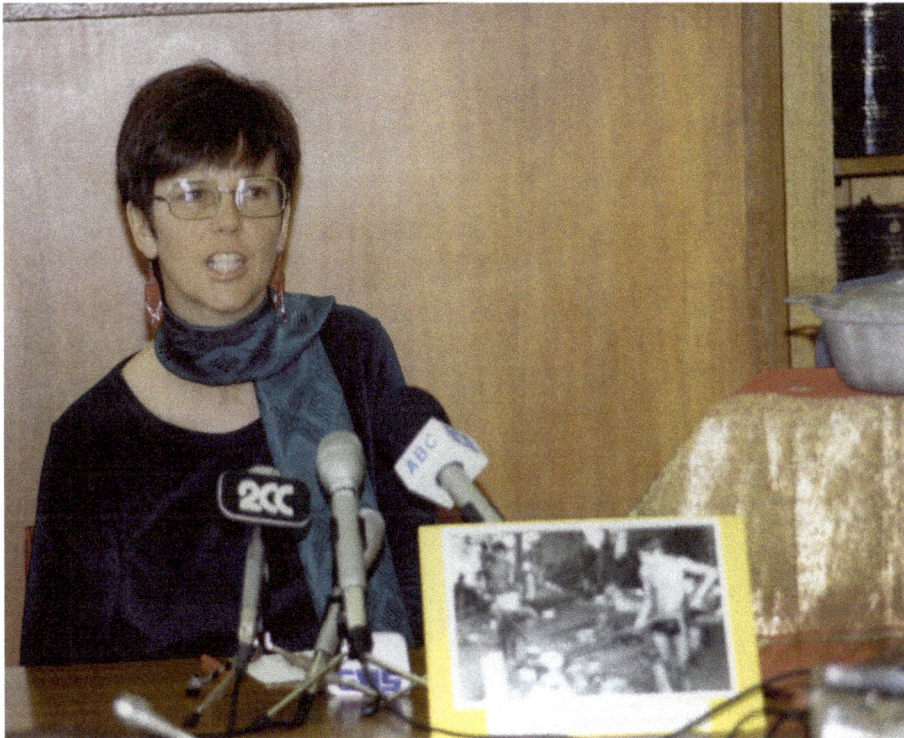

Figure 6 Janet Hunt Launches Development Dossier on Disarmament and Development 1987.

Source: ACFID.

Figure 7 Susan Harris Rimmer Speaking for ACFID at Rally for Peace held in Canberra 2001.

Source: Seselja, Loui.

The key was to get aid issues on politicians' agendas, and conventional broad-based global education was not going to do that. Added to this was the post-Cold War donor fatigue of the 1990s. This meant that the agenda had to be revitalised through campaigns like One World and Jubilee 2000 in the UK and elsewhere (Saunders 2009). The campaigns were successful and an important part of keeping aid on the agenda through the cynical 1990s and into the 2000s, when overseas aid volumes shot up to the same levels (as a percentage of GDP) as the 1970s, but without the postcolonial aid obligations of that era.

If the Dev Ed Unit was ACFID's signature activity in the 1970s, by the 1990s and into the 2000s it was campaigning. In 1989 the One World Campaign was launched (ACFOA 1989b). The focus was on environment and development, poverty, disarmament and human rights. Fifteen member agencies came on board, together with a $300,000 grant from AusAID (Ross 1991). The campaign opened with the global television documentary *Our Common Future*, which led to 10,000 signing up, five times more than planned for (ACFOA 1989b), and even a resolution of support in the Australian Parliament (Tickner 1989). Later in the year, ACFID put a scenario to Geoffrey Robertson, a prominent human rights lawyer, who had a very popular television program on social issues called *Hypotheticals*. The format was a panel of public figures, experts and politicians responding to a rapidly shifting hypothetical situation orchestrated by Robertson, which made for good television. ACFID persuaded AusAID to cover the production costs of the ensuing program *Beggar Thy Neighbour*, which looked at aid and human rights. It was a television success, getting development issues to a mass audience. A kit for schools followed (Hunt 2011).

The second major ACFID campaign was Make Poverty History, which was conceived by British NGOs in 2003 as a campaigning coalition that would mainly focus on the G8 summit in July 2005 to be held in the UK (Harrison 2010). Over time it outgrew those humble beginnings and became a global campaign over the next 10 years. In Australia it had its own identity separate to ACFID or individual NGOs, with ACFID being a member of the campaign coalition and offering some staff and secretarial support.

The One World Campaign represented the shift that had been underway for some time of ACFID moving out of global education as such and to an arms-length campaigning model for getting development messages out. The same change was also being seen in the agencies themselves, with the early 1990s marking a period of change, when there was a broad shift from global education to campaigning. Twenty years of ACFID's involvement in global education was not without its controversies, but the work of the first five years and the semi-autonomous Dev Ed Unit set the scene for public and government engagement. This early work set ACFID up as a key voice in public debates, and gradually saw it take a greater coordination rather than operational role in campaigns and global education.

Global education in the 2000s

Global education was internationally strong for about 15 years up to the mid-1980s, when it declined in part due to a conservative backlash, particularly in the UK with the Thatcher government (Fujikane 2003), which saw global education as 'condoning indoctrination and politicisation of the educational experience' (Bracken et al. 2011, p. 2). In the 2000s, the Blair government in the UK saw advantages in supporting global education as it was important in maintaining the strong constituency for aid, so it was well resourced with NGOs being encouraged to put resources into it as well (Dominy et al. 2011; Weber 2013). In Australia ACFID members continued to do work on global education with AusAID providing some funding, but with more strings attached. AusAID began to approve the material being used, even for projects being funded under the usually much looser ANCP (AusAID 2013), and in 2014 even went so far as to drop public awareness raising as an accreditation criterion (DFAT 2014; Purcell 2015).

The 2000s represented a shift away from the 1970s and 1980s and critiques of contemporary development models to a narrower focus on aid more directly, and taking a more positive and less critical approach to the topic – what Bryan (2011) calls the 'de-clawing' of global education. This reflected a broader shift among NGOs globally, whereby they were more constrained in criticising government policy due to tighter regulatory and financial strings, and Lissner's 'middle-of-the road' NGOs were less inclined to fund the more radical advocacy organisations (Ni Chasaide 2009; Biccum 2011; Lang 2012; Lissner 1977; Weber 2013). In 2015, however, following massive cuts in the official aid program and polling that showed historically low levels of public understanding of development issues, there were signs of change. The 2015–20 ACFID Strategic Plan moved ACFID to a more direct engagement with the public on the challenges of human development to try to build the development constituency, much in the same way that ACFID and AWD did in the 1970s but without the same levels of resources.

Conclusion

In the 20 years that ACFID had a global education program it had achieved a lot but also had trodden on many toes. The leadership and vision of the early years was that global education should not only bring development issues to the eyes of the public, and from a government perspective provide a constituency for aid programs, but it should also challenge the basic injustices of the global order. This latter direction of course challenged the 'comfort zones' of agencies, which had been built on the altruistic notion of helping those in need, to being in solidarity with and being prepared to challenge a fundamentally unjust economic order. In the end this last 'ask' was probably a step too far.

Balancing both the challenging of key issues of development and keeping the aid constituency on side for over 20 years was no small feat. The Dev Ed program in 1972 was built on two key events: the public revulsion to the Australian government's inaction to what was happening in Bangladesh and the massive public response to the AWD global education program. This gave the impetus for the new Dev Ed Unit to start with a radical edge and to challenge the prevailing views of development, developing countries and social justice. This was the heady period of social change in Australia and globally. The Dev Ed program set an agenda and had the public and governments sitting up and taking notice. This was demonstrated by the two national global education conferences in 1973 and 1978, which galvanised support especially in the education sector to put the messages out in school and the community on issues of social justice.

Of course this agenda was very challenging to both agencies and government, especially among those agencies that had the idea of development built on non-political stances and values of non-interference on matters of aid and politics. There was always an inherent tension with ACFID and its Dev Ed Unit, which was only resolved in the 1980s with a shift in direction to campaigning. In the early 1990s, the global education program had largely achieved what it had set out to do. There were strong education programs among member agencies, Dev Ed centres were flourishing in the states, and the education curriculum in schools had a much richer analysis of development and developing country issues.

The campaign model was a move away from what may be described as grassroots activism on social justice issues more generally in the mould of AWD to a more focused approach looking at specific issues more clearly directed by agencies and ACFID. The debate that occurred within ACFID and across NGOs more broadly was that while campaigning is important to focus on particular questions in the short term, something was lost in not having an ongoing program of global education with the general public to keep a higher awareness of social justice issues. The drop in public support for aid in the 2010s may be a result of this shift in focus.

In the 2000s, with governments more sensitive to public criticism, the global education and advocacy space for peak agencies such as ACFID has closed somewhat. ACFID is also very sensitive that they still have a place at the table to express a voice even if it is behind closed doors, lest they be excluded in the same way that CCIC has been in Canada (Smillie 2012). The advocacy space and campaigning is now filled, not with voices railing against injustice but rather looking to have strong and growing aid programs, and generally avoiding structural issues altogether. There are, however, signs of change as ACFID in 2015 moves to a more direct engagement with the public about broader development challenges beyond aid and levels of aid.

04

From Women in Development to Gender Justice?

Why, at a time when race prejudice is being overcome, and when the
prestige of another keyword 'anti-colonialism' is serving diverse interests,
why do we resign ourselves so easily to the maintenance of other privileges
of which women only are the victims [and] protective measures consolidate
their inferior status ... Equality of rights is a man's affair.

— Lefaucheux 1959, p. 452

Including women into aid and development activities has been difficult ever since official aid programs started in the 1950s and 1960s. While Third World women have been clamouring to be included and were leading drivers in the UN processes since the 1950s, Western development agencies, including NGOs, have been very slow to incorporate women's needs into their development programs, and even less inclined to look at the gender issues in power relations between men and women in developing countries, let alone gender minorities.[1] The same story applies to ACFID, which has struggled to adequately take on board women and gender in development throughout much of its history.

It can be argued that the focus of most Australian international NGOs on gender has moved little beyond women and development type activities such as microfinance and livelihoods, which can be used to entrench existing inequality as much as being empowering or liberating. ACFID's engagement with gender and development issues in the early years was driven by the major UN Women's Conferences,[2] if government funding was available, or if the regulators insisted on compliance with such legislation as the Equal Employment Opportunity Act.

---

1   Here I refer to those who identify themselves as gay, lesbian, transsexual, transgender, and other sexual minorities who are regularly and systematically marginalised and oppressed in many, if not most, developing countries.

2   Mexico City, Copenhagen, Nairobi and Beijing. ACFID was represented at three, but curiously not Copenhagen.

Apart from those times, the history of ACFID and its members had been one of little progress in advancing the cause of women in developing countries until possibly the 2000s, and nothing at all on gender and sexual minorities (Kilby and Crawford 2011). This chapter will track the 'progress' over 40 years of gender largely being resisted by the mainstream development agencies, the hard work of a few individuals in keeping gender on the agenda, and the continual revisiting of the same gender issues by NGOs.

Women and development pre-1975

How men and women, boys and girls in the community are recognised in aid and development activities has been an issue for the UN since the early 1950s, mainly through the work of the UN Commission on the Status of Women (CSW) (Jain 2005). For development agencies, recognising and working on women and development issues did not come to the fore until the early 1970s. The International Women's Year activities of 1975 and the associated Mexico City Women's Conference brought the issue of women's rights to a much broader audience, and set in train a set of processes that led to the idea of gender and women's rights, ostensibly as a central plank in development, having a much greater focus.

Before 1975, there had been a raft of statements and declarations on the rights of women dating back to the UN's formation in 1945, and the League of Nations before that (Lefaucheux 1959; UNGA 1963b; Boserup 1970; Jain 2005). The Inter-American Commission on Women, which was formed in 1928, was active in working for women's roles in development through the 1950s (Meyer 1999; Charlesworth and Chinkin 2013); the CSW was established in 1946; and in 1961 US President Kennedy set up a US Commission on the Status of Women (Harrison 1980; Freeman 1999; Jain 2005). In Africa, activists sponsored by the UN Economic Commission for Africa (ECA) in the 1960s had put women at the centre of ECA's analyses as early as 1966, and were implementing a prototype of 'women-in-development' projects well before its official recognition in the West in the 1970s (Quataert 2013, p. 3). The CSW was pushing for women's political rights from 1946, with a Convention on the Political Rights of Women passed by the UN in 1952. Lakshmi Menon from India, who was the head of CSW (1949–50), had already being lobbying UNESCO on the importance of girls' education (Peppin-Vaughan 2013; UNESCO 1951), which was finally officially recognised as a development priority in the Millennium Development Goals (MDGs) some 50 years later. In the 1950s and 1960s, CSW shifted its focus to looking at women's economic and social development to mirror the major development trends at the time and, in 1962, the UN Secretary-General asked CSW to report on the role of women in the social and economic development plans of member states (Krook and True 2012; Jain 2005).

Of course these changes were not met with open arms, and there was a lot of resistance from member states. For example, a British Foreign Office view from 1954 was that CSW's push for women's rights was 'woolly, half-baked and impractical' (Laville 2012, p. 487). CSW, therefore, was largely alone in the UN system on women's rights, with the other major agencies such as the International Labour Organization (ILO) and FAO relegating women to being virtually second-class citizens by advocating what would be seen now as an anachronistic gendered division of labour, with women being confined to domestic roles (Quataert 2013; Jain 2005). Women and development was a virtual unknown in bilateral development programs, except for some pioneering work in Sweden in the mid-1960s (Nanivazo and Scott 2012).

The 1966 Declaration on the Elimination of Discrimination against Women (DEDAW) was a major breakthrough in the UN system in terms of women's rights, with its pioneering argument that the 'discrimination of women impeded development' (Fraser 1995, p. 78). This declaration was later given teeth in the form of the Convention on the Elimination of All Forms of Discrimination against Women (CEDAW) in 1979 (INSTRAW and UNIFEM 1995; Peters 1996). The 1966 declaration had its origins in a draft declaration put to the UN General Assembly (UNGA) in 1963, when a group of 22 developing and Eastern European countries introduced a resolution at the UNGA calling for the drafting of a resolution on women's discrimination. This was at the peak of UN work on the first Development Decade and the broad commitments being made to Third World development. It is also worth noting that no Western countries were involved in the drafting or presentation of the resolution, a point that challenges the commonly held notion that the leadership on women's rights and development came out of the West, or that it represents an agenda of Western feminists (Schech 1998; Haggis and Schech 2000; Escobar 2011; Shain 2013).

The draft DEDAW Resolution of 1963 also called on member states to appoint national commissions on the status of women. In 1967, following the Declaration, the UN Secretary-General was tasked to report back to the General Assembly on the progress of the work of member states' national commissions. In 1972, following the appointment of national commissions, the UN proposed that countries should also put in place national long-term programs for the advancement of women (United Nations Economic Commission for Africa 1973). The first country to actively seek to include women in its development programs was Sweden in 1964, when it enacted legislation that mandated government assistance to women in development programs as part of its aid program (Tinker and Zuckerman 2014). Sweden was followed by the US in 1973 with the Percy Amendment 'requiring that particular attention be given to integrating women into national economies to improve their status and to assist the overall development effort' (Snyder 1995, p. 98). More broadly, the UN also recognised the gap, and both men and women were seen as important in the development process. The 1970 UN International Development Strategy called for the 'full integration of women into the development effort' as part of the Second Development Decade Plan (quoted in Jain 2005, p. 43).

Despite this high level of debate on women's rights at the UN through the 1960s and 1970s, there was no mention of women in development in the ACFID records at the time. It seemed that in the 1960s and 1970s the women's movement and the development agenda occupied seemingly parallel universes. One explanation might be that liberation theology of the 1960s, which was very male focused and gender blind, drove a lot of development discourse and, in particular, global education thinking among NGOs (Connolly 1997).

In 1970 Ester Boserup's groundbreaking work *Women's Role in Economic Development* (1970), based on her own observations in India and Senegal and the work of the ECA in the 1960s, put the issue of women and development to a much wider audience (Turner and Fischer-Kowalski 2010; Quataert 2013). It put a challenge to Western donors when she argued for 'women's integration into the development process as equal partners with men' (Drolet 2010, p. 213). In the United States Boserup's message, and the work of the ECA, led to Congress adopting the Percy Amendment (Snyder 1995), which included the establishment of a Women in Development (WID) office within USAID (in 1974). However, it was not until a US Accounting Office audit of policy compliance in the 1990s some 20 years later that USAID began to systematically comply with that Congressional directive (Miazad 2002). Similarly, the DAC convened an expert group on women in development in 1975, but the work was slow to be realised, not least in Australia where it paid lip-service at best until well into the 1990s (ADAB 1979; ADAB 1983; Snyder 1995).

The issue of women's marginalisation in development was not new even in the 1970s, particularly to women's groups in developing countries which advocated for women's rights around urbanisation, modernisation, the role of religion, intra-family patriarchal power structures, the status of women in society, and reproductive health, among many others, all of which are still relevant in the twenty-first century (Tinker and Bo-Bramson 1976). Luisbu N'Kanza from Zaire feared:

> that International Women's Year would turn out to be nothing more than just a glorified Mother's Day, and called for action that would show that women were tired of feeling powerless and wanted a share in national and international decision making. Sexism as practices by individuals and institutions was [to be] condemned (quoted in Tinker and Bo-Bramson 1976, p. 143).

The Mexico City Women's Conference (and the associated civil society tribune) was a momentous event, bringing together 8,000 women from all over the world. It 'introduced activists to the potential of pursuing their interests through the UN at a time when there were few international venues for women's rights' (Bunch 2012, p. 214). The key outcome of the Mexico City Conference was the building of a network, which the UN Conference enabled:

> Women discovered their 'brand': in every country women and girls were treated as an inferior minority. In over 200 formal and informal meetings, emerging leaders formed new friendships. Recognizing that power is taken, not given, they forged a network for change (Persinger 2012, p. 192).

The Mexico City Conference also led to a World Plan of Action around three broad objectives, one of which was the integration and full participation of women in development.[3] The plan was criticised for continuing to leave women as passive victims of 'underdevelopment', with women being seen as 'mothers, workers and citizens' rather than as having a broad range of identities and voices (Bignall 1997; Zinsser 2002, p. 149). But it was a first step as the World Plan of Action also offered guidelines for governments and the international community to follow for the next 10 years, with a set of minimum targets to be met by 1980.

The conference not only brought women's development issues to the fore but also went well beyond Boserup's economic role of women to put the structural discrimination issues that women faced in all societies onto the agenda (Koczberski 1998; Moghadam 2000; Fraser 2012; Jahan 2012; Funk 2013). It also highlighted the differences in priorities of Third World women, which were about underdevelopment and the role of race, class, caste and gender in women's marginalisation, and First World women, whose primary concerns were around gender equality (Jain 2005).

> Serious tensions and divisions surfaced, exploding any notion of 'sisterhood', 'common cause', or 'women' as one unified political agent. Simultaneously, confronting these tensions initiated a reassessment of feminist visions under the human rights rubric and through the gender lens (Quataert 2011, p. 635).

---

3   The three broad objectives were full gender equality and the elimination of gender discrimination; an increased contribution by women in the strengthening of world peace; and the integration and full participation of women in development. These three objectives each reflected the particular interests of the First, Second and Third World respectively, a feature of UN conferences at the time.

It would not be until the Nairobi Women's Conference in 1985 that these different positions would begin to come together and a global feminism emerge (Moghadam 2000). This was in part because the Non-aligned Movement had a strong women's caucus, which had already met in New Delhi prior to the Nairobi conference to agree on a position that 'linked women's inequality to underdevelopment and unjust international relations' (Jain 2005, p. 83). It was rather ironic that at Beijing in 1995 it was Western feminists who brought out issues of marginalisation due to gender and race, caste, sexuality and the like, which mirrored the concerns of Third World women 20 years earlier without explicitly acknowledging them (Çağatay et al. 1986; Baden and Goetz 1997; Moghadam 2000).

Women and development in Australia

Despite these momentous global events on gender, Australian development NGOs were very slow to recognise the role of patriarchy and power in these marginalising processes on women in the countries where they worked, and so the mainstream development NGOs tended to be followers rather than leaders on the issue of women and development.[4] This lack of interest and engagement by the development NGOs was in contrast to a long history of women's NGOs in Australia dating back to the 1890s, with the women's suffrage movement and the state councils of women representing Australian women's groups (Foley 1985; Lake 1996). For example, in 1958 the Social Science Research Council, with government funding, commissioned a year-long study into the status of women in Australia, which was undertaken in 1959–60, well before DEDAW in 1967 obligated Australia to do such studies (MacKenzie 1962).

The National Council of Women was also very active in the early 1970s and, while its focus was mainly involved with the Australian domestic scene, its work did 'stray' into the international arena. For example, it sponsored a conference on Population, Development and the Role of Women in October 1973, with delegates from across the Asia-Pacific region, but with no ACFID staff or member agency involvement (National Council of Women 1973). What is clear is that women and development was not part of the aid discourse in Australia in the 1960s and into the 1970s, despite the issue being important abroad at the time, with developing-country women calling for the recognition of their rights and the issues that affected them (Tinker et al. 1976; Reid 2012). Likewise, the history of official aid in the 1970s was devoid of reference to women's roles in development processes and the consequent disadvantages they faced. To be fair,

---

4 After the 1995 Women's Conference in Beijing the term gender and development was adopted.

however, aid policy at the time was devoid of references to the involvement of people more generally, particularly as aid recipients (Wilkinson 1976; Viviani and Wilenski 1978).

The records of the early years of ACFID and its Dev Ed Unit were remarkably silent on the issue of women's rights until the Mexico City Women's conference of 1975, when ACFID sent a representative to the NGO Forum, and the *Development News Digest* 'discovered' women after some years with a special issue on International Women's Year (ACFOA 1975c).[5] Despite some work from 1974 to 1978 on advancing women and development issues among ACFID member agencies following International Women's Year and the Mexico City Women's Conference, progress was limited. Neither women's rights nor gender were on the program at the Tasmanian Summer School, the major development conference at the time (ACFOA 1978b). The first mention of women and development in ACFID's Standing Policy was not until 1983 when a sentence on involving women in aid programs was added (ACFOA 1983f). This followed AusAID's recognition of women and development in a policy statement in 1980 (ADAB 1980).[6]

ACFID and the Mexico City Women's Conference

As mentioned above, it was the International Women's Year and the Mexico City Women's Conference that prompted ACFID to look at women's rights issues. In 1974, as part of the planning stage for the Mexico City conference, ACFID secured a relatively small grant of $900 from the International Women's Year Secretariat to undertake research on women in Australian NGOs and how they saw women and development in their work (Whitlam 1975; Reid 1975). The research was undertaken by ACFID staff in early 1975 through a mail survey of all ACFID members covering their policies and practices regarding women's employment in their agencies and women's participation as aid recipients in agency programs. From this survey a report was produced: *Aid in a Changing Society* (Moore and Tuckwell 1975). This report set the context for examining the role of women in development through the lens of the NGOs' philosophy; as such, it was critical of the ACFID member agencies as a whole, finding their philosophy somewhat paternalistic to both their approach to women as staff in their organisations as well as to aid recipients.

---

5   The first issue was in 1972.

6   There has never been an ongoing subcommittee in ACFID's structure looking at women's rights or gender justice. At best there have been ad hoc working groups, with gender being generally subsumed under development education or policy, rather than given prominence in development practice work.

> Nowhere did the agencies recognise the different problems of women within their own organisations or as recipients of their aid, and [there is] little evidence of support for projects based in favour of increasing women's independence (Moore and Tuckwell 1975, pp. 7–8).

Given the flurry of activity around International Women's Year, with a secretariat and National Women's Advisory Committee advising and funding projects of Australian domestic NGOs and community groups to address the rights and roles of women throughout society (Reid 1975a), the dismissive response of ACFID members to women's issues evident in the survey was both surprising and disturbing. It possibly reflected a broader disconnect of development NGOs with the aims and activities of the women's movement and domestic women's NGOs at the time. It also probably reflected a disconnect between gender issues and the broader social and liberation movements in developing countries of the time, which were generally patriarchal in their structures and practices. Gender was seen as secondary in the broader struggle to avoid possible divisions within the movements (Sigmund 1990; Graham 2003; Viterna and Fallon 2008). Meer (2005) talks specifically about the case of South Africa and the anti-apartheid movement, but the same issues were found in Latin America, where gender and women's issues were seen as divisive and to be dealt with after the broader 'struggle' had achieved its aims (Hassim 1991).

Moore and Tuckwell's (1975) report suggested that the management and boards of NGOs reflected a paternalistic view of development while the activists in organisations failed to see the importance of the gender dimension in social justice and liberation struggles, and male staff and activists tended to avoid 'gender'. Needless to say their report created a furore at the 1975 ACFID Council, which was already divided over the issue of global education. There was a move from a handful of agencies to have the report pulped. As it was a report to government through the International Women's Year Secretariat, ACFID Council agreed that instead of withdrawing the report it should have a strong disclaimer from ACFID on the cover, and that the ACFID Executive Committee would decide how the report was to be used (ACFOA 1975d; Moore 2011). The report, however, had already been printed and distributed without a disclaimer and so the resolution had little practical effect.

The Mexico City Women's Conference itself and Australia's leadership in it was very important in advancing women's rights. While there was a strongly worded Australian government brief articulating its support for women's rights in development, it was far from certain whether the brief reflected either the views of AusAID or the Australian NGOs of the time:

> Since aid is a grim necessity due to the injustices in the old international order, women in donor countries could profitably make sure that programs

and projects do not make women in recipient countries more marginal and dependent and that they do not impose western cultural sex-role stereotypes (Australian Government Brief quoted in Moore 1975).

While Australia developed a National Plan of Action in 1978, there is little reference in it to the second key plank of the Mexico City Conference on the participation of women in development until the Copenhagen Women's Conference of 1980.

The Mexico City Women's Conference, however, did put women and development on the agenda of ACFID and AusAID, albeit tenuously, as it was to be another 10 years before women and development was to become more of a mainstream issue for either of them. As a response to the Women's Conference, AusAID appointed two relatively junior women and development officers to advise on the aid program but offered little high level policy direction to guide them. The role of the WID advisers in AusAID was to appraise projects against WID principles and make suggestions to the desk officers. As the WID policy framework was sketchy at best, it was up to desk officers whether they took the advice of the WID adviser or not. In 1976 AusAID adopted policies specifically taking into account the particular needs of women at the design, implementation and appraisal stage of development projects (ADAB 1979). These included guidelines for appraisal, more projects targeting women, more women students in the scholarship program, and a women's affairs committee was set up which reported regularly to the UN Economic and Social Commission for Asia and the Pacific (ESCAP).

These policy guidelines, however, were poorly implemented and the 1979 AusAID report to the DAC went on to say that it was too hard to measure the effects of Australia's aid program on women or the extent to which they had been included (ADAB 1979, p. 19). Four years later in another report to the DAC, AusAID reported that little had changed on the issue of women and development, with the low level of demand from recipient countries for WID projects being given as the reason for the lack of progress. An example was that the low number of women on scholarships had barely moved since 1978 (ADAB 1983, p. 12). In the mid-1970s AusAID had little policy direction on social inclusion of any kind, let alone women, as it struggled with its own internal divisions (Viviani and Wilenski 1978).

ACFID was concerned that with the new Coalition government in 1975 the 'temporary' women and development unit in AusAID would be closed down, and so ACFID regularly lobbied Andrew Peacock, the foreign minister at the time, to keep the positions (ACFOA 1976d; Batt 1977). While the positions remained it was not until Dr Ruth Pfanner from the United Nations joined AusAID in 1980 that the role of women in development was taken more seriously.

The policy direction on women and development until then was generally embedded in statements by the foreign minister, for example, when Andrew Peacock in 1976 said that Australia's aid took into account the special problems of women in developing countries (ADAB/DFAT 1980, p. 127). In the AusAID 1978–79 *Annual Report* a couple of paragraphs under the heading 'Women in Development' indicated that women's projects from developing countries 'will receive particularly sympathetic consideration' (ADAB 1980, p. 16). There was also a symbolic gift in 1979 of $100,000 over five years to the UN Voluntary Fund for Women (administered by ESCAP) for the Asia-Pacific region. It was not until a chapter on women and development in the 1984 Jackson Committee report on the aid program, drafted by Ruth Pfanner and pushed by Professor Helen Hughes, a member of the committee, that this issue was put firmly on the AusAID agenda. Following this, detailed policies were developed and funding was provided (Jackson Committee 1984; Pfanner 2012).

Within ACFID there was also little progress despite the global interest of developing country women's groups and local NGOs at the time. In the late 1970s ACFID still struggled with the issue, with only a few tentative steps being made around realising women's equality and rights. In 1976 there was a half-day consultation with Germaine Greer on women in development with 80 women from NGOs attending and 10 from AusAID. In the same year ACFID put out the 'We Women' resource kit for NGOs (ACFOA 1976i). But, as mentioned above, two years later women and development was completely overlooked at the Tasmanian Summer School in 1978. In 1977 the ANCP's appraisal criteria included a focus on self-reliance, women, and social justice. Of course the women's projects supported at the time were invariably handicrafts and small-scale income generation, with little about women's rights. Apart from these largely women-led gestures, ACFID and its members really did not heed the exhortation of the Mexico Women's Conference, and women seemed to become more marginal in development programs. This was due largely to the paternalist attitudes of the time, which continue to some extent to this day (Kilby and Crawford 2011). After Kate Moore left ACFID in 1978, women and development fell off the ACFID agenda until after the 1980 Women's Conference in Copenhagen.

In Australia, the National Women's Advisory Council (NWAC), set up in 1978, had the task of not only oversighting women's inclusion in the domestic sector through a broad policy and coordination role (Sawer 1998), but it also had a brief to work with DFAT in preparing for the Copenhagen Women's Conference around women and development issues. This did not happen in any real sense. There was certainly no interaction with either AusAID or ACFID on women and development until 1982 when, after a submission from AusAID, the NWAC recommended a WID fund in the aid program (National Women's Advisory Council 1984). Bob Whan, the ACFID executive director at the time, reflected in

1981 that there seemed to be no space for men in the WID work when he was thinking of strengthening ACFID's work in the area (Whan 2008). On the other hand, there did not seem to be much push by the male leadership of NGOs to be included in that space either, and 35 years later the ACFID gender equity working group is still largely made up of women.

The Copenhagen Conference

Globally, a number of shifts were occurring, which started at Mexico City but were taken forward in key locations. In the United States the Carter administration put a greater focus on women in USAID programs, setting up a WID office and showing some improvements in its women's programs. The critics of WID, however, argued that these programs were supporting unfair and unequal systems and were training women as clients and ignoring the structural issues they faced (Jaquette and Staudt 2006). This was the context in which the Copenhagen Women's Conference was held where there were clear divisions. A strong anti-Western theme came through in both the Conference and the NGO Forum. The sharp difference between Third World and First World women at the forum made participants feel uncomfortable and begin to question the usefulness of these forums (Çağatay 1986; Margolis 1993; Kapadia 1995; West 1999; Zinsser 2002). The key areas of difference between feminists from the North and South, like at Mexico City, were about whether gender could be separated from issues of nationality, race, and class, and about the differing priorities of 'development' for the Third World feminists and 'equality' for Western feminists. These divisions put some pressure on the solidarity of the global women's movement.

The Copenhagen Women's Conference itself, however, made important progress and sharpened the focus on women in development. It recognised that women's agency and self-reliance should be supported. The disadvantages that rural women faced were also key elements of the Program of Action (Zinsser 2002). The Australian delegation took a lead 'to promote integration of women in development and support and complement efforts made by governments at national level' (ADAB/DFAT 1980, p. 128). It also took a lead on the issue of power and patriarchy.

> Australia and New Zealand were persistent in pressing for independent recognition of male power as a cause of women's low status, and of the ways women were exploited because of their reproductive roles ... but the Program of Action contains few references that are feminist in this anti-patriarchal sense (Jaquette 1995, p. 55).

ACFID was caught out by Copenhagen. While the Australian delegation included domestic and Indigenous NGOs and an AusAID representative, there was no one from ACFID on the delegation (Office of Women's Affairs 1981). At Copenhagen the Australian delegation initiated a resolution on women and development assistance programs; it also co-sponsored resolutions on battered women (Office of Women's Affairs 1981). While the conference was not seen as a success,[7] the Australian government, however, made it clear that it supported the positive changes emerging from the Copenhagen Women's Conference, in particular the resolutions it sponsored and co-sponsored. In an interesting aside, a resolution noted that women's disadvantage was based on a number of 'isms': racism, neo-colonialism, imperialism, as well as the very contentious Zionism. As part of the negotiations the Australian delegation tried to have the term 'sexism' added to the list of causes of women's disadvantage.

> Inequality for women in most countries stems to a very large extent from mass poverty caused by underdevelopment which is a product of imperialism, colonialism, and neo-colonialism and also of unjust economic relations. The unfavourable status of women is aggravated in many countries by *de facto* discrimination on the grounds of sex (footnote: many countries call this sexism) (Office of Women's Affairs 1981, p. 29).

Australia also co-sponsored resolutions on 'battered' women (domestic violence) and women with disabilities, two issues that were to wait almost another 30 years to be recognised in aid programming by either AusAID or ACFID and its members. An important outcome was that developing countries recognised for the first time that there was an issue with domestic and gender-based violence, and agreed with a call for the UN to look into it (Office of Women's Affairs 1981, p. 30). Australia and Asian countries worked to strengthen the reference to rural women, given the focus of Australia's development assistance program at the time. Australia also formulated a resolution on women in development assistance programs, which was co-sponsored by Pacific countries. This resolution emphasised the need for women to be involved in development aid planning, policy and implementation. The interests of women were to be taken into account in all projects and programs; more resources to be allocated to women's programs; capital funding to be given for skills and income generating activities; and involvement of women, including women affected by these programs, in the planning. While there is no evidence that this resolution

---

7   There were divisions around Zionism and Palestinian rights, with Australia, the US and Canada voting against the final resolution on these grounds. This decision by Australia to vote against the resolution was not made by the delegation, which recommended approval with reservations on the Zionism clause. Instead, it was taken at the highest levels of government, probably at Cabinet level, and the decision to vote against it was mainly about Australia's relations with the US and the US Alliance in the context of the Cold War.

was then adopted in Australia's aid policy, the issue of women in development was beginning to get onto the agenda, and not merely remain as a sector to be funded.

While ACFID was not represented at the Copenhagen Conference or the NGO Forum, the events surrounding the conference stirred ACFID into action. There was a much more concerted push and a stronger lobby in ACFID by a group of mainly Melbourne-based women who had been meeting since 1979 on the issues of getting women and development issues on the ACFID agenda (Poussard 2012). In 1980, following the Copenhagen Women's Conference, the ACFID Council passed a resolution that member agencies review internal policies with regard to participation and rights of women, and that the ACFID secretariat support them in this (ACFOA 1980b). In 1981 a group of member agency women held a conference in Melbourne and put out the Lowanna Declaration on Women and Development, which led to the establishment of the Women and Development Network of Australia (WADNA) in 1982 (Kennedy 1992).

Also in 1981, a Women in Development Interim Committee of ACFID was established. ACFID applied for a special purpose grant from AusAID to fund its women in development awareness raising activities. A major women in development workshop was held and ACFID lobbied for a specialist WID fund (ACFOA 1981e).[8] At the same time, the National Council of Women was recommending that government engage more with NGOs on the issue of women and development (National Women's Advisory Council 1982).

At the 1982 ACFID Council there was a resolution to study the effects of aid on women (ACFOA 1982a). In the end the study did not occur, probably due to fears of another controversial report like Moore and Tuckwell's of 1975 being produced. Through 1983 the push for stronger women and development policies and work among NGOs continued, with a conference in July at ANU looking at issues facing women and development (ACFOA 1983d). Russell Rollason, the executive director of ACFID, speaking at the conference noted that 'men from agencies are not participating in the women and development discussion, and they [the men] are not hearing the concerns being brought from the third world' (Rollason 1983, p. 142). He went on to say, rather optimistically, that great strides had been made in ACFID on its approach to women and development since 1974. What he did not say, however, was that most of this progress had happened in the previous two years due mainly to the drive of WADNA. While ACFID had missed the boat with mainstream Australian women's organisations, WADNA did link with them and was able to advance the women and development agenda among mainstream agencies and prompt ACFID into more action. At one point

---

8   In New Zealand a special WID fund was set up in 1983 with a greater government matching grant (Lowe 1993).

there was a suggestion that the mainstream Australian women's organisations be represented on WADNA's governing body. While that did not happen, they were nevertheless very supportive (Poussard 2012).

Despite the action from WADNA, other changes in ACFID were still slow in coming. ACFID's standing policy first mentioned WID in 1983 by way of an additional sentence on 'involving women in aid programs' (ACFOA 1983f, p. 1). Interestingly, it was not in the first draft of the policy and came three years after AusAID's policy statement on women and development (ACFOA 1983b). In 1983 both New Zealand and Australia gave special consideration to women and development through their subsidy schemes with a higher 75 per cent government match (ACFOA 1983b; Lowe 1993). The problem with this approach was that a lot of the women's projects at the time (and even now) were naïve, assuming that either women's participation was enough, or that promoting the type of work that men were not interested in and could be done by women would produce meaningful change. Of course, this avoided the messy and political business of addressing the causes of structural inequality (Mayoux 1995).

In preparation for the 1984 Nairobi Women's Conference another survey of ACFID members was undertaken (ACFOA 1984c). When ACFID discussed the proposed review of women in aid agencies, the executive with memory of the furore 10 years earlier noted that the issue was sensitive and that the executive should retain editorial control over the final report (ACFOA 1985b). *The Role and Status of Women in ACFID member agencies* report by Aida Maranan was important in that it showed a clear change over the previous 10 years with respect to women staff in NGOs, with recruitment policies resulting in more women in management and project officer positions. The report did point out, however, that this led to a 'dichotomy between the in-Australia role and status of women and the overseas concern for women and development' (Maranan 1985, p. 2). The focus of ACFID member agencies was on recruitment and affirmative action and more hiring of women to top positions but less on improving field practice. 'When you look back 30 years a lot seems to have happened; but when you stand in the middle as we do now things seem to be moving awfully slowly' (p. 2).

The Nairobi Women's Conference

The Nairobi Conference of 1985 represented a breakthrough in NGO activism with 14,000 NGO representatives (Patton 1995, p. 62). The big issues at the conference were solutions to growth and Third World debt. In addition the Forward Looking Strategy from the conference:

integrated issues on the basis of gender language: the participation of women in development and recognition that current development strategies actually damaged women and their status (Patton 1995, p. 73).

The conference was a major step forward for women in development, and saw a sea change with the adoption of a goal of 'transformation of women's status in society, to enable them to participate fully in reorienting the development process itself' (Sweetman 2012, p. 392). It also recognised that 'the development strategies [then in place] actually damaged women and their status' (Patton 1995, p. 62). Most important was the reconciliation between Third World and First World feminists and the emergence of a global consensus (Çağatay et al 1986; Moghadam 2000). This consensus was in part due to the effects of the Thatcher and Reagan governments' responses to the global debt crisis, of austerity and the implementation of neoliberal policies required of Western donors. Consensus was also partly due to the role of the network of Southern-led development feminists DAWN (Development Alternatives with Women for a New Era), which had the aim of 'reorienting the economic discussions scheduled for the Third Women's World Conference in Nairobi … and help reveal the nature and structure of power' (Quataert 2013, p. 12).

The Nairobi Conference also prompted further activity in both AusAID and ACFID; there were a number of training workshops for AusAID staff on women in development and a procedure on implementing its Women in Development policy (Reid 1985). ACFID also sent three women to Nairobi who then did a speaking tour to ACFID members on their return. ACFID, however, was still playing catch up in terms of development practice. It did not seem to see the women and development implications for good aid practice, let alone advancing women's rights. In a major report on aid effectiveness the executive summary had the phrase 'especially women' (probably added at the last minute), but there was no mention of women or women in development in the main report despite the coverage of Nairobi at the time (ACFOA 1986b).

A much sharper government policy on women and development and affirmative action prompted ACFID into action on agency staffing policies. In 1987 ACFID passed a policy statement on equal employment opportunity for member agencies to adopt. Elizabeth Reid, speaking to it, noted that women working in Australian NGOs (much like Australian society more broadly) were occupationally and hierarchically clustered, receiving both lower pay and less access to decision-making within member agencies (ACFOA 1987a). As a result, in 1988, ACFID prepared an Affirmative Action Manual for all agencies, but it was not until 1994 that it passed its own affirmative action policy with regard to the secretariat's practices, including having 30 per cent of women on all committee structures, paid paternity and maternity leave, and a sexual harassment policy (ACFOA 1994a).

The 1990s and the Beijing Women's Conference

By 1990, in the lead up to the Beijing Women's Conference, ACFID started to push harder on having a comprehensive women and development policy. In 1992 the ACFID Council passed a resolution that by 1995 all agencies undertake a WID review, have specific action plans, and the agency head be responsible for integrating WID and having affirmative action plans in place. ACFID would have a women and development subcommittee, and a WID adviser whose role would be to look at the barriers for WID integration – for example, cultural values, traditional roles, competing demands of family and livelihood, lower status of women, and so on – and also establish a women's network (ACFOA 1992a; ACFOA 1992b). With some of the key people leaving the network to form the International Women's Development Agency (IWDA) in 1985, WADNA had largely collapsed by the 1990s. IWDA was aimed to showcase good gender and development practice in aid programs and advocate for gender inclusion policies in government programs.

An early task of the WID adviser was an affirmative action audit in which 28 agencies were surveyed. The results were an improvement on the 1975 and 1985 surveys and, as it was a self-reporting survey, perhaps agencies at least saw the importance of being seen to be doing something. Sixty-three per cent said they gave WID a high priority above all other sectors but, when that figure was unpacked a little, over half of the respondents had some women-only programs; a similar percentage had no WID guidelines; less than half of the sample indicated they had consulted with women's groups; and only 11 per cent had programs that could be described as gendered, that is, dealing with 'feminist' issues related to power and structural inequality (Mitchell 1994). The 1993–94 gender audit revealed slow progress since the 1985 Maranan study, and ACFID members, like other sectors in Australian society, were also behind internationally on equal employment opportunity practice with respect to women. For example, while 88 per cent of International Council of Voluntary Agencies (ICVA) members had paid maternity leave, only 60 per cent of ACFID agencies had maternity leave, and mostly unpaid (Mitchell 1995).

The Beijing Women's Conference marked a further step forward from the Nairobi Women's Conference and introduced the terms 'gender' and 'empowerment' to reflect the power relations and patriarchy inherent in women's disadvantage and marginalisation. It accepted that women's rights were human rights (Chow 1996; Eyben and Napier-Moore 2009). It also introduced a grand vision of 'gender mainstreaming', so that women's issues were not on the edge but rather these issues of gender and women's marginalisation were central in government and

NGO policy and practice (Bunch and Fried 1996; Chow 1996; Timothy 2005). The conference, however, was not without its critics, especially from the more conservative NGOs and governments which had reservations and objections, describing it in terms like 'feminist imperialism that reflects disrespect for religion and culture, an overzealous individualism, and an effort to impose Western values that destroy the family and local communities' (Bunch and Fried 1996, p. 203). This conservative backlash was to dog the implementation of the Platform of Action. There have been many attempts to revise the text at later CSW meetings, with many countries stepping away from the agreements they had made (Timothy 2005).

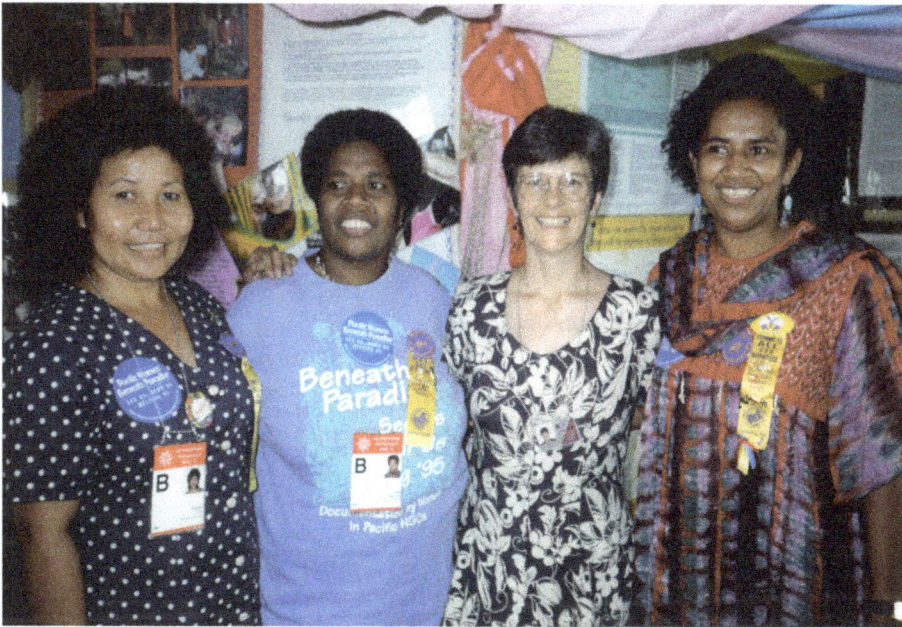

Figure 8 Janet Hunt and a Pacific women's delegation at Beijing.
Source: ACFID.

In development practice the idea of gender mainstreaming was seen as synonymous with women's inclusion, which had been around since the 1970s, and that 'women's empowerment as a central element in international development discourse' was the way forward (Eyben and Napier-Moore 2009, p. 285). The problem with the aid sector was that it was more concerned with doing what was doable rather than doing what was transformational. While women's empowerment was the headline word, in practice there was enough 'wriggle room' for it to be reinterpreted, shifting 'from transformation in societal relations as the core of empowerment, to becoming a technical magic bullet of micro-credit programmes and political quotas for women' (Eyben and Napier-Moore 2009, p. 287; Kilby 2011). The World Bank argued that women's empowerment was 'smart economics' and very quickly the 'meanings of empowerment associated with solidarity and collective action were being crowded out' (Eyben and Napier-Moore 2009, p. 294), and 'economic empowerment' was to be the new buzz word.

Another issue was the competing agendas at the Social Development Summit held in 1995 in Copenhagen. Unlike Beijing, it was a conference of bureaucrats more than activists. The Copenhagen Summit put poverty (and women's poverty) front and centre in preparing the groundwork for the Millennium Declaration and associated MDGs. This suited the aid bureaucrats as 'gender equity [was] potentially more threatening to the power and privilege of policymakers themselves in their own gender roles, in contrast to poverty, which relates to a constituency "out there"' (Eyben 2006, p. 597).

In short, the Beijing gender agenda was more transformational in its aims, and that is perhaps why its initial impetus in the 1990s has faded through the 2000s in favour of the MDGs. The other issue is the lack of unanimity on the Beijing Platform of Action and a push from religious and conservative quarters to water down or delete some provisions of the platform (Andersson and Togelius 2011; Quataert and Roth 2012). Quataert argues that '[g]ender equity – whether at home, or in family and personal status law, or in political life – has emerged as one of the major points of geopolitical confrontation for global power elites' (2011, p. 632). The implication is that advancing gender justice will be very difficult in the 2010s, with the main aim being to hold onto the important gains made in the 1980s and 1990s.

ACFID after Beijing

Beyond picking up the rhetoric of empowerment there was little change within ACFID on addressing the implications of the Beijing Platform of Action. While there continued to be gender training, there was little evidence of gender mainstreaming in NGO work (ACFOA 1997a; 1997d). Reports by AusAID and others about NGOs' work with gender were not encouraging, and by 1998 the ACFID gender group was waning (AusAID 1995a; ACFOA 1997d; Hunt 1998). It was another 10 years before gender was to be picked up with the same enthusiasm as in the early 1990s (Kilby and Crawford 2011). This was also the case in official and development agencies, both bilateral and multilateral, with Charlesworth (2005) arguing that in the UN there is 'a resistance to or a misunderstanding of gender mainstreaming ... [and] by referring to women and children [this] reinforces women's identity and value as mothers [only]' (p. 10). The United Nations Development Program (UNDP), which had been taking the lead on gender justice and rights-based development, struggled with little to show of gender mainstreaming as late as 2006, and even by 2009 there was not a supportive institutional framework (UNDP 2006; UNDP 2009). A similar story can be found in any number of bilateral and multilateral organisations 10 years after Beijing (Kilby and Crawford 2011). It was this poor report card that prompted a sharper focus by NGOs, bilaterals and multilaterals alike so that by the 2010s many development agencies had improved their track record on issues of gender, and certainly around basic human needs for women and girls.

By the 2010s, while gender still has some way to go to be fully mainstreamed into Australian NGO work, it was an issue that ACFID members were more than aware of and struggling with (Kilby and Crawford 2011). While there was still not a gender committee within ACFID despite the 1995 recommendation, there was an active gender equity working group which made sure ACFID member voices were heard, and that gender had been incorporated into the Code of Conduct under both good development priorities as well as respect for human rights. Gender was also one of three strategic areas for ACFID, the other two being human rights and civil society. 'Gender-transformative approaches that address the root causes of injustice, challenge harmful gender norms, and foster progressive changes in power relationships between women and men should be prioritised' (ACFID website, 2014).

ACFID has also taken a lead on gender-based violence. Forty years after it was raised as a key women's issue at Mexico City it has been more or less 'mainstreamed' into ACFID's work, with most members having gender-based anti-violence programs, and recognising their importance in development. The other key issue not being addressed by ACFID or most of its members is that of same-sex relationships and gender minorities, and the discrimination issues they face (Kilby and Crawford 2011). In the 2010s there has been a sharp rise in many developing countries' national legislation circumscribing same-sex relationships, and often with draconian penalties (Saiz 2004; Altman et al. 2012). While there has been progress on some gender issues within ACFID, such as gender-based violence, and a more strategic approach to women's rights, there remains a long way to go for ACFID to pick up the human rights and development issue of same-sex and gender minorities. Even in the 2010s ACFID members recognise their weaknesses in gender and gender mainstreaming with only about 10 per cent of ACFID member CEOs being women, and far fewer if special interest women and children's NGOs are excluded.

Conclusion

For much of its 50 years ACFID has been ambivalent to varying degrees of where it sees women's rights as part of its work. For the first 20 years progress was very slow. It certainly was led by a few women but not seen as central either to ACFID members or its own work. ACFID was not alone as most development agencies were slow to adopt a focus on women and development and later on gender and development, despite the pioneering work of mainly Third World women in the 1950s and 1960s, who were working through the various organs of the UN, most notably the CSW. Even when major agreements were made, such as those at the four major UN Women's Conferences, the implementation of the agreements through aid agencies has been slow to the point of being glacial. For example, the first move by the UN to prioritise the education of girls in developing countries was in the early 1950s, but not put into practice until 50 years later through the Millennium Development Goals. It was only when it became painfully aware that 10 years after the Beijing Women's Conference that mainstreaming gender and women's empowerment had still a long way to go that the issues were taken up more forcefully.

International NGOs and ACFID were likewise slow to respond, with resistance by some NGOs to engaging with women and development in the 1970s, and not a lot of support from the ACFID executive and secretariat staff until the 1980s. There was, however, a major push from key women within NGOs from the mid-1970s through the 1980s, and AusAID provided support to strengthen NGOs' gender work prior to the Beijing Women's Conference. The result of the Beijing Women's Conference on ACFID and its members was twofold. While it emphasised the importance of gender work in NGOs, it also led to an easing of emphasis and perhaps a feeling that 'we have done gender' so let's move on. It was not until the early 2010s that gender came back on the agenda with changes to the Code of Conduct and continuing criticism so that the pace of gender work picked up. Nevertheless, gender work is still seen as largely a women's issue to be run by women. While some tentative steps were being made in the 2010s, gender justice for same-sex and other gender minorities still has a significant way to go to be taken up by the majority of ACFID members.

05

Emergency Responses and Humanitarianism

Being involved in the responses of NGOs to humanitarian crises was more or less expected of ACFID from its early years. Responding to these disasters is an integral part of most NGOs' work, and ACFID has had a central coordinating and fundraising role in emergency work for 20 years from 1973 to 1993 through its International Disasters Emergency Committee (IDEC). This was then replaced by an Emergencies Forum, which then became a Humanitarian Reference Group (HRG), neither of which had a fundraising role. In the UK the Disaster Emergency Committee (DEC), the model IDEC initially adopted, went in a different direction and became an emergencies fundraising juggernaut, with its own media agreements against which individual agencies could not compete. In Australia the ACFID member agencies were nervous about this approach, and did not allow IDEC to institutionalise itself to anywhere near the same degree as in the UK. Perhaps Australia was too small a market for a permanent agency like DEC, and so IDEC ultimately folded.

Given the complexity involved in coordinating emergency appeals, it was a wonder that IDEC managed to last as long as it did, but at its peak in the 1980s IDEC appeals raised tens of millions of dollars. Three major events defined IDEC: the crisis in 1971 that led to the formation of the independent state of Bangladesh; Vietnam's invasion of Cambodia to overthrow the Pol Pot regime in 1979, and the associated famine response and rebuilding required; and the Ethiopian famine of 1984–85 and the role IDEC played in coordinating the Australian leg of Bob Geldof's Live Aid phenomenon. In the last two events, IDEC showed a huge capacity for coordination and management, which no individual agency could undertake. It was also a symbol of unity among agencies in that they were not seen to be competing: IDEC 'is a fundraising body for the agencies but not of the agencies' (IDEC 1981, p. 3).

Emergency responses often have to deal with complex emergencies where armed conflict, civil war, government inaction or cruelty is at the heart of the problem. While these issues did not come to haunt IDEC directly, as its members had the task of dealing with them, ACFID often had to take policy and advocacy positions about them. There were many mistakes made and lessons learnt in some of these humanitarian crises: Biafra (1969); Bangladesh (1971); Cambodia (1979); Ethiopia (1984); and Rwanda (1994). Alex De Waal rather unfairly refers to these mistakes as 'famine crimes' (De Waal 1997). Didier Fassin (2007) refers to them more pragmatically as the 'politics of life', where difficult choices are made on an almost daily basis in dealing with complex emergencies. This chapter will explore these often ethical issues in the context of the emergency work of ACFID and IDEC, and how they were managed.

NGOs and emergency work

Many of the major Australian and international NGOs were formed as part of a community response to emergency work in areas of armed conflict (OECD 1988; Smillie 1995; Barnett and Weiss 2008; Barnett 2011).[1] It was natural then that NGOs would continue the humanitarian principles of providing relief of suffering, even though much of their work was generally in long-term development. The number of NGOs and the public interest in emergencies, mainly through improved communications, led to a number of attempts in the 1960s to coordinate NGO emergency work so the public were not bombarded by appeals from a plethora of agencies, a concern of ACFID in the late 1960s (ACFOA 1967c, 1968a, 1971a).

In the UK a committee of five agencies was set up in 1963 to be an information source and coordinating body. This was at a time when there was a need within NGOs and government to work together to provide emergency relief for disasters overseas but no government departments dedicated to overseas aid. The first members of the new committee were the British Red Cross, the Oxford Committee for Famine Relief (now Oxfam); Inter-Church Aid (now Christian Aid); War On Want; Save the Children Fund; the Foreign and Colonial Offices; and the Refugee Council. Their main task was to quickly exchange information during a crisis, and to see how they could receive support and logistical help from the military, and medical and surgical aid from the British Medical Association and the Royal College of Surgeons (DEC 2012).

It was the advent of television that made large-scale emergency appeals possible, with the British NGO War on Want's successful television appeal following a disastrous cyclone in Sri Lanka in 1963. This success prompted UK agencies

---

1   This list was covered in Chapter 2: the Red Cross from the human suffering on the battlefield of Solferino in 1859; Save the Children from the allied blockade of Germany in 1919; Oxfam from the British blockade of Greece in 1943; CARE from the relief program to the displaced in Europe following World War II; and World Vision from looking after Korean war orphans in 1950.

to think about working more closely together to use the power of television to bring the immediacy of disasters to the general public, something that hitherto had not been possible. This was hurried along by a BBC threat not to publicise appeals for multiple agencies, and so they asked the committee to nominate a particular agency for a specific appeal (Taylor 1982). The Disasters Emergency Committee (DEC) came into being in 1964, with the same membership as the coordinating committee plus the addition of the Catholic agency CAFOD, and both the UNHCR and government having observer status. DEC was also recognised by the Charities Commission as an 'operative agency', which enabled it to raise funds. The chair of DEC was independent of its members and it had a secretariat (initially from the Red Cross). Key to its success was a close relationship from the outset with two major television networks, the BBC and ITV, which were included in decisions as to whether there would be an appeal or not. Donors were also able to make donations at selected banks and all Post Offices — a world first.

The division of the appeal funds was based on an equal amount going to each of the five DEC members, which were then free to spend it according to their own priorities. This way money could be raised rapidly and made available to agencies quickly; it also enabled anonymity of the donor if they wished (Disasters 1977). The first joint appeal was launched in 1966, raising £560,000 to help the survivors of an earthquake in Turkey which killed more than 2,300 people and caused massive destruction. Over the following 10 years DEC raised £8.5 million for disasters, but not without some controversy. This was mainly due to the fact that many emergencies are a result of armed conflict and are by definition political in nature, a theme that was to recur all too frequently.

The Biafran emergency

The Biafran emergency was the first very large-scale conflict-based emergency since World War II to which a large number of NGOs coordinated their response. In Australia a public appeal among a number of agencies raised a relatively modest $500,000 (Hayes 1970c); while in the UK the Biafran relief effort was the largest public response since DEC was established. It was soon to be a source of major controversy (Chandler 2001). An NGO consortium led by Oxfam and the Christian Churches, and in defiance of the British government and the International Committee of the Red Cross (ICRC) and without agreement from the Nigerian government, organised over 5,000 night flights in 1968 and 1969 with relief goods across Nigerian government lines to besieged Biafran civilians (Smillie 1995). Inevitably, the Biafran rebels benefitted from this: they were able to fly in arms in the shadow of the relief flights; and they received foreign exchange from the cash provided by NGOs for local purchases and the exorbitant landing fees NGOs were charged, which enabled the purchase of arms (Burnell 1991; Smillie 1995).

The DEC committee was divided and so did not launch an appeal, but the other agencies that supported the Biafran airlift had their own combined agency appeal (Burnell 1991). The general belief after the emergency was that the rebel commanders manipulated the situation to ensure continuing political support for their cause (Smillie 1995; De Waal 1997; Franks 2005; Cumming 2013); and there is no hard evidence that the Nigerian government would have stopped either humanitarian aid being provided or prevented refugees leaving. As a result, British and other NGOs have had to endure ongoing criticism that they were dupes of the rebel regime and extended the war by as much as 18 months (Burnell 1991; Smillie 1995). Alex de Waal referred to the NGO response to Biafra as 'a heroic debacle' (1997, p. 78) and Ian Smillie as 'an act of unfortunate and profound folly' (1995, p. 104). The most tragic part was that the Biafran emergency remained a humanitarian problem rather than a political one and so 'excuse[d] the UN and Western governments from direct involvement' (Smillie, p. 106).

The Biafran emergency and response also firmly established the role of NGOs as humanitarian players able to operate outside the control of government and speak out for what they saw as fundamental humanitarian injustices. The humanitarian agency Médecins Sans Frontières (Doctors without Borders) had its origins in French doctors who, returning from Biafra and disillusioned with the ICRC response, set up their own agency. MSF moved away from the notion of neutrality that had hamstrung the ICRC in favour of 'testimony in favour of the victims' (Fassin 2007, p. 516; Givoni 2011).[2] The situation in Biafra also introduced the idea of the complex humanitarian emergency, which was to dominate emergency thinking through to Rwanda nearly 30 years later. Complex emergencies challenge conventional views on development and what Duffield refers to as:

> [the] assumption of the universality of social progress, [as] a series of interconnecting movements leading from poverty and vulnerability to security and well-being: shared progress is the normal and long-term direction of all social change (Duffield 1994, p. 39).

2   Givoni goes on to argue that the formation of MSF was an 'outgrowth of the legitimacy crisis of the medical profession, and that its practice of witnessing has ultimately been a mode of ethical self-cultivation by means of which physicians could fashion themselves as more enlightened personae' (p. 43).

These complex emergencies involve contested politics and political movements which do not sit easily within the development ideals; and they ask aid agencies to make difficult choices in how resources are distributed among conflicting parties.

The background to IDEC

In Australia IDEC had its origins in the formation of ACFID in 1965, and the idea of a relief and development commission to have a coordinating role in relief work, with the British DEC Committee being in people's minds at the time as a model (see Chapter 2). When the relief and development commission folded in 1970 in favour of a simpler ACFID structure, it had already been directly involved in emergency appeals, the first of which was the ACFID–*Age* newspaper Vietnam Appeal in 1968. While this was not a large appeal by the standards of the time ($72,000), it was important as it leveraged government support for the ACFID secretariat in its early years. It also provided some ideas for a Disasters Relief Committee (ACFOA 1968a, 1968b), which the three larger agencies ACC, ACR, and the Red Cross supported but the other ACFID members were less enthusiastic (ACFOA 1968c). As there was little coordination of the separate agency appeals for Biafra, and later Bangladesh in 1971, the various appeals tended to alienate the public. The argument was growing for a separate, single appeal disaster mechanism which brought all the agencies concerned under a single umbrella, much like DEC in the UK (ACFOA 1971a, 1971c; Tiffen, et al. 1979).

Bangladesh and the beginning of IDEC

While ACFID was not directly involved in running appeals until 1974, it was very much involved in emergencies and provided information to agencies. For example, ACFID was the conduit for information on the Bihar famine of 1967, and it developed guidelines for material aid for the Peru earthquake in 1970 (ACFOA 1967c, 1970b). But it was the civil war in East Pakistan in 1971 that led to the formation of Bangladesh, and the related emergency when India was host to nearly 10 million refugees that led to a more hands-on role for ACFID.

Tensions had been building in East Pakistan for some time over how it was ruled from the Pakistan government based in West Pakistan. This came to a head in March 1971 when the West Pakistan-based government refused to accept the result of Pakistan's first democratic election in 1970, won by the Awami League from the East[3] (O'Dwyer 1971a; ACFOA 1971b; Zaheer 1994). East Pakistan then unilaterally declared independence with the name Bangladesh. The Pakistan military responded by brutally suppressing the nascent uprising and forcing the provisional Bangladesh government into exile. This brutal attack led to a breakdown of markets, food hoarding, and all the other elements that inevitably lead to a famine (Zaheer 1994; Raghavan 2013). There was a mass outflow of refugees from May 1971 so that by October of that year there were nearly 10 million refugees in camps in India and 30 million displaced internally (O'Dwyer 1971a; ACFOA 1971b; Zaheer 1994). The actions by the West Pakistan government were roundly condemned internationally, including a motion in the UK Parliament accusing West Pakistan of genocide (Zaheer 1994). The refugee flow over these months was greater than all refugees to India to that point, including those during Partition (Government of India 1971; Smillie 1995). This situation was intolerable and the immediate crisis was only alleviated when India invaded East Pakistan in mid-November 1971. The war came to an end a little over a month later at the end of December (Zaheer 1994; Raghavan 2013). The provisional government, which had been operating in exile in India, took over and on 11 January 1972 the newly independent nation formally changed its name to Bangladesh.

The international aid community had been in place in East Pakistan dealing with the aftermath of a cyclone and so were in a good position not only to provide relief assistance but also to report on the atrocities of the Pakistan authorities and undertake the massive rehabilitation program that was required (Smillie 1995). Coming so soon after Biafra, 'Bangladesh was perhaps the beginning of a recognition that major emergencies were likely to be a continuing phenomenon' (p. 107), and that NGOs would be an integral part of any response. It also marked the beginning of the development of strong national NGOs in developing countries, when Faisal Abed returned to Bangladesh from London in January 1972 to rebuild villages in the district of Sullah. In one year, 14,000 houses were built, and Abed registered the Bangladesh Rural Advancement Committee (BRAC), now the world's largest NGO (Ahmed and French 2006; Ahmed et al. 2012).

This crisis galvanised the public in Australia so that by August 1971 $1.1 million had been raised, double the Biafran appeal (Hinton 1971). The Australian government was lukewarm to providing support to alleviate the refugee crisis, probably due to its alliance with the US and their continual support of Pakistan throughout the conflict. It avoided public comments, providing only $500,000 in emergency aid to India despite a strong bilateral aid relationship. General

---

3   At the time Pakistan was geographically divided into two parts separated by India as result of the 1947 Partition: East Pakistan and West Pakistan. The centre of power was in the West but the larger population lived in the East.

Cullen as chair of ACFID visited the refugee camps in India in mid-1971 and found the situation deplorable; he felt that the Australian government response was 'sorely lacking' (Cullen 1971). The public backlash at government inaction was such that cabinet spent five hours on it, possibly the first (and only) time that a specific aid appeal had been thrashed out at that level. Further pressure was added through a hunger strike and a very large demonstration at Parliament House in Canberra (ACFOA 1971b). The issue of a humanitarian response to a crisis on a large scale was very new to government in a postcolonial environment, and it seemed unable to either judge the public mood or see itself as having responsibility to respond, particularly as India was the largest recipient of Australian aid at the time. This was a far cry from the 2010s where humanitarian responses are an everyday role for defence forces, and the Australian government is usually among the most generous of donors (Hollway et al. 2011; Kovács and Spens 2011; Rolfe 2011).

It was the Bangladesh crisis that forced ACFID members to reconsider the earlier idea of setting up a disasters emergency committee to coordinate agencies' fundraising (O'Dwyer 1971a). By late 1971 ACFID was in the process of forming IDEC (ACFOA 1971b; O'Dwyer 1971d). The NGOs were initially sceptical, and the issue of which agencies would be in IDEC was, and continued to be, an ongoing source of tension (ACFOA 1975e). In early 1972 an interim IDEC committee was set up. It employed a consultant to lobby government for more support for Bangladesh, which by then had been established as a newly independent country (ACFOA 1972a). In April 1972 an Oxfam UK representative briefed ACFID on how DEC functioned. But the simple proposition that five agencies were to receive the funds, whether they had any programs in the disaster area or not, was not seen as viable in the ACFID context (Taylor 1982). It was in October 1972 that IDEC was formally established (ACFOA 1972c), with the founding members being Austcare, ACR, ACC, CAA, AFFHC, and the Red Cross. In 1974 IDEC became a permanent standing committee of ACFID (ACFOA 1974a).

The first major appeal for IDEC was the Ethiopian famine appeal in 1974, referred to by some as the 'hidden famine' as the Ethiopian Emperor Haile Selassie did not want it publicised. In mid-1973 the Ethiopian government was aware of the situation but would not allow public appeals. However, it accepted shipments of food under the condition that the shipments were not publicised; but leaks to a newspaper and a BBC documentary showed that one million people were in dire need (Keller 1992, p. 611). This famine took the lives of 200,000 people by the end of 1973, and led to the overthrow of the Haile Selassie regime by military coup in 1974. The events of 1973 and 1974 were to be tragically repeated again 10 years later when the military government themselves were responsible for hiding the story of a famine.

In 1974, a full-scale relief effort was underway and the associated IDEC appeal raised $1.2 million. This was the first appeal that enabled direct deposits to selected banks, which proved a great success, with nearly half of the appeal income coming through the banks. The issue to dog IDEC throughout its life was poor coordination among the Australian state branches of IDEC members, which were given the job of promoting the appeal in those states (Evans 1974). Overall, however, the appeal demonstrated the success and efficiency of the model, with the Ethiopian Appeal having a cost of fundraising of less than 5 per cent of funds raised (ACFOA 1975g). It is worth noting that the cost of fundraising always presents problems in appeals as people expect their money to go to the appeal and do not expect there to be a fundraising cost, or at least one that they should bear. This was taken to the rather absurd limit when Bob Geldof promised zero administration cost in the 1985 Live Aid appeal. This meant that the program was run by well-meaning but inexperienced volunteers, which inevitably led to waste, poor judgements, and avoidable mistakes (De Waal 2008).

In 1975 the IDEC structure was streamlined with a standing committee made up of representatives of the five major agencies – the Red Cross, ACR, ACC, Austcare, AFFHC – plus two other members who were on the committee on a personal basis elected from council. There was also a promotions/marketing committee for IDEC and provision for a government observer, given that government was also becoming a source of IDEC appeal funds. As for the vexed issue of which NGOs were to get the funds, and in what proportion, it was agreed the five permanent member agencies would receive half of any appeal (down from the earlier 75 per cent) with the balance open to all, including the original five agencies, on a competitive basis. The criteria were the quality of the agencies' projects and their capacity to deliver in a particular country or context. This shift from 75 per cent of the appeal going to the major agencies to only half sowed the seeds for the ultimate demise of IDEC, as it was the reputation of the larger agencies which IDEC depended on; but these larger agencies felt they were in effect subsiding the smaller ones and could possibly do better with their own appeals.

East Timor

The East Timor crisis of 1975 was the first real test for IDEC and how it functioned. East Timor had been a colony of Portugal until 1974 when, rather than having a staged decolonisation process, Portugal effectively abandoned East Timor after its revolution that year. While the left-leaning Fretilin party had won local elections in March 1975 and had been able to form a shaky coalition with the right-leaning UDT party to govern East Timor, this broke down in May 1975 following Indonesian pressure on UDT. A civil war between Fretilin and UDT broke out in August leaving up to 3,000 dead. Indonesia responded with an invasion in December 1975 and formal annexation in July 1976 (Carey 1999; Cotton 2001; Cabasset-Semedo and Durand 2009).[4]

A humanitarian crisis emerged throughout 1975. In September, as the crisis deepened, ACFID called on the Australian government to help end the crisis and assist humanitarian refugees (ACFOA 1975j) (see Chapter 6). At the time, IDEC considered an appeal but the Red Cross, which chaired IDEC at the time, objected on the grounds that this would mean helping Fretilin and so be seen to be partisan in the conflict. Other IDEC agencies as well as non-IDEC member World Vision launched their own appeal under the auspices of ACFID. The fact that non-IDEC members were part of this appeal pointed to the tenuous position the Red Cross had taken, but they stood firm on what they saw as a neutrality issue and withdrew from ACFID in January 1976 (ARC 1976), but still remained a member of IDEC (Taylor 1982). With the funds raised, the NGOs chartered a barge with relief supplies from Darwin in mid-November 1975. The appeal was coordinated by an ACFID staff person in East Timor (Richards 1975; ACFOA 1975k; Sullivan 2013). The review of ACFID in 1979 found that 90 per cent of member agencies agreed with the ACFID position on East Timor and the associated appeal, making it one of the least divisive of the issues that ACFID faced at the time (Tiffen et al. 1979).

While the East Timor appeal was not large by IDEC standards – $350,000 – and only half of that was from the public (ACFOA 1976h), the experience highlighted the fragility of IDEC when a member could have the right of veto. By 1977 IDEC appeals were beginning to wane, perhaps because there were too many of them, or because support from the press and the public was not adequately assessed before launching an appeal. The Indian cyclone appeal in 1977 raised only $172,000, even with the advantage of benefitting from a non-IDEC World Vision TV crew raising the profile of the appeal in the last week (ACFOA 1977b; Werner 1978). Another appeal for Africa, also in 1977, was rejected by the Red Cross, but it went ahead and used the IDEC post box, with other agencies being recipients.

The experience from the East Timor appeal prompted a generally positive review of IDEC in 1977, but there were three issues of concern: which emergencies were suitable for IDEC appeals and which were not; there was little feedback from the recipient agencies of the IDEC grants; and, finally, some of the goods that were sent under the IDEC umbrella were not appropriate to the particular context (Tiffen et al. 1979). Not having favourable media coverage was a bugbear for IDEC, as it was those issues that attracted media attention, particularly with

---

4   For a full account of the international manoeuvrings around the process for Indonesia's annexation of East Timor, including the US and Australia's complicity, see James Cotton (2001).

a celebrity involved, that were successful and attracted public support, but did not necessarily reflect the most pressing need (Werner 1978). The issue of the risk involved in starting an appeal was eased to some extent in 1978 when AusAID agreed to provide $20,000 in seed funding for promotions for each appeal to help get them off the ground (Taylor 1982). In 1981 the rules were changed so that the vote for launching an IDEC appeal went from being unanimous among members to a 75 per cent majority; and, further, that after six weeks of an IDEC appeal, member agencies could then run their own appeals (ACFOA 1981e). There was also a rule of thumb that if a story was on the front page of national papers for three days running then it was worth opening an IDEC appeal, but this practice was not always followed (Vincent 2012). It was the appeals of Cambodia in 1979–80 and Ethiopia in 1984–85, which showed the power of media and celebrity coming together, that were to be the big success stories for IDEC.

Cambodia

The background to the crisis lay in the brutal Khmer Rouge regime in Cambodia from 1975–79, which was involved in border disputes with Vietnam, leading to a flood of refugees into Vietnam. This led to a series of Vietnamese military incursions into Cambodia in mid-1978, a full-scale invasion in late December to overthrow the Khmer Rouge government, and the capture of Phnom Penh on 7 January 1979. A new government of Khmer Rouge defectors supportive of Vietnam was installed and the horrors of the Pol Pot regime were exposed to the world's media (Fein 1993). Not only was there genocide throughout the previous five years, but the Khmer Rouge also destroyed all food crops and grain stores in its retreat. While there was some debate as to whether this destruction by the Khmer Rouge caused a famine, from mid-1979 there were certainly serious food shortages, and at one point a fear of three million people starving (ACFOA 1979g; Murlis 1980). This prompted a massive international humanitarian response on an unprecedented scale.[5]

In Australia, IDEC set up a Kampuchean emergency appeal in mid-September 1979, with television personality Leonard Teale as its chair. Teale went to Cambodia in October on an IDEC emergency charter with a television crew, and a barge with relief supplies from Singapore followed shortly after (ACFOA 1979a). The Australian public's response was such that within two months it had raised $6 million. Within one year this had grown to over $10 million, the largest humanitarian appeal up to then, with only 3 per cent in administration and fundraising expenses (ACFOA 1979h, 1980a; Touche-Ross 1980; Alston

---

5   For example, in the UK, the Oxfam Relief Consortium for Cambodia grew to 32 international NGOs, and in period 1979–80 provided $75 million worth of assistance (Burnell 1991).

1980b). The $10 million was also matched by $14 million from the government, bringing the overall appeal to $24 million, making it the largest appeal IDEC was to have (Ross 1980; ACFOA 1980a). Even after the emergency period was over in 1981, and despite the exclusion of Cambodia by the UN and Western aid community at the time, foreign affairs minister Andrew Peacock had made it known to ACFID that the government was prepared to provide aid to Cambodia through NGOs, despite the government's public pronouncements at the time (Vincent 2012).

Figure 9 Christine Vincent from IDEC and Christine Brown from ACC reporting on relief to Cambodia.
Source: Fairfax Media.

Of course the Cambodian Appeal was not without controversy, the most significant being the withdrawal of the Red Cross from IDEC in December 1979 following ACFID and ACFID agencies making statements of a 'political nature' in the context of the Cambodian Appeal (Alston 1979). This may have been to do with ACFID tacitly supporting the Vietnamese invasion when it was critical of Australian government calls for Vietnam to withdraw and the suspension of aid to Vietnam following the invasion. ACFID was also quick to note the government's inconsistency when it continued aid to Indonesia following its invasion of East Timor in 1975 (ACFOA 1979a, 1979b, 1979d, 1979h). ACFID was to continue its advocacy on Cambodia through the 1980s, particularly on the issue of the Khmer Rouge holding a seat at the UN (ACFOA 1981f). The issue of continuing to recognise the Pol Pot regime was something which divided the government as well, with foreign minister Peacock and the department arguing against the suspension of aid to Vietnam and the continuing recognition of the Pol Pot regime at the UN, while Malcolm Fraser, the prime minister, did not want to alienate his US and ASEAN allies by taking the more pragmatic approach of condemning Vietnam. It reached the point that foreign minister Peacock twice offered his resignation to the prime minister (Kelly 1980; Radok 1981).

Like all humanitarian action in such a politically charged field, both sides of the conflict used some of the aid to prosecute the war, most notably in the Khmer Rouge-controlled camps in Thailand (with some Thai complicity), as did those backed by the Vietnamese government. As McFarlane points out: 'It is hard to escape the conclusion that humanitarian action contributed greatly to the consolidation of both sides in the conflict, sustaining and increasing their capacities to continue the conflict' (1999, p. 546), which harks back to the events in Biafra. In the context of Cambodia, however, there had to be a humanitarian intervention as doing nothing was not an option. It was really up to the Thai and Vietnamese governments – and their great power patrons the US and the Soviet Union – to more actively support humanitarian principles and give the NGOs a better space in which to operate.

Given the scale of the response over a very short period of time, ACFID was severely stretched. Almost all ACFID staff were involved and, as it had been two years since the previous IDEC appeal, some of the procedures and structures had lapsed. While IDEC had little choice given the circumstances, a review found that the appeal had been launched in haste with insufficient preparation, so some of the procedures were sloppy or poorly implemented (ACFOA 1981f).[6] Overall, however, the appeal was a huge success and set the groundwork for a longer term engagement of Australian NGOs in Cambodia for the 10 years before the final political settlement of 1991. From 1983 the immediate disaster was over and NGOs were involved in rehabilitation programs. Given the protracted negotiations for a political settlement, they were effectively acting as proxies for governments (Brown and Zasloff 1998; Pierdet 2012). The Australian government kept its links to the Cambodian regime open through a large rehabilitation funding package for NGOs each year from 1984, as it was their way of maintaining contact through the period of the international standoff until the UN transition process in 1990.

---

6   For example, some agencies seemed to have appropriated the IDEC donor lists. World Vision received IDEC money without being a member. The record of numbers of people who donated to banks was not captured, and AFFHC did not spend its funds on the emergency but held them until the rehabilitation stage, which caused tensions among IDEC members on the slow rate of disbursement (ACFOA 1981f).

Ethiopia and Live Aid

The two IDEC appeals for the Ethiopian famine from late 1984 to 1985, taken together, were on a similar scale as the Cambodian appeal and raised over $10 million. Like Cambodia, the Ethiopian famine was complex in its causes and was also a result of Cold War-related conflict as much as drought. Unlike Cambodia, however, it took nearly two years and the passion of a minor rock star Bob Geldof for the situation in Ethiopia to strike a chord with the public. IDEC had its first African Appeal with a focus on Ethiopia in 1980 at the same time as the Cambodian Appeal was still running. Despite parallel appeals, it raised $660,000 (IDEC 1980; Taylor 1982). In 1983, as the situation worsened, there was another appeal for Ethiopia in July, but it was not a success due to a lack agency enthusiasm (IDEC 1983; ACFOA 1983c). While the rains had failed in 1982 and 1983, these were in the northern parts of Ethiopia where the conflict was. While donors were sceptical of Ethiopian government reports, the Ethiopian government still refused to let independent media cover the story (Keller 1992; Dercon and Porter 2010). At the same time the US government, under the Reagan administration, had cut their food aid to Ethiopia in 1983 and completely stopped it in 1984, possibly in order to topple the Soviet-allied Marxist regime (Clay 1991).

The famine was also a function of the counterinsurgency strategies employed by the Ethiopian government involving the denial of people's access to their land through 'villagisation' (confining them to restricted 'village' areas), thus limiting the support the insurgency could rely upon. This effectively 'tipped a chronically poor peasantry over the edge into outright starvation' (De Waal 2008, p. 44). The Ethiopian government were also deliberately attacking food supplies in the rebel-held areas (Keller 1992, p. 620). From mid-1984 the Ethiopian government began to resettle 1.5 million people from the north (the source of the insurgency) to the south, to collectivised farms (Niggli 1986; Keller 1992). It was this counterinsurgency operation that triggered the famine, which in turn gave an excuse for more resettlement. De Waal (1991, p. 5) estimates that the resettlement program killed 50,000 people, and 400,000 people died in the famine. Half of these deaths were due to human rights abuses that caused the famine to strike earlier and harder than would otherwise have been the case.

As the Ethiopian government was 'starving out the rebels', it was not until September 1984, after the 10th anniversary of the overthrow of Haile Selassie, that the media was let in (Clay 1991, p. 149). By then 300,000 people had died as a result of drought and the counterinsurgency policy of the Ethiopian government, prompting the Michael Buerk BBC documentary, which led to the mass appeals and responses in late 1984 and 1985. This television report resulted in Bob Geldof, from the little-known rock band the Boomtown Rats, and Midge

Ure, from the much better known Ultravox, to write the song 'Do they know it's Christmas'. Geldof quickly put together a 45-member super group, Band Aid, to record the song in November 1984. It became the biggest selling record of the time, with 3.5 million copies sold and over $9 million raised globally from record sales alone (McDougal 1986; De Waal 2008). This success prompted another round of famine appeals, culminating in the Live Aid concerts in mid-1985.

Figure 10 Bob Geldof and Midge Ure arrive to record 'Do they know it's Christmas', November 1984.

Source: Larry Ellis, Getty images.

De Waal argues that the Ethiopian government was very successful in manipulating foreign donors and the media in the Ethiopian appeals of 1984 and 1985. While the government was using the 'famine' as a weapon in its war with rebel provinces, the donors either did not understand this or turned a blind eye to what was going on. For example, food aid to government-held areas of Eritrea and Tigray in 1985–86 provided perhaps 5 per cent of the diet of the famine stricken population; 20 per cent of the townspeople's needs, and 100 per cent of the militia's food needs (De Waal 1997, p. 136). This harks back to Catholic Relief Services channelling USAID food aid to the South Vietnamese military and their families in 1968 during the war in Vietnam (Lissner 1977). This still left a significant proportion of those in need without food 'behind the lines' in the bitter conflict, so part of the relief effort was to ensure that these people were not left out. A cross-border operation of shipping food and other relief needs from Port Sudan through a clandestine route across the border into the rebel held areas of Tigray and Eritrea in the North of Ethiopia was set up.[7]

It was in this complex political context that IDEC held another appeal for Ethiopia in October 1984, but it was not until December 1984 that the IDEC Ethiopian famine appeal gained real traction, on the back of the Band Aid phenomenon, and raised $3.3 million (ACFOA 1985a). Live Aid followed in mid-1985 with concerts in the UK, USA and elsewhere (including Australia) telecast globally as a massive fundraising event. In Australia it was agreed that the Live Aid funds would go to IDEC. Russell Rollason, ACFID executive director at the time, recalls a series of often colourful evening phone conversations with Geldof, when he argued against the money raised in Australia going directly to the Band Aid Trust which would then implement projects. Geldof argued that the Australian agencies could not be trusted not to waste it. Rollason countered that there would be no tax relief for the donors if the money did not go through Australian agencies, and this is what changed Geldof's mind (Rollason 2013; IDEC 1985a).

IDEC set up an Oz for Africa Telethon which stretched ACFID's resources to the limit. The bulk of the Oz for Africa income was on the night of the concert unlike earlier appeals which ran over at least six weeks or even longer (ACFOA 1985a). Over the following days the donation letters overwhelmed even the Canberra GPO, and IDEC had to use an unoccupied office in the building as a makeshift mailroom. Christine Vincent tells the story that in the centre of the room was a box into which anonymous cash in envelopes were thrown, and at the end of the day when this was tallied it was over $30,000. Another $1 million came in later in the year in a follow-up appeal so that when the Oz for Africa appeal was closed it had raised $6.5 million (IDEC 1988). The more complicated part of the appeal was the division of money: IDEC simply could not use the existing IDEC rules. Rather, the project submissions went to the UK and, as it was before the age of email, the proposals were sent by very long telexes which were then approved by the Live Aid project committee. Generally, what the Australian agencies put up was accepted by Live Aid.[8]

Another, less successful, part of the Live Aid phenomenon was related to Live Aid's focus on funding the logistics of delivering relief aid. Bob Geldof came out to Australia in 1985. In the process he met the prime minister, Bob Hawke, and persuaded him to donate to the Red Cross two military Hercules transport planes destined for the scrap heap with refurbishment and running costs paid for with Oz for Africa funds (Collier 1985). It was not until March 1986 that

7   The author coordinated the Australian contribution to this operation from 1985–89.
8   The only project rejected was $200,000 for truck tyres, as Live Aid had already purchased what they thought was more than enough.

one of the Hercules made it to Asmara in Ethiopian-controlled Eritrea with a film crew in tow to make the film *Wings Over Africa*, and depict the role of the Australian Hercules in the relief effort (Fogarty 1986a; IDEC 1986b, 1986c). In the end the plane flew and the film was made and broadcast,[9] and most of those involved relieved that the very expensive saga of the Hercules was over.

Figure 11 Oz for Africa Hercules being handed over.
Source: ACFID.

The third part of the Geldof appeal was Sport Aid in mid-1986, which raised a further $37 million and took place in 89 countries simultaneously, with the money raised in Australia also to come to IDEC. In Australia, Sport Aid was to prove an expensive failure when the TV sports shows failed to pick it up to garner pledges through their endorsement and promotions. IDEC paid out $232,000 in expenses for a return of $540,183 (IDEC 1986a). In 1988, when it was proposed to run Sport Aid again in Australia, there were no takers to run it: too many fingers had been burnt (Rollason 1988). This pointed to the inherent risky nature of global fundraising events: when they work, they work well, but the risks can be very big indeed.

---

9   The postscript to the story, however, was that the co-pilot was accused of spying in August and the plane grounded (Fogarty 1986b). The filmmaker entered a two-year dispute with IDEC over a final payment before being settled (Butterworth 1987).

Globally, the Band Aid phenomenon was a great success with a total of $144 million raised for relief work in Africa when it was wound up in 1990 (Geldof 1991).[10] Kenyon observed at the time that its success was a mix of the market and altruism: 'the facility of the enterprise to derive advantage from the moral ambiguities attending good works and chartable actions' (Kenyon 1985, p. 3), which raise some uncomfortable questions around celebrity marketing (Davis 2010). George Harrison and Ravi Shankar attempted a similar event 12 years earlier with the Concert for Bangladesh, but it did not have the same global impact. It may have been the mix of perceived need, communications technology, and the sheer drive and certainty of Geldof that made Band Aid work. Speaking of his trip to Africa in 1985 Geldof said:

> The journey was not some jaunt into a personal heart of darkness nor was it a dilettante's voyeuristic dip into the pitiless pain and degradation of others. It was a trip to refocus my outrage (Bob Geldof quoted in Regan 1986, p. 75).

In its own way, Band Aid spelt the end of IDEC. The all-absorbing workload put a strain on ACFID resources, which had essentially started with the Cambodia crisis in 1979 and had not let up for the following seven years. Among ACFID members there was dissatisfaction with what was referred to as the 'gezinter'[11] method of dividing funds more or less equally among an increasing number of agencies, and the part-time nature of the IDEC secretariat meant that mistakes were made. Talk of a full-time secretariat similar to DEC in the UK, and matched grants for distribution (to ensure agencies put their own resources in) came to nothing (IDEC 1985a, 1985b, 1986b, 1986d, 1991b). A number of appeals in 1988 and 1989 were unsuccessful, with the final IDEC appeal, the 1991 African Crisis appeal, raising $171,000 but costing $110,000 to run (IDEC 1992). The Red Cross again withdrew from IDEC as did CAA, which would only participate if there was a full-time secretariat (Rollason 1991; Armstrong 1991b); and AusAID stopped using IDEC as a channel for its relief money, preferring to go through agencies directly (IDEC 1991a). Even the Rwanda genocide and the massive relief appeal that followed in 1994 could not spur IDEC to reform.

The issue with which IDEC struggled was having a formula that worked. When the Band Aid largesse was available, membership of IDEC grew very rapidly, which upset those agencies that were specialist relief agencies. A number of proposals were put forward, including splitting the funds from an IDEC appeal equally between those that had international capacity, like the Red Cross or Oxfam, and those that had a local capacity in the country concerned, and

---

10   Band Aid raised $8 million, Live Aid $80 million, Sport Aid $30 million, as well as spin-offs such as School Aid and Fashion Aid.
11   A contraction of 'goes into', that is, divided equally.

be proportionate to their income from the Australian community (Henry 1985), and other ideas which were variations on that theme. IDEC struggled on with a number of small appeals that did not bring in much money relative to their costs until the disastrous African Crisis appeal of 1992, after which nobody wanted to call another appeal. All of the proposals for reform involved some agencies giving up their influence and income from IDEC. It seemed to reach a point where if particular agencies could not benefit then no one should. Also there was a lack of hard-headedness about whether an appeal would gain traction, and for this strong media links were required, but after a decade of more or less continuous African appeals the public interest had waned. So when the Rwanda crisis occurred in 1994, even though IDEC was still 'on the books', it played no part in it despite Rwanda's important role in redefining humanitarian responses for NGOs.

Questioning NGO humanitarian responses – the Rwanda crisis

By the time Rwanda and the Great Lakes crisis came in 1994 IDEC was out of the picture, but ACFID was certainly involved. Like the development debates, the critiques of humanitarianism which were less prominent in the 1970s and 1980s were starting to emerge (De Waal 1997; Macrae 1998; Stockton 1998). While many myths had been built about humanitarian NGOs and their competence, more serious questions were now being asked about the nature of their response and NGOs' responsibility in humanitarian crises. Like Biafra in the 1960s, and Cambodia and Ethiopia in the 1980s, NGOs found themselves on different sides of ongoing and complex conflicts, which had at times unsavoury international dimensions with realpolitik and the Cold War determining many donor state responses (Macrae 1998). This was no less the case in Rwanda, where much of the relief work was with refugees and those displaced from the community that perpetrated the genocide; this led to many questioning the nature of the humanitarian response (Pottier 1996; Storey 1997).

The key question was what role do NGOs as humanitarian organisations have in these complex emergencies? In Biafra in 1969 it was to run an 'unauthorised' airlift to the population in rebel areas against the wishes of both the Nigerian and British governments; in the case of Cambodia the new government of Cambodia was not recognised by the West but NGOs worked with it; and in the case of Ethiopia most of the people in need were in areas controlled by the rebels, and the Ethiopian government used aid as a weapon. On top of this, the messages of celebrity fundraising generally avoided discussing the inherent political complexity (De Waal 2008; Richeya and Ponte 2008). The next big disaster in Rwanda pushed these ethical dilemmas to another level and led to some major changes in how humanitarian aid was delivered.

The Rwanda crisis is among the worst genocides on record in terms of the percentage of the population killed as result of direct government policy (Dallaire and Dupuis 2004). It had its origins in an ongoing civil war that had been underway since 1990. In April 1994 the Rwandan government seized an opportunity, and over the following three months the army and government-run militias initiated and led the massacre of between 800,000 and one million Rwandan people, or 20 per cent of the population (Storey 1997; Dallaire and Dupuis 2004). Most of the dead were from the Tutsi ethnic minority, hence the reference to the massacre as genocide. However, members of the majority Hutu group opposed to Hutu extremists were also killed. As a result a rebel army, the Rwandan Patriotic Front (RPF), which had been at war since 1990 with this regime and its predecessor, restarted its offensive to take the country and ultimately succeeded in defeating the government forces and taking power shortly after the massacres in July 1994 (Reyntjens 2011). This led to a massive 'refugee' crisis as members of the former regime and their supporters fled to neighbouring Zaire and Tanzania, as part of an organised program by the defeated government so a base to regroup could be developed (De Waal 1997, p. 195). These camps quickly came under control of the former regime's forces and were run by committees made up of former government, military and business leaders who had been responsible for the genocide. This was something that aid workers were slow to grasp in terms of the dynamics of camp politics (Storey 1997; Pottier 1996). The focus of the relief effort was to these camps, rather than the situation inside Rwanda, and it overlooked the genocide itself. By late 1995, 20 times more aid was going to refugees outside the country rather than to displaced persons and rebuilding communities within the country.

> In a number of ways, some NGOs (as well as official donors, such as the UN agencies) lent support to the forces of the deposed genocidal regime, especially after they had fled to neighbouring countries. This support was manifest in the following ways: the choice of where to work; the type of support offered, and the structures and people with whom the NGOs worked and some public statements made by NGO representatives [which portrayed the genocide merely as an ethnic squabble] (Storey 1997, p. 386).

There were questions of prolonging the conflict and giving succour to murderers with a disproportionate amount of aid going to these camps, such as in Goma, rather than for rehabilitation inside Rwanda (De Waal 1997; Storey 1997). De Waal argues that Oxfam's and other calls for a ceasefire at the time were inconsistent with international law obligations to stop the genocide, and that defeating the military perpetrating it was the only way it would stop. This was a clear case for a 'just war'. De Waal went on to argue that Oxfam's view of providing relief before, or at least at the same time as, providing justice and dealing with the genocide, meant the agencies effectively 'fulfilled a charitable imperative but violated the spirit of international law' (1997, p. 198). This caused a lot of questioning in the NGO community as to how they ended up in a situation where attacks on NGOs and the humanitarian framework they had adopted could happen (Macrae 1998).

> At issue is not only protecting the quality of [food] rations, but the basis of rights and international responsibilities; protecting these values, not simply cash flow, is likely to be the major challenge for the relief community in coming years (p. 315).

The intense competition for funding and media coverage among international NGOs in the camps in Goma 'undercut the collective action necessary to protest the misuse of aid' (Cooley and Ron 2002, p. 7). Two hundred NGOs descended on the Goma camps, which held 800,000 refugees, and competed for $1 billion in relief funds. Given the scale of the operation there was little space to raise concerns about who was running the camps, and whether NGOs were effectively offering protection and safe havens to the perpetrators of the genocide, suspected war criminals, and the re-emergent Hutu militias (Cooley and Ron 2002).

Hugo Slim, however, reminds us that the negligence or inaction of NGOs in these contexts is because of the negligence and inaction of those in political power:

> It would therefore, be morally negligent if excessive agonising by or about relief agencies (the groaning of the white man and his burden) shouted out the accusations of blame which should be put squarely where they are most obviously due: with the killers, the rapists, the dispossessors and their political leaders who initiate and sustain the policies of excessive and unjust violence in today's wars and genocides (1997, p. 247).

Humanitarian codes of conduct

The NGO community responded to these ethical dilemmas by adopting the Red Cross Code of Conduct, which included principles of impartiality and neutrality, and the Sphere standards, which covered standards of service delivery to refugee camps and the like. The problem is that the Code of Conduct seems to avoid what it was meant to address and that is the political nature of most humanitarian emergencies: 'humanitarian action is political action ... [and] human rights abuses are invariably an intimate part of famine creation' (De

Waal 1997, pp. 1–2). While the Sphere standards probably made sense, asking all NGOs to take the same stance of neutrality and impartiality seemed odd and often at conflict with human rights law and rights-based approaches to development, which argue for giving voice and advocating against injustice. Given the history of ACFID and Australian NGOs supporting 'liberation' movements through the 1970s and 1980s, and the withdrawal of the Red Cross from ACFID over perceived partisan humanitarian interventions in various conflicts, reconciling people's human rights in conflict situations with helping perpetrators of injustice (as what happened on the borders of both Cambodia and Rwanda) can lead to deep ethical dilemmas, and possible irreconcilable differences among NGOs.

The Emergencies Forum and the Humanitarian Reference Group

Following the demise of IDEC the Emergencies Forum was established in the early 2000s. It had a coordinating role rather than a fundraising or operational role, and it later became the Humanitarian Reference Group (HRG). It was during the mid to late 1990s that emergencies such as the East Timor crisis (ACFOA 1999b), Bougainville (through the 1990s), and the PNG Aitape Tsunami (1998) occurred. ACFID took a lead in coordinating the emergency response to all of these and, similar to the 1975 response to East Timor, set up a temporary office in Darwin in 1999 to coordinate NGO relief efforts with the UN. This included the response of global partners of Australian NGOs, which was challenging in terms of a number of issues such as which agency was the lead in the response.

The Emergencies Forum became the HRG to provide a more formalised structure for agencies to share information, improve coordination between agencies, and develop tools/events to share with the wider humanitarian sector. The HRG has members approved by the ACFID Executive and is the primary NGO coordination mechanism for emergency appeals and responses (ACFID 2014b). Teleconferences are convened in response to an emergency and are attended by AusAID as well as by regional counterparts such as New Zealand agencies upon request and need. Regular teleconferences are not only a mechanism to facilitate a coordinated emergency response but they also provide a forum for discussing particular NGO capacity, local needs and how they may be delivered, funding issues and opportunities for joint messaging (Lipner 2010).

Figure 12 Cartons of emergency supplies piled high, with RAAF aeroplane in background, during the relief operation to assist Aceh, Indonesia.
Source: Dan Hunt.

The Indian Ocean tsunami

It was the 2004 Indian Ocean tsunami with 230,000 lives lost and over one million left homeless which brought the HRG into its own. The scale of the disaster and the public response was even greater than that of the 1980s Cambodia and Ethiopian appeals, but without the same level of political complexity (Athukorala and Resosudarmo 2005; Rodriguez et al. 2006; Telford and Cosgrave 2007; Kilby 2008; Jayasuriya and McCawley 2010). One hundred million dollars was donated within the first 10 days. When the appeal was over the total was $377 million, of which World Vision alone raised over $110 million (ACFID 2006; Abraham 2007; Clarke 2007). This completely overwhelmed the agencies, which had never experienced this level of support for an emergency, and many had to set up separate sections internally to manage the tsunami program for a number of years. While there was no consolidated IDEC-type appeal, ACFID took on a coordinating and, most importantly, a public accountability role for the NGOs. As foreign minister Downer said at the time: 'we are in this together

… like peas in a pod' (O'Callaghan 2013). The scale of funding was so great that both the government and ACFID were mindful of putting reporting processes in place to ensure maximum accountability and reducing opportunities for media scandals to put at risk the reputation of the response. This resulted in the ACFID secretariat doing more than information sharing and coordination, but also collating and reporting on the work of all agencies involved in the response on a quarterly basis to the public and government (ACFID 2006).

There were also longer term effects.

> The 2005 Asian tsunami transformed the aid and development sector. It placed unprecedented demands on many agencies to manage effective humanitarian response and reconstruction efforts, dramatically lifted public donations and increased media scrutiny of how those donations were spent (ACFID 2010a, p. 3).

Of course the irony was that in the past IDEC bore most of the pressure and demands at these times, but it was too long in the past for the NGOs to remember the role it played. The role of the HRG groups was beefed up in 2008 to become a more formal ACFID advisory committee in response to the increasing operational and policy challenges in this area. Its work was:

> to coordinate emergency response systems, work closely with ACFID's Executive Committee on policy and advocacy, and further collaborate on operational activities/policy such as disaster risk reduction, protection, civil military coordination and human security issues (ACFID 2013c).

By 2010 there was even talk of a return to an IDEC-type arrangement with a joint funding/consolidated funding mechanism. Many 'argued that this approach would help enhance NGO credibility in the eyes of the public' and would also hold NGOs more accountable for their actions, decrease competition, and increase the potential for a more complementary response, thereby enhancing efficiencies of scale and scope (Lipner and Henley 2010, p. 22). By ACFID's 50th anniversary in 2015, however, nothing had come of this idea.

Conclusion

The 50 years of ACFID's engagement, and that of its member agencies, in humanitarian work has seen it involved in the major emergencies of the time; from the controversial Biafran airlift in 1968 to the Indian Ocean Tsunami in 2004, and a number of large-scale emergencies in between: Bangladesh, East Timor, Cambodia, Ethiopia, Rwanda and others. Each of these posed its own unique challenges, and in many ways each challenged the nature of humanitarianism.

As Fassin put it, the 'politics of life' are where difficult choices and decisions are made. These 'politics of life' decisions can often compromise the values of an NGO and sometimes the integrity of a particular intervention, and can create ethical and moral dilemmas for NGOs and their staff. ACFID did not shy away from these debates, nor did it resolve them, as they are the enduring legacy of humanitarian interventions. While ACFID's hands-on role through IDEC may have lasted only 20 years, and may not have been the great success expected, ACFID still continues to be a leading source of information and networking on humanitarian issues for its members and the government.

06

Human Rights

The huge and widening gap between the poorer and wealthier nations of the world and between rich and poor people within nations, which result in deprivation of basic human rights for more than half the world's population, constitutes a denial of natural justice and is a continuing threat to world peace.

— ACFOA 1966c, p. 1

The promotion of human rights has underpinned ACFID's work over its 50 years. From its first standing policy of 1966 (excerpt quoted above) to its work on the self-determination of peoples – whether it be in the context of apartheid in South Africa, the decolonisation and invasion of East Timor, or the isolation of Cambodia and Vietnam by the West in the 1980s – the advocacy work of ACFID has always been couched in the language of people realising not only their civil and political rights but also their economic, social and cultural rights. At the 1971 ACFID Council, Governor-General Sir Paul Hasluck in opening the Council noted that 'you may have to demonstrate clearly that it is to Australia's interest both for posterity and for peace to have a different pattern of economic relationships [with developing countries] from what we have now' (ACFOA 1971a, p. 4). These were interpreted as words of encouragement for supporting economic and social rights coming from a former foreign minister in the conservative Menzies government. By the 2000s the rights work of ACFID had moved to a more direct development focus, building on the Declaration of the Right to Development and focusing on the idea of a rights-based approach to development. This latter shift was a response to the more instrumentalist approaches to development, which have become the norm in many development circles and were epitomised by the World Bank's damaging structural adjustment programs of the 1980s and 1990s.

A focus on human rights moved NGOs away from more simplistic notions of charity and working just to meet the basic human needs of aid recipients to the notion that 'needs can be met out of charitable intentions, but rights are based on legal obligations' (Cornwall and Nyamu-Musembi 2004, p. 1417). The strength of a human rights framework is that it links the donor (government or NGO) to the recipient NGO, recipient government, and recipient communities and individuals in a network of obligations and responsibilities which traditional aid programs do not do (Manzo 2003; Cornwall and Nyamu-Musembi 2004; Uvin 2004; Ensor and Gready 2005). The other part of human rights work has been to argue for a more just set of international relationships, such as ACFID's support for many of the many struggles for self-determination of the 1960s, 1970s and later.

This chapter will track ACFID's history on human rights, and in particular the important role of the work on East Timor from 1975 until its independence in 1999 and beyond, which drove ACFID's human rights work at the time. First, however, the chapter will set the context for human rights and development and how it emerged from a series of UN meetings and processes.

The origin of rights and development

Human rights approaches to development are based on the central idea of the obligations of states and the international community to ensure that citizens of developing countries can claim their economic, social and cultural rights, together with their civil and political rights, and that all of these are fulfilled. While the 1986 Declaration of the Right to Development was an attempt to bring these two streams of rights together (UNGA 1986) it has been largely ignored by Western donors, in part because of the possible international obligation on the levels of aid that donors may face. The Declaration's passage through the UN at the height of the neoliberal structural adjustment policies in the mid-1980s was no coincidence. The Vienna Declaration and Program of Action of 1993 cemented the Right to Development within the existing human rights framework, and the Millennium Declaration of 2000 brought human rights and development into mainstream development work. While the MDGs seem technocratic and carefully avoid human rights language, they are very much informed by the Millennium Declaration and the Right to Development (Slim 2002; Alston 2005; Schmitz 2012).

The idea of linking human rights with development came out of the anti-colonial struggles of the 1950s and 1960s. Developing countries were both finding their voice and being frustrated by the poor response by Western countries to the lofty ideals of the first Development Decade of high aid volumes to drive high growth rates, neither of which eventuated (Pearson 1969; Tomasevski 1993; Weber 2013). A series of human rights instruments were agreed to by the UN in the 1960s: the Convention on the Elimination of All Forms of Racial Discrimination (CERD) in 1965; the International Covenant on Economic, Social and Cultural Rights (ICESCR) and the International Covenant on Civil and Political Rights (ICCPR), both in 1966; and in 1967 the Declaration on the Elimination of Discrimination Against Women (which became CEDAW in 1979).

The 1960s also marked the first Conference on Human Rights held in Tehran in 1968. It was here that developing countries asserted economic development and the freedom of peoples and nations as being the priority (Alston and Robinson 2005; Burke 2008). 'The achievement of lasting progress on the implementation of human rights is dependent on sound and effective national and international policies of economic and social development' (UN 1968, para. 13). This was a major step as it moved the international community away from the rights of the individual, which the West had prioritised, and set in place a binary around human rights. What should be prioritised: civil and political rights or economic, social and cultural rights (Burke 2008)? The adoption of the ICESCR and CERD in 1965 and the Tehran conference of 1968 was seen as representing 'a shift from the Western-inflected concept of individual human rights to a model that emphasized economic development and the collective rights of the nation and its people' (Burke, p. 276). Burke (2008) goes on to note that the West saw it as somewhat ironic, however, that Iran should host the conference with the Shah's reputation for the denial and abuse of the civil and political rights of his people at the time.

This shift in the UN to focus on priorities set by developing countries led to the idea of a New International Economic Order (NIEO) of the early 1970s. It aimed to give developing countries a greater say on the trade and investment activities within their borders and the ability to act as a bloc on common issues to redress what was seen as a new economic colonisation by the West (Bhagwati 1977; Rothstein 1979; Burke 2008). '[I]t was in the act of [these] struggles that rights were articulated and came to form the basis for action for social justice' (Eade 2006, p. 1421). NGOs were very active in supporting the NIEO of the 1970s, with 'critiques of large scale bilateral and multilateral development projects on the basis of who benefits from them and who bears the cost' (Tandon 2000, p. 321), suggesting that the aid programs of the time were part of the economic colonisation of which the developing countries were so wary of. The irony is that by the 2010s much of the ideals of the NIEO had come about with developing countries through the G20 being very much in control, but the economic colonisation was coming from within the developing countries group with the rise of China's aid program being a potent example (see Chapter 10).

The 1970s saw a concerted push from developing countries for the recognition of the human rights principles they championed in the 1960s (economic and social rights), so that by 1972 the idea of a right to development emerged. By 1977 the first draft Declaration of the Right to Development was tabled (Alston and Robinson 2005; Burke 2008; Tadeg 2010), with its emphasis on 'establishing a fair international economic order' (Tadeg 2010, p. 327). The shift was from not only recognising the state's responsibility to its citizens, but also the collective obligation of all states to 'create a just and equitable international environment for development to occur' (Eade 2006, p. 1422). In the end what came out in the 1970s 'was a bloodied compromise between the industrialised North and the developing South' (Davis 2009, p. 176). As far as the West was concerned: 'Growth dominated development, and civil and political rights dominated human rights' (Alston 1981, p. 63).

The push for a greater focus on economic, social and cultural rights had a major setback in the 1980s as the power of growth-oriented structural adjustment policies in response to the debt crisis pushed by Western donors became dominant, in particular from the World Bank and the International Monetary Fund. This effectively rolled over both the NIEO and the Right to Development in favour of what became known as the Washington Consensus (Davis 2009, Williamson 1993). This 'consensus' was a neoliberal view of the world in which developing country governments reduced their role in society in favour of the market, with privatisation, liberalisation and deregulation being the dominant set of norms.

Rights-based development

The UN processes and debates of the early 1960s lead ACFID to see development from a rights perspective at its formation in 1965, much earlier than government. ACFID was therefore part of the ongoing lobbying and advocacy to gain recognition for developing countries' economic and social rights. Forty years later, in the 2000s, ACFID picked up rights-based development as an approach and urged AusAID to take it up as well (Miller 2010). Even though it was not called rights-based development in the 1960s and 1970s, many of the principles of good development practice of local control and participation advocated for at that time have become part of the rights-based development principles of the 1990s and 2000s (Kindornay et al. 2012).

A focus on participatory development and human rights were common themes of ACFID's magazine the *Development News Digest* through the 1970s and a key focus of the major development education conferences of 1973 and 1978. As a result, the definition of development which came out of the ACFID review of 1979 is clearly couched in rights-based development language:

> Development is a process which enlarges the action space for persons and groups in their own societies ... with a common objective the development of peoples and of human potential in a climate of justice, self-determination, participation, and sustainability (ACFOA 1979i).

ACFID and human rights: The early years

In its early years ACFID adopted a set of principles that amounted to a nascent rights-based approach in how human needs and poverty should be responded to, which were about participation, local control, and accountability (ACFOA 1966). It was the humanitarian crises of the time, however, that brought rights to the fore in the context of often violent struggles for the right to self-determination. These shaped how humanitarianism and rights were seen within NGOs more generally, and ACFID in particular. The Biafran crisis of 1967–69 saw NGOs first take an active approach in providing emergency relief independent of government (see Chapter 5). While the ACFID secretariat was not part of the Biafran airlift and associated appeals, its members were and so it was ACFID's first involvement in what Chandler calls 'modern human rights-based solidarity movements' (2001, p. 683). The experience of Biafra and, a couple of years later, Bangladesh pointed to the strong role that NGOs could take in advocating for the rights and social justice issues involved in self-determination struggles.

While the focus on rights was strong throughout the 1970s, with the 1976 ACFID Standing Policy affirming human rights even more clearly than the 1966 policy (ACFOA 1976c), there were tensions within ACFID at the time on how rights were seen and advocated. The recognition and respect of human rights were major themes of the Tasmanian Summer School and led to the formation of the Human Rights Council of Australia in 1978, initially operating out of the ACFID office in Canberra (Curtis 1977; ACFOA 1978b, ACFOA 1998b). While the Harries Report on Australia's relations with the Third World in the late 1970s argued that any discussion of economic rights in an aid context was 'misplaced humanitarianism' (Harries Committee 1979, p. 156), ACFID argued that economic and social rights must be part of the development mix and have a strong focus on self-determination, the main focus of economic rights at the time (ACFOA 1978b; Okolie 1978).

While the right to self-determination was created in the context of decolonisation, it was later taken up in the context of minority and indigenous rights, and this is where ACFID ran into arguments about the sovereignty of the 'governing' state. The main example was East Timor and Indonesia's claims of sovereignty over it (Hannum 2011), but also Eritrea and New Caledonia where ACFID argued the case for self-determination, and South Africa where ACFID argued against apartheid and for the inclusion of the black majority in the political process. In all these cases, ACFID supported local representatives of these movements in Australia to make their case to the Australian government and, more widely, to the United Nations (Rollason 2013).

East Timor

It was the issue of East Timor and its fight for independence that was to be probably the most important and defining part of ACFID's human rights work for more than 25 years (Purcell 2013; Walsh 2014). The East Timor work was at times contentious within ACFID and in its relations with the Australian and Indonesian governments to the point that, even in the 2010s, some Australian NGOs are still not allowed to set up offices in Indonesia as a result of the stance they took on East Timor in the 1970s through to the 1990s. The background to the East Timor crisis was its rapid decolonisation by Portugal in 1974 and the push for early local government elections in March 1975, which led to an unstable coalition and an attempted coup in August 1975. With the pretext of instability on its border, Indonesia invaded East Timor in December 1975 and took the country over in a brutal occupation, which was to take hundreds of thousand lives and continue for the following 25 years (Ramos-Horta 1987; Dunn 2003; Cristalis 2009).

ACFID was one of the first international aid agencies involved and sent a delegation on behalf of Australian NGOs in October 1975 to report on the increasingly dire situation in East Timor (Dunn 1975; ACFOA 1975b; ACFOA 1975i, 1975k). ACFID and its members had been highly supportive of East Timor's independence, and had passed a resolution supporting self-determination, which sparked a protest from Indonesia even prior to the invasion (ACFOA 1975c). After the report of the delegation that visited in October 1975, ACFID launched an appeal which raised enough funds to send a barge with emergency supplies from Darwin to Dili in November on behalf of a number of its members, but notably not the Red Cross (see Chapter 5).

Despite the overwhelming support of ACFID's members over its stance on East Timor (Tiffen et al. 1979), the Red Cross argued that ACFID was taking a political or partisan role and, as a result, withdrew its membership of ACFID but stayed on as an observer. It only rejoined as a full member of ACFID in 2013 (ACFOA 1976b; Sullivan 2013). The questions raised about whether ACFID was partisan, and a view that it had inherited a 'left wing' agenda,[1] led ACFID to be forceful in stating that it was non-partisan, its advocacy was on the basis of human rights and the right to self-determination and, in the case of East Timor, it was not favouring a particular political group (Walsh 2014).

ACFID continued its advocacy on the plight of the East Timorese and provided implicit support for East Timor's self-determination (ACFOA 1979e, 1979f, 1980c, 1981e, 1982b). Following the humanitarian calamity and famine in East

---

1   This included accusations from right-wing organisations such as the National Civic Council that ACFID supported communism or had communist sympathies.

Timor of 1977–79 as part of Indonesian actions against the resistance movement (de Acolhimento 2005; Walsh 2012; Robinson 2009), there was a push in 1979 for more Australian government support for East Timor. In their submission to the government at the time, ACFID noted that there was some inconsistency in Australian government policy in cutting aid to Vietnam over its invasion of Cambodia, but not criticising Indonesia's invasion of East Timor, let alone halting aid (ACFOA 1979b). Internationally there was also a polarised view, with Catholic Relief Services of the US still taking a strident anti-communist line and restricting humanitarian aid to East Timor even after it was heavily criticised for channelling US food aid to the South Vietnamese military a decade earlier (Walsh 2014; Flipse 2002; Howell 2014).

The work of ACFID around the Indonesian invasion and subsequent famine was not without its critics. In 1977 ACFID commissioned a report into East Timor in which eminent persons were to conduct hearings from affected people in East Timor and elsewhere, which was to support ACFID's advocacy work (Walsh 2014). The report took nearly three years to complete and was only handed over after much urging from ACFID. The Traille report was surprisingly (at least to ACFID) critical of ACFID's position. The report argued against supporting the right for self-determination. It was supportive of the Indonesian invasion and claimed that the refugees were not strictly speaking refugees but Portuguese citizens. It was also implicitly critical of ACFID's advocacy, arguing that the independent monitoring of aid was an unacceptable political string. Most notably, however, the report made little reference to the famine that had been underway for the previous two years (ACFOA 1980c; *The Canberra Times* 1981). While ACFID felt it could not withhold the release of the report, especially after former prime minister Gough Whitlam called for its release (Whitlam 1981), it did so with a comprehensive rebuttal, particularly around errors of fact. ACFID also argued vigorously that the research was not balanced, particularly in terms of the various points of view, the nature of the evidence sought, and which groups were chosen to be given a hearing (ACFOA 1981e). While it prompted a spirited debate between ACFID and the authors of the report in the letters column of *The Canberra Times* (Whan 1981; Traille 1982; Alston 1981; Rivett, 1981), the Traille report was a complete failure as a way of getting the evidence out of what was actually happening in East Timor (Walsh 2014).

The 1980s and the human rights office

In the 1980s ACFID broadened its human rights work beyond East Timor, and established a human rights office in Melbourne in 1985. While the human rights program was in some sense a strategic response to what was happening in East Timor, for ACFID to have a broader credibility on human rights it had to expand its work beyond East Timor and show that it was not anti-Indonesian

(Walsh 2014). A key element was promoting people-to-people relations, and links were made with human rights organisations and other NGOs in Indonesia through the 1980s. A very good working relationship was established with them and 'in a trial and error sort of way it worked out beautifully' (Walsh 2014).

The office began working on human rights issues around the Sri Lankan conflict, as well as Burma, and to a lesser extent West Papua (ACFOA 1998b). The other important role that the human rights office had was a regular dialogue with the Australian government from 1984. Whether these consultations were a way for government to neutralise NGO voices or not, they did enable an international NGO perspective to be brought to DFAT and prompt the engagement of DFAT in the human rights issues of the day. This was probably helped by having a sympathetic Labor government and a human rights lawyer in the form of Gareth Evans as foreign minister for part of that time.

The human rights office had a chequered life with frequent calls for it to be closed down on the basis of cost or there being more pressing priorities. In 1987 the ACFID executive tried to close down the office as a budget measure, but it was overruled by the ACFID Council, and funds were found to keep it operating. In 1990 there was another review of the human rights program with the result that the office was more directly brought into the structure of ACFID (ACFOA 1998b). The 1993 World Conference on Human Rights in Vienna was a watershed for NGOs in general and ACFID in particular. As part of the preparatory work, human rights NGOs of the region, including ACFID, brought their issues to a preparatory meeting in Bangkok, and from there these issues had a global airing in Vienna (Purcell 2009; Walsh 2014). Vienna also confirmed that all human rights were of equal importance and thus laid the groundwork for rights-based development touched on earlier in this chapter (Kindornay et al. 2012, Davis 2009).

East Timor was also reaching a turning point in the late 1980s and early 1990s, especially following the Dili massacre of 1991. With the increased and more effective Timorese resistance through the 1990s, there was an upsurge of support for East Timor's self-determination (Sherlock 1996; McWilliam 2005; Novais 2007). By the late 1980s Indonesian President Suharto was having trouble maintaining the fiction that all was fine in East Timor, while still not allowing in any Western observers. In 1989 a three-person ACFID delegation visited Dili for a day on the way to another meeting, and met with Bishop Belo, the Catholic Bishop of Dili, to confirm that he was making a public call for self-determination and would appreciate ACFID's support. This opening up of East Timor enabled more people to observe human rights abuses, including the filming of the Dili massacre of 1991, which prompted international public outrage (Novais, 2007) and led to ACFID being banned from Indonesia for a time (Jarret 1994; Walsh 2014).

Figure 13 José Ramos-Horta, leader of the East Timorese Independence movement, speaking at ACFID, May 1984.

Source: Fairfax media.

Over the next eight years, the work of ACFID and NGOs more broadly on the situation in East Timor resulted in constant pressure on the Indonesian and Australian governments. After President Suharto resigned in 1998 the way was open for an independence referendum, which was held in 1999. ACFID had representatives on the Australian official observer mission led by former deputy prime minister Tim Fisher (Schulze 2001; Walsh 2014). While the poll overwhelmingly supported independence, it led to a humanitarian emergency when the Indonesian army and Indonesian-backed militias went on a rampage, destroying much of East Timor's infrastructure. It was only after an armed, but generally non-violent, intervention by a multinational military force led by Australia that the situation was stabilised to enable an interim UN administration to prepare the country for an orderly handover to an East Timorese government in 2002 (Traub 2000; Chopra 2002; Fernandez 2011). Thus ended nearly 25 years of advocacy work by ACFID for the right to self-determination of the people of East Timor.

Aboriginal and Torres Strait Islander land rights

The other important driver of ACFID's human rights work were the Aboriginal land rights struggles of the 1960s through to the 2000s. These struggles resulted in Aboriginal and Torres Strait Islanders' political rights gradually being recognised in a number of laws in Australia in the early 1960s, culminating in the 1967 constitutional amendment removing discriminatory references from the Australian Constitution to enable the Commonwealth government to make laws with regard to Aboriginal and Torres Strait Islanders and overturn any discriminatory state law.[2] There is still, however, no formal recognition of Aboriginal and Torres Strait Islander peoples in the Australian Constitution.

The gap that remained was in the area of traditional land rights, which would not be recognised until 1993. It had become an international issue as early as the late 1960s, when international NGOs such as the WCC and a number of ACFID members provided grants to Aboriginal organisations in 1969 to fight for their land rights (Hill 1972). The Campaign Against Racial Exploitation was set up in Australia in the early 1970s as an anti-apartheid and anti-racism network with strong links and support from ACFID (*The National Times* Editorial 1975; Hill 1975b; ACFOA 1975a). From the early to mid-1990s ACFID was also very active around Native Title rights following the High Court's Mabo and Wik decisions.[3] It was out of some of this work and the support of ACFID that Australians

---

2   The referendum resulted in Clause 127 excluding Aboriginal and Torres Strait Islander people from the census being deleted; and the deletion of discriminatory references to Aboriginal and Torres Strait Islander people in Clause 51, which covers the lawmaking functions of the parliament. The right to vote had already been provided for in federal legislation in 1962 (National Archives of Australia).

3   The Mabo decision (High Court of Australia 1992) confirmed Murray Islander people's rights to their traditional lands; and the Wik decision (High Court of Australia 1996) confirmed Aboriginal peoples' land rights to pastoral leases on mainland Australia.

for Native Title and Reconciliation (ANTaR) was formed. It continues to this day working on reconciliation with a focus on constitutional recognition of Aboriginal and Torres Strait Islanders.

The issue of fighting for Australian Indigenous rights has always had its critics in ACFID, who argued that ACFID be only involved in international social justice issues. Generally, however, a large majority of members have always supported ACFID being involved in Australia's Indigenous issues, and have provided direct assistance themselves (Tiffen et al. 1979; Hubbard 1981; ACFOA 1990c). In the 2000s, this work continues with an ACFID Aboriginal and Torres Strait Islander Working Group, and ACFID's development of a Practice Note for working with Indigenous Australians (ACFID 2014a).

From the Right to Development to rights-based development

Western donors often have trouble with the language of rights, preferring the language of aid which suggests aid is a favour being granted (often in the donor's own interest) rather than an obligation of the international community – the basis of the Right to Development. Some of the key principles of the Right to Development discussed above were taken up at the 1995 World Summit for Social Development at Copenhagen (Hamm 2001; Eyben 2006). While the Right to Development had at best a lukewarm acceptance by the donor community (afraid their aid budgets may be locked in), it did provide the basis of the move to rights-based development which has since been picked up, for a time at least, by UN agencies such as UNDP and by NGOs in the early 2000s (Chapman et al. 2009; Kindornay et al. 2012).

While bilateral donors may accept there is a Right to Development, this is aspirational at best and is not about a right to development assistance or in any sense a legal obligation: 'Donor countries do not wish to be legally obliged to provide aid' (Piron 2005, p. 20). This was in part a reason for the move to rights-based development as an alternative (Davis 2009; Tadeg 2010). However, even when taking this path aid recipients must shift, in the eyes of the donor, from being the subject of development to being citizens who participate in the process of a development assistance exchange. In such an exchange there are necessary processes to ensure justice, participation, empowerment and agency (Davis 2009).

The idea of rights-based development emerged in the late 1990s as an attempt to implement some of the principles of the Right to Development. Some of these principles have been around since the 1960s (Hudson 2002; Schmitz 2012).

Perhaps 'it is "old development" wine served up in new, rights-based bottles' (Kindornay at al. 2012, p. 479). The change to a rights discourse in the 1990s, however, provided an important antidote to the one-size-fits-all neoliberal structural adjustment policies that were more or less forced upon developing countries in the 1980s,[4] and the consequent loss of the once strident voice of developing countries. The language of rights provided some space to argue the case for the poor, not in terms of being a beneficiary of donor largesse but from the standpoint that the right to agreed basic standards of service and access is universal, and there are obligations on us all to ensure these are provided. This, however, points to a weakness of rights-based development and there is the assumption that rights-based approaches will favour the poor and marginalised, which may not be always the case. As Philip Alston points out: 'the consequences of highlighting rights will depend very significantly on the power relations that exist within the society or the group [and] the promotion of a rights approach ... could well reinforce the rights of those who already have power' (Alston 2005, p. 805). Another problem is what seems to be a disjunction between principle and practice:

> the right to development defines development by international human rights and their accompanying obligations, [while] donors tend to see 'rights-based approaches' as offering new analytical and program tools for assisting poverty alleviation within existing development assistance structures (Davis 2009, p. 179).

The implication of this argument was that there are no obligations attached to these rights. There is also a conflict of rights-based approaches with what has been called 'new managerialism', whereby results-based management and value-for-money principles are central to recent approaches to aid delivery. As Hudson (2002) put it: 'While civil society groups have made rights-based approaches a key priority in their own discussions of aid effectiveness, donor and partner country responses have been lukewarm' (p. 497). The effect was that rights-based approaches have struggled to gain traction.

Rights-based approaches, optimistic as they are, also challenge the view of many developing countries, which have argued since the 1960s that sacrifices of civil and political rights were required to achieve rapid development and advances in economic, social and cultural rights. There was a point in the 1970s when some commentators, and even governments at the time, regarded authoritarian regimes as useful or possibly essential for development, as evidenced by the successes of Malaysia, Taiwan, Singapore and South Korea. In the 1980s,

---

4   Enormous capital flows into the United States following the oil shocks of the 1970s had the effect of dramatically reducing the availability of capital to poor and middle-income countries, thus forcing them to the IMF and World Bank for credit (Arrighi 2010).

arguments for the suppression of civil and political rights continued to receive a sympathetic airing, as they may have to be sacrificed for the realisation of economic and social rights, which was central to the Asian values debate of the 1980s and 1990s (Espiritu 1986; Mauzy 1997; Korey 2001; Kraft 2001). While the West preferred international law to focus on civil and political rights, the rise of China as a major donor in the 2000s has now provided an option for those developing countries not agreeing with human rights conditionality from the West (Donnelly 1989; Kjøllesdal and Welle-Strand 2010; Shepherd Jr. and Nanda 1985).

By the early 1980s there was a more detailed examination of economic, social and cultural rights, with an associated shift in thinking from economic development to human development. This shift was in response to the top-down development policies at the time and the harmful effects they were having on local communities (Alston 1981; International Commission of Jurists 1981). In response to these debates, some official donors were arguing for a middle ground and 'to "civilise" global capital via a rights-based development approach' (Davis 2009, p. 174). ACFID also made these links to development and moved from advocacy for self-determination of the 1970s and 1980s to seeing basic human needs as a right (Rollason 1987). This was a forerunner of the process through the 1990s that led to the development of the Millennium Development Goals. Bill Hayden, the foreign minister at the time, labelled these arguments as a 'new type of imperialism' (quoted in Rollason 1987), which was a little surprising given that it was developing countries themselves that were making these links, not Western NGOs as Hayden seemed to be suggesting.

While the Right to Development makes clear links to economic and social rights, such as the right to food, health care, education, and the civil and political right to participation and the like, they were never seen as obligatory, simply because it is very hard to agree on a specific standard affordable to all. Davis (2009) commented that 'it pushes states to focus on substantive basic needs and social justice' (p. 175). These were second- and third-generation rights,[5] and for this reason developing countries tended to see these as bargaining chips with the West for more aid to counter the ill effects of globalisation and to counter accusations of poor civil and political rights in developing countries. Tadeg (2010) pointed out that the 'danger posed by globalisation to existing

---

5   First-generation human rights deal essentially with liberty and participation in political life. They are fundamentally civil and political in nature and serve to protect the individual from excesses of the state; second-generation human rights are related to equality, and guarantee different members of the citizenry equal conditions and treatment. The term 'third-generation human rights' includes group and collective rights, such as the right to self-determination; the right to economic and social development; the right to peace; the right to a healthy environment; and the right to intergenerational equity.

human rights structures … renders individual states, acting alone, unable to satisfy the obligations imposed by international human rights instruments' (p. 326).

The UN moved this process along following the Social Development Summit when the Secretary-General in 1997 mandated that human rights were to be mainstreamed in all UN programs. The UN human rights office produced a Common Understanding to guide agencies in rights-based approaches (UNDG 2003). In its most basic form a rights-based approach puts human dignity at the centre and spells out the rights of people and the obligations of government and others to assist in meeting those rights. The guide also outlined the mechanisms of participation and accountability to help the poor and marginalised claim their rights and hold those obliged to meet those rights to account (Winter 2009; Lundy and McEvoy 2012). The idea was to 'frame poverty in the language of international human rights standards and transform passive recipients of aid into empowered rights-holders' (Schmitz 2012, p. 525).

ACFID actively promoted rights-based development through the 2000s. In 2009 it undertook a major study into how Australian NGOs realised rights in their work, and from that developed a program to strengthen members in their human rights work. This resulted in a Practice Note being developed spelling out what a rights-based approach might look like for ACFID members, some of the principles that underpin it, and some ways to assess if it is effective (Winter 2009; ACFID 2010b; Law et al. 2012).

Human rights in the 2000s

The progress of human rights through the 2000s has been mixed. While The Millennium Declaration has its basis in human rights, the MDGs that emerged are more instrumental in their nature. Kuruvilla et al. (2012) stated that although 'human rights and the MDGs are clearly linked and constitute shared global commitments, in practice there is surprisingly little that connects them' (p. 148). For Philip Alston (2005) the MDGs and human rights were seen as 'ships passing in the night' (p. 755), ignoring the broad social, economic and political structures which led to rights being denied. After a push for broader recognition and respect for human rights in the early 2000s, the gloss had faded by the 2010s. Despite these instrumental approaches to depoliticising rights-based development (such as the MDGs) it still seems to be on the wane. At the Busan DAC conference in December 2011 'emerging powers of the South [set] the agenda to one that is no longer the people centred and participatory development approach … that the DAC played such an important role in creating [in 1996]' (Eyben 2013, p. 89). The rise of Southern economic and political powers like China and the rest of the BRICS[6] have moved the global development agenda away from rights towards a more clearly economic growth focus within the sovereign state, 'claiming rights is a political process and ... rights are often negated and denied in the first place by structural inequalities and dominant power relations', which are largely determined by the sovereign state (Ako et al. 2013, p. 49).

The implications of rights-based development also dampened NGO enthusiasm, due mainly to the burden on partners to meet their obligations and the difficulty in engaging in national advocacy to hold sovereign governments to account when these governments are hostile to civil society and advocacy. In brief, there has been a lukewarm response from donor and recipient governments alike, in an aid environment which has been moving more sharply to results-based aid schemas (Kindornay et al. 2012; Schmitz 2012). What is emerging is 'an unresolved tension between a principled human rights approach, where rights are seen as non-negotiable, and an instrumental development approach where rights are subject to cost–benefit analysis' (Waldorf 2013, p. 714). If rights-based approaches are taken too literally then agencies can get tangled up in endless discussions about how to approach a particular problem, and which human rights are being dealt with, rather than the broad principles of the approach. The exceptions seem to have been in the area of child rights and disability, where rights-based approaches have made some headway and are increasingly being used. This is in part because there are specific human rights conventions in place, and in part because advocacy about them in most cases is less of a threat to the state and its laws (Whitehead et al. 2011; Lundy and McEvoy 2012; Njelesani et al. 2012; UNICEF 2012; Arts 2013).

While AusAID has generally been unwilling to consider human rights more broadly beyond specialist human rights programs in its aid program, some cracks did emerge. The focus on disability by the Labor government in 2008 resulted in the first direct linking of aid to a human rights convention, and in this way recognised the important processes of rights-based development (Purcell 2009). More broadly, though, despite the Joint Parliamentary Committee on Foreign Affairs, Defence and Trade recommending a rights-based approach in 2010 (JCFADT 2010, p. 134), with numerous submissions supporting it, including a presentation from 17 agency heads, the 2011 review of the aid program explicitly rejected a rights-based approach. The review's main arguments against a rights-based approach was that *inter alia* it would risk placing 'other rights above the poverty objective ... and could open the Australian Government to unpredictable demands' (Hollway et al. 2011, p. 113), which more or less restated concerns

---

6   Brazil, Russia, India, China and South Africa.

made by AusAID 10 years earlier (AusAID 2001). While these objections are not insurmountable this report and the government response to it, as well as the DAC walking away from it at Busan, effectively closed off debate on the issue.

Conclusion

Respect for human rights has been an important driver of ACFID's work since its founding in 1965, an era when the main human rights conventions were being negotiated and finalised. ACFID being a social development peak body tended to look at human rights as universal, and that recognising economic, social, and cultural rights were necessary for the fulfilment of civil and political rights. As far as ACFID was concerned it was not a matter of generations of rights or a priority of one set of rights over another. The second important focus that ACFID, and NGOs more broadly, took was in support of self-determination as part of the decolonisation process and ending bloody internal conflict. This started with Biafra in 1968 but continued with East Timor, Eritrea and others. In later years ACFID took up the idea of rights-based development as an outcome of the Right to Development, and a way of realising economic, social and cultural rights which had been bogged down in the UN system since the 1970s.

It was the issue of East Timor's self-determination, however, that focused the human rights work of ACFID. Prior to that there was some generalised advocacy on human rights in South Africa and Latin America. The ACFID Tasmanian Summer School had led to the formation of the Human Rights Council of Australia, but it was East Timor that had advanced the issue within ACFID. While some had seen ACFID as partisan in this work, it was a small minority; and over 25 years the work on East Timor brought to the public eye the human rights abuses that occurred, including the devastating famine of 1978–79 and the events surrounding the Dili massacre in 1991. The human rights office set up in 1985 broadened its work beyond East Timor and took up the cause of human rights abuses in Sri Lanka and other countries.

In the 2000s rights work continued with the idea of rights-based development as an approach adopted for a period. In the 2010s the idea of promoting the advancement of international human rights any further has waned, in part due to much stronger nationalistic sentiment combined with the effects of globalisation, increasing inequality, and an increased movement of people internally as well as internationally, all of which have put some pressure on how international conventions are recognised in the context of local sovereignty pressures. The challenge for ACFID in the future will be how to keep the human rights agenda in the public and government eye when national interests of both First and Third World countries are being put ahead of human rights in so many contexts.

07 | Engaging with Government

ACFID was relatively slow in its early years in developing a fruitful engagement with government on aid and development policy, with little substantial engagement until the mid-1970s. This was frustrating for them at the time as NGO engagement with government in public policy is an important reason for their existence as public benefit organisations, a role often taken on by peak bodies such as ACFID. This engagement presents both risks and opportunities for NGOs. This chapter looks at the opportunities that emerged when the Australian government saw an advantage in cooperating with NGOs. Chapter 8 will look at the risks that occurred when later governments not only saw little advantage in engaging with NGOs but were also in some quarters even hostile to the very notion of engagement.

Australian governments of the late 1960s and early 1970s had not formed a policy on aid and development much beyond the Colombo Plan of 1950, which soon morphed into being part of a Cold War strategy of winning 'hearts and minds', and later in the 1960s the war in Vietnam filled the foreign policy space (Oakman 2010; Howell 2014). For other developed countries, and the United Nations more broadly, the 1960s was a period of closer engagement with development NGOs as part of the first Development Decade, so that by the late 1960s NGO funding schemes had been established in a number of donor countries and NGOs were actively engaging with their respective governments on aid and development policy (Brodhead et al. 1988). By the 1980s government funding of NGOs had expanded (OECD 1988) to the point that questions were being raised as to whether it was too much. Michael Edwards called it 'too close for comfort' (Edwards and Hulme 1997), and in the 1990s the 'dependency' of NGOs on government funding was being hotly debated (Van der Heijden 1987; Drabek 1992; AusAID 1995a; Steen 1996).

Of course the timing of these changes differed from country to country, depending to a large extent on the political cycle and the relevant government's views on NGOs and their role. This chapter will look at the increased engagement by government with NGOs, from the first Development Decade UN commitments, and track how this engagement led to greater funding of NGOs through official aid programs (Gubser 2012). Chapter 8 will then track how a growing scepticism of NGOs by government, particularly after the end of the Cold War, led to varying levels of disengagement of governments with NGOs in many countries, including Australia.

The international experience

Government funding of NGOs started in the 1950s with the US government funding international NGOs in 1951 and Sweden in 1952 (OECD 1988). The US funding of NGOs was unique in that it rapidly increased in the mid-1950s, more than 10 years ahead of most other donor governments. In 1954 the Agricultural Trade Development Assistance Act, otherwise known as PL480 (Public Law 480), became the Food For Peace program under president John F Kennedy (OECD 1988). The PL480 program mandated that the majority of food aid be used to meet humanitarian food needs, either for direct feeding or to be sold to raise cash for development work, and be delivered through NGOs or the World Food Programme. The PL480 program grew rapidly, and for agencies like CARE and Catholic Relief Services in the US it became their major source of income. This was also a time when the US government used NGOs, and even created them in the case of the Asia Foundation, as part of its Cold War strategy (Department of State 1966; Howell 2014; Marchetti and Marks 1974; Pergandi 2002; Flipse 2002).

In the other OECD countries government funding of NGOs started in the 1960s with Germany, Netherlands and Norway in 1965, and Canada in 1968 (Herbert-Copley 1987; OECD 1988; Brouwer 2010; Smillie 1995). This followed a push by the UN for greater engagement of governments with NGOs and the successful global Freedom from Hunger Campaign as part of the first Development Decade. In 1968 an NGO division was established in the Canadian International Development Agency (CIDA), which started making matching grants on a 1:1 basis to agencies to support their work. In its first year this scheme sent $5 million to 50 projects undertaken by 20 agencies, which by 1985 had grown to 2,400 projects by 200 agencies (Brodhead et al. 1988; Brouwer 2010).

In the UK there was some ambivalence about government funding from both government and NGOs, with prime minster Heath saying in 1970 that providing aid to NGOs was 'undesirable' (Burnell 1987, p. 14). By 1973, however, 10 per cent of the UK's official aid was provided through NGOs, most probably boosted by the one-off funding to the Bangladesh emergency (Cole-King 1976; Hilton 2012). In 1975 a Joint Funding Scheme based on the Canadian model was set up by the UK Labour government, and in 1977 the four largest agencies received block funding from government (Hilton 2012). There was some nervousness among UK NGOs of government funding. The major agencies had set an upper limit of 10 per cent of their funding coming from government, as they felt their reputation with their developing country partners might be put at risk. The experience from the US was that USAID funding of NGOs had exacted a price in terms of their reputation for supporting US foreign policy and, in the case of Vietnam, US wars (Lissner 1977; Burnell 1987; Diamond 1992; Ekbladh 2011; Pergandi 2002; Flipse 2002).

The focus of donors on funding NGO programs was due in part to the failure of large-scale bilateral projects and questions as to whether these projects benefitted the poor. NGOs were also seen as good managers of food aid: in 1981 the US Congress mandated that a minimum of 12 per cent of the US food aid commitments go through NGOs (OECD 1988). By 1985, of the $4.5 billion given as grants by NGOs in the OECD, around one third of the funding was from government (OECD, p. 81). When compared with 1975 the level of aid delivered by NGOs as a proportion of GDP had not changed significantly, but the funding from Overseas Development Assistance (ODA) had risen more than tenfold, 'from some $100 million in 1975 to over $1.1 billion in 1985' (Van der Heijden 1987, p. 103). In Canada the amount of ODA through NGOs doubled between 1975 and 1985 to 8 per cent of ODA (Herbert-Copley 1987). By the mid-1980s other official aid agencies started to also subcontract NGOs to undertake bilateral projects; however, there were costs. In the US in particular, where program and block grant funding was lowest, the effect of the contracts governing these grants limited NGO ability to speak out:

> these NGOs have put at risk their ability to speak out on important issues, their freedom to identify projects based on local input, and their general independence of action. They find themselves responding increasingly to donor demands and guidelines rather than to the relationships and networks they had developed in the field (Hellinger 1987, p. 136).

This issue of government constraining the voice of NGOs by virtue of their funding contracts still continues (see Chapter 10).

The Australian government and ACFID 1965–74

As discussed in Chapter 2, while the Australian government may have had some input into the formation of ACFID in 1965, and with the impetus from the UN for governments to engage more effectively with NGOs, it was the driving force of Sir John Crawford that made it happen. However, the day-to-day relations of NGOs with government in the 1960s were not close. Apart from covering some of the core costs of ACFID from 1967, and the volunteer program, there was no NGO funding from government outside of small grants for emergencies until 1974 when the ANCP started. As a result the relationship of NGOs with government through the 1960s and early 1970s was at best distant and at worst acrimonious. The major issue which was to dog ACFID for its first 15 years was the granting of tax relief for donations for overseas aid work. This issue was to be the source of bitter dispute between ACFID and government throughout its formative years.

While liaison with government was a reason for ACFID's formation, its influence on official aid policy was relatively weak in the 1960s, and its policy dialogue on aid could be described as a dialogue of the deaf, or at least to the deaf. Any policy influence ACFID had up until the mid-1970s was mainly through a series of conferences (ACFOA 1965b, 1966g, 1969a) but these generally had little effect on the aid program, and ACFID's access to government was limited. This was probably because the government in the 1960s did not have a culture of engagement with the community sector as such (beyond industry groups), and the whole notion of overseas aid in a broader policy sense was very new. Official aid at the time was still rooted in strategic Cold War imperatives and trade promotion rather than development (Viviani and Wilenski 1978; Waters 1999). ACFID's work on the Bangladesh crisis of 1971 and the McMahon government's intransigence in responding to the crisis was a case in point (O'Dwyer 1971a).

> International aid has introduced a completely alien element into this world of debate of security and trade interests ... [and so] arguments on aid policy are always framed in the national interests, and they never rest their case on moral or humanitarian arguments (Arndt 1969, p. 46).

From 1973 the relationship improved under the Labor government and, following its fall in November 1975, the Coalition government of Malcolm Fraser maintained the engagement with NGOs and ACFID but not the growth in funding. While general funding to NGOs did not grow much in real terms, the Fraser government did not reverse any of Labor's funding initiatives for NGOs, which were relatively small compared with other DAC counterparts (OECD 1988). The Fraser government was more engaged in policy dialogue and used NGOs for specific programs, mainly around Cambodia in the early 1980s when bilateral relations were not possible. Most importantly, the Fraser government introduced tax deductibility for donations for international development work in 1980 (Howard 1979; Alston 1980a). In 1983 the new Labor government then rapidly expanded funding to NGOs until the mid-1990s, when the growth in funding stopped and questions were raised about NGO dependency on government and whether they were the most effective channels of official aid (AusAID 1995a). This next section will look at the relationship with government over those first 30 years from the days of hostility to the building of government funding schemes and the 'golden age' of NGO funding in the 1980s. The cooling of relations with government came in the 1990s, initially with the Labor government but continued with the Coalition government under John Howard, with a drop in funding to NGOs from the peak of the early 1990s until the 2010s, when NGO funding as a proportion of the aid program again increased for a period. The 1990s and 2000s will be looked at in more detail in Chapter 8.

The fight for tax deductibility

In the 1960s the same arguments on tax deductibility for donations to NGOs were also happening on the international stage. While the notion of tax relief to charities has a long history going back to 1799 in the UK, when charities were given an exemption from paying tax under the new tax laws of that year (Scharf and Smith 2012), the idea of giving a tax deduction to the benefactor for their donations to charities was more recent. The US was the first to offer tax relief for donations in 1917, and other countries much later (Lissner 1977; Wolfe 2013). The introduction of exemptions from other taxes, such as value added taxes and employment taxes, also had a positive effect on the commercial arms of NGOs such as Oxfam Great Britain and its very large network of shops (Lissner 1977).

By the mid-1960s, the idea of providing tax relief for donations to international NGOs was gaining some traction. The UN work around the first Development Decade and the Freedom from Hunger Campaign put NGOs and their work to the fore, and various forms of tax relief for NGOs were being introduced in a number of countries. By 1967 Canada, the United Kingdom, and New Zealand all had some degree of tax relief for donations for NGO development work (Perkins 1967), and by 1975 only Sweden, Switzerland and Australia were among the OECD countries had not provided tax relief for donors who gave to development NGOs (Lissner 1977). The Freedom from Hunger Campaign had been granted tax deductibility as Australia's commitment in support of the UN resolution on the first Development Decade in 1959. The campaign itself, however, got underway in 1961 as a five-year campaign (Lockwood 1963), but in Australia did not start until 1962. As the campaign was expected to run until 1967, it should have had tax deductibility for all of that time. So it came as quite a surprise when in mid-1964, after only two financial years of operation, the campaign's tax deductibility was arbitrarily withdrawn. The argument of the government at the time was the rather spurious one that the agreement was made in 1959, and that the tax relief was from then and not from the commencement of the campaign in 1962. This led to outrage, and AFFHC was a reluctant party to the early meetings around the formation of ACFID due to the bitterness engendered and the perceived duplicitous nature of the government

(Webb 1964a). The Freedom from Hunger Campaign was probably a victim of its own success when treasury calculated the tax revenues foregone from donations to the campaign.

As a result, one of the major activities of the ACFID executive in those early years was regular lobbying for tax relief, with many meetings and letters (ACFOA 1966a, 1966d, 1969c, 1969d, 1970a; Crawford 1966, 1969; Perkins 1967). In 1966 ACFID met with prime minister Harold Holt to discuss the tax relief issue and presented comprehensive arguments, and there was regular follow up with the government over the following years. The main objection from government was that tax relief was given to enable Australians, through private donations, to either help other Australians through charity work, and thus relieve government of some of the burden, or to provide an incentive to use private services instead of government services (such as health and education), and again relieve government of some burden. This was the so-called 'in Australia test': tax relief was given to Australian organisations for the support of Australians so there was a direct benefit to government in providing tax relief, and there was no cost to government as the opportunity cost of the taxes forgone was more than covered by savings in expenditure. For overseas aid there is no obvious quid pro quo: providing tax relief to the donors to international NGOs to the tax office was a 'haphazard subsidy' with no direct benefit to Australia (*Current Affairs* Bulletin 1967, p. 202).

Another argument that featured in the US was that tax deductibility gives an effective expenditure priority for government spending in which government has no say, as there are no associated appropriations linked to the tax forgone (Whitaker 1974). The paradox was that while these arguments were going on, donations for the work of agencies in PNG were tax deductible as it was regarded at the time as being part of Australia (Hinton 1969). The Labor government of 1972 was no more sympathetic, preferring to provide direct grants to NGOs, which they started to do in 1974, rather than give tax relief to the donors. It was not until 1980 that general tax relief to NGO donations was granted following a one-off tax relief for donations to the Cambodian appeal, which had exceeded all expectations (see Chapter 5).[1]

An aspect of the tax relief debate at the time was the eligibility of donations for global education in Australia, so that Australians through the education system and through community activities were made aware of the issues of poverty

---

1   An interesting aside was that at the time there was a campaign by AFFHC supporters who sent small sums of money to the Treasurer to make up for its contribution for overseas aid the government was so worried about. These donations came back to ACFID and presented a headache as to what to do with them (Solomon 1972c).

and development (see Chapter 3). In the UK there had been a long battle in the 1960s to have global education included as a legitimate activity of NGO use of tax deductible funds under the Charities Act. In 1963 the Charities Commission even suggested development aid itself may not be a 'charitable' act but the UK House of Lords, which supported NGOs, resolved that it was. In 1969 global education came to the attention of the Charities Commission as AWD was seeking to undertake global education as part of a broader consortium under VCOAD. The Charities Commission ruled it ineligible, and so a separate entity was set up to enable this work to occur without a tax exemption (McDonald 1972; Weber 2013).

While overseas aid can be seen as having a public benefit, advocacy was seen in some jurisdictions as having a partisan or sectional benefit, and as such was a direct engagement in political processes. In both the US and the UK in the mid-1970s advocacy for aid policy change was allowable for a tax exemption if it was an adjunct to an NGO's primary purpose (Whitaker 1974; Lissner 1977; Crowson et al. 2012). Canada followed suit in the 2000s (Carter and Man 2011). From 1974 Oxfam gave 5 per cent of its income to global education work (Black 1992). However, NGOs that did not undertake advocacy directly related to development work, such as AWD, had their tax privileges revoked (Hilton 2012). There was a double standard here, as some charities were allowed to advocate for changes to laws, such as those dealing with disability, while those dealing with child poverty or social injustice were not allowable (Lissner 1977, p. 118). Nightingale argued that such legislation invariably has the effect of blackmailing agencies into avoiding policy debate, thus inhibiting their natural development, and so 'imposes alien ways on them [so that] a good charity may *ipso facto* be a worse organisation' (Nightingale 1973, p. 52).

In Australia global education and campaigning had been included as an eligible activity for tax exemption since 1980, when it was introduced for overseas aid activities, until it was questioned by the Howard government in 2007. Under British common law, which has been largely adopted in Australia, the courts have added to the list of purposes which were accepted as charitable over the years.[2] While the argument for tax deductibility for overseas aid can be and has been argued under the relief of poverty, NGO advocacy and policy work could only come under the notion of an 'other purpose beneficial to the community'. In most countries tax deductibility can be used for advancing a

---

2   In 1891 Lord McNaughton, in the Pemsel case, classified these charitable purposes under four 'heads':
   i.   the relief of poverty;
   ii. the advancement of education;
   iii. the advancement of religion; and
   iv. other purposes beneficial to the community
        (Culyer, Wiseman et al. 1976, p. 33; Cordery and Baskerville-Morley 2005).

public benefit rather than a sectional or partisan one. In the UK, the Charities Act more narrowly defined policy advocacy as being part of the political process and so donations for advocacy were ineligible for a tax exemption. The Australian advocacy NGO AidWatch had their tax deductible status revoked in 2007 on the grounds that their policy advocacy was part of the political debate rather than aid as such. This was challenged in the High Court of Australia which ruled that the arguments of the Charities Commissioner in the UK did not apply to Australia due to their differing constitutional arrangements. It then went on to argue that it did meet the charitable purpose of being 'beneficial to the community' (McNaughton's fourth Head) in that 'the generation by lawful means of public debate ... concerning the efficiency of foreign aid directed to the relief of poverty, itself is a purpose beneficial to the community' (High Court of Australia 2010, para. 47). The effect of this decision was that donations used for advocacy and global education could still receive a tax exemption, thus broadening the definition of a charitable purpose (Martin 2011; Turnour 2011; Williams 2012; see also Chapter 3).

Engaging on policy debates

While ACFID had been engaging on broad policy through the regular conferences it ran from 1966 to 1972, the engagement with government did not really gain traction until the work of the Dev Ed Unit outlined in Chapter 3. The newly elected Labor government in 1972 provided new impetus for this engagement as, unlike its predecessor, it was open to dialogue with NGOs. The reasons for engaging with government are complex: at one level influencing aid policy is of itself a good thing and was what Crawford had in mind in 1963 when he first floated the idea of a council of development NGOs. Lissner also argues that engagement with government on aid policy is important to NGOs as it maximises agency 'respectability and leverage' and fulfils the desire 'to be taken seriously' (1977, p. 203). In his drive to establish ACFID in the early 1960s, Crawford was certainly aware of the importance of leverage. The desire, however, for the NGOs to be taken seriously by government on policy matters probably emerged later, and arguably through ACFID's engagement with the Labor government between 1972 and 1974. In the 1970s there had also been some input into the aid policy of the major parties when ACFID had the opportunity, and this bore fruit in that many of the aid initiatives by the Labor government between 1972 and 1975 were driven to some extent by ACFID's agenda. Similarly, ACFID had an input into Liberal Party policy in 1975 (Sullivan 1974b; Sullivan 2013).

Lissner (1977, p. 105) suggests that NGOs, in their relationship with governments, have an 'inferiority complex' due to their perceived relatively weak financial position and organisational power vis-a-vis government. NGOs, however, also had to deal with a perception by government of being 'amateurish, inefficient and lacking in hard-nosed financial and technical competence', with the churches feeling this particularly hard, being missionary-based, 'starry-eyed and pious' (Lissner 1977, p. 108). Even 40 years later, in the 2010s, NGOs still talk of being professional and needing to professionalise, even when its purpose and what it might mean for them is not that clear (Lang 2012; Wright 2012; Martinez and Cooper 2013). The downside is that the 'professionalisation' of NGOs puts them into an 'industrial–bureaucratic mode', which is useful in gaining access to government and intergovernmental forums, but comes with an opportunity cost to the NGOs' capacity to be truly independent and voluntary in character and true to their Weltanschauung, or world view (Lissner 1977; Lang 2012).

Arguments about the quantity of government aid have been ritual for ACFID throughout most of its history. This is particularly during the preparation and handing down of the national budget, with regular analysis and lobbying being an ongoing strategy for the agency. When there are mooted or real aid budget cuts, this lobbying work can become intense as cuts are seldom restored, and certainly not in the short term. The aid budget cuts of 1976, 1986 and 1996 were major issues for ACFID. It was not until after the September 11 terrorist attacks in New York and Washington that the aid budget was restored to nearly the levels (as a proportion of GDP) of the 1970s. In 2013 and 2014 this increase in aid came to a halt when an incoming Coalition government made some sharp cuts and brought the ODA to GDP ratio of aid to the lowest levels ever.[3]

In 1976 the ACFID campaign against aid cuts was broad based and had a great deal of community support, due in part to the work of the ACFID Dev Ed Unit and AWD, which was still very active at the time. The campaign started following a 13 February meeting of ACFID with foreign minister Peacock who flagged cuts in aid, the disbanding of the Aid Advisory Board, and moving AusAID to being an aid bureau within the Department of Foreign Affairs (ACFOA 1976g). The government's view at the time was that aid policy was a function of foreign policy (Viviani and Wilenski 1978), thus sparking an ongoing debate with ACFID. The relationship of aid and foreign policy was also a key question in the three independent aid reviews held over the following 35 years (Jackson Committee 1984; Simons et al. 1997; Hollway et al. 2011). In a one-day consultation with AusAID in 1976, ACFID made it clear that it saw the closing down of AusAID and the cutting of aid as retrogressive, but to no avail (ACFOA 1976a, 1976f). In 2013 history was to repeat itself when AusAID was fully merged with DFAT (a more thorough integration than that of 1976), and a real cut in aid levels was made.

---

3   The ODA/GDP ratio fell from 0.33 to 0.22.

The vigour of the response from the NGOs and the public in 1976 to what was essentially a slowdown in the growth of aid showed the strength of public support for official aid at the time (Barker 1976). The feedback from sympathetic officials was that ACFID had not made enough lobbying noise before the budget. ACFID felt that that might have been counterproductive, but did agree after the cuts were announced that lobbying should have been earlier as a precursor to the campaign (Sullivan 1977b).[4]

In 1985 when there was another sharp round of budget cuts the response from NGOs was somewhat muted despite a campaign launched by ACFID (Rollason 1985). One reason for the poor response by NGOs to the cuts was the quality of aid debate: aid going to regimes with poor human rights records was being criticised, the main example being the aid program in the Philippines being used to support counterinsurgency operations in Mindanao, and propping up the Marcos regime (ACFOA 1982a, 1983e). The other point was the focus of the official aid program, which was on infrastructure with little support for basic human needs and community-based approaches outside of the ANCP. In this environment neither the public nor the NGOs were prepared to run an aid cuts campaign with any enthusiasm (Birch 1985; ACFOA 1985a).

Another reason may have been that the NGOs had received a substantial increase in their funding from AusAID, and perhaps ACFID was reluctant to bite the hand that feeds. From the public interested in aid, there had been a visceral dislike of the Fraser government in 1975 and how it came to power, and perhaps they were reluctant to be too critical of the relatively new Labor government 10 years later. A similarly muted response came from ACFID in 2013, when an incoming Coalition government cut not only against the forward estimates but also within that financial year, followed by another round of deeper cuts a year later. This may also have been to do with a lower level of tolerance by government more generally for vigorous criticism of their policies, both within Australia and globally, which was becoming more evident in the 2010s (Edgar and Lockie 2010; Lang 2012; Gray 2013).

The big policy debates that ACFID engaged in through the early 1980s were about Australia's aid relations with countries that violated their citizens' human rights, namely in South Africa and the Philippines, and also to press for closer relations with countries that were perceived as Cold War enemies, in particular Vietnam and Cambodia. In the case of Vietnam and Cambodia ACFID was particularly scathing of government policy, which tended to support Pol Pot allied groups at the expense of the Vietnamese-backed government in Cambodia

---

4   An ACFID file note recorded that the department was offering a much bigger aid cut, arguing that they could break some existing bilateral agreements, but in the end the aid level achieved was higher than what the department suggested, and no bilateral agreements were broken.

(ACFOA 1979a, 1982, 1984b). Given the genocide by Pol Pot and the Khmer Rouge, ACFID and the aid-supporting public saw this policy position as Cold War cynicism at its worst. Interestingly, in 1985 a small number of Australian NGOs set up a Joint Office in Pnom Penh funded by AusAID and supported by ACFID, which was to be later staffed by a former DFAT officer who also had a role in laying the diplomatic groundwork for bringing Cambodia in from the diplomatic cold and Australia's recognition of Cambodia (ACFOA 1985d; Ashton 1989).[5]

Government funding of NGOs

Government funding of NGOs was a major area of engagement for ACFID and, like its work on tax, it had a direct financial interest for its members. In the 1960s government funding for NGOs in Australia lagged behind its international counterparts and was for one-off activities such as volunteers and emergency relief (Webb 1971; Burnell 1991, p. 209; OECD 1988). In 1963 total NGO funding from the general public was well over £3 million, and not that far short of the £5 million the Australian government gave to its main overseas aid program, the Colombo Plan (Anderson 1964). Even by 1973 there was no systematic government support for NGO programs in Australia, while globally government grants to NGOs were being recognised as a mainstream aid activity (Lissner 1977; OECD 1988). However, in both the UK and Australia, while private aid flows made up more than 10 per cent of the total aid provided from all sources (Cole-King 1976; Lissner 1977), the official funding of NGOs was still tiny, and in Australia a miniscule 0.17 per cent of the aid budget in 1975. This was at a time when the global average of official aid to NGOs was 3 per cent, and Canada was providing 4 per cent of its official aid program through NGOs (Herbert-Copley 1987).

The Labor government in Australia (1972–75) started to change this and put in place a broad funding scheme for NGOs that recognised their contribution to development by providing a matching subsidy for their work. This was to become the Australian NGO Cooperation Program (ANCP), which has continued in its basic form ever since, so that by 2013 the funding of the program had grown to over $100 million. Despite these initiatives it was not until the mid 1980s that official aid to Australian NGOs began to come near the level of other OECD donors.

---

5   Whether it was wise for NGOs to be involved in this sort of diplomatic work, even if it was about ending a conflict, is another matter. It harks back to accusations in the US of the Peace Corps and other NGOs' involvement in foreign policy (McCarthy 2000; DemMars 2001).

The Australian NGO Cooperation Program

The Australian NGO Cooperation Program's genesis was in 1973 when ACFID put a submission to the newly elected Labor government seeking matching grants to NGO-funded work in developing countries. ACFID suggested a set of criteria for demonstrating local participation; and also for ease of administration, that the ANCP fund groups of NGO projects as a country/region or sector program (ACFOA 1973c). In 1974 the submission was updated and called for a committee to assess projects, which came about in 1977 (ACFOA 1974). There were concerns at the time that the proposed subsidy scheme may lead to NGOs' loss of independence in their own work, as they became more dependent on these proposed government subsidies, the implications of which would come back to haunt them in the 1990s (AusAID 1995a; Hunt 1995d). These concerns of too much government funding for NGOs were already in the minds of international counterparts (Lissner 1977), who were to become more vocal in the 1980s and 1990s as government funding of NGOs continued to grow (see Chapter 8). In the mid-1970s ACFID was very clear in its preference for program support rather than government picking and choosing those projects that suited its interests (Harris 1975).

Two of the criteria for entry into the ANCP program were to be an ongoing issue for some NGOs. The first was a quality of aid argument that the funding should be for development work only and that the welfare activities of many agencies such as direct child sponsorship, orphanages and the like should fall outside the scheme. The second was that the evangelical work of missionary agencies should also not be supported. The basis of the argument linked to the tax deductibility debates that the aid program should not be funding welfare in other countries, nor should the government be supporting the religious activities of NGOs. Despite these criteria being made clear from the earliest days of the ANCP (ADAA 1977a, 1977b), in the 2010s these two issues still dog those agencies that want to do their traditional missionary and welfare work and garner either a government subsidy or a tax break for their donors in order to do it (Purcell 2013).[6]

With the advent of the Fraser government in 1975, the ANCP was streamlined and more open processes put in place (ACFOA 1976a). The real problem, however, was that the program was chronically underfunded. For example, in 1976 the ANCP subsidy on offer was $250,000 for $26 million of NGO aid being sent abroad, giving an overall subsidy level of a miserly 1 per cent (ACFOA 1976e). In 1977 there were consultations of 25–30 NGO representatives and government, which the foreign minister opened, to try to sort out the ANCP as well as the volunteer

---

6   This is a regular issue of the CDC and accreditation reviewer workshops the author is involved in.

scheme (Peacock 1977). The main issues raised were how the annual allocations to the ANCP were made so there was equal opportunity among NGOs to access the funds, and developing an option for program funding (Sullivan 1977a). Not surprisingly, some 40 years later these same issues are still being discussed.

The key features of the scheme in the mid-1970s were that half of the NGO funding of a project would be a government subsidy; NGOs that were part of statutory bodies were initially allowed (but later disallowed); the NGO must be identifiably Australian; and there was evidence of the NGO's capacity to undertake the programs. These criteria would be looked at via an agency profile covering the governance of the NGO, evidence of community support, a priority to overseas aid, a track record, and clear links to partners. If the agency was accepted into the program, projects were then appraised against criteria including a focus on self-reliance, the involvement and targeting of women, and social justice (ADAA 1977). In the 2010s, while the process was more rigorous, these remain the key criteria for assessing agencies to participate in the ANCP program.

By 1977 the scheme had a governance body with the rather grand title of the Committee for Development Cooperation (CDC), but with a focus confined to NGO aid only. The committee met four times a year with three representatives each from government and the NGOs. Fifteen NGOs were part of the scheme in 1977, and they put up 45 projects for a limited pool of funds, plus a special allocation of $500,000 for the South Pacific. The funds available remained a problem so that only two thirds of the projects submitted could be funded. This meant that if agencies did not apply at the start of the year, they were not funded (Batt 1977). The 1979 Harries Committee report argued against any further funding of NGOs, contending that the case made by ACFID for NGO funding was very weak (Harries Committee 1979; ACFOA 1978d). Harries' poor view of NGOs may have contributed to the muted response to the appeals to government to increase its funding levels to NGOs.

By 1979 AusAID was working on how to iron out the persistent problems of inadequate funding for the ANCP, and Neville Ross from AusAID, who would later be a Chair of ACFID, was instrumental in building the funding base of NGOs over the following 10 years. Ross had come from the NGO scene and was also associated with churches as a minister of religion in his former life. He saw reform from within AusAID as a way forward and set out to strengthen NGO–government cooperation. One of his first acts was to hold a two-day consultation to have 1 per cent of ODA go through NGOs (Ross 1979). In 1980 this work came to fruition with a one-third increase in the ANCP pool and the granting of tax deductibility for donations to NGOs (Alston 1980c). The result was that the percentage of the official aid program going to NGOs doubled from 0.17 per cent in 1975 to 0.36 per cent, but it was still the lowest among the OECD donors

(ACFOA 1981b). This increase, however, was the first of what was to be a steady series of increases of NGO funding from AusAID over the following decade, and represented a honeymoon period of the relationship of ACFID and its members with AusAID. By 1982 NGO funding had jumped to 1 per cent of ODA, in part boosted by the large grants to NGOs for their work in Cambodia at the time (Guilfoyle 1982); by 1995 grants and subsidies through NGOs reached a peak of 7 per cent of the official aid program (ANAO 1996). The NGOs favoured block grants for their work and, while some progress had been made, the funding model was still administratively clumsy. By 1982, 50 per cent of Canada's NGO programs were block grants, the Netherlands 82 per cent, and UK 71 per cent (OECD 1988, p. 87). In Australia the process was slow and even by the 2010s the focus was to fund only the 10 larger, more capable, agencies through multi-year block grants.

The incoming Labor government of 1983, like its predecessor in 1973, favoured increases in funding for NGOs. It also took advantage of the fact that NGOs were well placed to fund those countries and regions which governments could not fund directly due to the political restrictions of the Cold War. One example of this was in Cambodia where, to some Cold War warriors, the Vietnamese invasion was somehow seen to be worse than the depredations of Pol Pot and the Khmer Rouge (Brown et al. 1996). The way through this impasse was for AusAID to fund the reconstruction of Cambodia through Australian NGOs, which in turn worked with the Vietnamese-backed Cambodian government and provided access to the Cambodian government for informal government contacts. Another example was the case of the Eritrean independence movement, the EPLF, who controlled a large section of Eritrean territory. Likewise, in Ethiopia, a rebel movement was the effective governing body for much of the province of Tigray (De Waal 1997). As the famine of 1984–85 worsened, AusAID was putting larger and larger amounts of famine relief through NGOs which were working in these areas in what were known as 'cross-border' operations (see Chapter 5).

These types of programs were possible because in a Cold War environment the sovereignty of countries that might be considered to be on the 'other side' did not feature as an issue. These efforts were seen as not only humanitarian but also as a step towards the end of these communist regimes. By the 2000s, with end of the Cold War, the West was much more reluctant to publically support similar cross-border operations in places such as Burma (South 2012; Decobert 2013). The growth in official funding of NGOs, however, still remained low in the early 1980s, and the issue ACFID and AusAID faced was how to increase it to match the demand from agencies so it was at a similar level to other donor countries.

In 1984 the Jackson Committee report into aid funding called for an immediate doubling of aid to NGOs 'with further rises to depend on increased public support and better administrative capacity' (1984, p. 12). This resulted in an increase of funding not only through the existing ANCP but also through new mechanisms such as the bilateral NGO (BiNGO) scheme and the Women and Development fund, which was mainly directed through NGOs (Jackson Committee 1984; ACFOA 1984a). The push to have NGOs more closely involved in bilateral aid work was also strong given the criticisms made of infrastructure projects and integrated rural development projects at the time (Porter et al. 1991). The approach was to have much bigger projects directly funded from country programs within AusAID (Bartsch 1982). The basic rationale was that as government could not do the community development side of large bilateral projects they would support NGOs to do it instead. What emerged was that AusAID was engaging NGOs in an ad hoc manner to ameliorate the worst effects of its bilateral projects and thus providing a further expansion of funding to NGOs, which prompted debates on NGO aid effectiveness and quality.

Quality of aid

The aid quality debates about government aid prompted ACFID to make sure its own house was in order, so in 1985 it set up a Development Project Appraisal and Evaluation Unit to look at the quality of NGO programs and prepared resources and training for NGOs to use for better aid programming. This was a way for ACFID to engage with AusAID on the quality of aid debates in the 1980s, which have continued ever since (ACFOA 1985a). The ANCP was also adapted to promote quality NGO projects and encourage NGO funding to the least developed countries in the Pacific.[7] It seemed that NGOs were being supported by governments for a plethora of responses ranging from emergency relief to bailing out failed bilateral projects. Despite the NGO rhetoric, however, for some sceptics there seemed to be little hard evidence that NGO projects were any better than bilateral or multilateral ones (Najam 1998).

ACFID had been working on demonstrating the effectiveness of NGO programs since the mid-1980s (ACFOA 1984d, 1986a, 1987b). Despite these moves by ACFID and others to improve NGO aid quality, by the 1990s there was a questioning of the effectiveness of NGOs, and the idea that perhaps government had put too many eggs into the NGO basket, in part based on exaggerated claims by the NGOs themselves as to their effectiveness (Edwards and Hulme 1995). As Herbert-Copley (1987) put it at the time: 'The point is not that NGOs are ineffective, but rather that exaggerated and unsubstantiated claims to effectiveness may in the long run do more harm than good' (p. 26). Doug Hellinger may have

---

7   For these 'quality' projects 20 per cent of the ANCP pool would go to these quality and geographic criteria on the basis of a 75 per cent subsidy compared to the prevailing 50 per cent matching grant for the general ANCP (ACFOA 1983f).

been prescient in 1987 when he wrote: 'Within a few years it is probable that the decade of NGOs will be declared over, and perhaps a failure, and a new development fad will take its place' (p. 142).

Picking up from Lissner's work of the mid-1970s, there was an emerging group of NGO critics who felt that NGOs were being co-opted to a government agenda. This was also bringing their developing country partners into the loop: 'Southern NGDOS tended to emulate their northern "partners" and often be more intimately linked to the aid system than to the wider society' (Fowler 2000, p. 640). Bebbington (2005) talks about how this process occurred with a Dutch co-financing scheme leading

> to a certain depoliticization of poverty, in which poverty discussions are increasingly separated from questions of distribution and social transformation, and in which poverty reduction becomes something sought through projects rather than political change (p. 940).

The phrase 'engaging with civil society' was to dominate the government NGO discourse, when of course what was really intended was a closer engagement of NGOs and community groups with the broader government agenda. Some of this was about democratisation and some was about the privatisation of services within the emerging neoliberal agenda of the 1980s (Clark 1992; Fowler 1992; Edwards and Hulme 1997; Fowler 2000). Through the work of the Dev Ed Unit, ACFID was in the 1970s at the forefront of the criticism of official aid programs and the neocolonial agenda it seemed to represent. By 1990 there was not much ACFID felt it could say or do about the prevailing aid philosophy beyond noting that global education was 'less doctrinaire' than in the past (Mavor 1993a, p. 2). This seemed to suggest that either the fight had gone out of ACFID or more likely that fighting was counterproductive.

The argument NGOs put to the aid quality debate, and what they offered that was different, was the 'value added' argument of being better able to reach the poor and provide a safety net for the prevailing neoliberal economic models. These tensions were felt more sharply in developing countries where local NGOs and social movements had fundamental objections to the direction aid and development was going, which also spilled over to their NGO donors in developed countries, which were increasingly becoming involved in government projects. This prompted critics to question the added value:

> Having set NGOs up to be sources of development alternatives, researchers soon adopted a more critical view as it became clearer that NGOs were actually not that good at promoting participation, addressing poverty, understanding the needs of the poor or – therefore – doing much that was especially alternative (Bebbington 2005, p. 937).

The real issue, however, was one of scale, driven by an assumption that if you did something on a small scale you could do it on a larger scale. Of course, when this was found to be not possible the questions of NGO effectiveness, or rather their usefulness in larger bilateral programs, began to emerge (Atack 1999). This led to governments in the 1990s reducing their engagement with NGOs, a theme that will be picked up in Chapter 8.

Conclusion

The history of the engagement of government with NGOs had its origins in the first Development Decade of the 1960s, when aid as development assistance was more formally institutionalised in the donor community following the decolonisation period of the 1950s. NGOs were seen as an important part of this process by the UN as early as 1963, and this was slowly picked up by donor governments over the next 10 years, with Australia being somewhat slower than most (UNGA 1963a). These initiatives prompted the formation of ACFID, with a positive relationship with government being part of the 'DNA' of ACFID. After a slow start through the 1970s the Australian government's relations with ACFID and NGOs blossomed through the 1980s with rapid increases of funding and an expanded architecture for funding Australian NGOs. While this mirrored global trends at the time, by the late 1980s there was a questioning of the closeness that NGOs had with government, with suggestions from government that NGOs were not delivering what they promised

What these debates did was to provide ammunition to sometimes sceptical governments that NGOs were too dependent on government funding and that the ODA largesse should be reined in. There was also a practical reason: NGO programs from a donor perspective are expensive to administer as the activities are generally much smaller than the multimillion dollar bilateral projects or the tens of millions dollar tranches to multilateral agencies that are the bread and butter of aid programs. These issues will be explored further in Chapter 8.

08

Dealing with Changing Government Priorities

Almost by definition NGO relations with government are fraught. On the one hand, NGOs believe that through their supporter base, values, and on the ground experiences they can advise governments on how they might run their aid programs. On the other hand, governments feel that they should get something back in return for the funding and tax breaks they provide to NGOs; and in particular by having 'the hand that feeds' not being bitten through NGOs' public criticism of government policy. Chapter 7 has spelt out the positive relationship that ACFID, and the NGO community more broadly, had with government through the 1980s. There was a high level of funding and cooperation in dealing with some of the complex humanitarian policy issues of the time. In the 1990s this was to change, with an international questioning of NGOs' role and usefulness in official aid programs. This did not mean that ACFID was beset with the broader structural problems which affected its work as happened in the late 1970s (See Chapter 1), nor did this questioning have any radical effect on its budget, such as happened to ACFID's counterparts in Canada and New Zealand in the 2010s. The questioning of NGOs did affect, however, ACFID's relationship with government in a number of key ways, and influenced the way ACFID worked in the 2000s.

The tension that these changes resulted in has to be managed and exhibits itself in a number of ways, ranging from the inevitable patron–client relationship that funding brings to the sometimes hostile relations that arise from differences in political ideologies between government and NGOs. Admittedly, ideological differences do not surface very often, or at least not enough to seriously affect relationships, but when they do NGOs often have difficulty in both understanding and managing these differences. This may have something to do with what Gaye Hart, a former president of ACFID, refers to as the 'sense of entitlement' among NGOs, or what Ian Smillie refers to (of some NGOs) as 'cloying paternalism and self-righteousness' (1995, p. 176). This sense of 'self-righteousness' comes from NGOs' values and work, and is something that governments and others outside the NGO orbit have trouble either understanding or accepting. Critics of NGOs, such as the Australian conservative think tank the Institute of Public

Affairs (IPA), deny any real legitimacy for NGOs, seeing them merely as another (self) interest group, and seriously question the relevance and effectiveness of NGOs' work, particularly their advocacy work (Johns 2000).

The period from the early 1990s to the end of the Howard government in 2007 was such a time for ACFID and its members, when their credibility and legitimacy were frequently questioned by government and at times by the media. This general scepticism started when government picked up on the international questioning by academics and others in the early 1990s of the legitimacy of NGOs and their perceived dependency on government funding. This was used against ACFID in the context of an NGO 'scandal' at the time (albeit involving a non-ACFID member).[1] Later in the 1990s, ACFID was challenged with what it saw as an anti-NGO stance of the Coalition government of the day. These differences are also invariably tinged with the personal proclivities and prejudices that individual politicians, bureaucrats and NGO staff bring to the table. ACFID came through this period, in which tough and robust politics were played, a little scarred but with its values still in place. Most importantly, the everyday work ACFID undertakes with its members, policy dialogue with government, and its broader representative role in a number of fora were largely unaffected and continued on in much the same way as they had before.

The 1990s: A period of questioning

The 1990s was a time when many in government and academia felt that NGOs had overstretched and oversold themselves in the previous decade. The early to mid-1980s saw NGOs bringing a new hope and vision to development practice, and with it a rapid increase in government funding in most Western countries to be 'the decade of NGOs' (Hellinger 1987, p. 142) or 'the Golden Age of NGOs' (Agg 2006). The growing popularity of using NGOs by the state was not necessarily always in the NGOs' interests, and there was the risk that 'engaging with the state and market would deprive [NGOs] of their autonomy and agency and thereby undermine their public legitimacy' (Miller et al. 2013, p. 137). The 1980s and 1990s were also the time of neoliberal social, economic, and development policies when centre-right governments were seeking to offload state responsibility to NGOs, and centre-left governments were exerting greater control over state/civil society interactions. In the 1990s the experiences in countries like Australia, the UK and Canada were similar, but these changes occurred at different times according to the political cycle (Smillie 1999c).[2]

---

1   A series of issues came up involving CARE Australia which are covered later in the Chapter.
2   In Canada and the UK it was a shift from centre right to centre left in 1993 and 1997 respectively, while for Australia it was the reverse in 1996.

By the mid-1990s the enthusiasm for NGO funding by donor governments was beginning to wane, and difficult questions were being asked by government critics whether the money was well spent, and by the more activist NGO supporters, whether increased government funding meant that NGOs' relations with government were getting too 'close for comfort' (Edwards and Hulme 1997; Smillie 1999a). From the NGO side there were also questions of the homogenisation of NGO practice brought about by government funding and its associated rules, and by globalisation (including of NGOs) more generally:

> It would appear that NGDOs are about to succumb to the homogenising forces of economic globalisation in favour of a market-inspired model of NGDO identity and behaviour. Such a model gives highest merit to values of individualism, competition, extraction, accumulation, exploitation and rivalry as the normative mode for relations between people and between people and nature ... undermining virtuous values such as trust, reciprocity, mutuality, co-operation and tolerance of difference (Fowler 2000, p. 644).

The argument that NGOs were heading down a corporate model of behaviour, while present in some NGO practices, was fairly weak overall as most business models were generally seen to be at odds with NGO values. There was, nevertheless, pressure to conform to quasi-business approaches (Lang 2012; Miller et al. 2013; Smillie 1999b). At the same time the argument of NGO 'dependency' on government funding arose almost as a mantra with little evidence to support it (Van der Heijden 1987, p. 103). In Australia NGO funding never reached any more than 8 per cent of the aid budget, and overall government funding to NGOs rose to a little over one third of their total income in the early 1990s (Smillie 1999b; AusAID 1995b; ANAO 1996).

Nikolova (2014) argues, however, that when government funding reaches around one third of an NGO's total, there can be a 'crowding out' effect on their public fundraising. The extent to which this effect occurred in Australia is unclear but it may explain the relatively flat level of fundraising from the public in the 1980s (Kilby 2014). While some agencies had large government contracts and received over half of their funding from the government, that level of funding never threatened the survival of those NGOs. And while NGOs did close their doors in the 1990s and 2000s, the loss of government funding was never a reason. Any dependency argument (in a survival sense) was fairly weak, but this is not to say 'sweating' on government contracts did not lead NGO managers and CEOs to have sleepless nights. The real issue that NGOs still have to deal with is relatively short funding time frames (usually three years) and the inflexibility of funding rules, which effectively imposes a cost on NGOs (Smillie 1999a).

The reason for the growth in the size and number of NGOs in the 1980s and 1990s was not as one-dimensional as some of the discussion at the time suggested, and went well beyond government funding. Charnovitz (1997) argues that the key reasons for the rise of development NGOs at the time were varied: they were to do with the growth of intergovernmental negotiations on domestic policy, which NGOs were asked to be part of; the end of the Cold War and an associated spread of democratic norms; globalised media and the much faster news cycles, which enabled messages to go out much faster than hitherto possible; and, finally, the resurgence of religious identities and the associated support they received from their compatriots in wealthier societies.

A report for the OECD on the changing NGO relations with OECD donors undertaken by Ian Smillie and others (1999) pointed to a complex set of factors not only driving the expansion of NGO work but also the NGO response to government funding. NGOs were seen to either succumb to the new global norms of managerialism – to do with strategic plans, key performance indicators and the like, often at the expense of flexibility, local control, and responsiveness – or they remained marginalised in what was rapidly becoming a more corporate environment with its 'explosive demand for documentation' (Mawdsley et al. 2005, p. 78). The other issue was the contracting culture of government whereby NGOs were seen to be public service contractors often at the expense of their values and mission (Smillie 1995, 1999b; Atack 1999; Najam 2000; Lang 2012). This was a growing phenomenon in the 1980s whereby, on top of receiving the block grant or subsidy from government to support NGOs' own work, NGOs were also bidding for and winning government contracts in their own right. Such NGO contracting was common in the US, Canada, Italy and Switzerland. For example, Swiss NGOs raised only 14 per cent of their income from the public in the mid-1990s with the rest coming from government contracts (Smillie 1995, p. 171).

The big concern with this shift to government contracting was whether NGO values were compromised when '[they] were being asked to provide Band-Aids to cover up deep wounds' at the expense of dealing with deeper structural issues (Smillie 1995, p. 173). The other side of the dependency argument was that the largesse from foreign donors led to local NGOs in developing countries crowding out the state to the point where NGOs were becoming a major, if not the major, provider of services such as health and education in countries like Bangladesh. In the dominant neoliberal policy framework of the 1990s, service provision in developing countries was being 'privatised' to NGOs through official donor funding (Smillie 1995; Besley and Ghatak 1999; Clark 1995; Wright 2012; Cumming 2013). NGOs saw an advantage in this role as Miller at al. (2013) argue: 'NGOs are more likely to have influence in invited spaces [as] their legitimacy is based on their expertise and the dependence of the state on their role in delivery' (p. 147).

The ACFID 25th anniversary conference of 1990, 'Through the Looking Glass – Australian NGOs and Third World Development' (ACFOA 1990a), recognised the influence and importance of these rapid changes then in train, the challenges they represented and, to some extent, the problems they foreshadowed for NGOs and ACFID that were to emerge over the following 15 years. As Doug Porter put it at the time:

> one tends to conclude the issue [of NGO effectiveness] has less to do with how NGOs can enhance local institutional capacity than how donor NGOs can limit the disruptive effects of [their] existing activities. What emerges is a growing hostility from NGO partners to the project approach and the bargaining relationships inadvertently caused by their offers of aid … NGOs risk being captured by their own rhetoric … [To overcome this] NGOs should remain at the margins, but not be marginal (Porter in ACFOA 1990a, p. 4).

This 'growing hostility' or, more correctly, tensions around demands from the international NGOs' own government donors, which their NGO partners in the Third World were having to deal with, was to be an ongoing issue for ACFID and its members. It was about who was setting the agenda, especially as the larger NGOs became more globalised and 'corporate' in their structures (Cumming 2013). In this context it probably was impossible to meet Porter's call for NGOs to remain at the margins without becoming marginal. ACFID needed to be at the centre of the policy debate, where it was a leader, but invariably the politics of funding got in the way.

A couple of trends were emerging: on the one hand, the argument was that NGOs were too close to government and beholden to them in terms of funding and, by extension, beholden to their policies and 'new managerial' practices as well; on the other hand, the corporate pressures on NGOs led them to globalise and be part of international networks and so lose touch with their local activist and Third World partner base regardless of government funding (Ensor 2013). There were also questions of NGO effectiveness, with some research suggesting that NGOs were no better than government at similar resource levels, with their effectiveness being in specific 'niche' areas but not more broadly; and while they did reduce poverty in the areas they worked it was not significant in the larger scheme of things (Agg 2006, p. 5). This finding was fairly unremarkable and what would be expected of NGOs, but maybe it also pointed to the fact that NGOs oversold themselves in what they could do, rather than not being effective in what they actually did (Smillie 1999a).

As NGOs were still taking what was seen as a largish chunk of the official aid program in the early 1990s, governments felt obliged to question NGO effectiveness in spending that money. As many indicators of effectiveness could be contested and expensive to measure, one approach was to develop much tighter processes and contractual arrangements in which project outputs and 'tangible' outcomes were more clearly identified and enumerated in advance, and so there were fewer block grants available to enable NGOs (and their partners) to make their own decisions on how the funds should be spent. There was also a prevailing belief that good design was at the heart of a good project (AusAID 2000), despite ACFID's obvious rejoinder that responding to the (ever changing) local context may also have something to do with the success of projects.

The 1990s marked the beginning of what might be referred to as the 'instrumentalising' of aid, where context seemed to be forgotten in favour of simplistic frameworks being applied to complex social and political environments (Smillie 1999b). This approach was to continue, more or less, for the following 20 years based on what would seem to be a couple of rather odd premises: first, people were the objects of development rather than subjects and, second, what worked in one place or context should work anywhere. While this was the approach of the failed integrated development projects of the late 1970s and early 1980s, the official view was that these projects were too complex and poorly designed rather than that they were trying to apply common approaches across different contexts, which simply would not work (Porter et al. 1991).

ACFID in the 1990s

In the 1990s, after the rapid changes that ACFID and its members went through in the 1980s in response to the increased demands on it at the time, it had the challenge of maintaining and building its constituency after the success of NGOs acquiring government funding in the 1980s. A feeling emerged among some NGOs that they could do without ACFID, and this was to some extent exemplified by the failure of IDEC (Smillie 1999b; see Chapter 5). There was also a new player on the block who also thought they could do without ACFID. CARE Australia, in one way or another, was to dominate NGO policy and to some extent NGO politics through much of the 1990s, particularly between 1993 and 1996 when Gordon Bilney was the minister for Development Cooperation and Pacific Island Affairs in the Keating Labor government. This also coincided with key changes in AusAID as Philip Flood, a career diplomat, became director general of AusAID in early 1993, and in 1996 became secretary of the Department of Foreign Affairs and Trade. He, like Bilney, brought a natural scepticism towards NGOs, which quickly permeated AusAID. In hindsight, 1993 was a 'perfect storm' for ACFID: there was a new minister and a new director general of AusAID, neither of whom were naturally sympathetic to NGOs, and a major NGO 'scandal' was brewing which had implications for all NGOs.

The events surrounding CARE Australia were probably only a catalyst as the changes in relationships between ACFID and government would probably have occurred anyway, such was the mood of government to NGOs at the time, and not only in Australia (Smillie 1999b). CARE Australia was established in 1987 as a member of CARE International. It sought to quickly establish a strong Australian presence under the leadership of the former Coalition prime minister Malcolm Fraser as chair of the board. CARE, like World Vision 20 years earlier, decided to go it alone and not be a member of ACFID, as CARE Australia did not agree with some of ACFID's advocacy and policies. With that, however, they were also not party to the Code of Ethics which had become mandatory for all members since 1989 (see Chapter 9). Even though CARE Australia was not a member of ACFID, a number of public incidents affecting CARE Australia resulted in collateral damage to ACFID and its members. The first of these was the very public resignation from the CARE board in 1991 of Clyde Cameron, a former Whitlam government minister over what he saw as excessive salaries and perks enjoyed by CARE management (Egan 1991). The second was questions by the auditor-general of CARE's handling of food aid in the late 1980s and into the 1990s (Auditor-General 1993). The government was slow to respond, in part because CARE was not critical of government in the same way ACFID and other NGOs were, and because Malcolm Fraser, a former prime minister, was chair of CARE (Rollason 2013). ACFID rather presciently observed that a 'scandal involving CARE had major implications for aid, the government, and NGOs' and briefed minister Bilney to that effect in 1992 (ACFOA 1992c). In 1993 the delayed reporting to AusAID of a theft of a substantial amount of Australian government funded food aid from a warehouse in Mozambique brought matters to a head, causing further tensions and ongoing calls for CARE to join ACFID and be party to the Code (Bilney 1994; Mavor 1993b; ACFOA 1994d).

The 1993 auditor-general's report prompted not only reviews of CARE's reporting, but also AusAID's extended it to all NGOs reports, with Bilney accusing NGOs of not reporting on or acquitting AusAID funds, citing 415 reports from 61 NGOs dating back to 1985 not being recorded as received (Bilney 1993). Of course the idea that AusAID failed to process most of these reports was not considered or acknowledged, and the NGOs had to wear the opprobrium and resubmit hundreds of reports.[3] This incident together with growing AusAID antipathy to ACFID led to a worsening of relations (Rollason 1993) so that by 1994 ACFID's own performance as a peak body was being questioned (Russell 1994). If this was not enough, in 1994 a disgruntled former CARE staff person accused CARE

---

3   At the time, the author was given the task of resubmitting very many such reports for Oxfam.

of extravagant wastage and inflating food aid prices purchased with government funds in order to cover its overheads (Broughton 1994). This story culminated in a major television exposé and public controversy in February 1995 (Vincent 1995; Smillie 1999b). These events put ACFID in a difficult position of having to manage the fallout over an agency which was not a member when Bilney began querying the standards and effectiveness of NGOs more generally. All of this put the spotlight further on the probity of NGOs (Thornton 1996; Cohn 1995; Millar et al. 2004) and had a 'profound effect on the relationship between the government of Australia and the Australian NGO community' (Smillie 1999b, p. 42).

As a result of ACFID's poor relationship with government and the fact that CARE was not a signatory to it, the existing ACFID Code of Ethics was largely ignored and, by implication, seen to be ineffective. In 1995 Bilney set up a new a committee, with parliamentary oversight and a minority NGO membership, to develop a code of conduct for NGOs, which was to be administered and run by AusAID. While the NGOs provided important input into the development of the Code they fought hard for it to be administered from ACFID, and after many months of argument ACFID finally won the day and kept control of it (see Chapter 9). The Code was to represent a sea change for ACFID and its work, shaping it and giving it direction for the next 20 years (Tupper 2012). CARE joined ACFID and signed up to the code in 1996 and, as a member, ACFID backed CARE and its work, including in 1999 when CARE Australia staff were imprisoned in Serbia (Eggleton 1996; ACFOA 1996b). The lesson from this and other cases demonstrates a point that McCarthy raises, which has also affected ACFID in other contexts:

> bad practices by one organisation can tarnish the image of all. In the environment in which NGOs often function, there is no room for hairsplitting or rationalisation. In that environment, a tarnished image can threaten the work of organisations and the safety of [their] workers (2000, p. 10).

This experience with AusAID in the mid-1990s affected the relationship NGOs had with government, and ACFID at times had to fight to have its voice heard and its funding secured. ACFID, however, still provided important input and policy advice and even leadership in key development issues of the time, including gender, HIV/AIDS, environment and development, and human rights, and was part of government delegations to the major global conferences of the 1990s.[4] ACFID continued to have access to the minister and provided input to Treasury in its role as representing Australia on the board of the IMF and World Bank, and to DFAT on human rights issues.

---

4   Rio Earth Summit of 1992; Vienna Human Rights Conference 1993; Beijing Women's Conference 1995; and the Copenhagen World Summit for Social Development 1995.

In late 1994, at the height of the CARE issue, AusAID questioned ACFID about its own performance as an agency and what it saw as the large number of agencies outside of ACFID – Red Cross, CARE, and Fred Hollows Foundation being the main ones – and all for quite different reasons (Rollason 2013). AusAID suggested reducing the subsidy it provided to support the ACFID secretariat from a ratio of around twice the level of member contributions to equal contributions from both ACFID members and AusAID (Russell 1994; Terrell 1994). In the end the agreement was that over the life of the four-year agreement the AusAID contribution would fall from 1.9 to 1.5 times the member contributions, with the AusAID grant being capped at $500,000. By the 2000s the AusAID contribution was less than half of ACFID's running costs, which was probably wise given the effects on CCIC (Canada) and CID (New Zealand) of sudden funding cuts to their core operations by their respective governments.

The other key event at the time was the NGO Effectiveness Review undertaken in 1994, with the final report being released in 1995 questioning NGOs' 'dependency' on AusAID funds (AusAID 1995a; ANAO 1996). The project assessment part of the review was very rigorous, sampling 10 per cent of the projects funded under the ANCP to NGOs over five years, and testing them on a number of dimensions, including effectiveness, gender inclusion, meeting objectives, and sustainability. Overall the review found that NGOs were very effective in their work (with gender being the notable exception), a finding supported by some international studies (Riddell 2007) but not others, for example a UNRISD report which found NGOs not particularly effective (Agg 2006).

In what ACFID called a 'perplexing' argument, the AusAID report also found that based on its review of international literature Australian NGOs were probably too close to government and should be less 'dependent' on it for their funding despite the high level of effectiveness of their work and the relatively low levels of government funding (ACFOA 1995d; AusAID 1995a). The review seemed to be saying that on the one hand there was clear evidence of the strength and success of the ANCP, while on the other hand suggesting that support to NGOs should be wound back. This scepticism by government of NGO work was also evident in an Australian National Audit Office (ANAO) report of AusAID's administration of NGOs programs the following year, which seemed to ignore the findings of the Effectiveness Review and picked up only on prevailing international views:

> there is an absence of a large body of reliable evidence on the impact and effectiveness of NGOs [and] … increasing evidence that NGOs do not perform as effectively as had been assumed in terms of poverty-reach, cost-effectiveness, sustainability, popular participation (including gender), flexibility and innovation (ANAO 1996, p. 2.19).

The ANAO obviously did not see the Effectiveness Review as constituting 'reliable evidence'. The effect of these adverse, or at best 'damned by faint praise', government reports was to put ACFID on the back foot, having to constantly defend its, and its members', legitimacy. The ANAO report also presented a difficulty for AusAID as it was roundly criticised by the ANAO in its management of NGO programs. The solution, for which AusAID sought help from ACFID, was that in addition to the Code of Conduct, a more formal accreditation process was to be put in place for all Australian NGOs wishing to receive AusAID funding (Hunt 2012). This accreditation process was to be administered by the existing CDC that oversaw AusAID's ANCP, and which already had quality assurance mechanisms through regular agency peer reviews, field visits, and evaluations, but without a formal accreditation attached to it (ACFOA 1997b; Hunt 2012). The accreditation process for NGOs was probably the most useful outcome of what, to many, was an unfortunate period.[5]

The Howard government

In March 1996 the Coalition government led by prime minister John Howard was elected. One of its first acts was to have a review of the overseas aid program. While the review recommended a greater focus on economic growth overall, it recommended a 'business as usual' approach with regard to NGOs (Simons 1997). This, however, was not the end of pressure on ACFID and the Australian NGOs, as the Howard government picked up on the ideological hostility to NGOs from some parts of the media, conservative politicians, and right-wing think tanks. This hostility was driven in part by the popularity of public choice theory with right-wing think tanks in their battles with the social democratic and liberal ideologies that were generally supportive of NGOs.

Public choice theory argued that while NGOs saw themselves as being public benefit organisations, as posited by Lissner (1977) and others (Kilby 2011; Salamon et al 1996; Staples 2012), they were in fact self-interested organisations seeking rents from government through the aid dollar (Johns 2000, 2003). The theory questions the existence, or at least the extent, of altruistic values and the promotion of a public benefit as the basis for the behaviour of NGOs. Its central argument is that self-interest is the driver of NGOs and their supporters (Staples 2007; Lissner 1977) who justify their actions by 'idealizing NGOs' (Williamson 2010, p. 23).

---

5   The other major outcome, the Code of Conduct, was arguably an expansion of what was already in place (see Chapter 9).

> Public choice economists make the … assumption − that although people acting in the political marketplace have some concern for others, their main motive, whether they are voters, politicians, lobbyists, or bureaucrats, is self-interest (Shaw 2002, p. 1).

Of course this theory hinges on the value systems of individuals and the extent to which they see a public interest as a greater good. Schroeder argues that 'individuals whose value system ranks [altruistic] values will be inclined to approach regulatory decisions differently, giving greater priority to other [non self-interest] values' (2010, p. 24.) When two completely different world views − one about self-interest and the other about a public interest − clash then it is hard to have a reasoned or reasonable debate, as the respective starting points (of the debate) are so different.

The public choice theorists also picked up on the arguments of the early 1990s that NGOs were not effective, and then provided an ideological underpinning of self-interest to argue for conditional relationships between NGOs and government (Williamson 2010). The conditions for government support of NGOs, according to these theorists, should be that if NGOs sign up to certain government programs they should acknowledge and adhere to the values inherent in that government program and even the values/policies of the government more broadly, even if the NGO's own values may be in conflict with them (Wright et al. 2011). The effect of these moves was that the whole notion of rights and entitlements of aid recipients, once thought settled, was again reopened. 'Accompanying the associated turn in politics has been a steady series of developments in policy, pulling back from entitlements based on rights, and moving towards programmes of obligation and conditionality' (Wright et al. 2011, p. 304).

AusAID tried to move its relationship with NGOs along the path pushed by public choice advocates through the early 2000s, and at one point tried to have a clause inserted in the Umbrella Contract with NGOs that signatories support AusAID policy, but this was quickly dropped when some of the major NGOs threatened to withdraw from the AusAID funding schemes (I. Davies 2012). Of course the point of much, if not most, NGO advocacy is to remind governments of people's rights and entitlements and seek to change policy. While there is lobbying for more NGO funding, much of global education and campaigning has been about policy change.

In Australia the right-wing think tank the IPA entered the fray. It was led by former Labor politician Gary Johns who argued:

> The surest way to maintain an open contest for influence on collective decision-making is for Government never to confer the mantle of public

authority on non-government organizations … [but] governments furnish access and resources to NGOs. In so doing, governments lend NGOs an authority beyond their actual legitimate claim (Johns 2000, p. 2).

This was a hard argument for the IPA to maintain as the NGOs and ACFID arguably had more influence, particularly with the Whitlam Labor government in the 1970s when they had little or no government funding. ACFID was rather more interested in the contest of ideas to improve policy for the benefit of aid recipients.[6]

Internationally the attacks on NGOs, particularly development NGOs, continued with the main players being the right-wing think tank the American Enterprise Institute and its *NGO Watch* website, which regularly reported on the work of NGOs.[7] *NGO Watch* had its origins in a 2003 conference, 'Non-governmental Organizations: The Growing Power of an Unelected Few', held at the American Enterprise Institute's offices in Washington but sponsored by the IPA in Australia (Jordan 2005; Kilby 2004; Hortsch 2010). The argument to emerge from that gathering was that participatory democracy has been at the expense of representative democracy. Gary Johns from the IPA argued that while NGOs may perform a useful role in non-democratic states, in democracies they can undermine the role of government and reduce or supplant the interest of the citizen with the interests of the NGO (Johns 2003). What was interesting is that none of the speakers at this conference chose to examine the role of corporate interests, corporate interest NGOs, and their advocacy with government by way of comparison (Kilby 2004).

What was also overlooked in these debates is that advocacy often comes from grassroots groups in poor countries, so there is a three-way tension: on the one hand the international NGO may want moderate change on an issue (Nelson 1997; Jordan 2005), while on the other the local groups may want international NGO support for something more radical, without necessarily understanding the delicate political relationship international NGOs may find themselves in:

> Because the ebb and flow of a successful campaign must match the rhythm of the political process, it often appears that trade-offs must be made, at least in the short term, between policy gains and strengthening grass roots associations. Lobbying actions sometimes can't wait for

---

6   The IPA is itself an NGO, albeit with diametrically opposed values, but had no public disclosure of its funding sources at all and, despite its claims, even took government contracts during that period (Tupper 2012).

7   *NGO Watch* was not very successful as any adverse reports they published tended to be trivial, and so it effectively provided a new audience for NGO arguments.

slower-paced grass roots education and participation efforts. Sometimes, the strategies preferred by the grass roots frame the issues so that they are hard to win (Covey 1995, p. 865).

The Howard government was very quick to pick up some of the principles of public choice theory and often referred to the NGO sector as 'single-issue groups', 'special interests' and 'elites', and Howard promised that his government would 'be accountable only to the Australian people' (Staples 2007, p. 4). It was as if these groups were somehow not made up of Australian people or did not represent them. The result was that the relationship with advocacy NGOs, particularly peak bodies across the country, soured so that by 2002 around two thirds of the national peak bodies were reporting tense relationships with government. Many had either lost their grants entirely, particularly in the environment sector, or they were severely cut back (Melville and Perkins 2003). Globally, the terrorist attacks of 11 September 2001 in Washington and New York provided more argument for a stronger centralised state and more controls on civil society organisations and NGOs, and as a result global funding to developing country advocacy NGOs was cut sharply (Parks 2008; Howell et al. 2008). At the same time NGO regulation through legislation such as the Patriot Act in the US and anti-terrorist legislation in other countries, including Australia, made it hard to operate in many countries, in particular those of the Middle East.

For ACFID, the late 1990s and early 2000s were difficult times with continual threats to both its funding and its advocacy positions. Internally, there were moves by a few agencies for ACFID to be split, with the larger agencies forming a separate grouping, an idea that had been first raised in the early 1990s (Smillie 1999b). There were some meetings about this but wiser heads saw the dangers of 'divide and rule' which the government had done with other national peak bodies, and ACFID remained to grow its membership over the following 10 years (Hunt 2012; Hobbs 2013). In the 1999 AusAID funding agreement with ACFID all mention of advocacy and global education was gone, with the focus being on a series of service functions for AusAID.

Effectively, ACFID's funding was split between member funding and AusAID funding with different purposes for each. AusAID was no longer funding into the core budget of ACFID as such, with the AusAID contract being of a performance-based purchaser–provider type (AusAID 1999). This led to changes in the policy and practice of the 'provider' to reflect the priorities of the 'purchaser', in this case AusAID: 'The coercive isomorphic pressures that encourage the adoption of specific policies and practices by a provider can lead to unwanted external scrutiny and interference in its internal processes and policies' (Cunningham 2010, p. 194). This occurs even if some of the funding is not only from government. While the activities can be quarantined the internal scrutiny of an agency by government may not be able make this distinction, and so agencies like ACFID are cautious in how they use non-government funding also.

The purchaser–provider arrangement is consistent with public choice theory '[which] concentrates government control over service delivery undertaken in non-state locations' (Wright et al. 2011, p. 300). The effect of constraining ACFID's public policy work was boosted by a much higher level of scrutiny by the foreign minister, which highlighted the inherent difficulty of arguing that separate funding sources could be used to justify ACFID's public stance on the public policy debates of the time. There was close scrutiny for overtly 'political content' in ACFID activities funded by AusAID (Ronalds 2010). For example, foreign minister Downer criticised ACFID's comments on West Papua and the World Trade Organization, suggesting they reflected political rather than humanitarian agendas (Downer 2000, 1999; Tupper 2000); and Sir Ronald Wilson's comments on Indigenous issues in the late 1990s were incorrectly linked in the press to his role as chair of ACFID and its government grant (Montgomery 2000). Despite this Graham Tupper, the executive director through much of this period, said that these pressures had little effect on ACFID's advocacy work at the time (Tupper 2012). Under Janet Hunt ACFID had already begun to wean itself off the high proportion of government funding so it could keep its independent voice and be relatively well insulated from arbitrary government cuts (Hunt 2012).

An issue that brought the relationship of ACFID and AusAID to a head was the seemingly trivial one of ACFID making a submission to the regular DAC's review of the Australian aid program (DAC 2005). This regular review happens to all DAC member countries, roughly every four years, and the process usually includes NGOs in a round table. In 2004 neither the NGOs nor ACFID were invited to a round table, but ACFID offered to make a written submission which the DAC then quoted from and cited in their report. While the submission was cleared with ACFID's executive committee it was not shown to AusAID prior to being submitted to the DAC. AusAID reacted very strongly to the submission, in particular to the sentence: 'High [staff] turnover can also lead to uneven and inconsistent approaches [and] constrains the development of constructive relationships with key partners [including NGOs]' (DAC 2005, p. 67), which AusAID misinterpreted as referring to it being unprofessional. AusAID attacked ACFID saying that ACFID could not be trusted, with implied threats to the funding of not only ACFID but also member agencies (Tupper 2012; de Groot 2013). While Graham Tupper had planned to leave ACFID prior to this incident, its effects were far reaching. His departure was seen as a circuit breaker and a more cautious approach was taken by ACFID in its relations with government until the advent of the Labor government in 2007, which was quite explicit in being open to criticism from NGOs as the Labor Party saw it as part of ACFID's job.

This period of tension with government also represented an important opportunity for ACFID. While the relationship with government was not as strong as it had been in the past, and the government funding of the NGO sector had declined in real terms through the late 1990s into the 2000s, public support for NGOs climbed steadily through the 1990s. There was an average growth of 11 per cent a year from 2000–04 (Chapman 2004; Kilby 2014). The strong growth pattern was to remain until 2010, when the ongoing effects of international economic crises saw personal savings increase at the expense of consumer spending which collapsed. This was reflected in a drop of donations to aid agencies but to a level (as a proportion of GNI) that was still much higher than it was in the 1980s and 1990s (Kilby 2014).

Experiences elsewhere

Internationally other NGO peak bodies had similar experiences to ACFID of faring badly under conservative governments, but some did far worse (Smillie 1999c, 2013; Cumming 2013). Both the Canadian NGO peak body CCIC and CID in New Zealand suffered a complete cut in government funding in 2010 due to what was seen as ideologically driven policy from conservative governments (CID 2011). CCIC had its three-year contract with CIDA ended and, after two months into a three-month temporary extension, CIDA without warning stopped providing funding. CCIC was forced to lay off most of the staff and close programs, including some of its work on codes of ethics (Buchanan 2012; Millar 2013; Plewes 2013). They also had to sell their office space in order to meet the cost of severance and other staff obligations.

> Unfortunately, it's hard not to see de-funding as yet another example of the 'political chill' message this government has been sending to the development community, says Gerry Barr CCIC's President and CEO. 'What we're experiencing here is punishment politics. Speak out against government policy and risk losing your funding' (CCIC 2010a).

CCIC, which was established in 1968 three years after ACFID, represented a similar number of NGO members as ACFID, and like ACFID had a long history of promoting and advocating for NGOs and their work, as well as monitoring and analysing federal policies on foreign affairs, aid, trade and peace building, all with CIDA funding its core activities (Plewes 2013). A few months after funding ceased, CIDA closed its subsidy scheme and put all of its NGO funding onto a competitive basis, thus breaking the strong sense of solidarity that Canadian

NGOs had built up. It also severely disadvantaged the smaller NGOs with less capacity to compete, and resulted in excessive delays in decisions being made and funding approved (Barr and Takacs 2010; CCIC 2011).[8] By 2012 CIDA had cut funding to some 75 NGOs, both local and international (Caplan 2012). This experience in Canada, not unlike in the Australian domestic NGO scene, was the result of an ideological shift which has seen a proliferation of ways individuals rather than groups could notionally input into policy while at the same time severely curtailing collective action (Laforest 2012). In 2012 in Australia a conservative Queensland state government was also cutting funding to local NGOs because of their opposing views on government policy (Hurst 2012).

In New Zealand there was a similar experience when CID, which had been funded through the official aid programme, was cut from $900,000 a year to $500,000 over two years (NZPA 2009; New Zealand Labour Party 2010). A year later it was cut to the point that it was having trouble functioning at all (Challies et al. 2011). In CID's case there was some warning as Janet Hunt had conducted a review in the early 2000s and noted that their funding base led them to being vulnerable to political shifts and they should diversify their income sources, but this advice was largely ignored (Hunt 2012). In Canada and New Zealand CCIC and CID had both recovered to some extent at the time of writing, and continue to function albeit at a reduced level. The issue, however, is that while they provide important services to their members, NGOs do not have the ear of government in the same way they had in the past, or the same input into policy.

ACFID in the 2000s

The Indian Ocean tsunami of 2004 provided a circuit breaker for ACFID. Given the scale of the response and the reputational risk involved for government and NGOs, both government and ACFID realised they needed each other. They started giving joint press conferences and the like on the response to the tsunami and the accountability mechanisms being put in place, with ACFID agreeing to coordinate reporting (O'Callaghan 2013). In one sense the tsunami enabled ACFID to engage with government on a new footing with the emphasis on lobbying rather than public advocacy. This did not mean that advocacy was not occurring through campaigns such as Make Poverty History, but there

---

8   In early 2011 the ongoing ideological battle with NGOs erupted into a political scandal when the minister responsible for foreign aid overturned a departmental recommendation for funding by inserting by hand the word 'not' into the text of a CIDA document, making it look as if CIDA opposed the grant (Bev Oda's serious transgression 2011; CCIC 2010b). This led to allegations of misleading parliament and a call for the minister's resignation (Herbert 2011). But the Conservative prime minster Stephen Harper backed the minister and she survived.

were fewer public attacks on government and much more direct lobbying for change, with a greater focus on the role of NGOs (O'Callaghan 2013; Lang 2012). ACFID, however, did keep the importance of aid on the agenda, with the Howard government committing to doubling the aid budget, and the subsequent Rudd government agreeing to increase it to 0.5 per cent of GNI against the wishes of his own party. This was due in part to a resurgence in aid due to global security issues following the terrorist attacks in the early 2000s, the traction gained by the MDGs, and more intense competition in the global aid space with the rise of non-DAC donors such as China and their influence.

While the relationship with the Howard government had improved from 2005, it blossomed with the Rudd Labor government in 2007. Not only was the prime minister very supportive of the aid program, but NGO funding from government also increased rapidly after some years of stagnation. There was also closer cooperation between ACFID and government, particularly on a disability focus for aid, a closer alignment with the MDGs, and ACFID agenda items such as the Ambassador for Women and Girls being agreed to and taken up. In 2013, with the election of the Abbott government, there was some nervousness about the relationship. However, the Coalition government is continuing the strong relationship with NGOs, seeing their role as being important in the aid program. The deep cuts to the aid program announced in 2013 and 2014 (a 20 per cent drop overall) and the fall in public support for aid, however, has prompted ACFID to review its approach to campaigning and to engage more directly with key constituencies on the effectiveness of aid and its overall importance (Purcell 2015). This approach resulted in some small victories around NGO funding but not a major reversal in policy. The focus of ACFID with conservative governments has been more on lobbying than on public advocacy. While this has been criticised, the view is that having a seat at the table is important in a policy sense.

Conclusion

While there has been a backlash against NGOs from governments around the world (Dupuy et al. 2014), ACFID and its members have survived most, if not all, the negative effects of that backlash. The challenge of relations with government is the same the world over: 'to maintain or revive an independent, distinctive and critical stance in a situation where [there is] danger of incorporation, an absence of alternative popular spaces, and a marginalisation of dissent' (Miller et al. 2013, p. 153). Since the early to mid-1990s there have been a series of questions raised by government as to the effectiveness, representativeness and accountability of ACFID and its members, which ACFID has generally weathered but not without some important changes in how it relates to government. While CCIC and CID folded when government arbitrarily cut the support they were receiving, they have survived but have been weakened in that they do not have the ear of government in the same way they had before. If government provides support for peak bodies to be the first port of call for advice and the like, then by virtue of this support they have a seat at the policy table. Without that seat, while peak bodies can represent a voice, the nature of the engagement by its very nature is more distant. The challenge, however is to avoid the inevitable co-option and agreeing to or accepting policies and conditions, or being silent on matters that one would or should not be silent on.

09

From a Code of Ethics to a Code of Conduct

The idea of NGOs being bound by a code of ethics or a code of conduct would not have been thought of in the early years of ACFID, but by the 1980s a number of events occurred that saw the development of NGO codes internationally as not only desirable but to some extent inevitable. The original code has broadened since the 1980s from a set of principles for NGO practice to a more normative focus on what constitutes good development practice across many dimensions. This has been quite a radical shift in NGO thinking on what they should be accountable for to their peers, supporters and aid recipients.

The original Code of Ethics was adopted in 1989 and over the following 25 years it has grown and developed. The current ACFID Code of Conduct is regarded as a benchmark for NGO standards globally, and has been drawn upon as a source by many NGOs and NGO peak bodies to develop their own codes to guide their operations and work (Obrecht et al. 2012). By 2010 there were over 300 worldwide national and international NGO codes of conduct and ethics (Warren and Lloyd 2009), with ACFID being a leader in their development. Comprehensive codes such as ACFID's also raise arguments of how NGOs may be constrained by being party to these codes in terms of the options they have and the choices they can make in how they do their work. This is why there are still some major Australian NGOs that are not code signatories as they believe it constrains their operations and how they can be true to their values.[1]

There are four major ethical dilemmas facing NGOs that codes may be able to help with, without necessarily providing an answer: whether to intervene in a particular context or not (Singer 2010; Doyle 2011); whose values and priorities drive an intervention – leading to arguments of Western imperialism (Mawdsley 2012; Barker 2013); what ethical compromises are acceptable in order to deliver aid to those who need it most – aid diversion and rent seeking (Gourevitch et al. 2012; Menkhaus 2012); and, finally, to what extent does

---

1   In Australia neither Compassion nor Médecins Sans Frontières (MSF), two of the larger NGOs, are code signatories.

helping individuals threaten a broader group or tacitly support broader human rights abuses – for example, aid to Khmer Rouge refugee camps in Thailand or aid to Hutu refugee camps in Goma (Slim 1997, 2014; De Waal 1997; Das 2010; see Chapter 5).

Codes of ethics and codes of conduct do not address all of these ethical dilemmas as some are in many ways intractable, but they should give some guidance as to how these and other issues are to be addressed. If it is hard for a code to be all encompassing and many of the code provisions may not be relevant in a wide variety of circumstances, such as advocacy or humanitarian response, it may be better to be guided by separate codes, such as the Humanitarian Code of Conduct (Tupper 2012).[2] The debate in Australia in the 2010s, however, is about the breadth of the ACFID code rather than the broad principles it enshrines which were developed in the late 1980s.

The challenge that the ACFID code has had to manage is that while codes of conduct and ethics are ostensibly about self-regulation, there is a very real risk that they are developed as an implicit or sometimes explicit response to meeting external agendas. Codes can thus compromise individual NGO values and practices in order to conform to a broader external vision or set of values, and so fall into the trap of managerial conformity at the expense of diversity and values (Gulrajani 2011; Roberts et al. 2005). Rudy von Bernuth from ICVA noted at the ACFID Council in 1997, when the new code of conduct was being debated, that while codes of conduct were in part about professional standards they were (not coincidently) also about efforts by governments, both North and South, to regulate NGOs in ways that NGOs may not like. Governments having an input or oversight of self-regulation is one way of achieving what is effectively a proxy for government regulation (ACFOA 1997b, p. 48). The other downside to codes, which Stephen Morrow pointed to at that time, was that over time codes may lead to a standardisation or 'coercive isomorphism, where NGOs all start to look the same' (Morrow 1997, p. i) and risk compromising the sector's diversity (DiMaggio and Powell 1983). These issues may seem inevitable, particularly when compliance with NGO codes coincides with government funding priorities, approaches and regulation; nevertheless, they still remain a risk for the autonomy of NGOs and peak bodies like ACFID.

The ACFID Code of Conduct had its origins in the ACFID Code of Ethics of 1989, one of the first NGO codes globally, with most other national development NGO codes taking a lead from it and introducing their own national codes in the early to mid-1990s. The Private Voluntary Organisation (PVO) Standards by InterAction for the United States' NGOs were developed in 1993 and would have

---

2   The full title is The Code of Conduct for the International Red Cross and Red Crescent Movement and NGOs in Disaster Relief.

used the ACFID Code as a reference point; CCIC in Canada based part of its 1993 code on the Australian Code, as well as using the template from InterAction of the US (CCIC 2000; Smillie 2013). In 1994 the Humanitarian Code of Conduct developed by the ICRC was also adopted by NGOs involved in disaster relief (Ebrahim 2003; Mowjee 2001). This chapter will look at the development of the ACFID Code, which was triggered in the mid-1980s by the different pressures that ACFID and its members had to respond to from government, external events, and internal pressures within ACFID (Syme 2008; ACFOA 1985f, 1985e).

NGO codes and their origins

Codes of ethics and codes of conduct are one way of setting standards and rules of behaviour among groups and organisations, most notably in the corporate sector but also in sectors such as health and education, while avoiding a 'command and control' approach by government (Kolk and Van Tulder 2005, p. 2). They serve to mediate the relationship between the public and private spheres and 'anticipate or prevent mandatory regulation' (p. 4). One of the earlier mooted codes was in India in the mid-1980s at around the same time the ACFID code was being thought of. The Indian NGO code did not get very far, in part because it was felt to have been driven by a government agenda to restrict the religious and more overtly political NGOs rather than meeting NGO priorities (Deshpande 1986). The ACFID Code of Ethics was a little different in that it had its origins not only in avoiding regulation by government but also in maintaining a sense of solidarity among its members and thereby broader support for NGO aid work. Like many other codes, it was developed during the march of neoliberalism through the 1980s when the questioning, if not the decline, in the role of government had left a gap in regulation. In the 1980s and 1990s, codes of ethics and codes of conduct were being developed across many corporate sectors to protect individual companies and whole industrial sectors from bad publicity and, probably more importantly, litigation as a result of poor behaviour. NGOs were no exception, having experienced their own share of scandals and public questioning (Gibelman and Gelman 2001; Smillie 1997; Lloyd 2005; Stalker 1982; van Eekelen 2013).

The major NGO codes as they have been developed, however, generally are much stronger in terms of possible sanctions and acceptable standards, than say business association codes (Kolk and Van Tulder 2005). This difference can probably be put down to the higher level of reputational risk that NGOs have; that is, they are expected to act more ethically than a profit-making corporation (Winston 2006). Bad publicity about what may be an isolated incident can have a disproportionate impact on the broader NGO sector, a point I will return to later in this chapter (see also Chapter 8). There was also an element of realpolitik involved. As NGOs were promoting corporate codes on issues such as labour, health or environmental standards, it was important that NGOs should be covered by a similar, if not a better, accountability regime in order to have credibility when calling for industry standards and codes (Braun and Gearhart 2004; Compa 2004).

The process of developing a code itself is also important for its effective socialisation among members: 'The legitimacy of a code is influenced by the process through which it was established, thus making the code creation process crucial to its final adoption' (Ebrahim 2003, p. 820). Negotiations around developing codes can go on for many years, something ACFID was to discover more than once, with three years seeming to be the norm. In the early 1990s, the focus of NGO codes was on maintaining ethical standards for their work, specifically in their relations with stakeholders. This led to a series of difficult questions needing to be addressed at the operational level with a range of stakeholders, such as donors and aid recipients. There is a risk that stakeholder pressure can paradoxically lead to a drift away from core ethical principles of behaviour when certain accountabilities are privileged over others. Like ACFID before them, InterAction in the US and CCIC in Canada took three years to negotiate their respective codes and another two years to allow members to become compliant (InterAction 2013; CCIC 2000).

The ACFID Code of Ethics

Since the 1970s ACFID, along with other international NGOs and UN bodies such as the ILO, had been asking for industry codes of ethics and conduct for companies working in developing countries following concerns around poor labour, environmental, and health standards. There had been examples of the use of child labour, the way infant milk formula was marketed, and lax environmental standards in the mining and timber industries, all in countries with poor regulatory regimes (ACFOA 1981a; Kolk et al. 1999; Sikkink 1986; Doh and Guay 2004). ACFID's role in those campaigns as well as its criticism of major companies working on Australian aid projects, such as the Zamboanga Del Sur project in the Philippines, raised the obvious question as to NGOs' own ethical behaviour in their aid work. Already questions were being asked of child sponsorship programs and how children were being portrayed to potential sponsors (ACFOA 1982a; Stalker 1982). There was also the broader issue the Jackson Committee raised, in having some common understanding by donors to all NGOs as to what their funds were being used for:

There could be an advantage in standardising voluntary agency definitions, accounting procedures, and agreed disclosure of information on administration and operation but such objectives should be pursued by and through ACFOA (Jackson Committee 1984, p. 111).

ACFID saw the idea of a code as meeting these concerns and had the discussion of a code put on its work program for 1985 (ACFOA 1985f). The need for a code was also spurred on by a dispute as to how some agencies were portraying others publicly and within ACFID. There had been a long running tension between what were seen at the time as the 'progressive' Christian agencies, which were long established in Australia, and World Vision which started in Australia in 1966 and joined ACFID in the mid-1970s. In the 1970s World Vision was seen as a conservative agency with a strong pro-US agenda, particularly around the war in Vietnam where it had its first project. Its focus on child sponsorship with strong religious messaging was also criticised (National Youth Council 1975; Hill 1975a; Henderson 1976, 1977; Webb 1977; Stalker 1982). World Vision felt at the time that a lot of this criticism was unfair and unfounded, and certainly by 1985 they had changed considerably. Despite these changes World Vision felt it was still not getting accepted by the other agencies for what it had to offer and so was thinking of leaving ACFID. This would have been a huge blow for ACFID's reputation and could have triggered an exodus of other more conservative agencies.

A special meeting was held with World Vision in Melbourne in December 1985. The idea of a code of ethics, which had been raised earlier in the year at the ACFID Council, was seen to be a way to stop member agencies criticising other members and to develop a common view on how stories were presented to the public in ways that respected the dignity of those portrayed – another ongoing issue for NGOs (ACFOA 1985e). This meeting provided some impetus for moving the development of a code of ethics along, and ACFID thought that given the high level of in-principle support for a code it could be finalised fairly quickly. The ACFID Quality of Aid Committee was tasked with drafting a code to be presented to the 1986 Council for adoption (ACFOA 1986a). In fact, it was to take three years for the code to be developed, in part because it was the first NGO code globally and so presented a wide range of unknowns. While there might have been a natural consensus on what constituted appropriate ethical behaviour among NGOs, the devil was in the detail, and there needed to be a long process of socialisation of the idea of a code, not to mention the reputational implications a code could have on signatories that were found to be in breach.

The first draft of the ACFID Code of Ethics went out for consultation in August 1986 (ACFOA 1986c) with the aim of its adoption in 1987. Initially it was to be a voluntary code of behaviour for agencies to trial and then be adopted as a Code of Ethics at the ACFID Council in 1988. In 1987 a revised draft was prepared and circulated outlining three principles for all ACFID members to accept: a commitment to humanitarian services; creative and trusting relationship with partners (avoiding arrangements that might seem to be paternalistic and patronising); and that people, rather than NGOs change their own lives. Signatories to the draft code were also required to provide to ACFID a report on their budget and an annual report with audited accounts including income received from government. They also had to commit to provide accurate information to the public; to not denigrate other agencies; to have monitoring and evaluation systems in place showing efficiently managed and effective programs; and to provide details of how they consulted with beneficiaries about their programs. Finally, the code required a statement by the board chair and CEO on compliance to these principles and procedures. While these principles and procedures might seem to be uncontroversial, the implications of what a too literal interpretation of them had for agencies' work was a concern for many. Just prior to the 1987 Council some member agencies baulked at the levels of specificity being sought by the code and sought some loosening of the language (ACFOA 1987c). These objections were overcome after a further year of negotiations and the Code was adopted in 1988, first as an interim code of behaviour with no compulsion (ACFOA 1988). After a year of operation it was finally approved as a Code of Ethics in 1989, with an ACFID committee established to monitor compliance (ACFOA 1989a).

There were a number of gaps in the early Code of Ethics, the most serious being the lack of an independent complaints and sanctions mechanism, and the lack of a set of standards on presenting NGO accounts to the public so they could be easily compared – a problem that still applies to many codes in other countries (Smillie 2013; Armstrong 1991b). These omissions were not oversights as such, but rather a set of difficult issues that would be best addressed once the code was agreed to and agencies had signed up. At the time this represented a huge step for agencies: to be compliant to a formal process imposed by themselves and to be accountable to each other. This is probably the main reason why the code took so long to be socialised and fully accepted. It is worth noting that it would be another 20 years before good practice standards for NGOs' in-country development work were put into the code, even though these principles were in the original code.

The Code of Ethics had its first cases of complaint in the early 1990s when agencies claimed other agencies' media releases misrepresented their work and did not respect the dignity of aid recipients in advertising (for example, images of starving babies as helpless victims). The process of resolving these complaints was slow and cumbersome, and they took up to a year (Rollason 1990; Hunt 1992), with the findings being that there was no breach of the code.

In these cases it was found that there had been inadvertent mistakes due to agency staff being unaware of the code, and it being poorly socialised across agencies (Loughland 1991).

The operation of the Code of Ethics Committee was also problematic with the ACFID executive director being involved in any referrals to the Committee, and thus creating an obvious perception of a conflict of interest, particularly if the complaint was made by or against a major member agency. While it was clarified that the executive director was not an *ex officio* member of the Committee their involvement still caused unease, as did the requirement for ACFID associate members to be compliant, but not have a representative on the Committee (ACFOA 1991a, 1991b, 1991c). Similarly, it was not clear as to how complaints could be received from the public (Ingram 1995), let alone from the partners of Australian NGOs in developing countries. Finally, despite the requirement of the Code to report on the level of compliance of agencies to its adherence, there was no mechanism in place to do so, and the Committee was not proactive in developing one. For example, the suggestion that there be common approaches to financial reporting and accounting, which was to become an issue in 1996, was first raised in 1985 by Russell Rollason as part of a response to issues raised in the Jackson Committee report (ACFOA 1985f), and again in 1991 by Community Aid Abroad (Armstrong 1991a), but was not addressed at either time.

An important and precedent-setting dispute arose in this period when an advocacy member of ACFID criticised a development organisation (also an ACFID member) of being involved in government education programs in PNG that disadvantaged local teachers and local NGOs (ACFOA 1995a). This case raised the thorny issue for the Committee of whether local NGOs could complain about international NGOs, and whether the code applied offshore. Waldon Bello, from a Southern advocacy organisation, had been very critical of Northern NGO advocacy work for not representing the views of affected communities (Lloyd 2005). These cases, however, come down to judgements about matters of degree of whether local communities were fairly represented or not (Lloyd 2005; Winston 2002). So the issue of offshore complaints was not fully resolved until the 2010 revision of the code when aid recipients were stakeholders in the code and could (and did) make complaints (Blunt 2013; ACFID 2013c).

Despite its strong normative wording, the code in its early years was for all intents and purposes a vehicle for dealing with complaints between agencies, rather than a set of minimum standards with which agencies would comply and be held accountable to. The complaints mechanism and the process of resolving them were not clear, and there were no clear guidelines on how agencies should adhere to the code. The issue of what was the most appropriate mechanism was to be an ongoing one. There were numerous 'tweaks' over the following 20 years, but in the early 1990s there was neither a workable process nor a strong sense of ownership by the members, despite them being signatories. The Committee only met on an 'as needed' basis, and it seems from the records that there were few meetings between 1992 and 1994. A survey of signatories in 1995 found that very few had complied with the code's reporting requirements, and there was a very low level of commitment of ACFID members to the code (ACFOA 1995b).

These experiences highlighted a need for an amendment to the code rules so that complaints could come to the Ethics Committee directly, a separation of the Committee from ACFID executive and staff, and for the Committee to be more proactive (ACFOA 1995b). This change was spurred on by an issue that emerged in 1994 and 1995, which further highlighted the weaknesses of the Code of Ethics. CARE Australia had not signed the code, as it was not an ACFID member, but it had complaints against it from other agencies which it did not directly address. This was compounded by allegations of impropriety with government funding which had been around since the early 1990s (Hunt 1992; ACFOA 1992d, 1993a, 1993c; McPhedran 1994) (see Chapter 8). On top of this, the Industry Commission Report of 1995 on NGOs, much like the Jackson Committee report 10 years earlier, had also recommended that common financial reporting standards to the public be part of the code (Industry Commission 1995, p. 161). The Code of Ethics Committee picked up these issues with a flurry of meetings in 1995 to work on them (ACFOA 1995a, 1995c), but it was all too late and minister Gordon Bilney intervened as the problems with CARE Australia deepened.

The Code of Conduct

The CARE media story in early 1995, the perceived poor reporting by NGOs to AusAID, related debates around NGO accountability, and the Industry Commission report, when put together prompted minister Gordon Bilney to take control of the code of ethics process. He proposed a code of practice with a much higher level of government control (Syme 2008; Hunt 2012). ACFID fought strenuously against the idea of government oversight right up to when the ACFID Code of Conduct was finalised 18 months later in October 1996 as a self-regulating model without any government input or control. Even though the Code of Conduct was 'sold' as something new, it was essentially a beefed up version of the existing Code of Ethics, with improved coverage of NGO governance, financial matters, improved compliance process, and greater autonomy from ACFID management.

Bilney had set the ball rolling by raising issues of the probity of the NGO sector as a whole, and he seemed to suggest the CARE case was merely the tip of the iceberg of NGO impropriety (Hunt 1995c; see Chapter 8). Bilney went on to argue that as the existing code did not apply to CARE and, rather than asking them to sign up to it, a new mechanism was needed. A Parliamentary Select Committee would now decide how NGOs might be better regulated in terms of codes (Bilney 1995a). In the end it was agreed that the existing code be the basis of the process, with the proviso that the existing Code of Ethics Committee not be involved, effectively signalling a lack of confidence in the existing ACFID process. The Parliamentary Select Committee was to be composed of AusAID staff, politicians from the two major parties, ACFID nominees, a representative of donors nominated by the Australian Consumers Association,[3] and chaired by an AusAID executive officer. After intense debate on the membership of the committee, the minister announced a Code of Practice Advisory Committee (COPAC) with an independent chair, Jim Ingram, a former head of AusAID who had resigned from public life. The NGO section of AusAID would act as the secretariat, and the Committee was to report on the implementation of the draft code of practice by September 1995 (Bilney 1995b; Lee 1995).

The COPAC report initially recommended a Code of Practice Committee to be chaired by a ministerial appointment, with three ACFID nominees and two others nominated by the minister (AusAID 1995b). This recommendation was rejected by ACFID (Hunt 1995a). Alternative structures were put forward, including adding a set of standards to an updated Code of Ethics (Hunt 1995b). In its final report, COPAC recommended an Interim Code of Conduct Committee (ICCC) independent of government to finalise a sector-wide code to cover all NGOs, not just ACFID members, with a chair approved by the minister (Ingram 1995). COPAC did not draft a new code but rather drafted a financial reporting structure and revised the existing Code of Ethics, passing these to the ICCC to consider as the basis for their ongoing development of a code. Despite arguing to the very end, ACFID had lost the fight to keep the process within the existing Code of Ethics Committee and have them beef up that code (ACFOA 1995e). Nevertheless, ACFID had retained effective control of the ongoing process and it kept the existing Code of Ethics Committee in place pending the finalisation of the new arrangement:

> ACFOA were not ready to dissolve the Ethics Committee and their Code until the principle of self-regulation and code ownership were clearly acknowledged as being in the NGDO domain of responsibility and the adequacy of the new Code of Conduct was tested (Syme 2008, p. 28).

---

3   This happened because a few months earlier *CHOICE* magazine printed a review of charities and their annual reports, both domestic and overseas, and as usual said they could be a lot clearer and provide better accountability to donors.

The ICCC first met in November 1995 with an independent chair nominated by ACFID and agreed to by the minister, four ACFID members including a representative of donors and specialist finance adviser, and one from outside the ACFID membership. The ICCC developed a new Code of Conduct with a new structure and presented it to ACFID in August 1996. Along the way there were a number of consultations with NGOs, which at times were quite heated. NGOs were very anxious, their main concerns being the idea of having an additional layer of accountability over and above what the domestic NGOs have; the unfairness of an imposition due to misdeeds of one agency; an implicit suggestion that NGOs could not be trusted; and, finally, the imposition of administrative demands on NGOs' limited resources. Even though ACFID had wrested control back, NGOs still saw the Code of Conduct as an imposition by government and a slap in the face for ACFID and the existing Code of Ethics (Franks 2013). There was still a feeling the NGOs could do it themselves and all that was required was for the existing code to be tweaked, a process already underway. What was not well understood was that the time for tweaking the existing code had long passed, even if that is arguably what the final outcome looked like – there was too much political capital invested in being seen to be doing something new and solving what was seen, at least by the minister, as an endemic problem.

The draft Code of Conduct fully incorporated the existing Code of Ethics but also drew from US InterAction's PVO Standards to add sections on governance and financial reporting. These were further strengthened by having a common financial reporting format for NGOs, which is still unique among international codes (ICCC 1996). The draft code went from the two pages of the existing Code of Ethics to four pages which, considering the scope of the code in the 2010s (40 pages), represented a relatively modest change. The ICCC also recommended a code of conduct committee to oversee the code, replacing the existing Code of Ethics Committee. The ICCC reported to both ACFID and the minister, but as the government had changed in early 1996 the new minister Alexander Downer did not see himself or the government as having a role in the ACFID Code. As a matter of principle the new Coalition government preferred self-regulation (Franks 2013; Syme 2008). In the end it was a change of government that brought the issue to a close.

The ACFID Council in 1996 formally accepted the ICCC report, adopted the Draft Code, and asked its members to sign up by July 1997. The Council also acknowledged the role of the Code of Ethics Committee through the process (ACFOA 1997c). This new iteration of the Code had more 'teeth' than the previous Code of Ethics, as it was not only a requirement for ACFID membership but also a requirement of the AusAID/NGO Umbrella Contract covering all AusAID funding of NGOs. Overall, the code was developed and implemented to achieve the accepted principles for good self-regulatory codes: coverage (ideally sector wide); an open consultative and public process of code formulation; balanced representation on the committee (ACFID and non-ACFID members plus consumer representation); transparency in reporting and compliance checking; strong sanctions and good enforcement; an independent chair; and independent external auditing (Franks 2013). The original Code of Ethics had some of these features but not all.

The Code of Conduct was formally launched by the Governor-General in 1998 after all agencies had formally signed up (Wilson 1997). By 1999 there were 118 signatories and a very busy committee that met six times that year and ran four seminars for member agencies. There was also a deliberate decision that there would be no AusAID funding for the administration of the code, but rather signatory fees (initially $200) would cover it (Syme 2008, p. 32). The new processes also overcame the long delays that complainants of the Code of Ethics had encountered, with the requirement that the Code of Conduct Committee must consider a complaint within 12 weeks of receiving it (ACFOA 1999a).

The politics of the process has meant that the importance and ground-breaking nature of the original Code of Ethics has been largely lost in ACFID's collective memory, and is not generally referred to as a precursor of the existing code in either the code itself or the broader ACFID context. This is unfortunate as the original Code of Ethics was the first NGO code anywhere, and its provisions and principles were essentially kept in full and expanded to include new areas and clarify and expand others. One could argue that the revision of the code in 2009 was far more comprehensive and nearly as traumatic for the code signatories as the 1995–96 process.

Implementing the code

The code was seen as one with teeth. It was signed by all ACFID members, including CARE Australia, which joined ACFID at the same time, as well as a number of non-ACFID members (ACFOA 1996b; Eggleton 1996). The early years of the code were devoted to having it work smoothly and achieve a certain level of minimum standards, particularly in financial and annual reporting before any further expansion of its scope. The early focus was on improved reporting, and by 2000 the primary goal of comparability of revenue and expenditure across NGOs had been largely achieved (Syme 2008). This was a huge step, something that CCIC in Canada was not able to do and has since regretted (Smillie 2013). In August 2000 a compliance monitoring working group was established to ease the workload on the secretariat and the full committee. Three code committee members met twice yearly to assess all reports submitted and follow up with those agencies that were finding it difficult to understand the minimum requirements. With these efforts full compliance by all code signatory NGOs had been achieved by 2004.

Most of the changes to the code in the early 2000s were 'tweaking' some content to reflect legislative and other changes and where it was felt the code should be in line with personnel and management practice, professional conduct and gender equity. A further refinement and clarification of financial reporting requirements was also made. Explicit links were made to other international codes such as the ICRC Humanitarian Code. While the Committee did not formally take advice from AusAID, as it was not an instrument of government, it did brief the government in bi-annual meetings. A subsequent lunch discussion, which included AusAID, covered any major sector-wide trends with potential implications for the code, and the Committee did keep an eye on what issues AusAID thought appropriate to consider (Franks 2013). Some of these 'messages' resulted in new clauses being added, covering child safety and protection and a 'no strings attached' clause with regard to the use of funds for party political and/or religious purposes.

In addition, the format of the code changed and a new guidance document was endorsed providing extensive information on how to implement code standards. The Code of Conduct Committee was also given new powers to initiate its own investigations, and experts were appointed to the Committee, most commonly to advise on fundraising and accounting standards. Given the Indian Ocean tsunami was such a large event, involving hundreds of millions of dollars of the public's money to be spent over a number of years, a tsunami reporting amendment was added to the code in 2005 to address that specific situation (Syme 2008; O'Callaghan 2013).

In 2008 a major review of the code was proposed, given it had been more than 10 years since the 'new' code was adopted. Fundamental issues regarding the code were emerging, in particular:

> maintaining the established principle of 'self-regulation' [and] ensuring 'Code credibility' through 'independence'. Self-regulation was and still is an important right of the NGDO sector that was 'won' after much uncertainty about the intentions of Government to regulate the Sector itself. It is cherished by the sector as a 'non-negotiable'. Credibility of the code is also non-negotiable, for without it, the Code would be merely an aspired [to] list rather than a substantive standard (Syme 2008, p. 6).

The specific issue that David Syme was referring to was a perceived conflict of interest that may occur when the body providing self-regulation was also the body promoting the sector and advocating for it (in this case ACFID). The role of peak bodies being an accreditor, code manager, custodian of standards, and advocate for member interests, however, is common in other sectors such as the health sector, for example, the Pharmacy Guild and the Australian Medical Association. There was no real suggestion at the time that this was a serious concern beyond the more general off-the-record type comments from AusAID that the code's compliance mechanisms were not as rigorous as its accreditation, but such a comment would be expected given the competing nature of the two processes.[4]

There was also a risk as code signatories which were not ACFID members (35 per cent of code signatories) were not coming to code training sessions to be updated on requirements. As a result, a significant minority (15 per cent) of NGO Code signatories said during the review that they would prefer a separate structure to administer the code (Syme 2008, p. 15). This was enough to prompt some members of the code Committee to argue that it may be better to set the code up as a body completely independent of ACFID, with no formal links, and possibly have a mandate beyond NGOs. How it would work was not spelt out but most probably as a separate NGO solely responsible for the code. The risks to ACFID were touched on by the report, the key one being that such a structural move away from the notion of self-regulation to a different form could, over time, lead to over-regulation, a duplication of AusAID's accreditation processes, and a blurring of the distinction between government regulation, self-regulation and standard setting.

This proposal for an independent body was rejected out of hand by the code Committee and the ACFID executive (Blunt 2013). The executive, however, while reiterating the governance of the code should not be changed, supported a full review and revision of the code given the increased risk profile of the NGO sector following the Indian Ocean tsunami and a mood for increased regulation of the broader NGO sector from the new Labor government. Such a review could also provide an opportunity for the code to take greater responsibility for government-funded programs, strengthen relationships more broadly, and meet some of the ongoing concerns about the effectiveness of the NGO sector (Khouri and Russell 2009). While issues of NGO effectiveness were not new (see Chapter 8) the idea of using the code to address it was an important, and to some extent a controversial, step as earlier iterations were about standards and principles of NGO operation rather than the effectiveness of the work.

---

4   It is probably worth noting that the budget for accreditation is around $6,000 per NGO per annum (in 2015), something that ACFID could not possibly afford for the code compliance costs for each of its 140 members.

The revised code went beyond a set of minimum standards and sought to embed the notion of good practice and continuous improvement, and at the same time built the compliance aspects and broadened the scope considerably. As with the previous major code revision in 1996, the process was tortuous with 40 drafts prepared (Blunt 2013). A steering committee for the review was made up of ACFID executive committee members rather than experts who it was felt may be more removed from the political exigencies of agencies. The result was a code embedded with a notion of progressive obligations; that is, agencies were expected to show improvement from year to year. The key elements were a stronger requirement that NGOs publicly reported they were code signatories; a more transparent complaints process; mandatory self-assessment; and a greater focus on partners and aid effectiveness. Overall the process elevated the understanding of the code, and the mandatory self-assessment was deferred for two years to 2012 to allow time for agencies to comply. The revised code suited the medium-tier NGOs, while the big NGOs often had the complication of global affiliate issues to contend with. The smaller NGOs found the code more complex to manage with their limited resources. Partial compliance is the most commonly reported self-assessment report, but it was expected the proportion of agencies being fully compliant would increase. With 140 separate obligations to comply with, however, full compliance still remains a daunting task to many agencies.

The downside was that the revised code of 2009 had grown to 40 pages from just two when it was the Code of Ethics and four pages of the original Code of Conduct. This level of complexity and specificity can be argued to be embracing a managerialist ethic that the NGOs and ACFID so trenchantly resisted in the early 1990s (Roberts et al. 2005; Gulrajani 2011; Morrow 1997). While the shift from the Code of Ethics to a code of conduct was regarded as a landmark shift in 1996, the 2009 revisions were far more radical and drilled far deeper into organisational practice, and possibly ran the risk of seeking an unnecessary conformity or more 'coercive isomorphism' within the sector (Morrow 1997, p. i). The other major shift, which addressed the issue of ACFID and non-ACFID members being code signatories, was that all code signatories must be members of ACFID. This resulted in a sharp increase of ACFID membership from a low of 69 in 2010 to 144 in 2014. This was important for ACFID's credibility and is in line with many other industry bodies that provide accreditation for practitioners. By keeping self-regulation in the same space as the policy driver, it is more likely the code will stay in touch with the sector rather than drift away from it, which would present a real risk.

Gaps in the code

There is an important set of challenges for NGO codes that have generally not been covered well, and the ACFID Code is no exception. These are to do with how agencies operate in developing countries and engage with the broad ethical challenges NGOs face, touched on at the beginning of this chapter. These challenges focus on how NGOs behave and deal with moral and ethical choices in working with local communities. The key one of these is the disruptive effect NGO programs can have on local communities, whether this is to do with distorting local priorities or favouring one group over another. While the code does ensure local participation, it is still a step short of the program being consistent with local priorities; and there is still no mention of duplication of services and activities either with other NGOs or with government. Generally, local partners have quite lot of influence over program content but not the broader issues of policy in a particular country or context (Elbers and Schulpen 2011). The risk is of a plethora of uncoordinated activities that are a drain on scarce local resources, particularly staff resources, leading to resentment (Barber and Bowie 2008; Rahmani 2012). The ethical question then is whether NGOs should be 'gap fillers' and only provide services as they push the state to take on the responsibility, as only the state can provide a social guarantee:

> NGOs should not allow key duty [bearers] to abrogate their responsibility to provide secure access to services that form the substance of basic rights where individuals cannot secure those rights effectively through their own activities (Donaghue 2010, p. 60).

One example of a code which attempts to address some of these issue is the NGO Code of Conduct for Health Systems Strengthening, which pledges to 'pursue practices that bolster the public sector in the countries in which they operate and encourage use of the public system as the platform for the delivery of services' (Bristol 2008, p. 2162). Part of this includes a commitment not to weaken local staffing by taking staff at much higher salaries from existing service providers for what is often short-term NGO work and so weaken what are often already over-stretched local systems. While this Health Systems Code is comprehensive, by 2014 there were still fewer than 60 signatories globally, and there were no review or sanction processes in place. Another example of how donors may be distorting priorities is how HIV has dominated development programs in Africa to the point that in Malawi in the early 2000s HIV programs overshadowed all other development work: 'AIDS in Africa is at risk of becoming a facile means of engaging with the continent's human development' (Deneulin and Rakodi 2011, p. 74). The challenge for donor country NGO codes such as the ACFID Code is how to be more proactive in looking at the effects NGO work has on existing local resources and processes.

A second area the code ignores is to do with how Western development NGOs tend to see liberalism as the norm, and a desired outcome in the situations where they work. This is the basis for many aspects of human rights work (see Chapter 6). However, when liberalism is the starting point there is little space for the priorities and values of inscriptive groups whose membership is not open ended, such as indigenous people's organisations, caste groups, and some religious groups (Eisenberg and Spinner-Halev 2005). In debating just outcomes in terms of development work and social change, a liberal ideal is often seen as the starting point and NGOs will work back from that to reach an agreed outcome (Kingsbury 2002). This goes to Lissner's (1977) point of NGOs being values-based organisations with a particular world view, or Weltanschauung. The ethical issue for various codes is how any clash in values is resolved given the power relations that exist between the donor NGO and the 'partner' NGO. This issue is not directly addressed in the ACFID Code and perhaps is too big for it. Nevertheless this issue is a dilemma NGOs (should) face.

The third broad policy area which codes do not address arises most acutely in humanitarian responses, but often in development programs as well. It is the 'do no harm' principle. There is often a situation where what is best to do as an individual NGO and what is best to do as a group of NGOs, in particular contexts, may be different. Collectively, a group of NGOs may be able to resist unjust situations such as those outlined at the front of this chapter, for example, relief camps controlled by belligerents in a conflict. Das (2010) refers to this as 'a collective problem of altruism' (p. 176), where there is an obligation on NGOs to take a more politically activist role but doing that may deny them access to the most needy. While the Humanitarian Code of Conduct does not address this question, Das (2010) argues that NGOs are morally required to act cooperatively to address any harm perpetuated on individuals by larger groups. The current ACFID Code does not address this issue. But guidance for NGOs who regularly encounter this issue would be important, with processes put in place to mandate collective responses. Whether a single national code can deal with these complex international situations is of course another question.

Conclusion

The story of the Code of Ethics and Code of Conduct is important in the history of ACFID and to varying degrees has been an important part of the latter half of ACFID's life. The development of the code serves to illustrate the changes that have taken place in NGOs over the past 30 years and how they have grappled with them. For the first 20 years (1965–85) of ACFID, members signed up to a set of principles by virtue of their membership, and how they interpreted or conformed to those principles was essentially up to them. This inevitably led to different interpretations of these principles in the 1970s and thus tension and conflict (see Chapter 3). In the 1980s, with increased government funding and an increased broader public profile (outside their own constituencies), NGOs were increasingly being subjected to the same harsh spotlight they themselves had been shining on government and public corporations. It was, therefore, inevitable in the 1980s era of neoliberalism and self-regulation that NGOs would think about codes of conduct. To its credit ACFID was the first global peak body to act in having a code of ethics in 1989.

The development of the code increased the level of prescription on how NGOs should be governed, interact with their stakeholders and, to some extent, how they implement their programs. Two very large NGOs are not code signatories (MSF and Compassion), ostensibly because they find the code obligations restricting on the way they work. On the other hand, being a signatory provides a powerful solidarity tool for NGOs to be able to be 'a sector rather than a collective'. The question remains, however, whether that is happening (Harris-Rimmer 2013).

The growth and complexity of the Code of Conduct in the 2000s raises the broader issue of maintaining diversity in the sector. While the broad ACFID membership of 2015 probably represents a similar level of diversity and numbers that the different categories of membership represented in the 1970s, the question remains whether ACFID has been hoisted by its own petard in the fight to defend NGOs against the inevitable march of managerialism in the 1980s and 1990s. Has it set a managerial agenda that may ultimately be counterproductive to the broad-based diverse set of NGOs which are its members? The real question for the Code as Harris-Rimmer (2013) notes is: 'when agencies are being asked how to be more ethical … it is not about each other, rather the question is: am I being ethical at doing what I do?'

10

The Australian Council for International Development in the Twenty-First Century: Challenges and Opportunities

The idea of NGOs coming together to engage with government on policy is unremarkable now, but it was very new in 1965 when there was little interest in debating aid policy by either the Australian government or any other government. In its 50 years ACFID has evolved through many changes in how aid should be delivered. It was a direct product of the aftermath of colonialism, the height of the Cold War and the optimistic hype of the first Development Decade of the 1960s, which was meant to herald a new era and had set a place for the then nascent international development NGOs. ACFID has emerged from its adventurous youth to the present with NGOs subject to many of the same dilemmas and contradictions that face all forms of aid.

The Cold War is now a distant memory, but in many respects global insecurity has worsened. The notion of a club of Western donors doling out aid to the former colonies of erstwhile allies for support in various conflicts is, to a large extent, also a thing of the past. The emphasis in the second decade of the twenty-first century is that aid should be used to help build a global order based on open trading relationships and more globalised economic processes, with increasingly powerful and confident development states such as China and India exerting their power and influence more directly. They are now major aid donors as well as emerging superpowers in their own right, seeking to shape global, economic and political processes.

NGOs, likewise, have come of age and are part of the development landscape rather than being treated as marginal players by governments as they were in the 1960s and 1970s. At the same time NGOs are being asked to account for themselves to their governments and their supporter publics in new ways, and their assertions of effectiveness are no longer taken for granted but are being constantly tested. The internet revolution and the 24-hour news cycle have meant that information is readily accessible, and readily forgotten, as new fashions in aid and development emerge and fade. All of this represents real challenges for ACFID. The days when it could push, what to many was, a radical agenda or 'the politics of the warm inner glow' are past (Evans 1989, p. 1). While public support for NGOs remains higher than it was earlier, the causes that NGOs support and how they are expressed in public debates have changed (Kilby 2014). The right to self-determination through the support of national liberation movements has given way to the more prosaic and local effects of achieving the MDGs or improving aid quality (Biccum 2011, Hilton 2012). One area of resistance to the aid-for-globalisation juggernaut that ACFID has been part of is the notion of rights-based development, which fundamentally challenges the justification and traditional ways of delivering aid (see Chapter 6). In the 2010s, however, even rights-based development seems to be struggling to gain traction, due in part to its complexity and also to the difficulty of having the necessary local level advocacy in the face of increasingly suspicious, if not hostile, host governments (Kindornay et al. 2012).

This chapter will explore these and other challenges facing ACFID in the 2010s, and how it advocates for social justice in a more complex aid and NGO environment, such as dealing with the 'security state'. The 'security state' has emerged as a successor to both the liberal welfare state of the 1960s and 1970s, and the neoliberal state of the 1980s and 1990s (Mitlin et al. 2007; Hallsworth and Lea 2011; Murray and Overton 2011; Howell 2014). It brings with it an intolerance of criticism of state policies by what are seen as unelected or unrepresentative NGOs. The question then becomes how to change advocacy messages so NGOs are listened to (Howell and Lind 2009b; Christensen and Weinstein 2013); and whether peak bodies, such as ACFID with their complex relationship with government and diverse membership, are well equipped to do this.

Another challenge is the rapidly changing aid scene in which aid volumes have increased sharply from the early 2000s in response to global security crises, then fallen again in the 2010s with the global financial crisis of 2008 onwards as more conservative governments in Europe and Australia respond to domestic fiscal pressures with more nationalistic ideologies. Traditional aid donors now have competition from the so-called 'non-traditional' donors led by China that want to work by a different set of rules; the main one being non-interference in the domestic policies of recipient governments. This shift challenges the global policy consensus that has been sought since the 1980s around democracy and what good governance might look like (Glennie 2011; Howell 2012a; Mawdsley 2012).

These donor dynamics of the 2010s have not only weakened the influence of the neoliberal juggernaut, which dominated in the 1980s and 1990s, but they have also meant that human rights and social justice issues have also been relegated, with many local voices in developing countries silenced by the rise of more nationalist and authoritarian regimes. These human rights issues are further complicated by a massive increase in labour mobility and remittances in a time of more restrictive migration policies globally, leading to increased human vulnerably from being a migrant, an issue that development NGOs have generally avoided (Ronalds 2013). Finally, the question arises as to whether there is a need for many of the larger NGOs to have a peak body at all, as they are more integrated into large global networks, such as CARE, Oxfam and World Vision. They all have their own advocacy priorities and machinery and may see locally based advocacy and the level of public support for it as less important.

A changing ACFID

In its early years, in the 1960s and 1970s, ACFID sat easily in the constructivist space of seeing the Third World as open to what Landolt calls 'norm diffusion': in some cases through aid, and in others through advocacy for a different type of aid dialogue (2004, p. 579). The argument put by NGOs and ACFID then was that aid programs, and philosophies which underpin them, should move away from the neocolonial positions of donors to provide greater support for self-determination and the NIEO. In the 1980s and 1990s, advocacy moved to challenge the neoliberal positions of donors and the conditions they set for recipient governments to receive their aid, which were about having smaller non-interventionist states in the developing world. This advocacy involved complex arguments which divided NGOs into those who advocated against the harsh structural adjustment regimes and those who sought to ameliorate its worst effects but still work from within a neoliberal framework (Biccum 2011; Lang 2012). Mitlen et al. (2007) refer to this period from around the mid-1990s into the 2000s as 'a period in which NGOs have had to come to terms with their entry, at scale, into the reform agenda' (p. 1709). The question became to what extent the neoliberal agenda should be resisted while at the same time being part of it by providing safety nets and the like. But perhaps this would lead to the worst of both worlds with an imposed set of values to produce what Biccum refers to 'as competitive cosmopolitan subjects' (2011, p. 1334; Christie 2012; McKinnon 2007). Where ACFID sits in the space is unclear due in part to the increased diversity of its membership (with an increase in smaller agencies with narrower agendas) and also to a less conducive advocacy space for debates around rights and self-determination.

The human rights agenda provided some counterweight to neoliberalism and anchored development in the local, but by the 2010s this had faded (Landolt 2004; Nelson 2007; Van Tuijl 2000). This was in part because of the return to a strong aid recipient nation state, which did not like being lectured to by middle-class activists in either their own countries or their Northern donor partners (Mawdsley et al. 2014). In a sense the NIEO had come to pass, and developing countries were now hostile to those NGOs who supported it in the 1970s. At the same time the Australian government was starting to constrain what ACFID could talk about in policy dialogues, and how public that policy dialogue should be. The change to a conservative Coalition government in 2013, and an aid program tied more tightly to diplomatic and strategic objectives, has meant that in the 2010s NGO concerns about human rights, basic needs and the MDGs have had less impact on government which places greater emphasis on economic growth and strengthening the private sector through the aid programs. This chapter will explore all of these issues and identify some trends for the future.

The State is back

Following the terrorist attacks of the early 2000s in New York, Madrid, London and Bali against the West and Western interests, there has been a shift in development policy from neoliberal calls for a smaller state to one that strengthens the state, particularly its security agencies, but also more generally. One result of the change in development focus to the 'securitisation' of aid was a backlash by both donor and recipient governments against civil society and NGOs, with much greater levels of regulation on what NGOs and other groups could say or do (van der Borgh and Terwindt 2012; Howell and Lind 2009a; Bloodgood and Tremblay-Boire 2011; Howell 2012b; NewsBharati 2012). Aid has been used as part of the global 'war on terror' to build national security apparatuses and to improve services, particularly education services in places like Afghanistan and Iraq (Fleck and Kilby 2006; Azam and Thelen 2008). This 'hearts and minds' strategy was to reduce the influence and role in education of the more fundamentalist forces linked to terrorism (Howell 2014). Another part of this shift has been to reduce the reach of NGOs and civil society, particularly those that might have even remote links to local groups seen as supporting terrorism. The anti-terrorist clauses in most government contracts are quite draconian and almost unenforceable.[1]

---

1   There is generally a requirement that there are no links with individuals and organisations on a very extensive terrorist list, with little support for verifying whether the data is correct or the names on the list are those being referred to. This places the onus on the NGO to verify what is usually beyond their capacity to do so.

This shift in approach by governments to NGOs, and an increased sense of nationalism among developing countries, has seen many countries not accepting civil society and NGOs as legitimate voices in political discourse. There are now stricter regulatory and funding apparatuses, including funding contracts that limit criticism of government policy by NGOs (Tiwana and Belay 2010). A study by Christensen and Weinstein found that over half of a sample of 90 developing countries either ban or restrict foreign funding of local NGOs, up from one quarter of the same list being restricted in 2005 (2013, p. 80). In Australia the restrictions have included the removal of tax deductible status of an advocacy NGO, later reinstated following a High Court appeal (see Chapter 8), and 'gag' clauses in government service delivery contracts preventing criticism of government policy. In developing countries the view of civil society and local NGOs as not being legitimate or desirable can manifest in ways ranging from physical harassment and intimidation through to the criminalisation of some NGO activities that are not in the 'interests' of the state (Christensen and Weinstein 2013).

> Stigmatisation of opponents in speeches, documents, and the media often precedes the judicial criminalisation. Stigmatisation can legitimise acts of criminalisation, while detentions and criminal trials can have a stigmatising effect (van der Borgh and Terwindt 2012, p. 1071).

In the 2010s Russia, for example, adopted laws that required politically active NGOs receiving foreign funding to submit quarterly reports and register with the Justice Ministry as 'foreign agents'; the United Arab Emirates cancelled the operating licenses of two international NGOs working on democratic governance; Ecuador and Zimbabwe have banned NGO projects funded by foreign governments and multilateral organisations; and restrictive laws were either put in place or being considered in India, Bangladesh, Cambodia, Honduras, Iran, Singapore, Ethiopia and Venezuela (Christensen and Weinstein 2013). In India in 2012, the government cancelled the registration of 4,000 NGOs receiving foreign funds – more than 10 per cent of all NGOs registered to receive these funds – largely on the basis of the advocacy stances they took (NewsBharati 2012). In the Pacific a very successful Churches Partnership program in Vanuatu funded by AusAID was halted for a period at the behest of the Vanuatu government in 2012 due to the advocacy stance it took (Thomas 2012).

As well as a response to the security state, this clamp-down on NGOs is also due to a backlash against the Western donor focus on governance, democratisation and strengthening civil society among aid recipient countries (Christensen and Weinstein 2013; Lewis 2010a; Verweij and Pelizzo 2009). These shifts can be seen as a return to more corporatist forms of government, where an authoritarian state relates to a few powerful interest groups (typically business or religious) at the expense of the broader civil society (Kilby 2004; Baccaro 2003; Kamal 2012;

Howell 2012b). This mirrors an earlier crackdown on civil society in the 1930s when many international and local NGOs' activities were severely curtailed with the rise of authoritarian governments (Davies 2008, Kilby 2004).

The other aspect of the return of the 'big State' is the nature of the dialogue with NGOs and peak bodies such as ACFID. Because both NGO legitimacy and funding are linked to the nature of engagement with the state, then any 'falling out' can have repercussions on the NGOs. The difficulties ACFID had with AusAID under the Coalition government of the late 1990s and early 2000s (see Chapter 8), and the cuts in government funding to CCIC in Canada and CID in New Zealand, for example, have had a salutary effect on the sector and resulted in a shift by ACFID more towards lobbying rather than 'noisy' public advocacy about specific government policy (Millar 2013; Brown 2012; O'Callaghan 2013). There are two issues at stake: the first is having a seat at the table, and the second is being listened to. These issues affect the nature of the dialogue and the legitimacy that is brought to the table by NGOs. ACFID has always had a seat at the table as it represents the interests of more than 140 NGOs with nearly $1 billion raised from the community for aid programs. At times ACFID's legitimacy has been put under question from some quarters, but generally it has had a hearing from government. Furthermore, as Chapter 1 pointed out, ACFID has had some important 'wins' over its 50 years.

At issue, however, is the level of compromise evident in the messages ACFID gives when it has a seat at the table; that is, whether NGOs are becoming unwitting carriers of the beliefs, policies and procedures of a global agenda which many of their partners in the Third World would oppose (Wallace 2009; Biccum 2011; Kamat 2004; Lang 2012). These beliefs are not necessarily in support of the narrow 'neoliberal' agenda of the 1990s. Few donors still argue for a smaller state and fewer bilateral aid recipients would accept the idea, but there is still a strong ideological focus of aid policy on the individual rather than the broader recipient community, and the obligations the state has to communities in delivering services and protecting community members' rights. NGOs can get caught up, almost inadvertently, in supporting a more individualist-based global agenda at the expense of the local:

> [T]hey achieve stability by conforming to and reinforcing global understandings of what policy and participation should look like – hence the remarkable isomorphism of these organizations' agendas and strategies (Watkins et al. 2012, p. 294)

These compromises are the effect, in part, of how the developmental state has emerged and chooses to relate to NGOs. These new state structures are referred to variously as neostructuralism (Murray and Overton 2011) and a new form of corporatism (Kilby 2004; Baccaro 2003). While Peck (2004) still refers to neoliberalism, he acknowledges that there may be many neoliberalisms, depending on local context, now based around the strong state. What these models all have in common is that the public benefit arguments of NGOs are generally ignored or suppressed in favour of particular interests, and so civil society and its NGO supporters are marginalised in this process (Murray and Overton 2011). The effect is that the social justice agenda and the calls for rights-based development have all but disappeared (Weber 2013; Howell 2012b). NGOs are restricted to offering 'pragmatic policy solutions within the confines of existing policy options instead of pursuing more general social, economic, and political change agendas' (Lang 2012, p. 91), or they risk being left out of the conversation as was the case for CCIC in Canada and CID in New Zealand in the early 2010s (Hobbs 2013; Purcell 2013; Smillie 2012; Murray and Overton 2011).

This broader shift in various national governance structures creates tensions for ACFID. In the 1970s what many saw as radical student rhetoric could pass as policy advice, but by the 2000s the tolerance levels of government to what it saw as unworkable, unrealistic, self-serving, or unhelpful advice was very low. The pressure on ACFID was not only to be 'on message' but also not to 'rock the (government) boat' by being too critical of its policies. ACFID's contract with AusAID in the 2000s was to provide policy advice and a forum for various consultations of government with NGOs, and so it is hard to be too publicly critical of government in this context. With around half of ACFID's budget being funded in one way or another by government, a precipitous cut in government funding, while not as catastrophic as the Canadian and New Zealand cases, would still limit ACFID in what it could do and, more importantly, possibly close avenues of dialogue with government, which is what frustrated CCIC in Canada (Purcell 2013; Hobbs 2013; Smillie 2012). Ian Smillie noted that the main effect of the CCIC cuts was to damage its members' sense of common purpose; but from the Canadian government's point of view the clear message was that:

> 'NGOs should be seen but not heard' … [but] civil societies' strength comes out of not just speaking out but from willingness of government and others to listen. When voices are silenced governments become deaf and lose the ability to discern (2012, p. 282).

Speaking out is not enough: being listened to is the other part of the equation. If the public or government mood is not to hear NGO messages then new strategies are required, and working out what they should be takes time. In Australia there was another aspect of this advocacy question, and that is whose voice should be heard, and how is legitimacy earned? There has been an ongoing view from some within government, which dates back to the 1990s, that the dialogue with NGOs should be restricted to those with whom it has its major partnerships, that is the (around) 10 largest NGOs,[2] as they have the largest constituency of Australian public support, accounting for about two thirds of funds raised (ACFID 2013). As discussed earlier (see Chapter 8), in the mid-1990s there was a move for the larger NGOs to separate from ACFID and have a separate forum with government, much like the British Overseas Aid Group (BOAG) in the UK (Hobbs 2013; Hunt 2012; Smillie 1999a).[3] In the early 2010s there were proposals that AusAID fund a facility, with matched funding from the 10 larger block-funded NGO partnership agencies, to look at aid quality and aid policy issues, both of which have been a central part of ACFID's mandate for most of its history (Purcell 2013). While these ideas did not eventuate, both examples point to the role of ACFID and NGO legitimacy, and how this legitimacy is demonstrated in the eye of government. Governments, in general, often do not like dealing with smaller, diverse and less broadly representative NGOs, even if they do represent an important niche constituency, such as those with disabilities, or a broader constituency but under-represented among the NGO cohort, such as women.

There is also another shift within NGOs, which also affects relationships with government and others, and that is the generational change in people who work for NGOs (Mitlin et al. 2007; Pearce 2010). Jenny Pearce notes:

> While those who worked in Northern agencies in the 1970s and 1980s were politicised by their experiences of injustice in the areas in which they worked, and by the radical political movements of the times, the new generation comes from Development Studies courses. This has reinforced the influence of those development-agency managers who see the development business as just that: another area of enterprise which must compete with other agencies in the same enterprise (2010, p. 630).

While many younger NGO workers would disagree with the idea that working with NGOs is just another development business, the new worker in development is, however, more sceptical of the student radicalism of the 1960s and 1970s. While they might be open to the ideas of social justice they have far fewer models from which to promote social change, so to some extent are left with no alternative but to argue for a 'tweaking' of policy within a dominant paradigm (Biccum 2011; Lang 2012). The effect is a new form of conformity. In the 1990s the notion of 'professionalism' had a sense of irony and possible resistance about it (Ross 1988; ACFOA 1994c; Meyer 1992), but by the 2000s professionalism is taken very seriously by NGO workers (McKinnon 2007; Tomlinson and Schwabenland 2010; Wright 2012). As ACFID stalwart Wendy

---

2   The number has varied over time from between five and 10, but at the time of writing it was the 10 largest NGOs.
3   British Overseas Aid Group (BOAG) is made up of the five biggest NGOs in the UK: ActionAid, Oxfam, CAFOD, Save the Children and Christian Aid.

Rose noted: 'the idea of professionalism can also "dumb us down" as we get caught up in being too "professional"' (2013). The real test is, perhaps, to ask whether we are making business cases or social justice cases to assess the work being undertaken (Tomlinson and Schwabenland 2010). Part of the social justice agenda is advocacy.

The advocacy agenda of the 2000s

In the 1970s and 1980s much of the advocacy agenda was about self-determination against unjust state regimes such as Biafra/Nigeria, Ethiopia/Eritrea, East Timor, Mozambique, South Africa, Bangladesh and others. By the 2000s the advocacy agenda was very much restricted to redressing some of the ills of modern (corporate or state) capitalism, and the relentless focus of aid policy on the individual to have a larger say in dealing with their own problems, whether it be through microfinance or user pays approaches in education or health care. While the welfare state has not vanished, it is questioned by many aid donors (Noel and Thérien 1995; Chang 2013). To some extent advocacy in the 2000s reflects some of these values, with a focus on access to trade markets for developing countries, improved health and education services, and increased and effective aid (Kamat 2004). There is now much less about rising global inequality and the poor, recognition of human rights, whether they be women's rights or workers' rights, but rather 'world poverty is turning from an international to a national distribution problem, and that governance and domestic taxation and redistribution policies are becoming more important than aid' (Pollard et al. 2011, p. 121).

The other question is whether the increasing levels of inequality will reach a 'flash point' at some stage, with increased internal, and possibly international, conflict. To some extent the rise of religious and other forms of fundamentalism and related terrorists attacks has been argued as a response to growing inequality (Benmelech et al. 2012; Krieger and Meierrieks 2010). While the link is debatable, the increased basic needs approach of the early 2000s through the MDGs and increased aid levels was seen as being in part a response to the threat of terrorism (Karnani 2011; Gore 2010; Bandyopadhyay et al. 2011; Azam and Thelen 2010). The problem, however, is that the MDGs have done little to counter the increasing marginalisation of minority groups and increasing inequality (Kabeer 2012; Fukuda-Parr 2010; Vandemoortele 2011). Vandemoortele points out that for every country that has reduced its levels of inequality, three others have increased levels (2011, p. 16). Studies suggest that development aid has a weak effect, if any, on actually decreasing inequality (Lundqvist 2014;

Chao et al. 2010), and an argument has emerged that if inequality is to be addressed then it needs to be much clearer in development targets such as the MDGs (Fukuda-Parr 2010).

While the question of rising inequality is being pushed within academia, NGOs and the UN, the reality is that with the election of more conservative and nationalistic governments, such as the Abbott government in Australia in 2013 and the Modi government in India in 2014, any advocacy in this area will have little traction, at least in the short term. The sharper emphasis on economic growth in national aid and development policies by these governments is more likely to result in further increases in inequality in developing countries, with the possibility of quite harsh social and political consequences. Piketty (2014) argues that the ever-rising concentration of wealth and patrimonial capitalism is not self-correcting and, if not directly dealt with by state policy, is counterproductive to the political order of the state in the long run and may directly or indirectly threaten global security as well.

The debates of the 1970s described by Lissner (1977) about the relationship and contradictions between NGOs supporting the fight for social justice and those providing services to the poor to fill the gaps left by government programs have faded. The focus in the 2010s is mainly on the supply of services either by government or by NGOs and how that is best done. Advocating for broader social change has largely slipped off the NGO radar, not because they are unaware of the issues but more because these issues do not gain traction with government or their supporter base. An advocacy focus on broad social change could jeopardise the effectiveness of other messages being given, or even NGO funding.[4] The challenge for the 2010s and beyond is how to link with activist movements to have a complementary approach to campaigning on social justice issues, to be more strategic in how that engagement occurs, and what role peak bodies like ACFID have in that process (Bennett 2004; Weber 2013).

There is also a marked difference from the campaigns of the 1970s and 1980s, which were about the injustices in nascent Bangladesh, and Australia's inaction; the anti-apartheid movement; East Timor; and World Bank lending policies, which all highlighted clear national injustices and the West's complicity (see Chapter 3). The main criticism of NGO advocacy in the 2010s is that it seems to be supporting a broader neoliberal paradigm. The argument is that the direction of the current aid program is generally fine, and it is just a question of increasing aid volumes and some tweaking around perhaps a closer alignment with the MDGs and the like (Biccum 2011; Kamat 2004; Lang 2012). The counterargument is that the globalisation battle is lost and all that NGOs

---

4   The cut in funding for CCIC has been put down to the fact it defends a member with a strong social justice focus (Weber 2013).

can do is to make sure the poor benefit rather than lose out from the changes that a more globalised world brings (O'Reilly 2010; Wallace 2009). The problem is, as mentioned above, the consequent inequality: '[In the 1940s] the renowned Indian political leader Dr Ambedkar predicted an intensification of the contradiction between political equality and economic and social inequity', and it seems little has changed (Alston and Robinson 2005, p. 5).

Figure 14 Make Poverty History Campaigners 2006.
Source: Michael Myers/OxfamAUS.

The question for ACFID in its advocacy is how to deal with this challenge, and how to promote a rights-based agenda in an aid and policy environment in which there is an assumed consensus on appropriate economic growth-based approaches. The alternative approach of rights-based development seems to have lost the traction it had in the early 2000s (see Chapter 6), when it was seen as a way to add structural issues to what many saw as fairly instrumentalist MDGs, framed in society averages rather than spelling out rights and obligations of all (Sarelin 2007; Nelson 2007). ACFID and others argue that the MDGs are very much set in a human rights frame, but this has been 'lost in translation' in moving to their implementation (ACFID 2009; Vandemoortele 2011).

Aid quality

The third issue that is a challenge for ACFID in the 2000s is the aid quality debate, which has become much sharper, more focused and more sceptical of the quality of NGO work than even at the height of the debates of the 1990s (see Chapters 1 and 8). ACFID had already begun work on NGO aid quality in the 1980s and set up the Development Project Appraisal and Evaluation Unit in 1985 in response to questions of NGO aid quality (ACFOA 1985a), and there has been a group of people undertaking this role in ACFID ever since. In the 2010s the Code of Conduct has provided a basis for expanding the work in this area, with quality criteria being slowly added.

While the reviews of the AusAID-funded NGO programs of the 1990s and early 2000s clearly demonstrated NGO work was effective, and presumably of good quality (AusAID 1995a, 2002; ACFOA 1995d; Fowler 1997), that evidence has been largely ignored, and others have argued that NGO aid more broadly was not effective (Boone 1996; Mosley 1986). In the 2010s the question of the effectiveness of NGOs and their work refuses to go away. There are still arguments that NGO aid is either not effective in reaching the poor or no better than bilateral aid (Nunnenkamp et al. 2009; Dreher et al. 2010). These arguments tend to ignore the evidence supporting NGOs; for example, from the IMF that NGO aid is effective compared with bilateral aid and it does reach the poor (Yontcheva and Masud 2005; Nancy and Yontcheva 2006). Roger Riddell (2007) has found that most studies show NGO work to be very effective in meeting their immediate objectives. The arguments that the long-term impact of NGO work may be weak can be countered by the fact that most of these impact studies tend to ignore the strong empowerment effects and local networking effect that NGO programs have, and so the broader impact may be understated.

The aid quality debate is linked to the cost-effectiveness debate. NGO programs, by virtue of being small compared with bilateral programs, are seen to have much higher transaction costs to administer if the same standards are to be applied. While these costs can be reduced by having multi-year agreements for block grant funding and quality assurance through accreditation, the pressure is still on donors to reduce costs. An easy way to do that is to reduce funding to NGOs with an argument that NGOs are either ineffective or no more effective than bilateral programs, which is what happened in the 1990s (see Chapter 8).

The Paris principles

It was the series of terror attacks of the early 2000s, mainly on Western targets, which built a new imperative for aid. This time, however, unlike the previous 40 years, aid had to be effective, provide good value for money and be an efficient use of resources (Doucouliagos and Paldam 2009; Brown 2012). In a 2010 study of DAC donors and UN agencies, Australia was ranked in the middle of a group of 30 donors and failed to make the top 10 in any of the four aspects of quality being examined (Birdsall and Kharas 2012).[5] This is partly to do with the criteria used but also with the disparate nature of the Australian aid program in how it deals with different issues and different agendas. Of course none of this was new. One way of dealing with the quality issue is to promote a common approach to how aid is delivered. Effectiveness was seen among the Western club of donors, the DAC, as the way forward and that was through the Paris Principles of Effective Aid.

In 2000 there were a number of meetings among DAC western donors to come up with the Paris Principles of Effective Aid, summed up by Armon:

> Aid at its most effective is harnessed to plans owned by beneficiaries, channelled through their own systems, with progress indicators agreed and reviewed by all stakeholders. It is harmonised, untied, long-term, and predictable, with strong mechanisms of mutual accountability built in (2007, p. 653).

Even though there have been some attempts to link human rights to the Paris Principles, this did not happen (Foresti et al. 2009; Eyben 2013). Another issue is that the short-run political considerations by government tend to militate against any transformational policy process being posited by the Paris Principles; and growth alone may not be enough to trigger the necessary changes (Booth 2012). By the 2010s, and the Busan DAC conference of 2011, the Paris Principles had all but disappeared, as economic growth and the need to accommodate the priorities of a set of Southern donors, the BRICS, had come to prominence. In particular China, as the main player in this group, acted as a counterbalance to Western donors and their interests (Glennie 2011; Mawdsley, Savage and Kim 2014; Eyben 2013). The implications for international NGOs and their aid programs remain unclear. Western donors may continue or even expand aid to NGOs and civil society as a counterpoint to the BRICS' programs, or they may wish to harmonise and reach a common understanding with the BRICS and downplay the role of NGOs and civil society.

The key challenges for the aid quality agenda for both NGOs and government is that development is a political process rather than a depoliticised technical one, which has been a result of the Washington Consensus of the 1980s. Whether the arguments against technocratic approaches can be won is doubtful, despite the evidence for example that the formation of alliances and partnerships

---

5   The four are maximising efficiency, fostering institutions, reducing the burden on recipient countries, and transparency and learning.

that challenge prevailing norms are far more effective than processes that '[skirt] around issues of overt contention' (Hughes and Hutchison 2012, p. 21). In a similar vein, Eyben argues for a move to 'relational aid' in which 'aid recipient countries [are seen] as real places rather than a category' instead of the current approach of 'substantialist aid' (2010, p. 390).[6] Of course these debates for NGOs are not straightforward, particularly in an environment when NGOs entering any sort of political debate, as noted above, is being increasingly frowned upon. On the plus side NGOs are, as Mitchell and Shmitz put it, driven by 'principled instrumentalism'; that is, they are flexible enough to adapt so their principles are not compromised but they are still able to do their work (Mitchell and Schmitz 2012). However, the question is: how far can principles be 'instrumentalised'?

In the future ACFID and its members will be facing the twin challenges of being more directly accountable for the effectiveness of their programs, probably in a technocratic sense, and so arguing the political economy of 'contention' referred to by Hughes and Hutchinson, and Eyben, will be increasingly frowned upon. This is especially so in an official aid program that is integral to foreign policy, and where the social space to speak out for those most marginalised will also be reduced. The result will be a further endangering of the quality of the aid program in terms of reaching the poor and marginalised. How effectively ACFID engages in this debate will be a measure of its own effectiveness.

Engaging with the emerging donors

Since the early 2000s the so-called 'emerging donors', the most prominent being China, represent a clear challenge to the erstwhile Western donors represented by the DAC. These donors include the BRICS, which have been involved in aid to their neighbours for many years. The volume of aid they are providing in the 2000s and 2010s has brought these donors to greater prominence so they are now being included in a greater number of aid forums, and they are acting as a bloc in forums such as the G20 and at the UN (Lieber 2013; Wade 2011; Harris-Rimmer 2013). This group has offered an important and increasingly effective counter to Western development policy, especially the policies of the World Bank and the IMF. Since the Asian economic crisis in the mid-1990s, the IMF has been weakened, particularly in the Asia Pacific where its poor policy advice and the conditions for a funding bailout were making matters worse and most Asian countries simply stopped taking IMF loans (Kilby 2012; Ito 2007). Since then

---

6   'A substantialist perspective sees the world primarily in terms of pre-formed entities in which relations among the entities are only of secondary importance. Substantialism allows us to observe, classify and ascribe essential properties to concepts, such as "international aid"' (Eyben 2010, p. 385).

China in particular has challenged the IMF in offering alternative financial support arrangements without IMF conditionality, for example to Angola and Chad, so that by the early 2010s China was a larger provider of adjustment loans and concessional finance to Africa than either the IMF or the World Bank. As Chin put it: 'The Chinese approach to development finance is not only different from that of the DAC regime, but it also undercuts the influence of the World Bank, [and] in some cases of potential lending' (2012, p. 212).

The BRICSs, and China in particular, see themselves as a counterweight to the dominance of the US (Harris-Rimmer 2013; Wade 2011). They put pressure on the role that civil society can play:

> Inviolable sovereignty in the World-Without-the-West rejects key tenets of "modern" liberal internationalism and particularly any notion of global civil society or public opinion justifying political or military intervention in the affairs of the state (Barma et al. 2007, p. 23).

Western donor policies aimed at strengthening civil society in developing countries have been around since the 1980s, either as a part of a broader neoliberal agenda to reduce the role of the state and have non-state actors take over some functions, or as part of the rights-based development agenda which sees civil society as a mechanism to hold local state actors to account. With the end of the Washington Consensus and its replacement by the 'Beijing Consensus' (Kjøllesdal and Welle-Strand 2010; Kennedy 2010; Dirlik 2006), with a greater role for government in development and a singular focus on rapid economic growth, the scope for NGO involvement is considerably narrower as service providers and most certainly as civil society organisations with a voice representing the poor and marginalised (Halper 2012; Spires 2011). The challenge for ACFID and its members in this rapidly changing, and threatening, context is how to support its partners in developing countries which have hitherto been largely silent.

Managing the political cycle

Aid policy tends to follow the political cycle: conservative governments support more mercantilist and business concerns for economic development with a strong growth focus while liberal–democratic governments follow more traditional human development and humanitarian concerns with an equity focus (Fleck and Kilby 2006). Conservative governments are also generally less generous as bilateral donors than liberal–democratic governments are (Brech and Potrafke 2014; Tingley 2010). Donors with fully independent aid agencies may be less prone to policy-based cuts (Bertoli et al. 2008; Fuchs et al. 2014). The relationship with NGOs is also reflected in the political cycle, with funding to NGOs being inclined to increase at a greater rate under liberal–democratic governments and decline, at least in real terms, under conservative ones. This has been the case to varying degrees over the last 50 years in Australia, Canada, the UK and the Nordic countries (Brown 2012; Smillie et al. 1999; Hilton 2012).

Since the 1960s Australia has had four independent reviews of aid, including the Harries Committee, which devoted a section on aid as part of a broader review of Australia's relationship with developing countries (ACFOA 1978d; Miller et al. 1980; Harries Committee 1979). Apart from Harries the other three reviews have all emphasised an important role for Australian NGOs in the official aid program (Jackson Committee 1984; Simons et al. 1997; Hollway et al. 2011). Harries argued that as aid was an expression of national interest there was little place for NGO aid beyond to it 'being a catalyst for wider public support', which is what the ANCP at the time was aimed at doing (Harries Committee 1979, p. 140). While government has tended to support the recommendations of these reviews, the emphasis on supporting NGOs has also followed the political cycle so that in the 1970s and 1980s the volume of aid provided through NGOs increased under Labor governments and had real falls (as a proportion of the aid program) under Coalition governments.

Figure 15 Young Australians from every federal electorate across for Make Poverty History Australia, March 2013.

Source: Sarah Pannell/Oaktree.

The challenge for ACFID is to manage the process of responding to and influencing government aid policy within the political framework of government, while at the same time ensuring the independence of NGOs to undertake their own work but being able to receive government support for that work. The argument by Harries in 1979 that government funding can be used to lever more funds from the Australian public was true. But it only went so far as there is also a role for NGOs in the broader official aid program, as the subsequent reviews pointed out (Jackson Committee 1984; Simons et al. 1997; Hollway et al. 2011). With the official aid program in the 2010s shrinking and more tightly integrated into the nation's foreign policy, the ability of NGOs to support partners in developing countries fighting for their rights or advocating policies at odds with their government's policies may be under some threat, as the door closes for broader NGO funding beyond the ANCP, and it has little prospect of growth in the context of a declining aid budget. In the ACFID strategic plan for 2015 onwards, there is a move to engage the public more directly on the broader challenges of human development as a way to build a constituency for aid, much like the global education programs of the 1970s (Purcell 2015). How well this plays out in a quite different global context will be interesting to see.

Conclusion

Over its 50 years ACFID has come full circle. From the early optimism for development and the role that NGOs might have in it, and from a strong global education focus in the 1970s, it has moved to building a strong relationship with government and issues-based campaigns of the 1980s. Since the early 1990s the relationship with government, and the role of ACFID, has grown more complex. While NGOs were more prominent, they are now also under more scrutiny. There is a threat that their 'voice' may be stifled with the rise of more nationalist and corporatist styles of government emerging in the 2000s. In its first 25 years, ACFID was able to speak freely and publicly on the issue of social justice, and to provide an important forum for its members to learn and share from each other. In the last 25 years, however, it has had to become more circumspect in its relations with government. As a forum ACFID now plays a much stronger role with its growing and more diverse membership, with the defining issue being the expanded Code of Conduct and its focus on aid quality and NGO accountability (see Chapter 9). The challenges in the 2010s are how to maintain that focus when there is a diminishing official aid program for NGOs; a narrowing of the political space in which partners can operate; and how ACFID can continue to be the rallying point for its members and a voice for social justice.

The opportunities for activism and promoting rights-based approaches have narrowed in the 2010s. There is reduced enthusiasm for them both in donor and recipient governments, which means that the social justice space that NGOs can carve out is limited, and can even threaten the survival of their partner NGOs in developing countries. Davies (2008) argues that the political threats to global civil society in the 2010s are on par with or even greater than they were in the 1930s, when the number of NGOs halved from a peak in the 1920s.[7] How a peak body like ACFID meets the challenge of these threats, when government concerns are more about policy alignment than social justice, and NGO partners are being squeezed by even sharper regulatory and funding pressures, remains to be seen.

The 50 years of ACFID have seen it move from an era of activism around self-determination, with East Timor being probably the stand out, to global education and advocacy, and dealing with greater engagement with government as both a funder in the 1980s and a regulator in the 1990s. Conflicts arose internally in the 1970s around global education and taking politically contentious stances on the social justice issues of the time and externally with government in the 1990s over high levels of NGO funding and questions of effectiveness and accountability. As a social justice organisation ACFID has to raise and advocate for these issues. The question is what is the most effective way to do it in a more hostile political environment, not only for NGOs globally but also for civil society more broadly?

The areas where ACFID has had mixed results are humanitarian programming and changing gender policies among its members. In the case of humanitarian and emergency programming IDEC was essentially a victim of its own successes (see Chapter 5). The Cambodian and Live Aid work showed what a coordinated approach through a single fund could do for disaster responses. But the politics of dividing up the money, and the perceived need to promote more and more humanitarian crises for little return after the public had long lost interest, led to some soul searching. ACFID found its niche as a coordinator and a forum for dealing with issues, including being a point of accountability, as was the case with the Indian Ocean tsunami. The unresolved issue of humanitarian programs is the ethical one for which there may not be an answer, and that is how to ensure those in most need are being reached without being enmeshed in the politics and ethical dilemmas of the conflict – lessons hard learnt from Biafra, Cambodia, and Rwanda.

ACFID has challenged its members on good gender practice since 1975, both within agencies and in their programs (see Chapter 4). The gains have been hard won and often lagged behind broader society and many of their NGO peers.

---

7   While the 1930s Great Depression was one cause of this drop, the political pressures on NGOs from authoritarian governments was also part of the explanation.

In the 2010s family and domestic violence is being seen as a development issue by ACFID members more broadly, but there may be some way to go for most of ACFID's members to see family violence as emerging from structural issues in society, and being prepared to advocate at that level. Within ACFID the issue of gender is still seen as a women's issue, with few men as gender activists involved.

ACFID has managed to continue to anchor itself in the founding principles of social justice and human rights, and the challenges outlined in this chapter and the book more broadly are certainly not insurmountable. ACFID led the world with its Code of Ethics, later to become the Code of Conduct, a code that continues to evolve. The growing membership of smaller NGOs, which may be less engaged in some of the broader issues, may also present a challenge to the executive and secretariat. But likewise such a broad membership is crucial for ACFID's credibility, as Sir John Crawford the founding president and Brian Hayes the first executive director in the late 1960s knew only too well. ACFID has proven very adept over the last 50 years at leading and challenging both government and its members, while surviving its own internal pressures and divisions. The Greek chorus referred to in Chapter 1 is still in good voice but with perhaps a subtler tune. This is the legacy of ACFID in 2015.

References

Abdel-Rahman, Ibrahim H. 1970. Discussion. In Colin Legum (ed.). *The First U.N. Development Decade and its Lessons for the 1970s*. Ch. 3. New York: Praeger.

Abraham, Anne. 2007. Tsunami swamps aid agency accountability: government waives requirements. *Australian Accounting Review* 17 (41):4–12.

Abrecht, Paul. 1968. Report Responses to the World Conference on Church and Society 1966. *The Ecumenical Review* 20 (4):445–463.

ACC. 1972. Report on the National Conference on Action for World Development. In *Records of the Australian Council for Overseas Aid*, MS9374, Box 31, Folio 152. Canberra: National Library of Australia.

ACFID. 2006. *NGO Report on the Asian Tsunami (26 December 2004 – 31 December 2005)*. Canberra: ACFID.

—— 2009. *Millennium Development Rights: How human rights-based approaches are achieving the MDGs; Case-studies from the Australian aid and development sector*. Canberra: ACFID.

—— 2010a. *Annual Report*. Canberra: ACFID.

—— 2010b. Human-Rights based approaches to Development. *Practice Note*. Canberra: ACFID.

—— 2013. *Annual Report*. Canberra: ACFID.

—— 2013a. ACFID Members Homepage. ACFID 2013. Available at www.acfid. asn.au/membership/our-members, accessed 14 May.

—— 2013b ACFID Website: Our Members, 2013. ACFID 2013. Available at www.acfid.asn.au/membership/our-members.

—— 2013c. *Annual Report*. Canberra: ACFID. Available at www.acfid.asn.au/ membership/our-members.

—— 2014a. Effective Development Practice with Aboriginal and Torres Strait Islander Communities. *Practice Note*. Canberra: ACFID.

—— 2014b. Humanitarian Reference Group. ACFID Website. Canberra: ACFID. Available at www.acfid.asn.au/about-acfid/standing-committees/humanitarian-reference-group-hrg, accessed 18 March.

ACFOA. 1965a. Minutes of Meeting of Voluntary Aid Organisations 6 and 7 April. In *Records of the Australian Council for Overseas Aid,* MS9347, Box 57, Folder 294. Canberra: National Library of Australia.

—— 1965b. Respective Roles of Government, United Nations and Non-Governmental agencies and Opportunities for Co-operation in overseas aid activities; conference, Development and Relief Commission of ACFOA 8–9 November. In *Records of the Australian Council for Overseas Aid*, MS9347, Box 2, Folder 9. Canberra: National Library of Australia.

—— 1965c. Minutes of First Council Meeting, August. In *Records of the Australian Council for Overseas Aid;* MS9374, Box 1, Folio 1. Canberra: National Library of Australia.

—— 1965d. Minutes of Executive Committee, 12 April. In *Records of the Australian Council for Overseas Aid,* MS9347, Box 57, Folder 294. Canberra: National Library of Australia.

—— 1965e. Australian Council for Overseas Aid Rules. In *Records of the Australian Council for Overseas Aid*, MS9347, Box 1, Folder 1. Canberra: National Library of Australia.

—— 1966a. Minutes of Council Meeting, 14–15 March. In *Records of the Australian Council for Overseas Aid*; MS9374, Box 53, Folio 274. Canberra: National Library of Australia.

—— 1966b. ACFOA: Its Objectives and Relationship with Government. In *Records of the Australian Council for Overseas Aid,* MS9347, Box 57, Folder 294. Canberra: National Library of Australia.

—— 1966c. ACFOA Standing Policy. In *Records of the Australian Council for Overseas Aid;* MS9374, Box 3, Folder 15. Canberra: National Library of Australia.

—— 1966d. Tax Deductibility for Donations to Overseas Aid. In *Records of the Australian Council for Overseas Aid,* MS9347, Box 13, Folder 1. Canberra: National Library Australia.

———1966e. Minutes of Special Meeting of ACFOA, 30 September. Melbourne. In *Records of the Australian Council for Overseas Aid*, MS9347, Box 57, Folder 294. Canberra: National Library of Australia.

——— 1966f. Letter from John Crawford to David Scott, 2 December. In *Records of the Australian Council for Overseas Aid*; MS9374, Box 1, Folio 1. Canberra: National Library of Australia.

——— 1966g. Addresses to Refugee and Migrant Services Conferences 22–23 February, Canberra.

——— 1967a. Minutes of Meeting with the Department of External Affairs, 13 November. In *Records of the Australian Council for Overseas Aid*, MS9347, Box 13, Folder 1. Canberra: National Library of Australia.

——— 1967b. Minutes of Executive Committee, 13 April. In *Records of the Australian Council for Overseas Aid*, MS9347 Box 13, Folder 1. Canberra: National Library of Australia.

——— 1967c. Minutes of Council Meeting, 7–8 June. In *Records of the Australian Council for Overseas Aid*, MS9347, Box 54, Folder 278. Canberra: National Library of Australia.

——— 1967d. *Not by Government Alone*. ACFOA (ed.). Melbourne.

——— 1968a. Council Minutes, 25–26 March. In *Records of the Australian Council for Overseas Aid*, Box 54, folder 276. Canberra: National Library of Australia.

——— 1968b. Minutes of Executive Committee Meeting, 24 March. In *Records of the Australian Council for Overseas Aid*, MS9347 Box 57, Folder 296. Canberra: National Library of Australia.

——— 1968c. Minutes of Executive Committee Meeting, 3 May. In *Records of the Australian Council for Overseas Aid*, MS9347 Box13, Folder 1. Canberra: National Library of Australia.

——— 1969a. *Proceedings of the Australian Role in Joint Ventures and Investment in Developing Countries of Asia and the Pacific*. In *Records of the Australian Council for Overseas Aid*, MS9374, Box 2, Folio 5. Canberra: National Library of Australia.

——— 1969b. Report of ACFOA Seminar on Education and Fundraising for Overseas aid in the 1970s, 20 June. In *Records of the Australian Council for Overseas Aid*, MS9347, Box 13, Folder 2. Canberra: National Library of Australia.

—— 1969c. Council Minutes, 21–22 June. In *Records of the Australian Council for Overseas Aid*, MS9347, Box 54. Canberra: National Library of Australia.

—— 1969d. Minutes of Executive Committee Meetings, 20 June and 10 December. In *Records of the Australian Council for Overseas Aid*, MS9347, Box 57, Folder 297. Canberra: National Library of Australia.

—— 1970a. *A Case for Tax deductibility on Overseas Aid Donations*. Melbourne: ACFOA.

—— 1970b. Council Minutes, 15–16 August. In *Records of the Australian Council for Overseas Aid,* MS9347. Canberra: National Library of Australia.

—— 1971a. Annual Council, 13–15 August. In *Records of the Australian Council for Overseas Aid*, MS 9347, Box 54, Folio 279. Canberra: National Library of Australia.

—— 1971b. Parliament House Hunger fast. Press release, 13 October. In *Records of the Australian Council for Overseas Aid,* MS9374, Box 51, Folder 265. Canberra: National Library of Australia.

—— 1971c. Submission on Co-ordination of Fund Raising for Major International Disasters, In *Records of the Australian Council for Overseas Aid,* MS9347 MSAcc10.179, Box 33. (Added 5 November 2010). Canberra: National Library of Australia.

—— 1972a. Minutes of ACFOA Executive, 24–25 March. In *Records of the Australian Council for Overseas Aid,* MS9347, Box 57, Folder 300. Canberra: National Library of Australia.

—— 1972b. The Education Centre Project Proposal (February). In *Records of the Australian Council for Overseas Aid,* MS9347, Box 36, Folio 13. Canberra: National Library of Australia.

—— 1972c. Launch of Disaster Emergency Committee. Press release, 13 November. In *Records of the Australian Council for Overseas Aid,* Box 51, Folder 265. Canberra: National Library of Australia.

—— 1973a. Minutes of Education Sub-Committee, 10 July. In *Records of the Australian Council for Overseas Aid,* MS9374, Box 37 Folder 178. Canberra: National Library of Australia.

—— 1973b. Council Minutes, 25–26 August. In *Records of the Australian Council for Overseas Aid,* MS9374, Box 54. Canberra: National Library of Australia.

—— 1973c. Submission to DFAT on Matching Grants to Voluntary Agencies. In *Records of the Australian Council for Overseas Aid,* MS9347, Box 31, Folder 153. Canberra: National Library of Australia.

—— 1973d. Australian Schools and the Third World. Paper for conference on Development Education, Canberra College of Advanced Education, 19–24 January. Canberra: ACFOA.

—— 1974a. Council Minutes, 31 August – 1 September. In *Records of the Australian Council for Overseas Aid,* MS9347, Box 57, Folder 300. Canberra: National Library of Australia.

—— 1974b. Minutes of Education Sub-Committee, 21 February. In *Records of the Australian Council for Overseas Aid,* MS9374, Box 37, Folder 178. Canberra: National Library of Australia.

—— 1974c. Minutes of Education Sub-Committee, 27 September. In *Records of the Australian Council for Overseas Aid,* MS9374, Box 37, Folder 178. Canberra: National Library of Australia.

—— 1975a. Minutes of the ACFOA Executive, 4 April. In *Records of the Australian Council for Overseas Aid,* MS9347, Box 57, Folder 300. Canberra: National Library of Australia.

—— 1975b. Letters, *Development News Digest* 13 (June): 1–23.

—— 1975c. Minutes of the ACFOA Executive, 1 August. In *Records of the Australian Council for Overseas Aid,* MS9347, Box 57, Folder 300. Canberra: National Library of Australia.

—— 1975d. Minutes of Annual Council, 23–24 August. In *Records of the Australian Council for Overseas Aid,* MS9347, Box 57, Folder 300. Canberra: National Library of Australia.

—— 1975e. Draft IDEC Constitution, 19 August. In *Records of the Australian Council for Overseas Aid,* Box 55, Folder 283. Canberra: National Library of Australia.

—— 1975f. Report of the Education Unit to Council, 18 August. In *Records of the Australian Council for Overseas Aid,* MS9347, Box 37, Folder 178. Canberra: National Library of Australia.

—— 1975g. Minutes of the ACFOA Executive, 6 June. In *Records of the Australian Council for Overseas Aid,* MS9347, Box 57, Folder 300. Canberra: National Library of Australia.

—— 1975h. Minutes of the ACFOA Executive, 7 July. In *Records of the Australian Council for Overseas Aid,* MS9347, Box 57, Folder 300. Canberra: National Library of Australia.

—— 1975i. Aid Agencies Gear up for Assistance to Timor. Media release, 20 September. In *Records of the Australian Council for Overseas Aid,* MS9347, Box 51, Folder 265. Canberra: National Library of Australia.

—— 1975j. East Timor ACFOA Position. Media release, 30 September. In *Records of the Australian Council for Overseas Aid,* Box 51 Folder 265. Canberra: National Library of Australia.

—— 1975k. Voluntary Agencies Team to Timor. Media release, 13 October. In *Records of the Australian Council for Overseas Aid,* MS9347, Box 51, Folder 265. Canberra: National Library of Australia.

—— 1976a. Minutes of Meeting of ACFOA Executive, 12 February. In *Records of the Australian Council for Overseas Aid,* MS9347, Box 57, Folder 300. Canberra: National Library of Australia.

—— 1976b. Minutes of Meeting of ACFOA Executive, 12 February. In *Records of the Australian Council for Overseas Aid,* MS9347, Box 57, Folder 300. Canberra: National Library of Australia.

—— 1976c. *Standing Policy.* Canberra: ACFOA.

—— 1976d. Submission to the Minister for Foreign Affairs, March. In *Records of the Australian Council for Overseas Aid.* MS9374, Box 31, Folio 153. Canberra: National Library of Australia.

—— 1976e. The end of ADAA. *Development News Digest* (15):1–31.

—— 1976f. The Power of Public Opinion: report of a one day consultation on ADAA and the future of Official Australian Aid, 12 April. In *Records of the Australian Council for Overseas Aid,* MS9374, Box 44, Folio 229. Canberra: National Library of Australia.

—— 1976g. Advice to the foreign minister on the disbanding ADAA, 17 March. In *Records of the Australian Council for Overseas Aid,* MS9374, Box 44, Folio 229. Canberra: National Library of Australia.

—— 1976h. Aid to East Timor Appeal Closed. Media release, 12 May. In *Records of the Australian Council for Overseas Aid,* MS9374, Box 51, Folio 265. Canberra: National Library of Australia.

—— 1976i. Education Committee Report to Council, 21–22 August. In *Records of the Australian Council for Overseas Aid*, MS9374, Box 55, Folio 284. Canberra: National Library of Australia.

—— 1977a. Some thoughts on the Review of ACFOA. In *Records of the Australian Council for Overseas Aid*, MS9347, MSAcc10.179, Box 46. (Added 5 November 2010). Canberra: National Library of Australia.

—— 1977b. Cyclone appeal money to India. Media release, 23 December, In *Records of the Australian Council for Overseas Aid*, MS9347, Box 51, Folder 265. Canberra: National Library of Australia.

—— 1978a. Minutes of the Review/Education Meeting, 14 June. In *Records of the Australian Council for Overseas Aid*, MS9347, Box 55, Folder 287. Canberra: National Library of Australia.

—— 1978b. Summer School shall not end. *Development News Digest*, 1–23 March. Canberra: ACFOA.

—— 1978c. Report to Council: ACFOA Education Program. In *Records of the Australian Council for Overseas Aid*, MS9347, Box 55, Folder 286. Canberra: National Library of Australia.

—— 1978d. Response to Harries Committee Report on Australia's Foreign Relations. In *Records of the Australian Council for Overseas Aid*, MS9347, Box 55, Folder 286. Canberra: National Library of Australia.

—— 1979a. ACFOA Attacks Government aid decision to Vietnam. Media release, 24 January. In *Records of the Australian Council for Overseas Aid*, MS9347, Box 51, Folder 265. Canberra: National Library of Australia.

—— 1979b. Private Aid to Vietnam continues. Media release, 25 January. In *Records of the Australian Council for Overseas Aid*, MS9347, Box 51, Folder 265. Canberra: National Library of Australia.

—— 1979c. Issues Raised by the ACFOA Review. In *Records of the Australian Council for Overseas Aid*, MS9347, MSAcc10.179, Box 46. (Added 5 November 2010). Canberra: National Library of Australia.

—— 1979d. Indo-Chinese refugees. Media release, 8 July. In *Records of the Australian Council for Overseas Aid*, MS9347, Box 51, Folder 265. Canberra: National Library of Australia.

—— 1979e. East Timor Meeting. Media release, 5 November. In *Records of the Australian Council for Overseas Aid*, MS9347, Box 51, Folder 265. Canberra: National Library of Australia.

—— 1979f. Agencies release report on East Timor Meeting. Media release, 2 August. In *Records of the Australian Council for Overseas Aid,* MS9347, Box 51, Folder 265. Canberra: National Library of Australia.

—— 1979g. DND 30 – Kampuchean papers, December. In *Records of the Australian Council for Overseas Aid,* MS9347, Box 83, Folder 74. (Added 30 January 1998). Canberra: National Library of Australia.

—— 1979h. Kampuchean Relief Appeal Report, 26 November. In *Records of the Australian Council for Overseas Aid,* MS9347, Box 84, Folder 79 (Added 30 January 1998). Canberra: National Library of Australia.

—— 1979i. ACFOA Review Stage Three. In *Records of the Australian Council for Overseas Aid,* MS9347, MSAcc10.179, Box 46. (Added 5 November 2010). Canberra: National Library of Australia.

—— 1980a. Kampuchean Relief Appeal Passes $10m. Media release, 12 June. In *Records of the Australian Council for Overseas Aid,* MS9347, Box 51, Folder 265. Canberra: National Library of Australia.

—— 1980b. Council Minutes, 27–28 September. In *Records of the Australian Council for Overseas Aid,* MS9347, Box 56, Folder 288. Canberra: Australian National Library.

—— 1980c. Report of ACFOA Commission of Enquiry on East Timor April with ACFOA critique (October). In *Records of the Australian Council for Overseas Aid,* MS9347, MSAcc10.179, Box 28, (Added 5 November 2010). Canberra: National Library of Australia.

—— 1981a. Submission to Industries Assistance Commission inquiry into general reduction in protection. In *Records of the Australian Council for Overseas Aid,* Box 31, Folder 153. Canberra: Australian National Library.

—— 1981b. Notes on briefing with Peacock, 14 January. In *Records of the Australian Council for Overseas Aid,* Box 46, Folder 242. Canberra: National Library of Australia.

—— 1981c. Minutes of Education Sub-Committee, 11 December. In *Records of the Australian Council for Overseas Aid,* Box 37, Folder 180. Canberra: Australian National Library.

—— 1981d. Council Minutes, 3–4 October. In *Records of the Australian Council for Overseas Aid,* MS9347, Box 56, Folder 289. Canberra: National Library of Australia.

—— 1981e. Notes Towards a criticism of the Report of the ACFOA-Initiated East Timor Commission of Enquiry. ACFOA East Timor Sub-Committee (ed.). Canberra: ACFOA.

—— 1981f. Kampuchean Appeal Report. In *Records of the Australian Council for Overseas Aid,* MS9347, Box 83, Folder 74. (Added 30 January 1998). Canberra: National Library of Australia.

—— 1982a. Council Minutes, 18–19 September. In *Records of the Australian Council for Overseas Aid,* MS9347, Box 56, Folder 290. Canberra: National Library of Australia.

—— 1982b. ACFOA Submission to the Senate Inquiry into East Timor. In *Records of the Australian Council for Overseas Aid,* MS9347, Box 31, Folder 153. Canberra: National Library of Australia.

—— 1983a. Submission to the Committee to Review the Australian Aid Program, 8 July. In *Records of the Australian Council for Overseas Aid,* MS9374, Box 50, Folio 262. Canberra: National Library of Australia.

—— 1983b. ACFOA Council Papers 24–25 September. In *Records of the Australian Council for Overseas Aid,* MS9347, MSAcc10.179, Box 53. (Added 5 November 2010). Canberra: National Library of Australia.

—— 1983c. National Aid Organisation call for aid to Ethiopia on Strict Conditions. Media release, 28 March. In *Records of the Australian Council for Overseas Aid,* MS9347, Box 45, Folder 236. Canberra: National Library of Australia.

—— 1983d. Women and Development. Media release, 12 July. In *Records of the Australian Council for Overseas Aid,* MS9347, Box 45, Folder 236. Canberra: National Library of Australia.

—— 1983e. Call for Australia to cut all miliary aid to Philippines. Media release, 5 October. In *Records of the Australian Council for Overseas Aid,* MS9347, Box 51, Folder 265. Canberra: National Library of Australia.

—— 1983f. Council Minutes, 18–19 September. In the *Records of the Australian Council for Overseas Aid,* MS9347, Box 56, Folder 291. Canberra: National Library of Australia.

—— 1984a. ACFOA Analysis of Aid Budget, 24 August. In *Records of the Australian Council for Overseas Aid,* MS9374, Box 50, Folio 262. Canberra: National Library of Australia.

—— 1984b. Aid Body Releases Study on Indochina. Media release, 4 May. In *Records of the Australian Council for Overseas Aid,* MS9347, Box 51, Folder 265. Canberra: National Library of Australia.

—— 1984c. Council Minutes, 18–19 September. In *Records of the Australian Council for Overseas Aid,* MS9347, Box 56, Folder 292. Canberra: National Library of Australia.

—— 1984d. Papers for Annual Meeting 15–16 September: ACFOA priorities 1984/85. In *Records of the Australian Council for Overseas Aid,* MS9347, MSAcc10.179, Box 32. (Added 5 November 2010). Canberra: National Library of Australia.

——1985a. Council Minutes, 14–15 September. In *Records of the Australian Council for Overseas Aid,* MS9347, Box 56, Folder 293. Canberra: National Library of Australia .

—— 1985b. Minutes of Executive, 21–22 February. In *Records of the Australian Council for Overseas Aid,* MS9347, Box 53, Folder 272. Canberra: National Library of Australia.

—— 1985c. Memo to Members: Notice of National Dev Ed officers conference to be held March 26–28, 18 February. In *Records of the Australian Council for Overseas Aid,* MS9347, Box 53, Folder 272. Canberra: National Library of Australia.

—— 1985d. Minutes of Executive, 22–23 August. In *Records of the Australian Council for Overseas Aid,* MS9347, Box 53, Folder 272. Canberra: National Library of Australia.

—— 1985e. Notes of Meeting at World Vision, 20 December. In *Records of the Australian Council for Overseas Aid,* MS9347, MSAcc10.179, Box 19. (Added 5 November 2010). Canberra: National Library of Australia.

—— 1985f. Papers for Annual Meeting 14–15 September: ACFOA priorities 1985/86. In *Records of the Australian Council for Overseas Aid,* MS9347, MSAcc10.179, Box 31. (Added 5 November 2010). Canberra: National Library of Australia.

—— 1985g. ACFOA Annual Report. In *Records of the Australian Council for Overseas Aid,* MS9347, MSAcc10.179, Box 37. (Added 5 November 2010). Canberra: National Library of Australia.

—— 1986a. Quality of Aid Committee Report, 21 February. In *Records of the Australian Council for Overseas Aid,* MS9347, MSAcc10.179, Box 19. (Added 5 November 2010). Canberra: National Library of Australia.

—— 1986b. *Improving Development the Effectiveness of the Australian Overseas Aid Program*. Canberra: ACFOA.

—— 1986c. Papers for Executive Committee, 21–22 August. In *Records of the Australian Council for Overseas Aid,* MS9347, MSAcc10.179, Box 19. (Added 5 November 2010). Canberra: National Library of Australia.

—— 1987a. ACFOA Council Resolution on Notice: Role and Status of women in agencies. In *Records of the Australian Council for Overseas Aid,* MS9347, Box 108, Folder 230. (Added 30 January 1998). Canberra: National Library of Australia.

—— 1987b. ACFOA Priorities 1987–88: Council Papers 12–13 September. In *Records of the Australian Council for Overseas Aid,* MS9347, MSAcc10.179, Box 36. (Added 5 November 2010). Canberra: National Library of Australia.

—— 1987c. Papers for Executive Committee, 11 September. In *Records of the Australian Council for Overseas Aid,* MS9347, MSAcc10.179, Box 20. (Added 5 November 2010). Canberra: National Library of Australia.

—— 1988. Minutes of the 1988 ACFOA Council. In *Records of the Australian Council for Overseas Aid,* MS9347 MSAcc10.179, Box 21. (Added 5 November 2010). Canberra: National Library of Australia.

—— 1989a. Council Minutes, 9–10 September. In *Records of the Australian Council for Overseas Aid,* MS9347, Box 54, Folder 282. Canberra: National Library of Australia.

—— 1989b. One World or None, Annual Report. In *Records of the Australian Council for Overseas Aid,* MS9347, MSAcc10.179, Box 45. (Added 5 November 2010). Canberra: National Library of Australia.

—— 1990a. *Through the Looking Glass – Australian NGOs and Third World Development*. Canberra: ACFOA/NCDS.

—— 1990b. Minutes of the Education Committee, 3 May. In *Records of the Australian Council for Overseas Aid,* MS9347, Box 182, Folder 115. (Added 21 September 1998). Canberra: National Library of Australia.

—— 1990c. Executive Director's Report to ACFOA Executive Committee, 7 September. In *Records of the Australian Council for Overseas Aid,* MS9347, MSAcc10.179, Box 49. (Added 5 November 2010). Canberra: National Library of Australia.

—— 1990d. Executive Committee Minutes, 3–4 May. In *Records of the Australian Council for Overseas Aid,* MS9347, MSAcc10.179, Box 49. (Added 5 November 2010). Canberra: National Library of Australia.

—— 1991a. Minutes of Ethics Committee, 26 July. In *Records of the Australian Council for Overseas Aid,* MS9347, MSAcc10.179, Box 25, 6–27 ACFOA Code of Ethics 1989–96. (Added 5 November 2010). Canberra: National Library of Australia.

—— 1991b. ACFOA Executive Committee Minutes, 9–10 May. In *Records of the Australian Council for Overseas Aid,* MS9347, MSAcc10.179, Box 49. (Added 5 November 2010). Canberra: National Library of Australia.

—— 1991c. ACFOA Executive Committee Report, 1–2 August. In *Records of the Australian Council for Overseas Aid,* MS9347, MSAcc10.179, Box 50. (Added 5 November 2010). Canberra: National Library of Australia.

—— 1992a. ACFOA Council: resolution on Women in Development in Australian NGOs, October. In *Records of the Australian Council for Overseas Aid,* MS9347, Box 108, Folder 237. (Added 30 January 1998*)*. Canberra: National Library of Australia.

—— 1992b. Proposal for a WID Adviser. In *Records of the Australian Council for Overseas Aid,* MS9347, Box 108, Folder 237. (Added 30 January 1998). Canberra: National Library of Australia.

—— 1992c. Brief for Meeting with AIDAB Executive. In *Records of the Australian Council for Overseas Aid,* MS9347, MSAcc10.179, Box 14. (Added 5 November 2010). Canberra: National Library of Australia.

—— 1992d. ACFOA Executive Committee Report, 7–8 May. In *Records of the Australian Council for Overseas Aid,* MS9347, MSAcc10.179, Box 50, (Added 5 November 2010). Canberra: National Library of Australia.

—— 1993a. AIDABExCom/ACFOA ExCom Meeting Brief, 10 June. In *Records of the Australian Council for Overseas Aid,* MS9347, MSAcc10.179, Box 8. (Added 5 November 2010). Canberra: National Library of Australia.

—— 1993b. Campaigns Committee Meeting Minutes, 29 March. In *Records of the Australian Council for Overseas Aid,* MS9347, MSAcc10.179, Box 41. (Added 5 November 2010). Canberra: National Library of Australia.

—— 1993c. ACFOA Executive Committee Report, 9–12 September. In *Records of the Australian Council for Overseas Aid,* MS9347, MSAcc10.179, Box 51. (Added 5 November 2010). Canberra: National Library of Australia.

—— 1994a. ACFOA Affirmative Action Policy. In *Records of the Australian Council for Overseas Aid,* MS9347, Box 108, Folder 232. (Added 30 January 1998). Canberra: National Library of Australia.

—— 1994b. ACFOA Executive Committee Report, 21–22 July. In *Records of the Australian Council for Overseas Aid,* MS9347, MSAcc10.179, Box 52. (Added 5 November 2010). Canberra: National Library of Australia.

—— 1994c. ACFOA Executive Committee Report Sept 8. In *Records of the Australian Council for Overseas Aid,* MS9347, MSAcc10.179, Box 52. (Added 5 November, 2010). Canberra: National Library of Australia.

—— 1994d. Umbrella Group Protects Aid delivery. Media release, 9 August. In *ACFID Files: CARE File 9–15.* Canberra: ACFID.

—— 1994e. ACFOA Executive Committee Report, 12–13 May. In *Records of the Australian Council for Overseas Aid,* MS9347, MSAcc10.179, Box 52. (Added 5 November 2010). Canberra: National Library of Australia.

—— 1995a. Minutes of Ethics Committee, 1 September. In *Records of the Australian Council for Overseas Aid,* MS9347, MSAcc10.179, Box 25, 6–27 ACFOA Code of Ethics 1989–96 (Added 4 November 2010). Canberra: National Library of Australia.

—— 1995b. Minutes of Ethics Committee, 19 October. In *Records of the Australian Council for Overseas Aid,* MS9347, MSAcc10.179, Box 25, 6–27 ACFOA Code of Ethics 1989–96. (Added 5 November, 2010). Canberra: National Library of Australia.

—— 1995c. Report of Ethics Committee to Council, September. In *Records of the Australian Council for Overseas Aid,* MS9347, MSAcc10.179, Box 25, 6_27 ACFOA Code of Ethics 1989–96. (Added 5 November 2010). Canberra: National Library of Australia.

—— 1995d. ACFOA's Response to the Review of the Effectiveness of NGO Programs. In *Records of the Australian Council for Overseas Aid,* MS9347, MSAcc10.179, Box 6, NGO Effectiveness Review File. (Added 5 November 2010). Canberra: National Library of Australia .

—— 1995e. Minutes of First Meeting of ICCC Nov 22. Records of the Australian Council for Overseas Aid, MS9347 MSAcc10.179, Box 26, (Added 5 November 2010) National Library of Australia, Canberra.

—— 1996a. Notes from meeting between Bill Armstrong, John Newsom, Janet Hunt and Andrew Thomson Parliamentary Secretary for Foreign Affairs, 13 November. In *Records of the Australian Council for Overseas Aid*, MS9347, MSAcc10.179, Box 2, Folder 3-4-1. (Added 5 November 2010). Canberra: National Library of Australia.

—— 1996b. Acceptance of ACFOA Code of Conduct, 29 November. In *Records of ACFID:* CARE Australia File 1-3-1. Canberra: ACFID.

—— 1997a. *One Clear Objective – poverty reduction through sustainable development: a response from ACFOA to the review of the Australian Oversea Aid Program*. Canberra: ACFOA.

—— 1997b. Maximising our Impact in Uncertain Times. Council Papers 1997, Annual ACFOA Council. In *Records of the Australian Council for Overseas Aid*, MS9347, MSAcc10.179, Box 1, Folder 6.2.15. (Added 5 November 2010). Canberra: National Library of Australia.

——1997c. Report of Code of Conduct Committee to Council, September. In *Records of the Australian Council for Overseas Aid*, MS9347, MSAcc10.179, Box 25, 6–27 ACFOA Code of Ethics 1989–96. (Added 5 November 2010). Canberra: National Library of Australia.

—— 1997d. Minutes of the Development Programs and Policies Committee, 6 June. In *Records of the Australian Council for Overseas Aid*, MS9347, MSAcc10.179, Box 30. (Added 5 November 2010). Canberra: National Library of Australia.

—— 1998a. Council Papers, 28 August. In *Records of the Australian Council for Overseas Aid*, MS9347 MSAcc10.179, Box 2. (Added 5 November 2010). Canberra: National Library of Australia.

—— 1998b. The Future of Human Rights in ACFOA: Council Papers, 28 August. In *Records of the Australian Council for Overseas Aid*, MS9347 MSAcc10.179, Box 2. (Added 5 November 2010). Canberra: National Library of Australia.

—— 1999a. Report of Code of Conduct Committee to Council, September. In *Records of the Australian Council for Overseas Aid*, MS9347, MSAcc10.179, Box 25, 6–27 ACFOA Code of Ethics 1989–96. (Added 5 November 2010). Canberra: National Library of Australia.

—— 1999b. Update on East Timor Crisis, September. In *Records of the Australian Council for Overseas Aid*, MS9347, MSAcc10.179, Box 28. (Added 5 November 2010). Canberra: National Library of Australia.

ADAA. 1977a. NGO Project Subsidy Scheme: information sheet. In *Records of the Australian Council for Overseas Aid*, MS9374, Box 45, Folio 233. Canberra: National Library of Australia.

—— 1977b. Guidelines for Schemes to Assist Voluntary Overseas Aid Projects of Eligible Australian Organisations. In *Records of the Australian Council for Overseas Aid*, MS9374, Box 45, Folio 233. Canberra: National Library of Australia.

ADAB. 1979. *ADAB Development Assistance Committee Australian Memorandum 1978*. Canberra: ADAB.

—— 1980. *ADAB Annual Review 1978–79, Development Cooperation: Australia's program of support for social and economic development of the Third World*. Canberra: ADAB.

—— 1983. *ADAB Development Assistance Committee Australian Memorandum 1982*. Canberra: ADAB.

ADAB/DFAT. 1980. *Development Co-operation: Australia's program of support for social and economic development in the Third World – Key Statements October 1975 – 3 November 1980*. Canberra: Commonwealth of Australia.

AFFHC. 1963. National Committee Minutes, in *Records of Australian Freedom From Hunger Campaign*, MS4529, Box 3, Folder 17. Canberra: National Library of Australia.

Agg, C. 2006. Trends in Government Support for Non-Governmental Organizations: is the Golden Age behind us?. In *Civil Society and Social Movements Programme Paper Number 23*. Geneva: United Nations Research Institute for Social Development.

Ahmed, Salehuddin and Micaela French. 2006. Scaling up: The BRAC experience. *BRAC University Journal* 3 (2):35–40.

Ahmed, Zu, Trevor Hopper and D Wickramasinghe. 2012. Hegemony and accountability in BRAC – the largest hybrid NGO in the world. In *AOS Workshop on Accounting, non-governmental organizations and civil society*, 12 July 2012 – 12 August 2012. London: London School of Economics (LSE).

AIS. 1972. Australians taking more interest in aid. *AIS Bulletin 7/18*. Canberra: Australian Information Service.

Ako, Matilda Aberese, Nana Akua Anyidoho and Gordon Crawford. 2013. NGOs, Rights-Based Approaches and the Potential for Progressive Development in Local Contexts: Constraints and Challenges in Northern Ghana. *Journal of Human Rights Practice* 5 (1):46–74.

Alston, Philip. 1981. Prevention versus Cure as a Human Right Strategy. Paper presented at Development, Human Rights, and the Rule of Law conference, 27 April – 1 May 1981, The Hague.

—— 2005. Ships passing in the night: the current state of the human rights and development debate seen through the lens of the Millennium Development Goals, *Human Rights Quarterly* 27 (3):755–829.

Alston, Philip and Mary Robinson (eds). 2005. *Human Rights and Development: Towards Mutual Reinforcement*. Oxford: Oxford University Press.

Alston, Richard. 1979. Letter to Red Cross, 5 December. In *Records of the Australian Council for Overseas Aid,* MS9374, Box 1, Folio 1. Canberra: National Library of Australia.

—— 1980a. Letter to Malcolm Fraser, 15 December. In *Records of the Australian Council for Overseas Aid,* MS9374, Box 3, Folio 15. Canberra: National Library of Australia.

—— 1980b. Alston correspondence, 8 April. In *Records of the Australian Council for Overseas Aid,* MS9374, Box 1, Folio 1. Canberra: National Library of Australia.

—— 1981. Letter to Editor, *The Canberra Times*, 4 December.

Altman, Dennis, Peter Aggleton, Michael Williams, Travis Kong, Vasu Reddy, David Harrad, Toni Reis and Richard Parker. 2012. Men who have sex with men: stigma and discrimination. *The Lancet* 380 (9839):439–445.

Altman, John C and John P Nieuwenhuysen. 1979. *The Economic Status of Australian Aborigines*. Cambridge: Cambridge University Press.

ANAO. 1996. Accounting for Aid – The Management of Funding to Non-Government Organisations: Australian Agency for International Development, Performance Audit. Tabled 29 August in *Audit Report No. 5, 1996–97.* Canberra: Australian National Audit Office.

Anderson, Nancy. 1964a. Australian Voluntary Foreign Aid Activities. *Australian Outlook* August: 127–142.

——— 1964b. Voluntary Aid Seminar 20–21 April: Review Paper Notes. In *Records of the Australian Council for Overseas Aid*, MS9374, Box 1, Folio 3, and Box 2, Folio 5. Canberra: National Library of Australia.

——— 1964c. Minutes of Meeting of Representatives of Societies engaged in voluntary foreign aid activities, University House Canberra, 27 July. In *Records of the Australian Council for Overseas Aid*, MS9374, Box 1, Folio 4. Canberra: National Library of Australia.

——— 2011. Interview with author, 22 May. Canberra.

ARC. 1976. Red Cross Withdraws from ACFOA. Media release, 9 January. In *Records of the Australian Council for Overseas Aid*, Box 51, Folder 265. Canberra: National Library of Australia.

Armon, Jeremy. 2007. Aid, politics and development: a donor perspective. *Development Policy Review* 25 (5):653–656.

Armstrong, Bill. 1981. Letter to David Pollard, 26 November, in *Records of the Australian Council for Overseas Aid*, MS 9347, Box 37, Folder 180. Canberra: National Library of Australia,

——— 2011. Interview with author, 7 April.

Armstrong, David. 1991a. Letter to Russell Rollason, 6 May, in *Records of the Australian Council for Overseas Aid*, MS9347, MSAcc10.179, Box 25, 6–27 ACFOA Code of Ethics 1989–96. (Added 5 November 2010). Canberra: National Library of Australia.

——— 1991b. Letter to Russell Rollason, 27 May, in *Records of the Australian Council for Overseas Aid,* MS9347, Box 185, Folder 130. (Added 21 September 1998*)*. Canberra: National Library of Australia.

Arndt, Heinz. 1969. Aid and the Official Conscience. *The Australian Quarterly* 41 (4):43–48.

——— 1970. Australian economic aid to Indonesia. *Australian Journal of International Affairs* 24 (2):124–139.

Arrighi, Giovanni. 2010. The world economy and the Cold War, 1970–1985. In Melvin P. Leffler and Odd A. Westad (eds). *The Cambridge History of the Cold War, Volume 3*. Cambridge: Cambridge University Press.

Arts, Karen. 2013. Countering Violence Against Children in the Philippines: Positive RBA Practice Examples from Plan – A Policy Brief. In Paul Gready and Wouter Vandenhole (eds). *Human Rights and Development in the New Millennium: Towards a Theory of Change*. Ch. 8. London: Routledge

Ashton, Jennifer. 1989. Cambodia: Development Needs. In *Records of the Australian Council for Overseas Aid*, MS9347, MSAcc10.179, Box 45. (Added 5 November 2010). Canberra: National Library of Australia.

Atack, Iain. 1999. Four criteria of development NGO legitimacy. *World Development* 27 (5):855–864.

Athukorala, Prema-chandra and Budy P Resosudarmo. 2005. The Indian Ocean tsunami: economic impact, disaster management, and lessons. *Asian Economic Papers* 4 (1):1–39.

Auditor-General. 1993. Audit Report No. 29. In *ACFID Files: CARE File 9–15*. Canberra: ACFID.

AusAID. 1995a. *Review of the effectiveness of NGO programs*. Canberra: AGPS.

—— 1995b. COPAC Draft Report, 23 August. In *Records of the Australian Council for Overseas Aid*, MS9347, MSAcc10.179, Box 26. (Added 5 November 2010). Canberra: National Library of Australia.

—— 1999. Agreement between the Commonwealth of Australia and ACFOA in relation to the supply of coordination and information services. In *Records of ACFID: ACFOA/AusAID Contract 1999–2004*. Canberra: ACFID.

—— 2000. Draft Assessment for Country Program-Funded Australian NGOs. In *Records of ACFID: AusAID QAG of NGOs Nov 2000 – Sept 2001*. Canberra: ACFID.

—— 2001. Putting Things to Rights: The Use of Foreign Aid to Advance Human Rights in Developing Nations. Submission to the Human Rights Sub-Committee of the Joint Standing Committee on Foreign Affairs, Defence and Trade on its Inquiry into the Link Between Aid and Human Rights. Canberra: AusAID.

—— 2002. Rapid Review of NGO Quality. In AusAID (ed.). *Work-in-Progress Report, Quality Assurance Group Report 5*. Canberra: AusAID.

—— 2012. *AusAID Civil Society Engagement Framework: Working with civil society organisations to help people overcome poverty*. Canberra: AusAID.

—— 2013. *AusAID-NGO Cooperation Program (ANCP) Development Awareness Raising Guidelines*. Canberra: AusAID NGOs and Business Branch.

AWD 1970. Challenge for Action: the official report of the 1970 conference on Action for World Development. Sydney: AWD.

Azam, Jean-Paul and Véronique Thelen. 2008. The roles of foreign aid and education in the war on terror. *Public Choice* 135 (3–4):375–397.

—— 2010. Foreign aid versus military intervention in the war on terror. *Journal of Conflict Resolution* 54 (2):237–261.

Baccaro, Lucio. 2003. What is Alive and What is Dead in the Theory of Corporatism. *British Journal of Industrial Relations* 41 (4):683–706.

Back, Kurt W 1988. Metaphors for Public Opinion in Literature. *Public Opinion Quarterly* 52 (3):278–288.

Baden, Sally and Anne Marie Goetz. 1997. Who needs [sex] when you can have [gender]? Conflicting discourses on gender at Beijing. *Feminist Review,* Summer:3–25.

Bandyopadhyay, Subhayu, Todd Sandler and Javed Younas. 2011. Foreign direct investment, aid, and terrorism: an analysis of developing countries. *Federal Reserve Bank of St. Louis Working Paper Series* (2011-004).

Barber, Martin and Cameron Bowie. 2008. How international NGOs could do less harm and more good. *Development in Practice* 18 (6):748–754.

Barker, Mark. 1976. Aid cuts shame us: bishops. *The Age,* 10 March.

Barker, Michael James. 2013. Bob Geldof and the Aid Industry: Do They Know it's Imperialism? *Capitalism Nature Socialism* 25 (1):96–110.

Barma, Nazneen, Ely Ratner and Steven Weber. 2007. A World Without the West. *The National Interest* 90 (July August):23–30.

Barnett, Michael N. 2011. *Empire of humanity: A history of humanitarianism.* Ithica NY: Cornell University Press.

Barnett, Michael and Thomas G. Weiss. 2008. Humanitarianism: A Brief History of the Present. In Michael Barnett and Thomas G Weiss (eds). *Humanitarianism in Question: Politics, Power, Ethics.* Ithaca, NY: Cornell University Press.

Barr, Gerry and Karen Takacs. 2010. Open letter to Bev Oda, Minister of International Cooperation, Canadian International Development Agency, 23 November. Ottowa: CCIC.

Bartsch, Sid. 1982. Report of NGO members of CDC to Annual Council. In *Records of the Australian Council for Overseas Aid,* MS9347, Box 46, Folder 238. Canberra: National Library of Australia.

Batt, Neil. 1977. Letter to Andrew Peacock Minister for Foreign Affairs, 7 July. In *Records of the Australian Council for Overseas Aid*, MS9347, Box 45, Folder 230. Canberra: National Library of Australia.

Bebbington, Anthony. 2005. Donor–NGO Relations and Representations of Livelihood in Nongovernmental Aid Chains. *World Development* 33 (6):937–950.

Benmelech, Efraim, Claude Berrebi and Esteban F Klor. 2012. Economic conditions and the quality of suicide terrorism. *The Journal of Politics* 74 (01):113–128.

Bennett, Austin E. 1969. *Reflections on Community Development Education.* Orono Maine: The Farm Foundation.

Bennett, W Lance. 2004. Social movements beyond borders: understanding two eras of transnational activism. In Donatella della Porta and Sidney Tarrow (eds). *Transnational protest and global activism*. Lanham: Rowman & Littlefield.

Bertoli, Simone, Giovanni Andrea Cornia and Francesco Manaresi. 2008. Aid effort and its determinants: A comparison of the Italian performance with other OECD donors. *Working Paper wp2008–11*. Florence: Università degli Studi di Firenze, Dipartimento di Scienze per l'Economia e l'Impresa.

Besley, Timothy and Maitreesh Ghatak. 1999. Public–private partnership for the provision of public goods: Theory and an application to NGOs. In *The Development Economics Discussion Paper Series No. 17*. London: LSE.

Bhagwati, Jagdish N. 1977. The new international economic order: the North–South debate. *MIT Bicentennial Studies*. Cambridge Mass: MIT Press.

Biccum, April. 2011. Marketing Development: celebrity politics and the 'new' development advocacy. *Third World Quarterly* 32 (7):1331–1346.

Bignall, Simone. 1997. Women in Development: A policy post-mortem. *Australian Feminist Studies,* 12 (26):321–331.

Bilney, Gordon. 1993. Letter to Russell Rollason 1 September. In *Records of the Australian Council for Overseas Aid*, MS9347, MSAcc10.179, Box 8. (Added 5 November, 2010). Canberra: National Library of Australia.

—— 1994. Food Aid Loss. Media release, 20 May. In *ACFID Files: CARE File 9–15*. Canberra: ACFID.

—— 1995a. Hansard report: Overseas Aid, 27 February, Australian Parliament, Canberra: AGPS.

—— 1995b. Letter to Janet Hunt 22 May. In the *Records of the Australian Council for Overseas Aid,* MS9347 MSAcc10.179, Box 26. (Added 5 November 2010). Canberra: National Library of Australia.

Birch, John. 1985. Address to Council. In *Records of the Australian Council for Overseas Aid,* MS9347, Box 53, Folder 272. Canberra: National Library of Australia.

—— 1983. Report on Quality of Aid Seminar; ANU Canberra 3–4 September. Records of the Australian Council for Overseas Aid, MS9374, Box 50, Folio 262. Canberra: National Library of Australia.

Birdsall, Nancy and Alexis Sowa. 2013. From Multilateral Champion to Handicapped Donor … and Back Again? *CGD Policy Paper 029,* August. Washington: Center for Global Development.

Birdsall, Nancy and Homi J Kharas. 2012. In Center for Global Development (ed.). *The Quality of Official Development Assistance Assessment 2009: Is Aid Quality Improving?* Washington: Brookings.

Black, Maggie. 1992. *A cause for our time: Oxfam the first fifty years.* Oxford: Oxfam and Oxford University Press.

Blackburn, Susan. 1993. *Practical Visionaries: a study of Community Aid Abroad.* Melbourne: Melbourne University Press.

Bloodgood, Elizabeth A and Joannie Tremblay-Boire. 2011. International NGOs and national regulation in an age of terrorism. *Voluntas: International Journal of Voluntary and Nonprofit Organizations* 22 (1):142–173.

Blunt, Cath. 2013. Interview with author. 7 November. Canberra.

Bocking-Welch, Anna. 2012. Imperial Legacies and Internationalist Discourses: British Involvement in the United Nations Freedom from Hunger Campaign, 1960–70. *The Journal of Imperial and Commonwealth History,* 40 (5):879–896.

Boone, Peter. 1996. Politics and the effectiveness of foreign aid. *European economic review* 40 (2):289–329.

Booth, David. 2012. Aid effectiveness: bringing country ownership (and politics) back in. *Conflict, Security & Development* 12 (5):537–558.

Bose, Sarmila. 2005. Anatomy of Violence: Analysis of Civil War in East Pakistan in 1971. *Economic and Political Weekly*: 4463–4471.

Boserup, Ester. 1970. *Women's Role in Economic Development.* London: George Allen and Unwin.

Bracken, Sean, Gareth Dart and Stephen Pickering. 2011. Evolution or Revolution? An Analysis of the Changing Face of Development Education in the United Kingdom. *Policy and Practice – A Development Education Review* (12).

Braun, Rainer and Judy Gearhart. 2004. Who should code your conduct? Trade union and NGO differences in the fight for workers' rights. *Development in Practice* 14 (1–2):183–196.

Brech, Viktor and Niklas Potrafke. 2014. Donor ideology and types of foreign aid. *Journal of Comparative Economics* 42 (1):61–75.

Bristol, Nellie. 2008. NGO code of conduct hopes to stem internal brain drain. *The Lancet* 371 (9631):2162.

Brodhead, Tim, Brent Herbert-Copley and Anne-Marie Lambert. 1988. *Bridges of Hope: Canadian Voluntary Agencies in the Third World*. Ottawa: The North-South Institute.

Broughton, Bernard. 1994. Fraudulent Practice of CARE Australia. Fax to Bilney, 22 May. In *ACFID Files: CARE File 9–15*. Canberra: ACFID.

Brouwer, Ruth Compton. 2010. When Missions Became Development: Ironies of 'Ngo-ization' in Mainstream Canadian Churches in the 1960s. *Canadian Historical Review* 91 (4):661–693.

Brown, MacAlister A and Joseph J Zasloff. 1998. *Cambodia confounds the peacemakers, 1979–1998*. New York: Cornell University Press.

Brown, Stephen (ed.). 2012. *Struggling for Effectiveness: CIDA and Canadian Foreign Aid*. Montreal: McGill-Queen's Press-MQUP.

Brown, Stephen, Duane Bratt and Christopher J Kukucha. 2012. Aid effectiveness and the framing of new Canadian aid initiatives. In Duane Bratt and C J Kukucha (eds). *Readings in Canadian Foreign Policy: Classic Debates and New Ideas*. Ch 26. Toronto: Oxford University Press.

Bryan, Audrey. 2011. Another cog in the anti-politics machine? The 'de-clawing' of development education. *Policy & Practice–A Development Education Review* 12 Spring.

Buchanan, Anne. 2012. Accountability and Aspiration: An Insight Approach for Organizational Ethics. PhD thesis. Ottawa: Faculty of Philosophy, Saint Paul University.

Bunch, Charlotte. 2012. Opening Doors for Feminism: UN World Conferences on Women. *Journal of Women's History* 24 (4):213–221.

Bunch, Charlotte and Susana Fried. 1996. Beijing '95: Moving women's human rights from margin to center. *Signs* Autumn:200–204.

Burke, Roland. 2008. From Individual Rights to National Development: The First UN International Conference on Human Rights, Tehran, 1968 *Journal of World History* 19 (3):275–296.

Burnell, Peter. 1987. Third World Charities in Britain and Official Funding. *Politics Working Papers*. Coventry: University of Warwick.

—— 1991. *Charity Politics and the Third World*. London: Harvester Wheatsheaf.

Butterworth, K. 1987. Letter to Kevin Power, 6 January. In *Records of the Australian Council for Overseas Aid,* MS9347, Box 192, Folder 164. (Added 21 September 1998). Canberra: National Library of Australia.

Byrne, William. 1974. Letter to Mick Sullivan (ACFOA), 18 November. In *Records of the Australian Council for Overseas Aid,* MS 9347, Box 36, Folder 13. Canberra: National Library of Australia,

Cabasset-Semedo, Christine and Frederic Durand. 2009. East-Timor: How to Build a New Nation in Southeast Asia in the 21st Century. *IRASEC Occasional Paper* (9):299.

Çağatay, Nilüfer, Caren Grown and Aida Santiago. 1986. The Nairobi Women's Conference: Toward a Global Feminism? *Feminist Studies,* 2 Summer:401–412.

Canberra Times. 1966. 'Committee on aid will go to Vietnam', 31 October.

—— 1971. 'Poet resumes fast for aid', 25 October.

—— 1981. ACFOA Report on Timor disclosed for first time, 29 October.

Caplan, G. 2012. Stephen Harper and the tyranny of majority government, 15 June. *The Globe and Mail*.

Carey, Peter. 1999. The Catholic Church, religious Revival, and the nationalist movement in East Timor, 1975–98, *Indonesia and the Malay World* 27 (78):77–95.

Carter, Terrance S and Theresa LM Man. 2011. The Evolution of Advocacy and Political Activities by Charities in Canada: An Overview. *The Philanthropist* 23 (4):535–544.

Casey, Richard. 1965. Letter to John Crawford, 5 March. In the *Records of the Australian Council for Overseas Aid,* MS9374, Box 1, Folio 1. Canberra: National Library of Australia.

Casey, Rick. 1973. Voluntary Agencies Plan Post-war Aid. *National Catholic Reporter* 9 (21):1.

CCIC. 2000. *Creating a Code of Ethics: Developing ethical standards for a sector.* Ottowa: CCIC.

—— 2010a. CIDA Funding to CCIC Threatened Canada's Foreign Aid Community Risks Losing Strong Voice for World's Poor. Media release, 1 June. Ottowa: CCIC.

—— 2010b. Canadian NGO confidence in CIDA funding standards undermined: CCIC calls for steps to restore trust in Canada's standards for aid spending. Media release, 15 December. Ottowa: CCIC.

—— 2011. Survey on the impacts of CIDA funding delays on civil society organizations, November Report. Ottowa: CCIC.

Chalmers, David. 2012. *And the crooked places made straight: the struggle for social change in the 1960s.* Baltimore: JHU Press.

Chandler, David G. 2001. The road to military humanitarianism: how the human rights NGOs shaped a new humanitarian agenda, *Human Rights Quarterly* 23 (3):678–700.

Chang, Ha-Joon (ed.). 2013. Hamlet without the Prince of Denmark: How Development has Disappeared from Today's 'Development'. In David Held and Charles Roger (eds). *Global Governance at Risk.* New York: John Wiley.

Chant, Sylvia and Cathy McIlwaine. 2009. *Geographies of development in the 21st century: an introduction to the global South.* Cheltenham: Edward Elgar Publishing.

Chao, Chi-Chur, Jean-Pierre Laffargue and Pasquale M Sgro. 2010. Foreign Aid, Wage Inequality, and Welfare for a Small Open Economy with Tourism. *Review of international economics* 18 (3):454–464.

Chapman, Jennifer, Valerie Miller, Adriano Campolina Soares and John Samuel. 2009. Rights-based development: the challenge of change and power for development NGOs. In Samuel Hickey and Diana Mitlin (eds). *Rights-Based Approaches to Development: Exploring the Potentials and Pitfalls,* Stirling: Kumarian Press.

Chapman, Rhonda. 2004. Investing in aid effectiveness: The contexts and challenges for Australian NGOs. *Development Bulletin* 65 August:57–62.

Charlesworth, Hilary. 2005. Not waving but drowning: gender mainstreaming and human rights in the United Nations. *Harvard Human Rights Journal* 18 (1):1–18.

Charlesworth, Hilary and Christine Chinkin. 2013. The creation of UN Women. In the *RegNet research paper series , 2013/7*. Canberra: Regulatory Institutions Network (RegNet).

Charnovitz, Steve. 1997. Two centuries of participation: NGOs and International Experience. *Michigan Journal of International Law* 18 (2):183–286.

Cheek, Timothy. 2012. Frank Dikötter. Mao's Great Famine: The History of China's Most Devastating Catastrophe, 1958–1962. *The American Historical Review* 117 (5):1565–1566.

Chin, Gregory. 2012. Two-Way Socialization: China, the World Bank, and Hegemonic Weakening. *Brown Journal of World Affairs*. 19(1):211–229.

Chopra, Jarat. 2002. Building state failure in East Timor. *Development and Change* 33 (5):979–1000.

Chow, Esther Ngan-ling. 1996. Making waves, moving mountains: reflections on Beijing '95 and beyond, *Signs* Autumn:185–192.

Christensen, Darin and Jeremy M Weinstein. 2013. Defunding Dissent: Restrictions on Aid to NGOs. *Journal of Democracy* 24 (2):77–91.

Christie, Ryerson. 2012. *Peacebuilding and NGOs: State–civil society interactions*. Routledge.

CID. 2011. Annual Report 2010–2011. Wellington: Council for International Development.

Clark, Charles. 2012. From The Wealth of Nations to Populorum Progressio (On the Development of Peoples): Wealth and Development from the Perspective of the Catholic Social Thought Tradition. *American Journal of Economics and Sociology* 71 (4):1047–1072.

Clark, John. 1992. Democratising Development: NGOs and the State. *Development in Practice* 2 (3):151–162.

—— 1995. The state, popular participation, and the voluntary sector. *World Development* 23 (4):593–601.

Clarke, Matthew. 2007. Raising the funds – spending the funds: a case study of the effectiveness of both roles of NGO's. In Andre MN Renzaho (ed.). *Measuring effectiveness in humanitarian and development aid: conceptual frameworks, principles and practice*. New York: Nova Science.

Clay, Jason. 1991. Western assistance and the Ethiopian famine: Implications for humanitarian assistance. In Richard E Downs, Donna O Kerner and Stephen P Reyna (eds). *The Political Economy of African Famine*. Philadelphia: Gordon and Breach.

Clemens, Michael and Todd J Moss. 2007. The Ghost of 0.7%, *International Journal of Development Issues* 6 (1):3–25.

Clunies-Ross, Anthony. 1963. *One Per Cent: the case for greater Australian Aid*. Melbourne: Melbourne University Press.

Cohn, Carol. 1995. Taking Stock of Charities. *Australian Accountant* 65:18–27.

Cole-King, Susan. 1976. Health Sector aid from Voluntary agencies: the British case study. *IDS Discussion Paper DP97*. Brighton: IDS.

Collier, Ian. 1985. Row over Planes for Africa, 26 December. *Daily Telegraph*.

Compa, Lance. 2004. Trade unions, NGOs, and corporate codes of conduct. *Development in Practice* 14 (1–2):210–215.

Connolly, John, R. 1997. Approaches to a Theology of Women's Liberation in Latin America. Paper presented at the meeting of the Latin American Studies Association. Guadelajara, Mexico, 17–19 April.

Cooley, Alexander and James Ron. 2002. The NGO scramble: Organizational insecurity and the political economy of transnational action. *International Security* 27 (1):5–39.

Cordery, Carolyn Joy and Rachel F Baskerville-Morley. 2005. Charity Financial Reporting regulation: a comparison of the United Kingdom and her former colony, New Zealand. In Working Paper 20. Wellington: School of Accounting and Commercial Law, Victoria University.

Cornwall, Andrea and Celestine Nyamu-Musembi. 2004. Putting the 'rights-based approach' to development into perspective. *Third World Quarterly* 25 (8):1415–1437.

Cotton, James. 2001. Against the grain: the East Timor intervention. *Survival* 43 (1):127–142.

Council for Cultural Cooperation. 1963. Youth and Development Aid. In *Series III – Out of School Education*. Strasbourg: Council of Europe.

Council of Europe. 1963. Strasbourg Seminar Report. In the *Records of the Australian Council for Overseas Aid,* Box 1, Folder 8. National Library of Australia, Canberra.

Covey, Jane G. 1995. Accountability and effectiveness in NGO policy alliances. *Journal of International Development* 7 (6):857–867.

Crawford, John. 1964a. Press Release following agency meeting, 27 July, In the *Records of the Australian Council for Overseas Aid,* MS9374, Box 1, Folio 4. Canberra: National Library of Australia.

—— 1964b. Letter to Jim Webb, 4 November. In *Records of the Australian Council for Overseas Aid,* MS9374, Box 1, Folio 1. Canberra: National Library of Australia.

—— 1964c. Opening address to Voluntary Aid Seminar April, in *Records of the Australian Council for Overseas Aid,* MS9374, Box 2, Folio 5. Canberra: National Library of Australia.

—— 1966. Letter to Treasurer (Holt), 26 January. In *Records of the Australian Council for Overseas Aid,* MS9374, Box 1, Folio 1. Canberra: National Library of Australia.

—— 1969a. Letter to Jim Webb, 4 June. In Records of the Australian Council for Overseas Aid; MS9374, Box 1, Folio 3. Australian National Library, Canberra.

—— 1969b. Letter Vaughan Hinton, 1 July. In Records of the Australian Council for Overseas Aid; MS9374, Box 1, Folio 1. Canberra: National Library of Australia.

—— 1971. Address to ACFOA Dinner, 13 August. In *Papers of Sir John Crawford,* MS 4514. Canberra: National Library of Australia.

—— 1972. Opening address to Council, 12–13 August. In the *Records of the Australian Council for Overseas Aid,* MS9374, Box 54, Folio 280. Canberra: National Library of Australia.

Cristalis, Irena. 2009. *East Timor: A Nation's Bitter Dawn*. London: Zed Books.

Crowson, Nick, James McKay and Jean-François Mouhot. 2012. *A Historical Guide to NGOs in Britain: Charities, Civil Society and the Voluntary Sector Since 1945*. New York: Palgrave Macmillan.

Cullather, Nick. 2010. *The hungry world: America's Cold War battle against poverty in Asia*. Cambridge MA: Harvard University Press.

Cullen, Paul. 1971. Letter to Billy McMahon 12 October. In *Records of the Australian Council for Overseas Aid*, MS9374, Box 2, Folio 13. Canberra: National Library of Australia.

—— 1974. Letter to Mick Sullivan, 22 November. In *Records of the Australian Council for Overseas Aid*, MS9374, Box 36, Folio 15. Canberra: National Library of Australia.

—— 1975a. Letter to William Keys, 5 August. In *Records of the Australian Council for Overseas Aid*, MS9374, Box 29, RSL Folio. Canberra: National Library of Australia.

—— 1975b. Letter to Brendan O'Dwyer, 5 August. In *Records of the Australian Council for Overseas Aid*, MS9374, Box 36, Folio 15. Canberra: National Library of Australia.

—— 1986. Letter to Pam Atkinson, 7 February. In the *Records of the Australian Council for Overseas Aid*, MS9374, Box 1, Folio 1. Canberra: National Library of Australia.

Culyer, Anthony J, Jack Wiseman and John W Posnett. 1976. Charity and Public Policy in the UK—The Law and the Economics. *Social Policy & Administration* 10 (1):32–50.

Cumming, Lawrence. 2013. Interview with author, 27 and 28 November. Canberra.

Cunningham, Ian. 2010. The HR function in purchaser–provider relationships: insights from the UK voluntary sector. *Human Resource Management Journal* 20 (2):189–205.

Current Affairs. 1967. 'Australian Aid Abroad'. *Current Affairs* Bulletin 40 (13).

Curtis, Neville. 1977. Council Paper 25, Report on Summer School – On What Terms: Australia's Future in the Pacific Region. University of Tasmania 20–25 January 1978. In Records of the Australian Council for Overseas Aid, MS9347, Box 38, Folder 187. Canberra: National Library of Australia.

DAC. 2005. *Peer Review of Australia*. Paris: OECD.

Dallaire, Romeo and Ray Dupuis. 2004. *Shake hands with the devil*. London: Arrow Books.

Das, Ramon. 2010. 'Aid Agencies, States, and Collective Harm'. In *Ethical Questions and International NGOs*, edited by Chris. Roche and Keith Horton, 175-191. Dordrecht: Springer.

Davies, Irene. 2012. Interview with author, 20 January. Canberra.

Davies, Thomas Richard. 2008. The rise and fall of transnational civil society: The evolution of international non-governmental organizations since 1839. CUTP/003 *Working Papers on Transnational Politics*. London: City University – Centre for International Politcs.

——— 2012. The Transformation of International NGOs and Their Impact on Development Aid. *International Development Policy Review* 1 (3) [online].

Davis, H Louise. 2010. Feeding the World a Line?: Celebrity Activism and Ethical Consumer Practices From Live Aid to Product Red. *Nordic Journal of English Studies* 9 (3):89–118.

Davis, Thomas WD. 2009. The Politics of Human Rights and Development: The Challenge for Official Donors. *Australian Journal of Political Science* 44 (1):173–192.

de Acolhimento, Comissão. 2005. Conflict-Related Deaths in Timor-Leste 1974–1999. The Timor-Leste's Commission for Reception, Truth and Reconciliation (CAVR) Report – Chega! Dili: East Timor.

DEC. 2012. *Our History*. Available at www.dec.org.uk/our-history.

Decobert, Anne. 2013. Humanitarian Resistance on the Thai-Burma Border. PhD thesis, School of Archaeology and Anthropology. Canberra: Australian National University.

de Groot, Jack. 2013. Interview with author, 14 January. Sydney.

DemMars, William E. 2001. Hazardous partnership: NGOs and United States intelligence in small wars. *International Journal of Intelligence and CounterIntelligence* 14 (2):193–222.

Deneulin, Séverine and Carole Rakodi. 2011. Revisiting Religion: Development Studies Thirty Years On. *World Development* 39 (1):45–54.

Department of External Affairs (ed.). 1966. Australia's aid to developing countries to 30 June 1966. Canberra: AGPS.

Department of State. 1966. 132. Memorandum From the Central Intelligence Agency to the 303 Committee. U.S. Department of State Office of the Historian. Available at history.state.gov/historicaldocuments/frus1964-68v10/d132.

Dercon, Stefan and Catherine Porter. 2010. Live aid revisited: long-term impacts of the 1984 Ethiopian famine on children. In *WPS/2010–38*. Oxford: Centre for the Study of African Economies.

Deshpande, VD. 1986. Code of Conduct for Rural Voluntary Agencies. *Economic and Political Weekly* XXI (30):1304–1306.

Develtere, Patrick and Tom De Bruyn. 2009. The emergence of a fourth pillar in development aid. *Development in Practice* 19 (7):912–922.

De Waal, Alex. 1991. *Evil Days; Thirty Years of War and Famine in Ethiopia: An Africa Watch Report*. Washington: Human Rights Watch.

—— 1997. *Famine crimes: politics & the disaster relief industry in Africa.* Bloomington: Indiana University Press.

—— 2008. The Humanitarian Carnival: a Celebrity Vogue. *World Affairs* 171 (2):43–55.

DFAT, 2014. Australian NGO Accreditation Guidance Manual, October. Canberra: DFAT.

Diamond, Larry. 1992. Promoting democracy. *Foreign Policy* 87 Summer:25–46.

DiMaggio, Paul J and Walter W Powell. 1983. The iron cage revisited – Institutional isomorphism and collective rationality in organizational fields. *American Sociological Review* 48:143–166.

Dirlik, Arif. 2006. Beijing Consensus: Beijing 'Gongshi.' Who Recognizes Whom and to What End?' Position Paper, *Globalization and Autonomy Online Compendium*. Available at www.globalautonomy.ca, accessed January 17. www.ids-uva.nl/wordpress/wp-content/uploads/2011/07/9_Dirlik.pdf.

Disasters. 1977. Viewpoints: inside the agencies. *Disasters* 1 (1):3–4.

Doh, Jonathan P and Terrence R Guay. 2004. Globalization and corporate social responsibility: how non-governmental organizations influence labor and environmental codes of conduct. *MIR: Management International Review.* 44 Special Issue:7–29.

Dominy, Guy, Ra Goel, Sean Larkins, Humphrey Pring and Hercules House. 2011. *Review of using aid funds in the UK to promote awareness of global poverty*. London: COI for DfID.

Donaghue, Kieran. 2010. Human rights, development INGOs and priorities for action. In Chris Roche and Keith Horten (eds). *Ethical Questions and International NGOs*. Dordrecht: Springer, pp. 39–63.

Donaldson, Linda Plitt and Kathleen Belanger. 2012. Catholic Social Teaching: Principles for the Service and Justice Dimensions of Social Work Practice and Education. *Social Work & Christianity* 39 (2):120–128.

Donnelly, Jack. 1989. Repression and Development: The Political Contingency of Human Rights Tradeoffs. In David P Forsythe (ed.). *Human Rights and Development : International Views*. Basingstoke: Macmillan Press.

Doucouliagos, Hristos and Martin Paldam. 2009. The aid effectiveness literature: The sad results of 40 years of research. *Journal of Economic Surveys* 23 (3):433–461.

Downer, Alexander. 1999. Letter to Ronald Wilson, 14 December. In *Records of ACFID: Correspondence to the Minister of Foreign Affairs and Trade 2000–2004*, File 3.1.1. Canberra: ACFID.

—— 2000. Letter to Ronald Wilson, 29 October. In the *Records of ACFID: Correspondence to the Minister of Foreign Affairs and Trade 2000–2004*, File 3.1.1. Canberra: ACFID.

Doyle, Michael W. 2011. International ethics and the responsibility to protect. *International Studies Review* 13 (1):72–84.

Drabek, Ann G. 1992. NGOs: do we expect too much? *Progress Reports on Health and Development in Southern Africa* Spring–Summer:40–4.

Dreher, Axel, Florian Mölders and Peter Nunnenkamp. 2010. Aid Delivery through Non-governmental Organisations: Does the Aid Channel Matter for the Targeting of Swedish Aid?. *The World Economy* 33 (2):147–176.

Drolet, Julie. 2010. Feminist perspectives in development: Implications for women and microcredit. *Affilia* 25 (3):212–223.

Duffield, Mark. 1994. Complex emergencies and the crisis of developmentalism. *IDS Bulletin* 25 (4):37–45.

Dunn, James. 1975. Report of visit to East Timor for East Timor Task Force October. In *Records of the Australian Council for Overseas Aid*, MS9347, MSAcc10.179, Box 28. (Added 5 November 2010). Canberra: National Library of Australia.

—— 2003. *East Timor: A rough passage to independence*. Sydney: Longueville Books.

Dupuy, Kendra E, James Ron and Aseem Prakash. 2014. Who survived? Ethiopia's regulatory crackdown on foreign-funded NGOs. *Review of International Political Economy* (ahead-of-print):1–38.

Dwivedi, Onkar Prasad and John Nef. 1982. Crises and continuities in development theory and administration: First and Third World perspectives. *Public Administration and Development* 2 (1):59–77.

Eade, Deborah. 2006. Review: Relationships for Aid by Rosalind Eyben. *Development in Practice* 16 (6):651-653.

Easterly, William and Claudia R Williamson. 2011. Rhetoric versus Reality: The Best and Worst of Aid Agency Practices. *World Development* 39 (11):1930–1949.

Ebrahim, Alnoor. 2003. Accountability in practice: mechanisms for NGOs. *World Development* 31 (5):813–829.

Ed Challies, E, Andrew McGregor and Lee Sentes. 2011. The Changing Landscape of International Development in Aotearoa/New Zealand. In *NZADDS Working Paper*. Auckland: NZADDS.

Edgar, Gemma and Frances Lockie. 2010. Fair-weather friends: why compacts fail non-government organisations. *International Journal of Sociology and Social Policy* 30 (7/8):354–367.

Development Decade. 1962. Editorial. *Freedom From Hunger Campaign News*. Rome: FAO.

Bev Oda's serious transgression. 2011. Editorial, 15 February. *The Globe and Mail*.

Edwards, Michael. 1999. International Development NGOs: Agents of Foreign Aid or Vehicles for International Cooperation? *Nonprofit and Voluntary Sector Quarterly* 28 Supplement 1:25–37.

Edwards, Michael and David Hulme. 1995. NGO performance and accountability in the post-cold war world. *Journal of International Development* 7 (6):849–856.

—— 1996. Too close for comfort? The impact of official aid on nongovernmental organizations. *World Development* 24 (6):961–973.

—— 1997. *NGOs State and Donors: Too Close for Comfort*. London: Save the Children Fund UK and MacMillan.

Egan, C. 1991. Call for review of aid body funding. *Weekend Australian*, 26–27 October.

Eggleton, Tony. 1996. Letter to Janet Hunt, 5 March. In *Records of ACFID: CARE Australia*, File 1-3-1. Canberra: ACFID.

Eisenberg, Avigail and Jeff Spinner-Halev. 2005. Minorities within minorities: equality, rights and diversity. Cambridge University Press: Cambridge.

Ekbladh, David. 2011. *The great American mission: modernization and the construction of an American world order*. Princeton University Press: New York.

Elbers, Willem and Lau Schulpen. 2011. Decision Making in Partnerships for Development Explaining the Influence of Local Partners. *Nonprofit and Voluntary Sector Quarterly* 40 (5):795–812.

Elkington, John and Seb Beloe. 2010. The twenty-first century NGO. In Thomas Lyon (ed.). *Good Cop Bad Cop: Environmental NGOs and their Strategies Towards Business*. London: Routledge, pp. 17–47.

Ensor, James. 2013. Interview with author, 11 October. Canberra.

Ensor, Jonathon and Paul Gready (eds). 2005. *Reinventing Development?: Translating Rights-Based Approaches From Theory Into Practice*. London: Zed Books.

Escobar, Arturo. 2011. *Encountering development: The making and unmaking of the Third World*. New York: Princeton University Press.

Espiritu, Caesar 1986. *Law and Human Rights in the Development of ASEAN : with special reference to the Philippines, Studies on Law and Development in ASEAN*. Singapore: Friedrich Naumann Stiftung.

Evans, Gareth. 1989. Opening Address to ACFOA: One World or None Annual Conference. In *Records of the Australian Council for Overseas Aid*, MS9347, MSAcc10.179, Box 45. (Added 5 November 2010). Canberra: National Library of Australia.

—— 2011. Cambodia Then and Now: Commemorating the 1991 Peace Agreement. Keynote Address. Paper presented at the Measuring Cambodia's Progress Toward Equality conference, 6 August, University of NSW Law School, Sydney.

—— 2013. Interview with author, 5 June. Canberra.

Eyben, Rosalind. 2006. The road not taken: International aid's choice of Copenhagen over Beijing. *Third World Quarterly* 27 (4):595–608.

—— 2010. Hiding relations: the irony of 'effective aid'. *European Journal of Development Research* 22 (3):382–397.

—— 2013. Struggles in Paris: The DAC and the purposes of development aid. *European Journal of Development Research* 25 (1):7–91.

Eyben, Rosalind and Rebecca Napier-Moore. 2009. Choosing words with care? Shifting meanings of women's empowerment in international development. *Third World Quarterly* 30 (2):285–300.

FAO. 1961. Report of the Conference of FAO Eleventh Session, Rome 4–24 November. Available at www.fao.org/dorep/x5572e/x5572e00.htm.

Fassin, Didier. 2007. Humanitarianism as a Politics of Life. *Public Culture* 19 (3):499.

Fein, Helen. 1993. Revolutionary and anti-revolutionary genocides: a comparison of state murders in democratic Kampuchea, 1975 to 1979, and in Indonesia, 1965 to 1966. *Comparative Studies in Society and History* 35 (04):796–823.

Fernandes, Angelo. 1970. The Role of the Church in Development. *The Ecumenical Review* 22 (3):222–250.

Fernandes, Clinton. 2011. *The Independence of East Timor: Multi-dimensional Perspectives –Occupation, Resistance, and International Political Activism.* Brighton: The Sussex Library of Asian Studies & Asian American Studies, Sussex Academic Press.

Fisher, Charles A. 1971. Containing China? II. Concepts and Applications of Containment. *The Geographical Journal* 137(3):301.

FitzSimons, Trish. 2009. Braided Channels: A Genealogy of the Voice of Documentary. *Studies in Documentary Film* 32 (2):131–146.

Fleck, Robert K and Christopher Kilby. 2006. How do political changes influence US bilateral aid allocations? Evidence from panel data. *Review of Development Economics* 10 (2):210–223.

Flipse, Scott. 2002. The latest casualty of war: Catholic Relief Services, humanitarianism, and the war in Vietnam, 1967–1968. *Peace and Change* 27 (2):245–270.

Fogarty, Quentin. 1986a. Telex to Russell Rollason, 8 April. In *Records of the Australian Council for Overseas Aid,* MS9347, Box 192, Folder 164. (Added 21 September 1998). Canberra: National Library of Australia.

—— 1986b. Letter to Buchanan, 3 August. In *Records of the Australian Council for Overseas Aid,* MS9347, Box 192, Folder 164. (Added 21 September 1998). Canberra: National Library of Australia.

Foley, Meredith Anne. 1985. The women's movement in New South Wales and Victoria, 1918–1938. PhD thesis. Sydney: Department of History, University of Sydney.

Foresti, Marta, David Booth and Tammie O'Neil. 2009. Aid effectiveness and human rights – strengthening the implementation of the Paris Declaration. *ODI Framework Paper*. London: ODI.

Fowler, Alan. 1992. Decentralisation for international NGOs. *Development in Practice* 2 (2):121–124.

—— 1997. *Striking a balance: A guide to enhancing the effectiveness of non-governmental organisations in international development*. New York: Earthscan.

—— 2000. NGDOs as a Moment in History: Beyond Aid to Social Entrepreneurship or Civic Innovation? quick view. *Third World Quarterly* 21 (4):637–654.

Frank, Andre Gunder. 1969. *Capitalism and underdevelopment in Latin America: historical studies of Chile and Brazil*. New York: Monthly Review Press.

Franks, Chris. 2013. Interview with author. 5 November. Canberra.

Franks, Suzanne. 2005. The neglect of Africa. *British Journalism Review* 16 (1):59–64.

Fraser, Arvonne S. 1995. The Convention on the Elimination of all Forms of Discrimination Against Women (The Women's Convention). In Anne Winslow (ed.). *Women, Politics and the United Nations*. Westport Connecticut: Greenwood Press.

—— 2012. Making History Word by Word. *Journal of Women's History* 24 (4):193–200.

Freeman, Jo. 1999. On the origins of social movements. In Jo Freemen and Victoria Johnson (eds). *Waves of Protest and Social Movements Since the Sixties*. New York: Rowman and Littlefield, pp. 7–24.

Freire, Paulo. 1970. *Pedagogy of the Oppressed*. New York: Continuum.

Fuchs, Andreas, Axel Dreher and Peter Nunnenkamp. 2014. Determinants of donor generosity: A survey of the aid budget literature. *World Development* 56:172–199.

Fujikane, Hiroko. 2003. Approaches to global education in the United States, the United Kingdom and Japan. *International Review of Education* 49 (1–2):133–152.

Fukuda-Parr, Sakiko. 2004. Millennium Development Goals: why they matter. *Global Governance* 10 (4):395–402.

—— 2010. Reducing inequality – The missing MDG: A content review of PRSPs and bilateral donor policy statements. *IDS Bulletin* 41 (1):26–35.

Funk, Nanette. 2013. Contra Fraser on Feminism and Neoliberalism. *Hypatia* 28 (1):179–196.

Geldof, Bob. 1991. *With Love from Band Aid*. London: Band Aid Trust.

Georgeou, Nichole and Susan Engel. 2011. The impact of neoliberalism and new managerialism on development volunteering: an Australian case study. *Australian Journal of Political Science* 46 (2):297–311.

Gibelman, Margaret and Sheldon R Gelman. 2001. Very public scandals: Nongovernmental organizations in trouble. *Voluntas: International Journal of Voluntary and Nonprofit Organizations* 12 (1):49–66.

Givoni, Michal. 2011. Humanitarian governance and ethical cultivation: Médecins sans Frontières and the advent of the expert-witness. *Millennium Journal of International Studies* 40 (1):43–63.

Glennie, Jonathan. 2011. Who should lead the aid effectiveness debate in the future. Speech at the first ODI Busan Debate, House of Commons, 6 July. London: ODI.

Golub, Philip S. 2013. From the New International Economic Order to the G20: how the 'global South' is restructuring world capitalism from within. *Third World Quarterly* 34 (6):1000–1015.

Gore, Charles. 2010. The MDG paradigm, productive capacities and the future of poverty reduction. *IDS Bulletin* 41 (1):70–79.

Gourevitch, Peter A, David A Lake and Janice Gross Stein. 2012. *The credibility of transnational NGOs: when virtue is not enough*. Cambridge: Cambridge University Press.

Government of India. 1971. Statistical Information relating to the Influx of Refugees from East Bengal into India till 31st October 1971. Calcutta: Ministry of Labour and Rehabilitation, Department of Rehabilitation, Branch Secretariat.

Govt of Malaysia. 1969. Memorandum of Malaysia's Development Experience and Problems of External Assistance. Presented to the Pearson Commission on International Development 9–12 April, Singapore. Kuala Lumpur: Government of Malaysia.

Gráda, Cormac Ó. 2011. Famines past, famine's future. *Development and Change* 42 (1):49–69.

Graham, Elaine. 2003. Feminist Theology, Northern. In Peter Scott and William Cavanaugh (eds). *The Blackwell Companion to Political Theology*. Ch. 15. Oxford: Blackwell.

Gray, Anthony. 2013. Government funding of non-governmental organisations and the implied freedom of political communication: The constitutionality of gag clauses. *Australian Journal of Political Science* 48 (4):456–469.

Gubser, Michael. 2012. The Presentist Bias: Ahistoricism, Equity, and International Development in the 1970s. *The Journal of Development Studies* 48 (12):1799–1812.

Guilfoyle, Margaret. 1982. Letter to Bob Whan from Acting Minister for Foreign Affairs, 18 May. In *Records of the Australian Council for Overseas Aid, MS9347*, Box 45, Folder 236. Canberra: National Library of Australia.

Gulrajani, Nilima. 2011. Transcending the great foreign aid debate: managerialism, radicalism and the search for aid effectiveness. *Third World Quarterly* 32 (2):199–216.

Haggis, Jane and Susanne Schech. 2000. Meaning well and global good manners: reflections on white western feminist cross-cultural praxis. *Australian Feminist Studies* 15 (33):387–399.

Hallsworth, Simon and John Lea. 2011. Reconstructing Leviathan: Emerging contours of the security state. *Theoretical criminology* 15 (2):141–157.

Halper, Stefan. 2012. *The Beijing consensus: Legitimizing authoritarianism in our time*. New York: Basic Books.

Hamm, Brigitte I. 2001. A human rights approach to development. *Human Rights Quarterly* 23 (4):1005–1031.

Hannum, Hurst. 2011. *Autonomy, sovereignty, and self-determination: The accommodation of conflicting rights*. Philadelphia: University of Pennsylvania Press.

Harries Committee. 1979. *Australia and the Third World: Report of the Committee on Australia's Relation with the Third World*. Canberra: AGPS.

Harris, A. 1975. Letter to Les Johnson, Director ADAA, 4 June. In *Records of the Australian Council for Overseas Aid, MS9347*, Box 46, Folder 238. Canberra: National Library of Australia.

Harrison, Cynthia E. 1980. A 'New Frontier' for Women: The Public Policy of the Kennedy Administration. *The Journal of American History* 67 (3):630–646.

Harrison, Graham. 2010. The Africanization of poverty: A retrospective on 'Make poverty history'. *African Affairs* 109 (436):391–408.

Harris-Rimmer, Susan. 2013. Interview with author, June 28. Canberra.

Hasluck, Paul. 1964. Australia and Southeast Asia. *Foreign Affairs* 43:51–63.

Hassim, Shireen. 1991. Gender, social location and feminist politics in South Africa. *Transformation* (15):65–82.

Hayden, Bill. 1990. Address at the opening of ACFOA Council. In *Records of the Australian Council for Overseas Aid,* MS9347, MSAcc10.179, Box 43. (Added 5 November 2010). Canberra: National Library of Australia.

Hayes, Brian. 1967a. Report on visit to Vietnam 23 July – 6 August 1967. In *Records of the Australian Council for Overseas Aid,* MS9347, Box 13, Folder 1. Canberra: National Library of Australia.

—— 1967b. Draft Report to Department of External Affairs, 17 October. In *Records of the Australian Council for Overseas Aid,* MS9347, Box 13, Folder 1. Canberra: National Library of Australia.

—— 1968. Letter to *The Age,* 9 May. In *Records of the Australian Council for Overseas Aid,* MS9374, Box 2, Folio 5. Canberra: National Library of Australia.

—— 1969a. Letter to members, 24 February. In *Records of the Australian Council for Overseas Aid;* MS9374, Box 13, Folio 1. Canberra: National Library of Australia.

—— 1969b. Future Role of ACFOA. Paper to Council, June. In *Records of the Australian Council for Overseas Aid,* MS9374, Box 13, Folio 2. Canberra: National Library of Australia.

—— 1970a. Letter to Paul Cullen, 19 March. In *Records of the Australian Council for Overseas Aid,* MS9374, Box 1, Folio 1. Canberra: National Library of Australia.

—— 1970b. Letter to John Crawford, 28 August. In *Records of the Australian Council for Overseas Aid,* MS9374, Box 1, Folio 1. Canberra: National Library of Australia.

—— 1970c. Letter to John Crawford, 3 April. In *Records of the Australian Council for Overseas Aid,* MS9374, Box 1, Folio 1. Canberra: National Library of Australia

Heater, Derek. 1984. *Peace through education: The contribution of the Council for Education in World Citizenship.* Lewes: Falmer Press.

Hellinger, Doug. 1987. NGOs and the large aid donors: Changing the terms of engagement. *World Development* 15 Supplement:135–143.

Henderson, Harold. 1976. Letter to Mick Sullivan, 3 June. In *Records of the Australian Council for Overseas Aid*, MS9374, Box 30, Folio 143 Canberra: National Library of Australia.

—— 1977. Letter to Mick Sullivan, 21 October. In *Records of the Australian Council for Overseas Aid*, MS9374, Box 30, Folio 143. Canberra: National Library of Australia.

Henry, Michael. 1985. Letter to Russell Rollason, 9 December. In *Records of the Australian Council for Overseas Aid*, MS9347, Box 198, Folder 186. (Added 21 September 1998). Canberra: National Library of Australia.

Herbert, Chantal. 2011. In defending Oda, Harper stands alone. *The Star*, 18 February.

Herbert, Harry J. 1973. The churches and the election. *Politics* 8 (1):158–161.

Herbert-Copley, Brent. 1987. Canadian NGOs: Past trends, future challenges. *World Development* 15 Supplementary:21–28.

Hewett, Andrew. 2013. Interview with author, 6 September. Canberra.

Hicks, David. 2003. Thirty years of global education: A reminder of key principles and precedents. *Educational Review* 55 (3):265–275.

High Court of Australia. 1992. *Mabo and Others v Queensland* (no. 2) (1992) 175 CLR 1.

—— 1996. *Wik Peoples v Queensland* (Pastoral Leases case) [1996] HCA 40; (1996) 187 CLR 1; (1996) 141 ALR 129; (1996) 71 ALJR 173 (23 December).

—— 2010. *Aid/Watch Incorporated v Commissioner of Taxation*, 1 December. In *HCA 42*, High Court of Australia. Canberra.

Hill, Helen. 1970. The Second United Nations. *The Nation*, 7.

—— 1972. Swiss chip in on the Yirrkala. *The Review*, July 1–7.

—— 1975a. Overseas Aid – posturing with the poor? *Nation Review*, 29 August – 4 September.

—— 1975b. Woolworths caught in a fish trap, *Nation Review*, 30 May – 5 June.

—— 1980. Australian Non-Governmental Organisations and the Third World. *Ideas and Action* (137):8–14.

Hilton, Matthew. 2012. International Aid and Development NGOs in Britain and Human Rights since 1945. *Humanity: An International Journal of Human Rights, Humanitarianism, and Development* 3 (3):449–472.

Hinton, Vaughan. 1968. Honorary Secretary's report, 25–26 March. In *Records of the Australian Council for Overseas Aid,* MS9374, Box 13, Folder 1. Canberra: National Library of Australia.

—— 1969. Report to Council, Minutes 21–22 June. In *Records of the Australian Council for Overseas Aid,* Box 54, Folder 277. Canberra: National Library of Australia.

—— 1971. Honorary Secretary's Report to Annual Council, 13–15 August. In *Records of the Australian Council for Overseas Aid,* MS 9347, Box 54, Folio 279. Canberra: National Library of Australia.

Hobbin, William. 1964. Letter to John Gorton, Treasurer, 19 June. In *Records of the Australian Freedom From Hunger Campaign,* MS4529, Box 1, Folder 4. Canberra: National Library of Australia.

Hobbs, Jeremy. 2013. Interview with author, October 7. Canberra.

Hodges, B. 1980. Letter to member agencies, 1 August. In *Records of the Australian Council for Overseas Aid,* MS9374, Box 36, Folio 13. Canberra: National Library of Australia.

Hollway, Sandy, Bill Farmer, Margaret Reid, John Denton and Stephen Howes. 2011. *Independent Review of Aid Effectiveness.* Canberra: Commonwealth of Australia.

Hortsch, Diana. 2010. Paradox of Partnership: Amnesty International, Responsible Advocacy, and NGO Accountability. The *Columbia Human Rights Law Review.* 42:119–155.

Howard, John. 1979. Letter to Richard Alston, 14 December. In *Records of the Australian Council for Overseas Aid,* MS9374, Box 46, Folder 242. Canberra: National Library of Australia.

Howell, Jude. 2012. Civil society, corporatism and capitalism in China. *Journal of Comparative Asian Development* 11 (2):271–297.

—— 2012. Shifting Global Influences on Civil Society: Times for Reflection. In Heidi Moksnes and Mia Melin (eds). *Global Civil Society – Shifting Powers in a Shifting World.* Uppsala: Uppsala University.

—— 2014. The securitisation of NGOs post-9/11. *Conflict, Security & Development* 14 (2): 151–179.

Howell, Jude and Jeremy Lind. 2009a. Changing donor policy and practice in civil society in the post-9/11 aid context. *Third World Quarterly* 30 (7):1279–1296.

—— 2009b. *Counter-terrorism, aid and civil society: before and after the war on terror.* Basingstoke: Palgrave-Macmillan.

Howell, Jude, Armine Ishkanian, Ebenezer Obadare, Hakan Seckinelgin and Marlies Glasius. 2008. The backlash against civil society in the wake of the Long War on Terror. *Development in Practice* 18 (1):82–93.

Hubbard, Rex V. 1981. Letter to Bob Whan, 18 September. In *Records of the Australian Council for Overseas Aid*, MS9347, Box 51, Folder 266. Canberra: National Library of Australia.

Hudson, Alan. 2002. Advocacy by UK-Based Development NGOs. *Nonprofit and Voluntary Sector Quarterly* 31 (3):402–418.

Hughes, Caroline and Jane Hutchison. 2012. Development effectiveness and the politics of commitment. *Third World Quarterly* 33 (1):17–36.

Hulme, David. 2013. Poverty and development thinking: synthesis or uneasy compromise? *BWPI Working Paper No. 180*. Manchester: Brooks World Poverty Institute.

Hunt, Janet. 1995a. Letter to ExCom, 11 August. In *Records of the Australian Council for Overseas Aid*, MS9347, MSAcc10.179, Box 25, 6–27 ACFOA Code of Ethics 1989–96. (Added 5 November 2010). Canberra: National Library of Australia.

—— 1995b. Memo to ExCom 21 August. In *Records of the Australian Council for Overseas Aid*, MS9347, MSAcc10.179, Box 26. (Added 5 November 2010). Canberra: National Library of Australia.

—— 1995c. Letter to Gordon Bilney 7 August. In *Records of the Australian Council for Overseas Aid*, MS9347, MSAcc10.179, Box 6, CEO's correspondence 4-4-5a. (Added 5 November 2010). Canberra: National Library of Australia.

—— 1995d. Discussion paper re ACFOA response to NGO Effectiveness Review to ACFOA Executive, 14 September. In *Records of the Australian Council for Overseas Aid*, MS9347, MSAcc10.179, Box 6, CEO's correspondence 4-4-5a. (Added 5 November 2010). Canberra: National Library of Australia.

—— 1998. Review of ACFOA Committees and Working Groups, August. In *Records of the Australian Council for Overseas Aid*, MS9347, MSAcc10.179, Box 42. (Added 5 November 2010). Canberra: National Library of Australia.

————— 2011. Interview with author, 15 October. Canberra.

————— 2012. Interview with author, 4 October. Canberra.

Hunt, Philip. 1992. Letter to Ian Harris, 1 September. In *ACFID Files: CARE File 9–15*. Canberra: ACFID.

Huntington, Samuel P. 1970. Foreign Aid for what and for whom. *Foreign Policy* (1):161–189.

Hurst, Daniel. 2012. NGOs told they are right to remain silent to keep funding. *Brisbane Times*, 21 August.

ICCC. 1996. Interim Code of Conduct Committee Report to the Minister of Foreign Affairs and ACFOA, August. In *Records of the Australian Council for Overseas Aid*, MS9347, MSAcc10.179, Box 27. (Added 5 November 2010). Canberra: National Library of Australia.

IDEC. 1980. IDEC Minutes, 25 June. In *Records of the Australian Council for Overseas Aid*, MS9347, Box 184, Folder 252. (Added 21 September 1998). Canberra: National Library of Australia.

————— 1981. Report on Future of IDEC, October. In *Records of the Australian Council for Overseas Aid*, MS9347, Box189, Folder 149. (Added 21 September 1998). Canberra: National Library of Australia.

————— 1983. Report on Public Relations Activities undertaken for the Africa Famine Appeal, 16 September. In *Records of the Australian Council for Overseas Aid*, MS9347, Box 184, Folder 124. (Added 21st Sept 1998). Canberra: National Library of Australia.

————— 1985a. IDEC Annual Report, 9 September. In *Records of the Australian Council for Overseas Aid*, MS9347, Box 189, Folder 150. (Added 21 September 1998). Canberra: National Library of Australia.

————— 1985b. Minutes of IDEC Meeting, 6 December. In *Records of the Australian Council for Overseas Aid*, MS9347, Box 189, Folder 150. (Added 21 September 1998). Canberra: National Library of Australia.

————— 1986a. Sport Aid: a Report, September. In *Records of the Australian Council for Overseas Aid*, MS9347, Box 180, Folder 111-6. (Added 21 September 1998). Canberra: National Library of Australia.

————— 1986b. Minutes of IDEC Meeting, 21 February. In *Records of the Australian Council for Overseas Aid*, MS9347, Box 189, Folder 150. (Added 21 September 1998). Canberra: National Library of Australia.

——— 1986c. Minutes of IDEC Meeting, 11 April. In Records of the Australian Council for Overseas Aid, MS9347, Box 189, Folder 150 (Added 21 September *1998)*. Canberra: National Library of Australia.

——— 1986d. Minutes of IDEC Meeting, 26 June. In *Records of the Australian Council for Overseas Aid*, MS9347, Box 189, Folder 150 (Added 21 September 1998). Canberra: National Library of Australia.

——— 1988. Financial Accounts. In *Records of the Australian Council for Overseas Aid,* MS9347, Box 188, Folder 141. (Added 21 September 1998). Canberra: National Library of Australia.

——— 1991a. Minutes of Annual General Meeting. In *Records of the Australian Council for Overseas Aid,* MS9347, Box 198, Folder 189. (Added 21 September 1998). Canberra: National Library of Australia.

——— 1991b. Minutes of IDEC Meeting, 4 June. In *Records of the Australian Council for Overseas Aid*, MS9347, Box 189, Folder 151. (Added 21 September 1998). Canberra: National Library of Australia.

——— 1992. Combined Agencies African Crisis Appeal Report, 6 April. In *Records of the Australian Council for Overseas Aid,* MS9347, Box 187, Folder 138. (Added 21 September 1998). Canberra: National Library of Australia.

Industry Commission. 1995. *Charitable Organisations in Australia*. Melbourne: AGPS.

Ingram, Jim. 1981. Letter to Bob Whan from ADAB, 26 August In *Records of the Australian Council for Overseas Aid,* MS9347, Box 45, Folder 236. Canberra: National Library of Australia.

——— 1995. COPAC Final Report. In *Records of the Australian Council for Overseas Aid,* MS9347, MSAcc10.179, Box 26. (Added 5 November 2010). Canberra: National Library of Australia.

——— 2010. Sir John Crawford. Paper read at the Biodiversity And World Food Security: Nourishing The Planet And Its People conference conducted by the Crawford Fund for International Agricultural Research. Canberra: Parliament House.

International Research and Training Institute for the Advancement of Women and UN Development Fund for Women. 1995. *Women and the UN: 1945–1995*. New York: INSTRAW and UNIFEM.

InterAction. 2013. *InterAction PVO Standards: Accountability; Transparency; Effectiveness.* Washington: InterAction.

International Commission of Jurists. 1981. Rural development and human rights in South-East Asia: conclusions of ICJ/CAP Penang seminar; and The Right to Development: its scope, content, and implementation. Papers presented at the Seminar on Human Rights and Development in the Rural Areas of South East Asia, December. Penang, Malaysia.

Irvine, Graeme. 1969. Letter to Brian Hayes, 20 May. In *Records of the Australian Council for Overseas Aid,* MS9374, Box 30, Folio 143. Canberra: National Library of Australia.

Ito, T. 2007. Asian currency crisis and the International Monetary Fund, 10 years later: overview. *Asian Economic Policy Review* 2 (1):16–49.

Jachertz, Ruth. 2012. *United Nations Food and Agriculture Organization, Wiley-Blackwell Encyclopedia of Globalization.* London: Wiley-Blackwell.

Jackson Committee. 1984. *Report of the Committee to Review the Australian Aid Program.* Canberra: Commonwealth of Australia.

Jahan, Rounaq. 2012. Sustaining Advocacy for Women's Empowerment for Four Decades. *Journal of Women's History* 24 (4):208–212.

Jain, Devaki. 2005. *Women, development, and the UN: A sixty-year quest for equality and justice.* Bloomington: Indiana University Press.

James, D Clayton. 1993. *Refighting the last war: Commanders and Crisis in Korea 1950–53.* New York: Simon and Schuster.

Jaquette, Jane S. 1995. Losing the Battle/Winning the War: International Politics, Women's Issues and the 1980 Mid-Decade Conference. In Anne Winslow (ed.). *Women, Politics and the United Nations.* Westport Connecticut: Greenwood Press, pp. 45–60.

Jaquette, Jane S and Kathleen Staudt. 2006. Women, gender and development. In Jane Jaquette and Gale Summerfield (eds). *Women and gender equity in development theory and practice: Institutions, resources and mobilization.* Durham NC: Duke University Press, pp. 17–52.

Jarrett, Frank G. 1994. *Evolution of Australia's aid program.* Canberra: National Centre for Development Studies.

Jayasuriya, Sisira K and Peter McCawley. 2010. *The Asian tsunami: aid and reconstruction after a disaster.* Cheltenham: Edward Elgar Publishing.

JCFADT. 2010. Inquiry into Human Rights Mechanisms and the Asia-Pacific. Canberra: Parliament of Australia.

Johns, Gary. 2000. NGO Way to Go: Political Accountability of Non-government Organizations in a Democratic Society. *IPA Backgrounder* 12 (3):1–15.

—— 2003. The NGO Challenge: Whose Democracy is it anyway?. In *Conference: Non-Governmental Organisations: the growing power of the unelected few, June 11*. Washington: American Enterprise Institute.

Jones, David Martin and Andrea Benvenuti. 2012. Menzies' Asia policy and the anachronistic fallacy. *Australian Journal of International Affairs* 66 (2):206–222.

Jordan, Lisa. 2005. Mechanisms for NGO accountability. *GPPi Research Paper Series* (3).

Juddery, Bruce. 1975a. Discussion on Dismissal Expected. *Canberra Times*, 23 August.

—— 1975b. Aid body refers dismissal to sub-committee. *Canberra Times*, 25 August.

Kabeer, Naila. 2012. Can the MDGs provide a pathway to social justice? The challenge of intersecting inequalities. In Isabel Ortiz, Louise Moreira Daniels, Sólrún Engilbertsdóttir (eds). *Child poverty and inequality new perspectives*. New York: UNICEF.

Kamal, Khairil Annuar Mohd. 2012. A New and Postmodern Theory of Malaysian Corporatism? Preliminary Conceptual and Theoretical Outline. *FEB Working Paper Series No. 1212*. Kota Samaraham Sarawak: UNIMAS.

Kamat, Sangeeta. 2004. The privatization of public interest: theorizing NGO discourse in a neoliberal era. *Review of International Political Economy* 11 (1):155–176.

Kanbur, Ravi. 2006. The economics of international aid. *Handbook of the Economics of Giving, Altruism and Reciprocity* 2:1559–1588.

Kane, Molly. 2013. International NGOs and the Aid Industry: constraints on international solidarity. *Third World Quarterly* 34 (8):1505–1515.

Kapadia, Karin. 1995. Where angels fear to tread?: 'Third world women' and 'development'. *The Journal of peasant studies* 22 (2):356–368.

Karnani, Aneel. 2011. *Fighting poverty together: rethinking strategies for business, governments, and civil society to reduce poverty*. New York: Macmillan.

Keck, Michelle. 2011. State funded NGOs in civil wars: the US case. *Contemporary Politics* 17 (4):411–427.

Keller, Edmond J. 1992. Drought, war, and the politics of famine in Ethiopia and Eritrea. *Journal of Modern African Studies* 30 (4):609–624.

Kelly, Paul. 1980. Pol Pot poses a dilemma for the Liberals. *The National Times*, 14–20 September.

Kennedy, Annie. 1992. Women in Development in Australian NGO Development Assistance. In *Records of the Australian Council for Overseas Aid*, MS9347, Box 108, Folder 237. (Added 30 January 1998). Canberra: National Library of Australia.

Kennedy, Scott. 2010. The myth of the Beijing Consensus. *Journal of Contemporary China* 19 (65):461–477.

Kenyon, Timothy. 1985. The Politics and Morality of Live Aid. *Politics* 5 (2):3–8.

Kerin, John. 1975. Adjournment Debate House of Representatives, *Hansard*. Canberra: Australian Parliament. 28 August.

Keys, William. 1975. Letter to Mick Sullivan, May 23. In *Records of the Australian Council for Overseas Aid*, MS9374, Box 29, RSL Folio. Canberra: National Library of Australia.

Khouri, Phil and Deborah Russell. 2009. *ACFID Code of Conduct Review – Stage 2 Report: Framing the Code*. Canberra: ACFID.

Kidd, James Robbins. 1964. Development Aid of Private Organisations in Canada. *Proceedings of the International Conference on Methods and Administration of Development Measures Initiated in the Field of Technical Assistance by Private Organizations in Western Donor countries*, 20–25 November. Berlin-Tegal: German Foundation for Developing Countries.

Kilby, Patrick. 2004. Nongovernmental Organizations and Accountability in an Era of Global Anxiety. *Seton Hall Journal of Diplomacy and International Relations*. 5(2):67–78.

—— 2008. The strength of networks: the local NGO response to the tsunami in India. *Disasters* 32 (1):120–130.

—— 2011. *NGOs in India: The challenge of women's empowerment and accountability*. London: Routledge.

—— 2012. The Changing Development Landscape in the First Decade of the 21st Century and its Implications for Development Studies. *Third World Quarterly* 33 (6):1001–1017.

—— 2014. Public support of development NGOs: a journey through the ages. In Stephen Howes (ed.). *DevPolicy Blog*, 9 April. Canberra: Development Policy Centre.

Kilby, Patrick and Joanne Crawford. 2011. Closing the Gender Gap: Gender and Australian NGOs. In *ACFID Research in Development Series Report No. 2*; Part of the ACFID-IHS Working Paper Series. Canberra: ACFID.

Kilcullen, David J. 2005. Countering global insurgency. *The Journal of Strategic Studies* 28 (4):597–617.

Kim, Kirsteen. 2011. Globalization of Protestant Movements since the 1960s. *The Ecumenical Review* 63 (2):136–147.

Kindornay, Shannon, James Ron and Charli Carpenter. 2012. Rights-Based Approaches to Development: Implications for NGOs. *Human Rights Quarterly* 34 (2):472–506.

Kingsbury, Benedict. 2002. First amendment liberalism as global legal architecture: Ascriptive groups and the problems of the liberal NGO model of international civil society. *Chicago Journal of International Law* 3 (1):183–195.

Kjøllesdal, Kristian Aamelfot and Anne Welle-Strand. 2010. Foreign Aid Strategies: China Taking Over? *Asian Social Science* 6 (10):3–13.

Knack, Stephen, F, Halsey Rogers and Nicholas Eubank. 2011. Aid quality and donor rankings. *World Development* 39 (11):1907–1917.

Koczberski, Gina. 1998. Women in development: a critical analysis. *Third World Quarterly* 19 (3):395–410.

Kolk, Ans and Rob Van Tulder. 2005. Setting new global rules? TNCs and codes of conduct. *Transnational Corporations* 14 (3):1–27.

Kolk, Ans, Rob Van Tulder and Carlijn Welters. 1999. International codes of conduct and corporate social responsibility: can transnational corporations regulate themselves? *Transnational Corporations* 8 (1):143–180.

Korey, William 2001. *NGOs and the Universal Declaration of Human Rights : 'A Curious Grapevine'*. Basingstoke: Palgrave.

Korf, Benedikt. 2007. Antinomies of generosity: moral geographies and post-tsunami aid in Southeast Asia. *Geoforum* 38 (2):366–378.

Kovács, Gyöngi and Karen M Spens. 2011. *Relief Supply Chain for Disasters: Humanitarian, Aid and Emergency Logistics.* Hershey PA: Business Science Reference.

Kowalski, Alexandra. 2011. When Cultural Capitalization Became Global Practice. In Nina Bandelj and Frederick F Wherry (eds). *The Cultural Wealth of Nations.* Redwood CA: Stanford University Press, pp. 73–89.

Kraeger, Patsy. 2011. NGO Mission Success: The Field Office Perspective. PhD dissertation. Phoenix: Arizona State University.

Kraft, Herman Joseph S. 2001. Human Rights, ASEAN and Constructivism: Revisiting the 'Asian Values' Discourse. *Philippine Political Science Journal* 22 (45):33–54.

Krieger, Tim and Daniel Meierrieks. 2010. Does Income Inequality Lead to Terrorism [online]. Available at SSRN 1647178.

Krook, Mona Lena and Jacqui True. 2012. Rethinking the life cycles of international norms: The United Nations and the global promotion of gender equality. *European Journal of International Relations* 18 (1):103–127.

Kuruvilla, Shyama, Flavia Bustreo, Paul Hunt, Amarjit Singh, Eric Friedman, Thiago Luchesi, Stefan Germann, Kim Terje Loraas, Alicia Ely Yamin and Ximena Andion. 2012. The Millennium Development Goals and human rights: realizing shared commitments. *Human Rights Quarterly* 34 (1):141–177.

Labouisse, Henry R. 1961. *An Act for International Development, A Program for the Decade of Development: Objectives Concepts and Proposed Program,* edited by the International Cooperation Administration. Washington, DC: Department of State Publication.

Laforest, Rachel. 2012. Rerouting political representation: Is Canada's social infrastructure in crisis? *British Journal of Canadian Studies* 25 (2):181–197.

Lake, Marilyn. 1996. Feminist history as national history: Writing the political history of women. *Australian Historical Studies* 27 (106):154–169.

Landolt, Laura K. 2004. (Mis)constructing the Third World? Constructivist analysis of norm diffusion: Feature review. *Third World Quarterly* 25 (3):579–591.

Lang, Sabine. 2012. *NGOs, Civil Society, and the Public Sphere.* New York: Cambridge University Press.

Laville, Helen. 2012. Woolly, Half-Baked and Impractical? British Responses to the Commission on the Status of Women and the Convention on the Political Rights of Women 1946–67. *Twentieth Century British History* 23 (4):473–495.

Law, Archie, Elisabeth Van Riedl and Danielle Celermajer. 2012. Measuring Social Change: Principles to guide the assessment of human rights approaches to development, *Research and Development Series* No. 5. Canberra: ACFID.

Lecy, Jesse D, Hans Peter Schmitz and Haley Swedlund. 2012. Non-governmental and not-for-profit organizational effectiveness: a modern synthesis. *Voluntas: International Journal of Voluntary and Nonprofit Organizations* 23 (2):434–457.

Lee, Pene. 1995. Letter to Gordon Bilney, 24 October. In *Records of the Australian Council for Overseas Aid,* MS9347, MSAcc10.179, Box 26. (Added 5 November 2010). Canberra: National Library of Australia.

Lefaucheux, Marie-Hélène. 1959. Some remarks and suggestions by way of a conclusion. Paper read at Women's Role in the Development of Tropical and Sub-tropical countries: Report of the XXXI Meeting of INCIDI, Brussels, 17–20 September.

Legum, Colin (ed.). 1970. *The first UN Development decade and its lessons for the 1970s.* New York: Praeger.

Lemaresquier, Thierry. 1987. Prospects for development education: Some strategic issues facing European NGOs. *World Development* 15:189–200.

Lewis, David. 2010a. Disciplined activists, unruly brokers?: Exploring the boundaries between non-governmental organizations (NGOs), donors, and the state in Bangladesh. In David Gellner (ed.). *From Varieties of Activist Experience: Civil Society in South Asia.* Ch. 8. New Delhi: Sage Publications.

—— 2010b. Political ideologies and non-governmental organizations: an anthropological perspective. *Journal of political ideologies* 15 (3):333–345.

Lieber, Robert. 2013. Multipolar or Multilateral? Diffusion of Power, the BRICS, and the United States. Paper read at Diffusion of Power, the BRICS, and the United States. APSA 2013 Annual Meeting, 22 August 2013.

Lindenberg, Marc. 1999. Declining state capacity, voluntarism, and the globalization of the not-for-profit sector. *Nonprofit and Voluntary Sector Quarterly* 28 Supplement 1:147–167.

Lindin, Eugene. 1976. *The Alms Race: the impact of American Voluntary Aid Abroad.* New York: Random House.

Lipner, Michele and Louis Henley. 2010. *Working Better Together: An NGO perspective on improving Australia's coordination in disaster response.* Canberra: APCMCOE and ACFID.

Lissner, Jorgen. 1977. *The Politics of Altruism: a study of the political behaviour of voluntary development agencies.* Geneva: Lutheran World Federation.

Lloyd, Robert. 2005. *The role of NGO self-regulation in increasing stakeholder accountability.* London: One World Trust.

Lockwood, John. 1963. 'The Call for Voluntary Service Overseas'. *Social Service Quarterly.* Autumn.

Loughland, K. 1991. Letter to Russell Rollason, 14 November. In *Records of the Australian Council for Overseas Aid,* MS9347 MSAcc10.179, Box 25, 6–27 ACFOA Code of Ethics 1989–96. (Added 5 November 2010). Canberra: National Library of Australia.

Lowe, David. 2013. Journalists and the Stirring of Australian Public Diplomacy: The Colombo Plan Towards the 1960s. *Journal of Contemporary History* 48 (1):175–190.

Lowe, Michelle. 1993. Women and Development. In Allen C Walsh (ed.). *Development that Works.* Palmerston North NZ: Amokura, Ch. D5.

Lundqvist, Jenny. 2014. *Foreign Aid's Impact on Income Inequality.* Lund: Lund University, Department of Economics.

Lundy, Laura and Lesley McEvoy. 2012. Childhood, the United Nations Convention on the Rights of the Child and Research: What Constitutes a 'Rights-Based' Approach?. *Child and Family Law Quarterly* 331:350.

MacFarlane, S Neil. 1999. Humanitarian action and conflict. *International Journal* 54(4):537–561.

MacKenzie, Norman. 1962. *Women in Australia.* Melbourne: F.W. Cheshire.

Mackin, Robert Sean. 2012. Liberation Theology: The Radicalization of Social Catholic Movements. *Politics, Religion & Ideology* 13 (3):333–351.

Macrae, Joanna. 1998. The Death of Humanitarianism?: An Anatomy of the Attack. *Disasters* 22 (4):309–317.

Maddison, Sarah, Clive Hamilton and Richard Denniss. 2004. Silencing Dissent: Non-government organisations and Australian democracy. *Discussion Paper Number 65, June.* Canberra: Australia Institute.

Manning, Chris and John Maxwell. 2011. Jamie Mackie: scholar, mentor and advocate. *Bulletin of Indonesian Economic Studies* 47 (2):183–193.

Manzo, Kate. 2003. Africa in the rise of rights-based development. *Geoforum* 34 (4):437–456.

Maranan, Aida. 1985. The Role and Status of Women in ACFOA member agencies: a survey report. Canberra: ACFOA.

Marchetti, Victor and John D Marks. 1974. *The CIA and the Cult of Intelligence*. London: Jonathan Cape.

Margolis, Diane Rothbard. 1993. Women's movements around the world: Cross-cultural comparisons. *Gender & Society* 7 (3):379–399.

Martin, Fiona. 2011. The legal concept of charity and its expansion after the Aid/Watch decision. *Cosmopolitan Civil Societies: An Interdisciplinary Journal* 3 (3s):20–33.

Martinez, Daniel E and David J Cooper. 2013. Assembling International Development Through 'Capture': The management and accounting control of non-governmental organizations (NGOs). Paper presented at the Seventh Asia Pacific Interdisciplinary Research in Accounting Conference, Kobe 26–28 July.

Mauzy, Diane K. 1997. The human rights and 'Asian values' debate in southeast Asia: Trying to clarify the key issues. *Pacific Review* 10 (2):210–236.

Mavor, John. 1975. The Future of the Education Unit. Discussion paper 7 July. In *Records of the Australian Council for Overseas Aid*, MS 9347, Box 38, Folder 186. Canberra: National Library of Australia.

——— 1993a. From the President. *ACFOA Annual Report*. In *Records of the Australian Council for Overseas Aid*, MS9347, MSAcc10.179, Box 37. (Added 5 November 2010). Canberra: National Library of Australia.

——— 1993b. Letter to Malcolm Fraser, 3 August. In *ACFID Files: CARE File 9–15*. Canberra: ACFID.

Mawdsley, Emma. 2012. The changing geographies of foreign aid and development cooperation: contributions from gift theory. *Transactions of the Institute of British Geographers* 37 (2):256–272.

Mawdsley, Emma, Janet G Townsend and Gina Porter. 2005. Trust, accountability, and face-to-face interaction in North–South NGO relations. *Development in Practice* 15 (1):77–82.

Mawdsley, Emma, Laura Savage and Sung-Mi Kim. 2014. A 'post-aid world'? Paradigm shift in foreign aid and development cooperation at the 2011 Busan High Level Forum. *The Geographical Journal* 180 (1):27–38.

Mayoux, Linda. 1995. Beyond naivety: women, gender inequality and participatory development. *Development and Change* 26 (2):235–258.

McCalman, Janya, Komla Tsey, Russell Kitau and Sue McGinty. 2012. 'Bringing us back to our origin': adapting and transferring an Indigenous Australian values-based leadership capacity-building course for community development in Papua New Guinea. *Community Development* 43 (3):393–408.

McCarthy, Nigel. 2000. Aid Workers, Intelligence Gathering and Media Self-Censorship. *Australian Studies in Journalism* 9:30–50.

McDonald, Stephen. 1972. *Action for World Development: the World Development Movement in the 1970s*. London: World Development Movement.

McDougal, Dennis. 1986. Live Aid Concerts Raised $82 Million, Audit Shows. *Los Angeles Times,* 23 January.

McGann, James and Mary Johnstone. 2004. Power Shift and the NGO Credibility Crisis. *Brown Journal of World Affairs* 11:159.

McGregor, Andrew, Edward Challies, John Overton and Lee Sentes. 2013. Developmentalities and Donor–NGO Relations: Contesting Foreign Aid Policies in New Zealand/Aotearoa. *Antipode* 45 (5):1232–1253.

McKinnon, Katharine. 2007. Postdevelopment, professionalism, and the politics of participation. *Annals of the Association of American Geographers* 97 (4):772–785.

McPhedran, Ian. 1994. Aid Agencies Brawl on Ethics and media. *Canberra Times*, 12 September.

McWilliam, Andrew. 2005. Houses of Resistance in East Timor: Structuring Sociality in the New Nation 1. *Anthropological Forum* 15 (1):27–44.

Meer, Shamim. 2005. Freedom for women: mainstreaming gender in the South African liberation struggle and beyond. In Fenella Porter and Caroline Sweetman (eds). *Mainstreaming Gender in Development: A Critical Review, Oxfam Focus on Gender Series*. Oxford: Oxfam.

Meier, Gerald. M. 1971. Development Decade in Perspective – 1965. In Ronald Robinson (ed.) *Developing the Third World: the experience of the nineteen-sixties*. Cambridge: Cambridge University Press, pp. 18–36.

Melville, Rose. 1999. The state and community sector peak bodies: theoretical and policy challenges. *Third Sector Review* 5 (2):25–41.

Melville, Rose and Roberta Perkins. 2003. Changing roles of community sector peak bodies in a neo-liberal policy environment in Australia. Wollongong: Institute of Social Change and Critical Inquiry, University of Wollongong.

Menkhaus, Ken. 2012. No access: critical bottlenecks in the 2011 Somali famine. *Global Food Security* 1 (1):29–35.

Meyer, Carrie A. 1992. A step back as donors shift institution building from the public to the 'private' sector. *World Development* 20 (8):1115–1126.

Meyer, Mary K. 1999. Negotiating international norms: The inter-American commission of women and the convention on violence against women. In Mary Myer and Elisabeth Prügle (eds). *Gender politics in global governance*. Ch. 4. Boston: Roman and Littlefield.

Miazad, Ossai. 2002. The Global Action and Investments for Success for Women and Girls (GAINS) Act. *Human Rights Brief* 9 (3):37.

Miles, Mathew. 1978. Development Education: report and recommendations by the Working Party of the Advisory Committee on Development Education. Overseas Development Paper. London: Ministry of Overseas Development.

Millar, Carla CJM, Chong Ju Choi and Stephen Chen. 2004. Global strategic partnerships between MNEs and NGOs: Drivers of change and ethical issues. *Business and Society Review* 109 (4):395–414.

Millar, Heather. 2013. Comparing accountability relationships between governments and non-state actors in Canadian and European international development policy. *Canadian Public Administration* 56 (2):252–269.

Miller, Chris, Marilyn Taylor and Joanna Howard. 2013. Surviving the 'Civil Society Dilemma': Critical Factors in Shaping the Behaviour of Non-Governmental Actors. In Jude Howell (ed.). *Non-Governmental Public Action and Social Justice*. London: Palgrave Macmillan. pp. 136–158.

Miller, Hannah. 2010. From 'rights-based' to 'rights-framed' approaches: a social constructionist view of human rights practice. *The International Journal of Human Rights* 14 (6):915–931.

Miller, JDB, Harold Crouch and Stuart Harris. 1980. Australia and the third world: A review symposium on the Owen Harries Committee Report. *Australian Journal of International Affairs* 34 (1):100–109.

Miller, John. 2009. Crawford, Sir John Grenfell (Jack) (1910–1984). In Diane Langmore (ed.). *Australian Dictionary of Biography*. Melbourne: Melbourne University Press.

Ministry of Overseas Development. 1965. *Overseas Development: the work of the New Ministry*. London: Her Majesty's Stationary Office.

Minogue, Noreen. 1974. Letter to Cullen, 27 November. In *Records of the Australian Council for Overseas Aid*, MS9347, Box 36, Folio 15. Canberra: National Library of Australia.

Minogue, Noreen and R Burns. 1975. Memo to Executive Committee of ACFOA on the role of Education Unit, May 27. In *Records of the Australian Council for Overseas Aid*, MS9347, Box 38, Folder 186. Canberra: National Library of Australia.

Mitchell, George E and Hans Peter Schmitz. 2012. Principled instrumentalism: a theory of transnational NGO behaviour. *Review of International Studies* 40(3): 487–504.

Mitchell, Suzette. 1994. General profile of Responding Agencies: Women in Development and Affirmative Action Audit. In *Records of the Australian Council for Overseas Aid*, MS9347, Box 108, Folder 238. (Added 30 January 1998). Canberra: National Library of Australia.

—— 1995. Gender and Development: Policy and Practice of ACFOA member agencies. In *Records of the Australian Council for Overseas Aid*, MS9347, Box 108, Folder 236. (Added 30 January 1998). Canberra: National Library of Australia.

Mitlin, Diana, Sam Hickey and Anthony Bebbington. 2007. Reclaiming development? NGOs and the challenge of alternatives. *World Development* 35 (10):1699–1720.

Moghadam, Valentine M. 2000. Transnational Feminist Networks Collective Action in an Era of Globalization. *International Sociology* 15 (1):57–85.

Montgomery, B. 2000. Guilt-free apology campaign: Sir Ronald. *The Australian,* 16 October.

Mookherjee, Nayanika. 2011. Mobilising Images: Encounters of 'Forced' Migrants and the Bangladesh War of 1971. *Mobilities* 6 (3):399–414.

Moore, Kate. 1975. Report: United Nations International Women's Year Conference and Tribune June–July Mexico City, 17 July. In *Records of the Australian Council for Overseas Aid,* MS9374, Box 36, Folio 13. Canberra: National Library of Australia.

—— 2011. Interview with author, 20 October. Canberra.

Moore, Kate and Sue Tuckwell. 1975. *Aid in a Changing Society: a handbook of the Australian Aid Debate.* Canberra: ACFOA.

Morrow, Stephen. 1997. The changing roles of International Development NGOs in Australia. *Development Issues.* Canberra: ACFOA.

Mosley, Paul. 1986. Aid-effectiveness: The Micro-Macro Paradox. *IDS Bulletin* 17 (2):22–27.

Mowjee, Tasneem. 2001. NGO–Donor Funding Relationships: UK Government and European Community Funding of the Humanitarian Aid activities of UK NGOs from 1990–1997. PhD thesis. London: London School of Economics and Political Science.

Moxon, Don. 1985. *Towards One World: World Development Education in Theory and Practice.* London: Christian Education Movement.

Murlis, John. 1980. An Analysis of Food Aid Information in Kampuchea to March 1980. *Disasters* 4(3):263–270.

Murphy, Hannah. 2012. Rethinking the roles of non-governmental organisations at the World Trade Organization. *Australian Journal of International Affairs* 66 (4):468–485.

Murray, Warwick E and John D Overton. 2011. Neoliberalism is dead, long live neoliberalism? Neostructuralism and the international aid regime of the 2000s. *Progress in development studies* 11 (4):307–319.

Najam, Adil. 1998. Searching for NGO effectiveness. *Development Policy Review* 16 (3):305–310.

—— 2000. The Four C's of Government Third Sector-Government Relations. *Nonprofit Management and Leadership* 10 (4):375–396.

Nancy, Gilles and Boriana Yontcheva. 2006. Does NGO aid go to the poor? Empirical evidence from Europe. *IMF Working Paper.* Washington: International Monetary Fund.

Nanivazo, Malokele and Lucy Scott. 2012. *Gender mainstreaming in Nordic development agencies: Seventeen years after the Beijing conference.* WIDER Working Paper WP091. Helsinki: UNU-WIDER.

Nation Review. 1975. Commentary, 18–25 July. p. 1028. In *Records of the Australian Council for Overseas Aid,* MS9374, Box 29, RSL Folio. Canberra: National Library of Australia.

National Archives of Australia. n.d. The 1967 referendum – Fact sheet 150. Available at www.naa.gov.au/collection/fact-sheets/fs150.aspx.

National Council of Women. 1973. Papers from the International Council of Women Regional Conference and the National Council of Women of Australia Triennial Conference. Sydney, 20 October – 1 November.

National Women's Advisory Council. 1982. *Annual Report 1981–1982.* Canberra: National Women's Advisory Council.

—— 1984. *Annual Report 1982–1983.* Canberra: National Women's Advisory Council.

National Youth Council. 1975. *Aid or obstruction: World Vision and the Third World: an investigation into World Vision Policy, Practice and Philosophy in New Zealand and the Third World.* Auckland: National Youth Council.

Ndikumana, Leonce. 2012. Applying evaluation to development and aid: Can evaluation bridge the micro-macro gaps in aid effectiveness?. Paper presented at AFD-EDN Conference. Paris, *26 March*.

Nelson, Paul J. 1997. Conflict, Legitimacy, and Effectiveness: Who Speaks for Whom in Transnational NGO Networks Lobbying the World Bank? *Nonprofit and Voluntary Sector Quarterly* 26 (4):421–441.

—— 2007. Human rights, the Millennium Development Goals, and the future of development cooperation. *World Development* 35 (12):2041–2055.

New Dawn. 1973. Rewriting the Aborigines' Role in Australian History. *New Dawn*, January.

New Zealand Herald. 2009. Aid groups say criticism brings cuts to funding. *New Zealand Herald,* 29 September.

New Zealand Labour Party. 2010. McCully brings axe down on aid NGOs. Media release, 9 June. Wellington: Scoop Independent News.

Newman, Janet, Kate McLaughlin, Stephen P Osborne and Ewan Ferlie. 2002. *The new public management, modernization and institutional change.* Routledge: London.

News and Information Bureau. 1972. *Australians Taking More Interest in Aid.* Canberra: Government of Australia.

NewsBharati. 2012. Kudankulam Effect: Government's Biggest Crackdown On Foreign Funding Of NGOs. *News Bharati.* Available at [Online] 30 August.

Newton-Turner, Helen. 1985. Australian agricultural aid to Africa – appropriate expertise: a report to the Australian Council for Overseas Aid. Canberra: ACFOA.

Ni Chasaide, Nessa. 2009. Development education and campaigning linkages. *Policy & Practice: A Development Education Review* (8):28–34.

Niggli, Peter. 1986. *Ethiopia: Deportations and Forced-Labour Camps.* Berlin: Berliner Missionswerk.

Nightingale, Benedict. 1973. *Charities.* London: Allen Lane & Penguin Press.

Nikolova, Milena. 2014. Government Funding of Private Voluntary Organizations: Is There a Crowding-Out Effect. *Nonprofit and Voluntary Sector Quarterly,* [Online before Print, 29 January] 0899764013520572.

Njelesani, Janet, Shaun Cleaver, Myroslava Tataryn and Stephanie Nixon. 2012. Using a Human Rights-Based Approach to Disability in Disaster Management Initiatives. Available at www.intechopen.com/books/natural-disasters/using-a-human-rights-based-approach-to-disability-in-disaster-management-initiatives.

Noel, Alain and Jean-Philippe Thérien. 1995. From domestic to international justice: the welfare state and foreign aid. *International Organization* 49:523–523.

Novais, Rui Alexandre. 2007. National Influences in Foreign News British and Portuguese Press Coverage of the Dili Massacre in East Timor. *International Communication Gazette* 69 (6):553–573.

Nunnenkamp, Peter, Janina Weingarth and Johannes Weisser. 2009. Is NGO aid not so different after all? Comparing the allocation of Swiss aid by private and official donors. *European Journal of Political Economy* 25 (4):422–438.

O'Reilly, Kathleen. 2010. The promise of patronage: adapting and adopting neoliberal development. *Antipode* 42 (1):179–200.

Oakman, Daniel. 2001. The Politics of Foreign Aid: Counter-Subversion and the Colombo Plan, 1950–1970. *Pacifica Review: Peace, security & global change* 13 (3):255–272.

—— 2010. *Facing Asia: a history of the Colombo Plan*. Canberra: ANU Press.

Obrecht, Alice, Michael Hammer and Christina Laybourn. 2012. Building a common framework: Mapping national level self-regulation initiatives against the INGO Accountability Charter. In *Briefing paper No. 131*. London: One World Trust.

O'Callaghan, Paul. 2013. Interview with author, 18 November. Canberra.

Odén, Bertil. 2010. The UN and development: from aid to cooperation. *Forum for Development Studies* 37(2): 269–279.

O'Dwyer, Barbara. 2012. Interview with author, August. Canberra.

O'Dwyer, Brendan. 1971a. Letter to Chidamabranathan (WUS), 15 June. In *Records of the Australian Council for Overseas Aid*, MS 9347, Box 14, Folder 4. Canberra: National Library of Australia.

—— 1971b. Letter to Newell, 21 April. In *Records of the Australian Council for Overseas Aid*, MS 9347, Box 14, Folder 4. Canberra: National Library of Australia.

—— 1971c. Letter to Irvine, 20 August. In *Records of the Australian Council for Overseas Aid*, MS9374, Box 14, Folio 5. Canberra: National Library of Australia.

—— 1972a. Editorial. *Development News Digest,* 1:1 June: 1.

—— 1972b. Letter to Hill , 3 July. In *Records of the Australian Council for Overseas Aid*, MS9374, Box 34, Folio 1. Canberra: National Library of Australia.

—— 1972c. Letter to Lindholm, 25 August. In *Records of the Australian Council for Overseas Aid*, MS9347, Box 34, Folio 1. Canberra: National Library of Australia.

—— 1972d. Letter to Rigelsford (Gordon and Gotch), 11 July. In *Records of the Australian Council for Overseas Aid*, MS9347, Box 34, Folio 1. Canberra: National Library of Australia.

—— 1972e. Paper to Education Sub-Committee on Proposed Educationalist Conference, 20 June. In *Records of the Australian Council for Overseas Aid*, MS9347, Box 37, Folder 179. Canberra: National Library of Australia.

—— 1972f. Letter to Watts, (ABC) 4 February. In *Records of the Australian Council for Overseas Aid,* MS9374, Box 38, Folio 183. Canberra: National Library of Australia.

—— 1973. Report on Conference on Development Education. *Development News Digest* 1(4) March: 1–16.

—— 1974. Address to ACFOA Council: Minutes 31 August – 1 September. In *Records of the Australian Council for Overseas Aid,* MS9347, Box 57, Folder 300. Canberra: National Library of Australia,.

—— 1975a. Editorial. *Development News Digest* 12 March.

—— 1975b. Letter to El Tinay, (WUS), 5 May. In *Records of the Australian Council for Overseas Aid,* MS9374, Box 35, Folio 10. Canberra: National Library of Australia.

—— 1975c. Talk for ABC Radio Heresies, 23 May. In *Records of the Australian Council for Overseas Aid,* MS 9347, Box 36, Folder 13. Canberra: National Library of Australia.

—— 2011. Interview with author, March 12. Melbourne.

OECD. 1988. *Voluntary Aid for Development: the role of Non-Governmental Organisations.* Paris: OECD.

Office of Women's Affairs. 1981. Copenhagen and Beyond: Perspectives on the World Conference and NGO Forum for the United Nations Decade for Women. Copenhagen, July 1980. Canberra: Office of Women's Affairs.

Okolie, Charles Chukwuma. 1978. *International Law Perspectives of the Developing Countries: The Relationship of law and economic Development to Basic Human Rights, NOK Legal Studies Services.* New York: NOK.

O'Neill, Onora. 2000. *Bounds of justice.* Cambridge: Cambridge University Press.

Opeskin, Brian R. 1996. The moral foundations of foreign aid. *World Development* 24 (1):21–44.

Parks, Thomas. 2008. The rise and fall of donor funding for advocacy NGOs: understanding the impact. *Development in Practice* 18 (2):213–222.

Parliament of the Commonwealth of Australia. 1991. You Have Your Moments: A Report on Funding of Peak Health and Community Organisations. House of Representatives Standing Committee on Community Affairs. Canberra: AGPS.

Patton, Charlotte G. 1995. Women and Power: the Nairobi Conference, 1985. In Anne Winslow (ed.). *Women, Politics and the United Nations*. Westport Connecticut: Greenwood Press.

Peacock, Andrew. 1977. Letter to Mick Sullivan, 13 July. In *Records of the Australian Council for Overseas Aid*, MS9347, Box 45, Folder 234. Canberra: National Library of Australia.

Pearce, Jenny. 2010. Is social change fundable? NGOs and theories and practices of social change. *Development in Practice* 20 (6):621–635.

Pearson, Lester B. 1969. *Partners in development: Report of the Pearson Commission on International Development*. London: Pall Mall.

Peck, Jamie. 2004. Geography and public policy: Constructions of neoliberalism. *Progress in Human Geography* 28 (3):392–405.

Peppin-Vaughan, Rosie. 2013. Complex collaborations: India and international agendas on girls' and women's education', 1947–1990. *International Journal of Educational Development* 33 (2):118–129.

Pergande, Delia T. 2002. Private voluntary aid and nation building in South Vietnam: The humanitarian politics of CARE, 1954–61. *Peace and Change* 27 (2):165–197.

Perkins, Harvey. 1965. Letter to Wilmot, 12 May. In *Records of the Australian Council for Overseas Aid*, MS9347, Box 1, Folder 1. Canberra: National Library of Australia.

—— 1967. Letter to John Gorton re tax deductability on behalf of ACFOA, 30 March. In *Records of the Australian Council for Overseas Aid*, MS9347, Box 13, Folder 1. Canberra: National Library of Australia.

Persinger, Mildred Emory. 2012. Unfinished Agenda. *Journal of Women's History* 24 (4):186–192.

Peters, Teresa L. 1996. International Refugee Law and the Treatment of Gender-Based Persecution: International Initiatives as a Model and Mandate for National Reform. *Transnational Law and Contemporary Problems* 6:225–250.

Petrou, Ioannis. 2012. The importance of the World Conference on 'Church and Society' and its methodology. An orthodox critical approach. *Synthesis* 1(1):83–92.

Pfanner, Ruth. 2012. Interview with author, 13 January, Canberra.

Philo, Greg. 1993. From Buerk to Band Aid. In J. Eldridge (ed.). *Getting the message: news, truth and power.* Glasgow University Media Group: Psychology Press.

Pierdet, Céline. 2012. Spatial and social resilience in Phnom Penh, Cambodia since 1979. *South East Asia Research* 20 (2):263–281.

Piketty, Thomas. 2014. *Capital in the Twenty-first Century.* Cambridge MA: Harvard University Press.

Piron, Laure-Hélène. 2005. Rights-based Approaches and Bilateral Aid Agencies: More Than a Metaphor? *IDS Bulletin* 36 (1):19–30.

Plewes, Betty. 2013. Interview with author, 22 November. Canberra.

Pollard, Amy, Andy Sumner, Monica Polato-Lopes and Agnès de Mauroy. 2011. 100 voices: Southern NGO perspectives on the Millennium Development Goals and beyond. *IDS Bulletin* 42 (5):120–123.

Porter, Doug. 1990. Address at the ACFOA Council, 7 September. In *Records of the Australian Council for Overseas Aid,* MS9347, MSAcc10.179, Box 43. (Added 5 November 2010). National Library of Australia, Canberra.

Porter, Doug and Kevin Clark. 1985. *Questioning practice: NGOs and evaluation:* Auckland: New Zealand Coalition for Trade and Development.

Porter, Doug, Bryant Allen and Gaye Thompson. 1991. *Development in practice: paved with good intentions.* London: Routledge.

Pottier, Johan. 1996. Why Aid Agencies Need Better Understanding of the Communities they Assist: the experience of food aid in Rwandan refugee camps. *Disasters* 20 (4):324–337.

Poussard, Wendy. 2012. Interview with author, 19 February. Melbourne.

Purcell, Marc. 2009. *Introduction: Rights in Sight: Australian Aid and Development NGOs on Human Rights.* Canberra: ACFID.

—— 2013a. Interview with author, 27 September. Canberra.

—— 2013b. Interview with author, 18 October. Canberra.

—— 2015. Interview with author, 10 April. Canberra.

Quataert, Jean H. 2013. A knowledge revolution: Transnational feminist contributions to international development agendas and policies, 1965–1995. *Global Social Policy*: [published online] 6 December.

Radok, S. 1981. IDEC Kampuchean Relief Appeal Public Report. In *Records of the Australian Council for Overseas Aid*, MS9347, Box 85, Folder 90. (Added 30 January 1998). Canberra: National Library of Australia.

Raghavan, Srinath. 2013. *1971: A Global History of the Creation of Bangladesh*. Cambridge MA: Harvard University Press.

Rahmani, Roya. 2012. Donors, beneficiaries, or NGOs: whose needs come first? A dilemma in Afghanistan. *Development in Practice* 22 (3):295–304.

Ramos-Horta, José. 1987. *Funu: the unfinished saga of East Timor*. Trenton NJ: The Red Sea Press.

Regan, Colin. 1986. Live Aid: a challenge to the 'experts'? *Trocaire Development Review*. Dublin: Trocaire.

Reid, Elizabeth. 1975. Papers of the International Women's Year Secretariat. In *Records Elizabeth Reid*, MS9262, Boxes 30–35. Canberra: National Library of Australia.

—— 1985. Report: Women in Development Training Workshops, May. Canberra: ADAB.

—— 2012. Interview with author, 18 January. Canberra.

Reimann, Kim D. 2006. A view from the top: International politics, norms and the worldwide growth of NGOs *International Studies Quarterly* 50 (1):45–68.

Rendall, Mary P. 1976. Development Education. *Pastoral Investigation of Social Trends*. Working Paper 5. Liverpool: Liverpool Institute of Socio-religious Studies.

Reyntjens, Filip. 2011. Constructing the truth, dealing with dissent, domesticating the world: Governance in post-genocide Rwanda. *African Affairs* 110 (438):1–34.

Richards, R.A. 1975. Report on ACFOA Operations in East Timor, 11 December. In *Records of the Australian Council for Overseas Aid*, MS9347, MSAcc10.179, Box 28. (Added 5 November, 2010). Canberra: National Library of Australia.

Richeya, Lisa Ann and Stefano. Ponte. 2008. Better (Red)™ than Dead? Celebrities, consumption and international aid. *Third World Quarterly* 29 (4):711–729.

Riddell, Roger C. 2007. *Does foreign aid really work?* Oxford: Oxford University Press.

Rivett, Ken. 1981. Letter to Editor. *The Canberra Times*, 16 December.

Roberston, G. 1975. Memo to ACFOA Council. In the Records of the Australian Council for Overseas Aid, MS9347, Box 36, Folder 176. Canberra: National Library of Australia.

Roberts, Susan M, John Paul Jones III and Oliver Fröhling. 2005. NGOs and the globalization of managerialism: A research framework. *World Development* 33 (11):1845–1864.

Robinson, Geoffrey. 2009. *If you leave us here, we will die: how genocide was stopped in East Timor*. Princeton: Princeton University Press.

Rodriguez, Havidan, Tricia Wachtendorf, James Kendra and Joseph Trainor. 2006. A snapshot of the 2004 Indian Ocean tsunami: societal impacts and consequences. *Disaster Prevention and Management* 15 (1):163–177.

Rolfe, Jim. 2011. Partnering to Protect: Conceptualizing Civil–Military Partnerships for the Protection of Civilians. *International Peacekeeping* 18 (5):561–576.

Rollason, Russell. 1983. Closing comments. Women Aid and Development Workshop, 15–17 July, ANU, Canberra.

—— 1985. Memo to Members: Stop the Aid Cuts Campaign, 19 March. In *Records of the Australian Council for Overseas Aid*; MS9374, Box 53, Folio 272. Canberra: National Library of Australia.

—— 1987. *Human Rights and Development*. Canberra: ACFOA.

—— 1988. Letter to Roy, 4 August. In *Records of the Australian Council for Overseas Aid*, MS9347, Box 195, Folder 172. (Added 21 September 1998). Canberra: National Library of Australia.

—— 1990. Letter to Loughlan Ethics Committee Convenor, 27 September. In *Records of the Australian Council for Overseas Aid*, MS9347, MSAcc10.179, Box 25, 6–27 ACFOA Code of Ethics 1989–96. (Added 5 November 2010). Canberra: National Library of Australia.

—— 1991. Letter to McLean, 19 July. In *Records of the Australian Council for Overseas Aid*, MS9347, Box 187, Folder 138. (Added 21 September 1998). Canberra: National Library of Australia.

—— 1993. Notes of Meeting with Phillip Flood. 12 June. In *Records of the Australian Council for Overseas Aid*, MS9347, MSAcc10.179, Box 8. (Added 5 November 2010). Canberra: National Library of Australia.

———— 1994. Letter to Gordon Bilney, 10 October. In *Records of the Australian Council for Overseas Aid,* MS9347, MSAcc10.179, Box 6. (Added 5 November 2010). National Library of Australia, Canberra.

———— 2013. Interview with author, 5 May. Skype. New Delhi.

Ronalds, Paul. 2010. Ethical Obligations to the Poor in a World of Nation States. In Keith Horten and Chris Roche (eds). *Ethical Questions and International NGOs: an Exchange between Philosophers and NGOs.* Ch. 2. New York: Springer.

———— 2013. Reconceptualising International Aid and Development NGOs. In Damien Kingsbury (ed.). *Critical Reflections on Development.* Ch. 6. Basingstoke: Palgrave Macmillan.

Rose, Wendy. 2013. Interview with author, 6 November. Canberra.

Ross, Edna. 1991. *One World Or-None: Campaign Final Report.* Canberra: ACFOA.

Ross, Neville. 1979. Letter to Bob Whan from ADAB , 6 November. In *Records of the Australian Council for Overseas Aid,* MS9347, Box 45, Folder 236. Canberra: National Library of Australia.

———— 1980. Letter to Bob Whan from ABAB , 18 July. In *Records of the Australian Council for Overseas Aid,* MS9347, Box 45, Folder 236. Canberra: National Library of Australia.

———— 1988. ACFOA 1988 and Beyond. In *Records of the Australian Council for Overseas Aid,* MS9347, MSAcc10.179, Box 39. (Added 5 November 2010). Canberra: National Library of Australia,

———— 1990. From the Chairman, ACFOA Annual Report. In *Records of the Australian Council for Overseas Aid,* MS9347, MSAcc10.179, Box 37. (Added 5 November 2010). Canberra: National Library of Australia.

———— 1992. ACFOA Annual Report. In *Records of the Australian Council for Overseas Aid,* MS9347, MSAcc10.179, Box 37. (Added 5 November 2010). Canberra: National Library of Australia.

Rothstein, Robert L. 1979. *Global Bargaining: UNCTAD and the Quest for a New International Economic Order.* Princeton: Princeton University Press.

Russell, John. 1994. Letter to Russell Rollason, 18 November. In *Records of ACFID: AusAID/ACFOA Agreements pre 2000.* Canberra: ACFID.

Saiz, Ignacio. 2004. Bracketing sexuality: Human rights and sexual orientation: A decade of development and denial at the UN. *Health and Human Rights* 7(2):48–80.

Salamon, Lester M and Helmut K Anheier. 1992. In search of the non-profit sector: The question of definitions. *Voluntas: International Journal of Voluntary and Nonprofit Organizations* 3(2): 125–151.

Salehyan, Idean. 2008. The externalities of civil strife: Refugees as a source of international conflict. *American Journal of Political Science* 52(4): 787–801.

Sarelin, Alessandra Lundström. 2007. Human rights-based approaches to development cooperation, HIV/AIDS, and food security. *Human Rights Quarterly* 29 (2):460–488.

Saunders, Clare. 2009. British Humanitarian, Aid and Development NGOs, 1949–Present. In Nick Crowson, Mathew Hilton and James McKay (eds). *NGOs in Contemporary Britain*. Basingstoke: Palgrave MacMillan.

Saunders, Malcolm. 1982. Law and Order and the Anti-Vietnam War Movement: 1965–72. *Australian Journal of Politics & History* 28 (3):367–379.

Sawer, Marian. 1998. Femocrats and ecorats: women's policy machinery in Australia, Canada and New Zealand. In Carol Miller and Shahrashoub Razavi (eds). *Missionaries and Mandarins: feminist engagement with development institutions*. London: Intermediate Technology Publications.

—— 2002. Governing for the mainstream: implications for community representation', *Australian Journal of Public Administration* 61 (1):39–49.

Sawer, Marian and David Laycock. 2009. Down with elites and up with inequality: market populism in Australia and Canada. *Commonwealth & Comparative Politics* 47 (2):133–150.

Scharf, Kimberley and Sarah Smith, 2012. Charitable donations and tax relief in the UK. In Gabrielle Fack and Camille Landais (eds). *Proceedings of the Charitable giving and tax policy: a historical and comparative perspective CEPR conference*. Paris: Paris School of Economics.

Schech, Susanne. 1998. Between tradition and post-coloniality: the location of gender in Australian development policy. *The Australian Geographer* 29 (3):389–404.

Schmidt, Heide-Irene and Helge Pharo. 2003. Introduction. *Contemporary European History* 12 (4):387–394.

Schmitz, Hans Peter. 2012. A Human Rights-Based Approach (HRBA) in Practice: Evaluating NGO Development Efforts. *Polity* 44 (4):523–541.

Schroeder, Christopher H. 2010. Public choice and environmental policy. In Dan Farber and Anne O'Connell (eds). *Research handbook on public choice and public law*. Cheltenham: Elgar, pp. 450-487.

Schulze, Kirsten E. 2001. The East Timor referendum crisis and its impact on Indonesian politics. *Studies in Conflict and Terrorism* 24 (1):77–82.

Schumacher, Ernst Friedrich. 1973. *Small is beautiful: A study of economics as if people mattered*. London: Vintage Books.

Scott, David. 1968. Comments on Development and Relief Commission. ACFOA Council meeting, 25–26 March. In *Records of the Australian Council for Overseas Aid*, MS9374, Box 13, Folder 1. Canberra: National Library of Australia,.

Selby, David and Fumiyo Kagawa. 2011. Development education and education for sustainable development: Are they striking a Faustian bargain? *Policy & Practice – A Development Education Review* Spring (12):15–31.

Sen, Binay R. 1962. World Freedom from Hunger Week. *Freedom From Hunger Campaign News*, 6–11.

Shain, Farzana. 2013. The Girl Effect: Exploring Narratives of Gendered Impacts and Opportunities in Neoliberal Development. *Sociological Research Online* 18 (2):9.

Shaw, Jane S. 2002. Public choice theory. In David Henderson (ed.). *The Concise Encyclopedia of Economics 1st Edition*, [online] New York: Liberty Fund Inc.

Shepherd Jr., George W and Ved P Nanda (eds). 1985. *Human Rights and Third World Development*. Westport, CT: Greenwood Press.

Sherlock, Stephen. 1996. Political economy of the East Timor conflict. *Asian Survey*, pp. 835–851.

Shragge, Eric. 2013. *Activism and Social Change: Lessons for Community Organizing*. Toronto: University of Toronto Press.

Sigmund, Paul E. 1990. *Liberation theology at the crossroads: democracy or revolution?* Oxford: Oxford University Press.

Sikkink, Kathryn. 1986, Codes of conduct for transnational corporations: the case of the WHO/UNICEF code. *International Organization* 40 (04):815–840.

Simons, Paul, Gaye Hart and Cliff Walsh. 1997. *One Clear Objective: Poverty Reduction through Sustainable Development*. Canberra: Australian Government Publishing Service and AusAID.

Singer, Peter. 2010. *The life you can save: How to do your part to end world poverty*. New York: Random House.

Slim, Hugo. 1997. Doing the Right Thing: Relief Agencies, Moral Dilemmas and Moral Responsibility in Political Emergencies and War. *Disasters* 21 (3):244–257.

——— 2002. Not Philanthropy But Rights: The Proper Politicisation of Humanitarian Philosophy. *The International Journal of Human Rights* 6 (2):1–22.

——— 2014. The Limits of Humanitarian Action. In Garrett W. Brown, Gavin Yamey and Sarah Wamala (eds). *The Handbook of Global Health Policy*. New York: Wiley-Blackwell, pp. 341–353.

Smillie, Ian. 1995. *The Alms Bazaar: altruism under fire – non-profit organizations and international development*. London: Intermediate Technology Publications.

——— 1996. Painting Canadian roses red. In Michael Edwards and David Hulme (eds). *Beyond the magic bullet: NGO performance and accountability in the post-cold war world*. West Hartford, CT: Kumarian.

——— 1997. NGOs and development assistance: a change in mind-set?, *Third World Quarterly* 18 (3):563–578.

——— 1999a. Australia. In Ian Smillie, Henny Helmich, Judith Randel and Tony German (eds). *Stakeholders: Government–NGO partnerships for international development*. London: OECD-Earthscan.

——— 1999b. At Sea in A Sieve?: Trends and Issues in the Relationship Between Northern NGOs and Northern Governments. In Ian Smillie, Henny Helmich, Judith Randel and Tony German (eds). *Stakeholders: Government–NGO partnerships for international development*. London: OECD-Earthscan.

——— 1999c. Canada. In Ian Smillie, Henny Helmich, Judith Randel and Tony German (eds). *Stakeholders: Government–NGO partnerships for international development*. London: OECD-Earthscan.

——— 2012. Tying up the Cow: CIDA, Advocacy, and Public Engagement. In Stephen Brown (ed.). *Struggling for Effectiveness: CIDA and Canadian Foreign Aid*. Montreal: McGill-Queen's University Press.

——— 2013. Interview with author, 8 November. Canberra.

Smillie, Ian, Henny Helmich, Judith Randel and Tony German. 1999. *Stakeholders: Government-NGO partnerships for international development.* London: Earthscan.

Snyder, Margaret. 1995. The Politics of Women and Development. In Anne Winslow (ed.). *Women, Politics and the United Nations.* Westport Connecticut: Greenwood Press, pp. 95–116.

Solomon, Geoffrey. 1971. Letter to Syd Einfeld, 20 December. In *Records of the Australian Council for Overseas Aid,* MS 9347, Box 14, Folder 5. Canberra: National Library of Australia.

—— 1972a. Memo to Agencies, 27 January. In *Records of the Australian Council for Overseas Aid,* MS9374, Box 13, Folio 3. Canberra: National Library of Australia.

—— 1972b. Letter to Johnston, 19 September. In *Records of the Australian Council for Overseas Aid,* MS9374, Box 14, Folio 7a. Canberra: National Library of Australia.

—— 1972c. Letter to Barb O'Dwyer, 11 October. In *Records of the Australian Council for Overseas Aid,* MS9374, Box 14, Folio 7a. Canberra: National Library of Australia.

Sommer, John G. 1977. *Beyond Charity: US Voluntary Aid for a Changing Third World.* Washington: Overseas Development Council.

South, Ashley. 2012. The Politics of Protection in Burma: Beyond the Humanitarian Mainstream. *Critical Asian Studies* 44 (2):175–204.

Spires, Anthony J. 2011. Contingent Symbiosis and Civil Society in an Authoritarian State: Understanding the Survival of China's Grassroots NGOs. *American Journal of Sociology* 117 (1):1–45.

Stalker, Peter. 1982. Please do not sponsor this child. *New Internationalist,* May.

Staples, Joan. 2007. NGOs out in the Cold: Howard government policy towards NGOs. In *University of New South Wales Faculty of Law Research Series.* Sydney: University of New South Wales.

—— 2008. Attacks on NGO 'accountability': Questions of governance or the logic of public choice theory? In Jo Barraket (ed.). *Strategic Issues for the not-for-profit sector.* Sydney: UNSW Press.

—— 2012. Watching Aid and Advocacy. In Helen Sykes (ed.). *More Or Less: Democracy And New Media.* Sydney: Future Leaders.

Steen, Odd Inge. 1996. Autonomy or dependency? Relations between non-governmental international aid organisations and government. *Voluntas: International Journal of Voluntary and Nonprofit Organizations* 7 (2):147–159.

Stockton, Nicholas. 1998. In defence of humanitarianism. *Disasters* 22 (4):352–360.

Stokke, Olav (ed.). 2013. *Aid and political conditionality*. London: Routledge.

Storey, Andy. 1997. Non-Neutral Humanitarianism: NGOs and the Rwanda Crisis. *Development in Practice* 7 (4) Double Issue:384–394.

Sullivan, Mick. 1974a. Memo to Barb O'Dwyer, 31 July. In *Records of the Australian Council for Overseas Aid*, MS9374, Box 36, Folio 15. Canberra: National Library of Australia.

—— 1974b. Letter to Pickering (Liberal Party), 25 June. In *Records of the Australian Council for Overseas Aid*, MS9374, Box 46, Folio 241. Canberra: National Library of Australia.

—— 1976. The Australian Experience: 30 years on. In Kate Moore and Sue Tuckwell (eds). *Aid is Simply not Enough*. Canberra: ACFOA.

—— 1977a. ADAB/NGO Consultation, 7–8 September. In *Australian Council for Overseas Aid: Manuscript Collection Aid*, MS9347, Box 45, Folder 234. Canberra: National Library of Australia.

—— 1977b. Note to File, 10 October. In *Records of the Australian Council for Overseas Aid*, MS9374, Box 46, Folio 241. Canberra: National Library of Australia.

—— 1978. Report to Executive on Summer School, 14 February. In *Australian Council for Overseas Aid*, MS9347, Box 38, Folder 187. Canberra: National Library of Australia.

—— 2013. Interview with author, 16 January. Brisbane.

Sweetman, Caroline. 2012. Introduction to Special Issue: Beyond Gender Mainstreaming. *Gender and Development* 20 (3):389–403.

Syme, David R. 2008. *An External Review of the ACFID Code of Conduct from Inception to July 2007, Stage 1, Current Situation Report*. Canberra: ACFID.

Tadeg, Mesenbet Assefa. 2010. Reflections on the right to development: Challenges and prospects. *African Human Rights Law Journal* 10 (2):325–344.

Tandon, Rajesh. 2000. Riding high or nosediving: Development NGOs in the new millennium. *Development in Practice* 10 (3–4):319–329.

Tarp, Finn. 2010. Aid, Growth, and Development. In George Mavrotas (ed.). *Foreign Aid for Development: Issues, Challenges, and the New Agenda*. Oxford: Oxford University Press.

Taylor, Greg. 1982. International Disasters Emergency Committee 1972–1982, September. In *Records of the Australian Council for Overseas Aid*, MS9347, Box 188, Folder 140. (Added 21 September 1998). Canberra: National Library of Australia.

Taylor, Keith W. 1965. Towards a New Foreign Aid Policy. *Australian Outlook* 19 (2):129–145.

Telford, John and John Cosgrave. 2007. The international humanitarian system and the 2004 Indian Ocean earthquake and tsunamis. *Disasters* 31 (1):1–28.

Terrell, Tim. 1994. Letter to Russell Rollason, 23 September. In *Records of ACFID: AusAID/ACFOA Agreements pre 2000*. Canberra: ACFID.

The Age. 1968. $72,000 from 'Age' readers presented to Overseas Aid officials for Vietnam. Article, 21 March. In *Records of the Australian Council for Overseas Aid*, MS9374, Box 2, Folio 5. Canberra: National Library of Australia.

The National Times. 1975. The Overflow Column: Charity at home, 25–30 August.

Thomas, Pam. 2012. Cluster Evaluation of AusAID Vanuatu Civil Society and Media Programs. Report to AusAID, 2 July. Available at dfat.gov.au/about.../vanuatu-media-strengthening-cluster-evaluation.doc.

Thorbecke, Erik and Finn Tarp. 2000. The evolution of the development doctrine and the role of foreign aid, 1950–2000. *Foreign aid and development: Lessons learnt and directions for the future*:17–47.

Thornton. 1996. Letter to Janet Hunt, July 17. In *Records of ACFID: CARE Australia File 1-3-1*. Canberra: ACFID.

Tickner, Robert. 1989. House of Representatives Votes and Proceedings No. 149, Parliament of Australia. Canberra. 2 November.

Tiffen, Rod, Steven Busby, J Ross and M Storz. 1979. *ACFOA Review: Stage 1 – Research Report* edited by CIT. Canberra: ACFOA.

Timothy, Kristen. 2005. 'Defending diversity, sustaining consensus: NGOs at the Beijing women's conference and beyond', *Journal of Women, Politics and Policy* 27 (1–2):189–195.

Tingley, Dustin. 2010. Donors and domestic politics: Political influences on foreign aid effort. *The quarterly review of economics and finance* 50 (1):40–49.

Tinker, Irene and Elaine Zuckerman. 2014. 'Women's Economic Roles and The Development Paradigm'. In Bruce Currie-Alder, Ravi Kanbur, David M Malone and Rohinton Medhora (eds). *International development: ideas, experience, and prospects*. Oxford: Oxford University Press.

Tinker, Irene and Michele Bo-Bramson. 1976. Proceedings of the Seminar on Women in Development, Mexico City, 15–18 June 1975. In Irene Tinker, Michele Bo-Bramson and Mayra Buvinic (eds). *Women and World Development*. New York: Praeger.

Tiwana, Mandeep and Netsanet Belay. 2010. *Civil Society: The Clampdown is Real; Global Trends 2009–2010*. Johannesburg: Civicus.

Tomasevski, Katarina. 1993. *Development Aid and Human Rights Revisited*. New York: Pinter.

Tomlinson, Frances and Christina Schwabenland. 2010. Reconciling competing discourses of diversity? The UK non-profit sector between social justice and the business case. *Organization* 17 (1):101–121.

Touche-Ross. 1980. Auditors Report of IDEC Kampuchea Relief Appeal, 19 September 1979 – 30 September 1980. In *Records of the Australian Council for Overseas Aid*, MS9347, Box 84, Folder 79. (Added 30 January 1998). Canberra: National Library of Australia.

Traille, John. 1982. Letter to Editor. *The Canberra Times*, 8 January.

Traub, James. 2000. Inventing East Timor. *Foreign Affairs*. 79:74.

Trebilcock, Michael, Robert Howse and Antonia Eliason. 2012. *The regulation of international trade*. London: Routledge.

Tupper, Graham. 2000. Letter to Alexander Downer, 16 October. In *Records of ACFID: Correspondence to the Minister of Foreign Affairs and Trade 2000–2004, File 3.1.1*. Canberra: ACFID.

Tupper, Graham. 2012. Interview with author, 5 September. Canberra.

Turner, Benjamin L and Marina Fischer-Kowalski. 2010. Ester Boserup: An interdisciplinary visionary relevant for sustainability. *Proceedings of the National Academy of Sciences* 107 (51):21963 –21965.

Turnour, Matthew. 2011. Some Thoughts on the Broader Theoretical Basis for Including Political Purposes within the Scope of Charitable Purposes: The Aid/Watch Case. *International Journal of Civil Society Law* 9(2):86.

United Nations. 1968. Proclamation of Teheran, the Final Act. In *International Conference on Human Rights, Tehran April 22 to May 13; U.N. Doc. A/CONF. 32/41 at 3 (1968)*.

UNDG. 2003. UN Statement of Common Understanding on Human Rights-Based Approaches to Development Cooperation and Programming (the Common Understanding). New York, UNDG.

UNDP. 2006. *Evaluation of Gender Mainstreaming within UNDP.* New York: UNDP.

—— 2009. *Gender Equality Institutional Assessment (GEIA).* New York: UNDP.

UNESCO. 1951. *Report of the Working Party for Planning Studies on the Access of Women to Education, in Preparation for the XV International Conference on Public Education to be Convened Jointly by UNESCO and the International Bureau of Education.* Paris: UNECSO.

UNGA. 1963a. Resolution A/RES/1943(XVIII) Dec 11: World Campaign against Hunger, Disease and Ignorance. New York: United Nations.

—— 1963b. A/RES/1921(XVIII). Draft Declaration on the Elimination of Discrimination against Women 5 December. New York: United Nations.

—— 1986. *Declaration on the Right to Development* Resolution A/RES/41/128, 4 December. New York: United Nations.

United Nations Children's Fund. 2012. *The Right of Children with Disabilities to Education: A Rights-Based Approach to Inclusive Education.* Geneva: UNICEF.

United Nations Economic Commission for Africa. 1973. *Women's Programme: National Commissions on Women and Development and Women's Bureaux.* Addis Ababa: United Nations Economic Commission for Africa.

Utting, Peter. 1994. *Between Hope & Insecurity: The Social Consequences of the Cambodian Peace Process.* Geneva: UNRISD.

Uvin, Peter. 2004. *Human Rights and Development.* Bloomfield: Kumarian Press.

van der Borgh, Chris and Carolijn Terwindt. 2012. Shrinking operational space of NGOs – a framework of analysis. *Development in Practice* 22 (8):1065–1081.

Van der Heijden, Hendrik. 1987. The reconciliation of NGO autonomy, program integrity and operational effectiveness with accountability to donors. *World Development* 15 Supplementary:103–112.

van Eekelen, Willem. 2013. Revisiting child sponsorship programmes. *Development in Practice* 23 (4):468–480.

Van Tuijl, Peter. 2000. Entering the global dealing room: reflections on a rights-based framework for NGOs in international development. *Third World Quarterly* 21 (4):617–626.

Vandemoortele, Jan. 2011. The MDG story: intention denied. *Development and Change* 42 (1):1–21.

VCOAD. 1966. Voluntary Committee of Aid and Development: Statement of Objectives and Principles. In *Records of the Australian Council for Overseas Aid,* MS9347, Box 1, Folder 1. Canberra: National Library of Australia.

Vernant, Jean-Pierre and Pierre Vidal-Naque. 1990. *Myth and Tragedy in Ancient Greece*. New York: Zone Books.

Verweij, Marco and Riccardo Pelizzo. 2009. Singapore: Does Authoritarianism Pay?, *Journal of Democracy* 20 (2):18–32.

Vincent, Christine. 1995. Memo to Excom: Sunday Program Report on CARE Australia, 24 February. In *ACFID Files: CARE File 9–15*. Canberra: ACFID.

——— 2012. Interview with author, 24 February. Canberra.

Viterna, Jocelyn and Kathleen M Fallon. 2008. Democratization, women's movements, and gender-equitable states: A framework for comparison. *American Sociological Review* 73 (4):668–689.

Viviani, Nancy and Peter Wilenski. 1978. The Australian Development Assistance Agency: a Post Mortem Report. In *National Monograph Series*. Brisbane: Royal Institute of Public Administration.

Wade, Robert H. 2011. Emerging world order? From multipolarity to multilateralism in the G20, the World Bank, and the IMF. *Politics & Society* 39 (3):347–378.

Waldorf, Lars. 2013. Getting the Gunpowder Out of Their Heads: The Limits of Rights-Based DDR. *Human Rights Quarterly* 35 (3):701–719.

Wallace, Tina. 2009. NGO dilemmas: Trojan horses for global neoliberalism? *Socialist Register* 40:203–219.

Wallace, Tina, Sarah Crowther and Andrew Shepherd. 1997. *Standardising development: influences on UK NGOs' policies and procedures.* Oxford: WorldView Publishing.

Walsh, Pat. 2012. What Australia doesn't want East Timor to know. *Eureka Street* 22(6).

—— 2014. Interview with author, 1 May. Melbourne.

Warren, Shana and Robert Lloyd. 2009. Civil Society Self-Regulation: The Global Picture. *Briefing paper No. 119.* London: One World Trust.

Waters, Christopher. 1999. A failure of imagination: RG Casey and Australian plans for counter-subversion in Asia, 1954–1956, *Australian Journal of Politics & History* 45 (3):347–361.

Watkins, Susan Cotts, Ann Swidler and Thomas Hannan. 2012. Outsourcing social transformation: development NGOs as organizations. *Sociology* 38:285–315.

Webb, Jim. 1964a. Letter to John Crawford, 3 July. In *Records of the Australian Council for Overseas Aid,* MS9374, Box 1, Folio 1. National Library of Australia, Canberra.

—— 1964b. Letter to Engel, 3 July. In *Records of the Australian Council for Overseas Aid*, MS9374, Box 27 OSB. Canberra: National Library of Australia.

—— 1964c. Letter to John Crawford, 18 December. In *Records of the Australian Council for Overseas Aid,* MS9374, Box 1, Folio 1. Canberra: National Library of Australia.

—— 1965. Letter to Perkins, March 9. In *Records of the Australian Council for Overseas Aid,* MS9374, Box 1, Folio 1. Canberra: National Library of Australia.

—— 1971. *Towards Survival: a Programme for Australia's Aid.* Melbourne: Community Aid Abroad.

—— 1974. Letter to O'Dwyer, 19 September. In *Records of the Australian Council for Overseas Aid,* MS9374, Box 36, Folio 13. Canberra: National Library of Australia.

—— 1977. Beyond Aid: A report of the seminar 12 years of Voluntary Aid held prior to the ACFOA Annual Council August 1976. In *Records of the Australian Council for Overseas Aid,* MS9374, Box 55, Folio 284. Canberra: National Library of Australia.

—— 2006. Interview with author, 9 December. Melbourne.

Weber, Nadya. 2013. A Comparative Study of the Shifting Nature of International Non-governmental Organization Global Education Programming in Canada and the United Kingdom. PhD thesis. Toronto: University of Toronto School of Graduate Studies.

Werner, A.G. 1978. Report to Council 20–22 October: IDEC Report. In the *Records of the Australian Council for Overseas Aid,* MS9347, Box 55, Folder 286. Canberra: National Library of Australia.

West, Darrell M. 2007. Angelina, Mia, and Bono: Celebrities and international development. *Development* 2: 1–9.

West, Lois A. 1999. The United Nations Women's Conferences and Feminist Politics. In Mary K Meyer and Elisabeth Prügl (eds). *Gender politics in global governance.* New York: Rowman & Littlefield.

Whan, Bob. 1981. Letter to Editor. *The Canberra Times,* 24 October.

—— 2008. Interview with author, Sydney.

Whitaker, Ben. 1974. *The Foundations: An Anatomy of Philanthropy and Society.* London: Eyre Methuen.

Whitehead, Richard, Ged Carney and Beth Greenhill. 2011. Encouraging Positive Risk Management: Supporting Decisions by People with Learning Disabilities Using a Human Rights-Based Approach. *Self-Harm and Violence: Towards Best Practice in Managing Risk in Mental Health Services*:215–236.

Whitlam, Gough. 1975. International Women's Year Grants: Press Statement No. 510, 6 June. In *Records of Elizabeth Reid,* MS9262, Box 35, Folder 14/32. Canberra.

—— 1981. Letter to Editor, *The Canberra Times,* 22 October.

Wilkinson, Alan. 1976. *The politics of Australian Foreign Aid Policy 1950–1972,* RSPAS. Canberra: Australian National University

Williams, George. 2012. The Australian Constitution and the Aid/Watch Case. *Cosmopolitan Civil Societies: An Interdisciplinary Journal* 3(3s) Special Issue [online].

Williamson, Claudia R. 2010. Exploring the failure of foreign aid: The role of incentives and information. *The review of Austrian economics* 23 (1):17–33.

Williamson, John. 1993. Democracy and the 'Washington consensus'. *World Development* 21 (8):1329–1336.

Wilson, Ronald. 1997. Letter to Governor-General Deane, 25 November. In *Records of the Australian Council for Overseas Aid,* MS9347 MSAcc10.179, Box 25, 6–27 ACFOA Code of Ethics 1989–96. (Added 5 November 2010). Canberra: National Library of Australia.

Winston, Morton. 2002. NGO strategies for promoting corporate social responsibility. *Ethics & International Affairs* 16 (1):71–87.

Winter, Sarah. 2009. *Rights in Sight: Australian aid and development NGOs on human rights.* Canberra: ACFID.

Wolf, Charles. 1957. Soviet Economic Aid in Southeast Asia. *World Politics* 10 (1):91–101.

Wolf, Siegfried O. 2013. The international context of Bangladesh Liberation War. *The Independent,* 29 March, 14–1.

Wolfe, Audra J. 2013. Giving Philanthropy a New History. *Historical Studies in the Natural Sciences* 43 (5):619–630.

Wright, Glen W. 2012. NGOs and Western hegemony: causes for concern and ideas for change. *Development in Practice* 22 (1):123–134.

Wright, Sharon, Greg Marston and Catherine McDonald. 2011. The Role of Non-profit Organizations in the Mixed Economy of Welfare-to-Work in the UK and Australia. *Social Policy & Administration* 45 (3) pp. 299–303.

Wu, Joyce. 2012. The People Follow the Mullah, and the Mullah Follows the People. In Christine De Matos and R Ward (eds). *Gender, Power, and Military Occupations: Asia Pacific and the Middle East Since 1945.* London: Routledge.

Wulfsohn, Michael and Stephen Howes. 2014. How reliant are Australian development NGOs on government funding? In S Howes (ed.). DevPolicyBlog. Canberra: Development Policy Centre.

Yontcheva, Boriana and Nadia Masud. 2005. Does foreign aid reduce poverty? Empirical evidence from nongovernmental and bilateral aid. In *IMF Working Paper WP/05/100,* Washington: International Monetary Fund.

Zaheer, Hasan. 1994. *The Separation of East Pakistan: the rise and realization of Bengali Muslim Nationalism.* London: Oxford University Press.

Ziai, Aram. 2011. The Millennium Development Goals: back to the future? *Third World Quarterly* 32 (1):27–43.

Zinsser, Judith P. 2002. From Mexico to Copenhagen to Nairobi: The United Nations Decade for Women, 1975–1985. *Journal of World History* 13 (1):139–168.

Zivetz, Laurie. 1988. *Appraisal, Monitoring and Evaluation: the NGO approach.* Canberra: ACFOA.

Index

www.ingramcontent.com/pod-product-compliance
Lightning Source LLC
Chambersburg PA
CBHW061238270326
41928CB00033B/3384